USING A LAW LIBRARY

A Student's Guide to Legal Research Skills

USING A LAW LIBRARY

A Student's Guide to Legal Research Skills

Second Edition

Peter Clinch

Information Specialist — Law, Cardiff University

With chapters and other contributions on researching the law of Scotland
by David R. Hart, Law Librarian, University of Dundee

BLACKSTONE
PRESS LIMITED

Published by
Blackstone Press Limited
Aldine Place
London
W12 8AA
United Kingdom

Sales enquiries and orders
Telephone +44-(0)-20-8740-2277
Facsimile +44-(0)-20-8743-2292
E-mail: sales@blackstone.demon.co.uk
Website: www.blackstonepress.com

ISBN: 1 84174 029 2
© Peter Clinch 2001
Chapters 9–13 © David R. Hart 2001
First edition 1992
Second edition 2001

British Library Cataloguing in Publication Data
A catalogue record for this book is available from the British Library

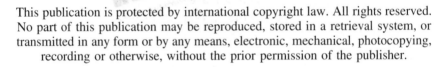

Typeset in 10/11pt Times by Style Photosetting Ltd, Mayfield, East Sussex
Printed and bound in Great Britain by Antony Rowe Limited,
Chippenham and Reading

Contents

PART 4 — KEEPING UP-TO-DATE

PART 5 — AIDS TO IMPROVE THE QUALITY OF YOUR RESEARCH

APPENDICES

Acknowledgements

This book is the product of over 30 years contact with the subject of law, first as an undergraduate, then as a local authority planner attempting to research and apply the law, and finally, as a librarian teaching students how to research it for themselves. The format and content of this book have been influenced by these experiences and I am indebted to all the people with whom I have come into contact, but particularly law staff, students and my library colleagues at various universities. Knowingly, and sometimes unwittingly, they have contributed to this work, by means of their interest, comment and 'off the cuff' remarks on the law and the difficulties of researching it. I must also pay tribute to those authors who have preceded me and whose work has influenced mine: John Pemberton, Adrian Blunt, Betty Moys, Derek Way, Robert Logan, Jean Dane and Philip Thomas, and John Jeffries and Christine Miskin.

For this second edition, I am especially grateful to David R. Hart (Law Librarian, University of Dundee) for writing chapters 9 to 13 on researching the law of Scotland, and providing contributions in other chapters where Scottish practice varies from that in England and Wales. I am sure his efforts 'to put a kilt on the book' will widen its appeal. Alex McLeod, Parliamentary Liaison Manager (TSO) has read and provided advice on the section on Bills of Parliament.

Acknowledgements and thanks are due to a number of people and organisations for permission to reproduce pages from their publications:

— Butterworth Law Publishers Co. Ltd (*All England Law Reports*);
— H.W. Wilson Co. (*Index to Legal Periodicals*);
— Legal Information Resources Ltd (*A Legal Thesaurus*);
— Sweet & Maxwell Ltd (*Current Law Case Citator, Current Law Statute and Statutory Instrument Citators*).

Crown copyright in the extracts from an Act and statutory instrument is acknowledged.

Notwithstanding this assistance freely given, any omissions or errors are entirely my responsibility.

I am also indebted to the staff of Blackstone Press, especially Heather Saward, for their understanding and professionalism.

Finally, I am indebted to my wife, Verity, for patiently enduring my preoccupation with the manuscript for a second time, and to Graham for his invaluable advice on all matters relating to information technology. To them I again dedicate the work.

Peter Clinch
November 2000

Table of figures

Introduction: about this book and how to use it

'Knowledge is of two kinds: we know a subject ourselves, or we know where we can find information upon it' (Samuel Johnson).

The study of law is changing. It is becoming less about learning mechanically the facts contained in books noted on lecturers' reading lists, and more about the ability to analyse a legal problem, identify and employ the written and computerised sources appropriate to its solution, and present the results of that analysis and research as a coherently organised, written or verbal presentation. This book is about the skill of legal research. The skills of analysis and communication are dealt with in two other Blackstone Press publications: *Learning Legal Rules* (Holland and Webb 1999) and *Learning Legal Skills* (Lee and Fox 1999).

The aim of this book, then, is to provide students studying English, Welsh, Scots, European Community and European human rights law with a basic knowledge of the research sources and techniques relevant to the literature of law.

This second edition has been expanded in several ways. First, the number of jurisdictions has been increased to include information on the research sources relevant to Scotland and Wales, both of which now, to quite different extents, enjoy government devolved from Westminster. In addition, the incorporation of the European Convention on Human Rights within the domestic law of the United Kingdom, by means of the Human Rights Act 1998, will result in greater need to research the legislation and case law of the relevant European bodies. For this reason, a new chapter has been added on the research sources for the Convention itself, and the case law and commentary which relate to it.

Secondly, the number and use of electronic databases has expanded considerably since the first edition was written. Details are provided of individual CD and internet databases (both free and those available only to subscribers). The distinction between paper and electronic sources reflected in the structure of the first edition has now become meaningless, so description of the contents of paper, CD and internet databases has been merged. Appendix 4 provides information on how to use CDs and the internet effectively for legal research. Electronic research sources change fast, in both their content and, internet sources in particular, their location. The information provided in this book is correct at the time of writing.

As an illustration of how quickly things change, there have been two unrelated developments in the months prior to writing this introduction, which could have far-reaching consequences for legal research in the UK. The first was the launch, in mid-March 2000, of an exciting new pilot internet service: BAILII (British and Irish Legal Information Institute). It provides free internet access to British and Irish legal materials. At its launch it contained 14 law databases, previously scattered over as many separate web sites. More databases are due to be added. This single site could eventually replace many of the web sites mentioned in the body of this book, so that researching the law using the internet becomes a one-stop event, as it is in Australia, from which the inspiration for this development has come. The web address of BAILII is:

http://www.bailii.org

The second development has been the increased promotion in the UK during early 2000 of the American database: Westlaw. Westlaw has been available for many years but only now have a number of well-established UK databases been added to its coverage, so that Westlaw UK has become a realistic addition to the sources which might be found through a university or college internet connection.

Experience shows that many students have great difficulty in developing adequate research skills for three reasons: first, they are confused by the distinction between publications containing the full and authoritative text of the law and publications which contain either unofficial versions or commentary; secondly, they are bewildered by the wide range of publications and databases containing legal information and have difficulty in matching the most appropriate source to the problem in hand; thirdly, some of the techniques required to correctly exploit these publications and databases appear complex and are a discouragement to further learning.

This book adopts the same two approaches in an attempt to overcome these difficulties, which were successfully applied in the first edition. First, it is clearly structured not only as far as the sequence of chapters is concerned, but in the way information is presented under standard headings for each source of legal information discussed. Secondly, wherever possible, use is made of diagrams and charts to outline the content and use of publications and provide step-by-step instruction in undertaking particular research problems.

The expansion in the number of jurisdictions covered in this second edition has necessitated dividing the book into more but shorter chapters. The heart lies in five parts.

Part 2 comprises eleven chapters on the source materials of the law for England, Wales and Scotland. Including information on researching the law of Scotland in this edition has proved a challenge. The jurisdiction has a long and distinctive history. Whilst there are many similarities between the law and sources of England and Wales on the one hand, and Scotland on the other, the bulk of the text on Scotland will be found in five chapters (9 to 13), but comments on Scottish variations, with cross-references will be found in chapters 4 to 8 also. The amount of repetition has been kept to the minimum through copious use of cross-references between the chapters.

Part 3 comprises three chapters on European Community law sources and a chapter on the research sources for European human rights law.

Part 4 comprises a single, short chapter which discusses how to keep up-to-date with legal developments, an aspect of legal research frequently neglected.

Wrapped around this core are Part 1, dealing with some initial steps in legal research, finding and using a law library, and the effective use of catalogues and indexes; and Part 5, covering how to record and present research results, including the discussion of methods to be used in extended research (such as for projects or final-year dissertations) to record progress and findings, and the purpose and techniques for the construction of footnotes and bibliographies (lists of references detailing the material you cite). Much of the information presented in Part 5 is often neglected by books and lectures on legal research, but knowledge and understanding of these techniques will improve your confidence in managing and presenting research.

The discussion of each source of legal information in Parts 2 and 3 is presented under a series of standard headings (except for chapter 17 on European human rights law, where the sources are too few to warrant the use of the headings). Each heading is further subdivided. This structure is applied quite rigidly, though where, in a very few instances, only a little information is to be conveyed, subdivision is not used. The guiding aim has been to ensure information is clearly presented and readily accessible. The standard headings and subheadings for each legal source discussed in chapters 3 to 16 are as follows:

A   Description — subdivided into a discussion of the **definition** and purpose of a particular original source material, a description of its **origin** and **structure**, information on its **publication and general availability** in libraries and details of the recommended form of **citation** (the way of referring to the source when writing about it).

B   Finding information — subdivided into paragraphs, each describing a different publication or database, containing either the text of the original sources described in section A or information to help you exploit them, with step-by-step instructions, often in diagrammatic form, on how to use key publications.

C   Answering research queries — an account, using diagrams and charts where possible, to illustrate which publications and databases described in sections A and B should be used to answer your most frequent research needs.

This rigid structure and the use of copious diagrams and charts makes the book appear more like a workshop manual than a conventional student text —

and that is as it should be, for skills are not learnt by reading books from cover to cover, but through the application of small amounts of book knowledge to resolve particular, practical difficulties or problems. As far as possible, each section of the book is self-contained, and through the system of subdivision it should be easy to find the particular information required to solve a research problem. Some publications and databases include information on more than one legal source so some duplication of text is inevitable, but every effort has been made to keep repetition to a minimum.

The use of diagrams and charts was a considerable innovation in the first edition. Very few law books contain illustrations of any kind but the authors of the increasing number of books on legal skills recognise that a diagram or chart is of more value to a student than pages of text or a lengthy verbal explanation. In the section on answering research queries (section C), cross-references are provided in the charts and diagrams to the discussion of particular publications in section B, so linking the research steps to be followed in solving a particular information need to the detailed use of particular publications.

One feature of this book which may come as a surprise is the lack of 'worked examples'. There are two reasons for this: first, the law changes with such rapidity and the details of a volume, page and/or paragraph number provided in indexes to publications or screen layout in a database alter so much, that it is difficult to follow the worked example even a short time after the exercise was compiled. Secondly, there is a temptation to select examples to illustrate as many research difficulties as possible, regardless of whether the difficulty is met frequently or rarely. Again, experience indicates that students find it easier to follow a step-by-step presentation of research *principles* rather than become faced with the *detail* of a particular legal problem.

A final remark. The first edition of this book was intended for use by students; it was not intended as a work of reference for law librarians and information officers. However, it has been gratifying to note how many trained staff have turned to the first edition for assistance. I hope they will find the second edition equally useful. Nevertheless, I must repeat what I wrote in the first edition: that the publication is intended for students, and as such, is not intended to be a comprehensive treatment but merely aims to highlight basic information sources and provide an introduction to legal research techniques. If you have difficulty with a legal research problem this book cannot answer, then do make use of the skill and experience of the staff of your local law library or information service — they are there to help!

PART 1

INITIAL STEPS IN LEGAL RESEARCH

Chapter 1

Finding and using a law library

1.1   WHERE IS YOUR NEAREST LAW LIBRARY?

As a law student you will have automatic access to the library in the university or college at which you are studying. But, if you are studying law following a distance learning or correspondence course at home, or wish to study during the vacations away from your term-time base, or are preparing a final year project or dissertation on a topic for which your usual law library has little material, you will want to discover the nearest law library which can provide the type and size of collection which will satisfy your research needs.

In its 1998 edition, the *Directory of British and Irish Law Libraries*, compiled by Pauline Fothergill for the British and Irish Association of Law Librarians, lists over 500 libraries, including academic libraries (the collective term for those in universities and colleges), public libraries, libraries of government departments, Inns of Court, national and local law societies, law firms and law courts themselves. Libraries are listed under each of the constituent countries of the British Isles, and then alphabetically by town, so it's easy to trace a library local to your base. Each entry gives details of the size of the collection, but most importantly a named contact. Before you set off to visit a law library other than one with which you are familiar, it is essential to contact the librarian beforehand, as many libraries outside the academic and public library service are private and normally available only to members. You may need to obtain permission to use them. Whilst you can walk straight into a public library you will discover that most will have only a very basic law collection. Normally you can use academic libraries for reference purposes only (that is, you can browse but you won't be able to borrow) unless you are a member of that educational institution, or you belong to another academic library which has made special reciprocal arrangements with the library you intend to use. Such a reciprocal scheme operates amongst a number of academic libraries in the London area, for example; it is called the London Plus Scheme and is available to part-time students registered at any one of the universities and colleges belonging to the scheme.

Although an increasing amount of information about the law is available in electronic format, the contracts and licences under which this information is made available to educational institutions usually mean that only if you are a registered member of that particular institution will you be allowed to access an electronic database, regardless of whether it is a CD or on the internet.

Check beforehand whether the library you wish to visit does, in fact, stock the publications you wish to use — the *Directory* provides only a very general idea of each library's stock. Opening hours are noted in the *Directory* but in view of expenditure cuts faced by all libraries, they may have been reduced, so that is another point to check.

In school or public libraries, the whole library service is usually centralised — all the books available to library users are kept in a single building. However, academic libraries frequently organise their collections quite differently, to take into account the needs of different groups of library users and the extent to which the university or college buildings are scattered over a geographical area. Some academic libraries have a single building housing the bookstock of all subjects; the law collection may be part of the main sequence of books, or it is sometimes set apart because the types of publication and the needs of law library users are rather different from those of other subjects. Other academic libraries may have a central library, with branches, frequently referred to as site, campus or departmental libraries, scattered over several buildings. Often these branch libraries are located close to the teaching departments they serve.

So, make a point of studying any leaflet guides or floor plans displayed in the library. If in doubt about where the law collection is shelved, ask library staff for assistance.

1.2   USING THE LAW LIBRARY

There is a strong chance that when you enter a law library for the first time you will experience bewilderment and apprehension, possibly leading to panic. Bewilderment at the hundreds of shelves, the numerous rows of books and personal computer (PC) terminals, apprehension at the thought of trying to find your way round the stock or through the databases, and panic that you will never be able to find the information you want in the time available.

Relax! Libraries are laid out in a logical way; there are catalogues to help you identify whether the library has the book you need and, finally, but most important of all, there will usually be an enquiry desk or information point where library staff will be available to assist you. Never be afraid to ask for help; it is an important part of the job of library and information staff to ensure, to the best of their ability, that customers' information needs are satisfied, regardless of whether they are for paper or electronic sources, so that they are encouraged to use the collections again in the future. Let's look at the paper and electronic sources a law library usually contains, starting with the paper followed, in section 1.2.9, with the electronic.

1.2.1   What is the general arrangement of the stock?

If you are attending a course of study at a university or college it is likely that during the early days of the first term you will be given a tour of the library. What follows in this chapter is meant to provide background information and a skeleton framework within which to set the detail of the particular library you are to use. There is a checklist in appendix 1 which you can use to find out how well you know how to use any law library.

Libraries usually contain two broad categories of material: books and periodicals (also called journals or, more popularly, magazines). They are usually shelved separately from one another. One reason for this is that periodicals comprise titles which are added to, more or less regularly, by the publication of new issues. So, space has to be left on the shelves between one title and the next to accommodate future issues. Some periodicals have new issues published as frequently as weekly and a few even daily.

Therefore, in law libraries you will find documents which are published in the same way as periodicals, such as Acts of Parliament, law reports as well as law periodicals, shelved separately from books.

1.2.2   How is each type of material arranged on the shelves?

Books are usually grouped according to their subject. This is achieved by means of a subject classification scheme. Several different schemes are in use; each employs numbers or a combination of numbers and letters to indicate the subject of a book. The classification number or mark — often abbreviated to class number or class mark — is placed near the bottom of the spine of each book. If you are familiar with school or public libraries you may have noticed they mostly use a scheme of numbers, the third and fourth separated by a decimal point. This is the Dewey decimal classification scheme. It is also used in some universities and colleges. Some law libraries use a special variation based on the Dewey scheme called the Moys classification, after the law librarian who devised it. Another scheme you will find in academic libraries is the Library of Congress classification scheme which uses a combination of letters and numbers. Whichever scheme your library employs the purposes of the classification are the same: to bring together on the shelves books on the same subject, and to indicate where in the library a particular book is to be found.

Periodicals may be arranged in one of several different ways: either by subject and then alphabetically by title within each subject, or just alphabetically by title. In some of the larger law libraries you may find periodicals arranged according to the jurisdiction (the geographical area over which the laws of a particular legislature or decisions of the courts extend) to which they usually refer. So, for example, English law periodicals will be shelved separately from European Community or French or United States periodicals.

Libraries often have separate sequences for a number of specialised groups of publications: reference books, such as dictionaries, general encyclopaedias, directories etc.; and bibliographic works — a large group of publications ranging from lists of the total publishing output of a particular country to lists of books and/or individual articles contained in periodicals on a particular subject, such as law. Government publications or the publications of international organisations such as the European Community, sometimes form a separate collection depending, in part, on how much of this huge publishing output is collected by the particular library.

You may also find another distinction made in the stock of the library: very large books (called 'folios', or 'quartos' in some libraries, or 'oversize' in others) may be shelved separately from ordinary size books. At the other end of the scale, some libraries, especially universities, keep very thin books (pamphlets) in a separate sequence. Recent changes in photocopying law mean that some libraries will stock photocopies made under licence of parts of books or articles from periodicals — these may be kept apart from the rest of the stock, perhaps in an area to which you will not have direct access so that you will need to ask staff to obtain the item you require.

1.2.3   Is all the stock of the library available for you to borrow?

Not all the stock of the library will be available for loan, and in law libraries in particular, where there is a very strong dependence on periodicals rather than books, a large part of the stock will be for use only in the library. However, libraries usually provide photocopying services, either self-service or undertaken by staff, where small sections of books or periodicals may be copied subject to the provisions of copyright law. Notices in the photocopy service areas will explain what is permitted under the law.

Usually you will be able to borrow copies of most books, though some of the more expensive or loose-leaf publications (which require regular updating by library staff) may be for use only in the library. Sometimes you will find several copies of the same basic text are available for loan, and each copy may be for a different loan period (the length of time you can borrow a book). The loan period is usually determined by the book's popularity — the level of demand for the title. Some libraries keep copies of the most frequently borrowed titles in a separate collection; you may have to ask library staff to obtain the book you require from this collection as it is sometimes placed behind a service desk or issue counter. The loan period for this stock may be very brief, perhaps just a few hours. The intention is that you may be required to read only one chapter of a book each week or fortnight, and you can borrow the book for a few hours, long enough to read the text required, return it to the library, and one of your colleagues on the course can then borrow the book. Often this collection contains copies of 'set' or 'recommended' texts for your course — copies which you should **buy** for your own personal use. Do not let the fact that the library has copies of recommended books prevent you from buying your own, because the number of students wishing to read a particular recommended book before an essay, assessment or seminar deadline, will usually far exceed the library's capacity to meet this peak in demand.

1.2.4   How do you discover whether the library has the book you require?

The key is the library catalogue. Many libraries now use computers on which to hold and display details of the stock, but in some libraries parts of the stock, frequently books purchased before the computer system was installed, will be recorded on microform or card catalogues. Microform catalogues comprise rolls or sheets of plastic film containing photo-reduced images of the details of books. The rolls or sheets of plastic are read using a piece of equipment called a microform reader. Card catalogues are contained in large banks of wooden drawers — the traditional image, along with leather-bound books, of a scholarly library!

No matter the medium by which the stock of the library is recorded and displayed, you will usually find at least three separate parts to the catalogue or ways of finding details about the stock:

(a)   *The author section* arranges details of the stock alphabetically by the authors' surnames. If no author's name is given in the book (perhaps it has been issued by a large organisation such as a government department) then an entry will be given under the name of the issuing body. Sometimes libraries also include for all books additional entries filed alphabetically by the title of the book, and this combined author and title catalogue may be referred to as a *name* catalogue.

(b)   *The subject section* is arranged alphabetically by subject and provides class marks where books on each topic are shelved.

(c)   *The classified section* arranges class marks in numerical or alphabetical order according to the classification scheme used, with details of the authors and titles of books allocated to each subject. This section of the catalogue is usually consulted only after you have found the appropriate class mark in the subject section, for the topic in which you are interested.

1.2.5   Which parts of the catalogue should you use to answer particular information needs?

If you know who wrote the book you are looking for, use the author section and remember to search by the first letter of the author's *surname*. If the library has books by more than one author of the same surname, search entries for the forename or initials of the author in whom you are interested.

Although an alphabetical arrangement of authors' names or book titles may sound straightforward enough to use, there are, unfortunately, two ways of organising the entries in alphabetical order. One uses a 'letter-by-letter' arrangement, the other 'word-by-word'. In 'letter-by-letter', any spaces between words are ignored and the whole name or title is treated as one long word. In 'word-by-word', the first word determines the overall order of entries and where two entries have the same first word, the second word determines the detailed order. Here are examples to illustrate the difference.

Letter-by-letter	*Word-by-word*
Law Centres Federation	Law Centres Federation
Law Commission	Law Commission
Lawler, S.D.	Law Reform Committee
Lawless, Clive	Law Society
Law Reform Committee	Lawler, S.D
Law Society	Lawless, Clive

If you know the title of the book but not the author's name and the library has a name or title catalogue, use it to find out if the book is in stock. *Ignore* an indefinite or definite article ('a', 'an', 'the' in English) at the beginning of the title.

If you wish to browse for books on a subject and you have no authors or titles in mind, use the subject section to find the appropriate class marks then either go to the shelves or use the classified section of the catalogue.

If you know the class mark for a subject you can go straight to the shelves and browse, but books in your chosen section may be on loan, and some may be shelved in other parts of the library because they are large size, or pamphlets or reference books. You will not have any idea, therefore, of what the full stock of the library may be. To obtain a full picture, it is better to use the classified section of the catalogue to identify particular authors and titles *before* you go to the shelves.

If the library has a computerised catalogue you will need to use a computer terminal with a screen and keyboard. Most systems provide users with a list of options, otherwise known as a 'menu', from which to choose the search path you wish to follow. Computerised systems often offer more ways of searching the database than the three outlined above and will also tell you the current position, whether, for example, the book you want is on loan, when it is due to be returned, or if it is on the shelves now. Some systems allow you to reserve or recall books you require which are presently on loan, by typing instructions at the computer terminal. Instruction leaflets are usually available to help you obtain the best results from using the library catalogue.

1.2.6   How do you discover if the library has the periodical you require?

Libraries with microform or card catalogues usually have a separate section of the catalogue devoted to a list, usually in alphabetical order by title, of the periodicals they keep in stock. This periodicals catalogue or 'holdings list' as it is sometimes termed, will give details of the particular issues and their dates of publication which the library keeps, and an indication of where on the shelves they are located.

If a library has a computerised catalogue then its periodicals catalogue may be within the title section of the book catalogue.

The way information is given about the issues of a particular title held by the library can sometimes cause a little confusion. Here is an example with an explanation.

New Law Journal v118 (1968) — v120 (1970), v124 (1974) -

This means the library stocks *New Law Journal* from volume 118 of 1968 to volume 120 of 1970, then there are some volumes not in stock, before the holdings of the title recommence at volume 124 of 1974 and continue *complete to the present*. Where some individual issues are missing from a set, too many to list individually on the public catalogue, the word 'incomplete' or 'incomp' may be given at the end of the entry.

1.2.7 Special points you should remember when searching the catalogue for law books

New editions of law books appear frequently because law is one of the most dynamic subjects in all knowledge. Libraries frequently retain old, out-of-date editions because they can have a value to those studying the development of law — legal historians. Entries for these books will, of course, appear in the library catalogue, so you should take particular care when using the catalogue *and* when searching the library shelves to obtain the particular edition of the work you may have been directed to either by a lecturer or in your reading. If no guidance has been given on the edition to use then a good rule of thumb is to consult the most up-to-date you can trace. You can check which edition is the latest available by using either publishers' catalogues or general lists of books such as *Whitaker's Books in Print* or its CD equivalent: *BookBank* (see 8.1B2.1) which virtually every library will possess. Publishers' catalogues may not be on public display in the library but ask library staff if you can consult copies kept to assist the library in purchasing its stock. The rule of thumb should also be borne in mind if you are tempted to purchase law books second-hand; make sure the edition on offer *is* the latest available, otherwise you may be parting with good money for a publication of little practical use.

Law books written by famous authors frequently continue to be known by the name of the original author even though that person died long ago. An example is Joseph Chitty, *Contracts*, first published in 1826 and now in its 28th edition. Joseph Chitty died in 1838. Subsequent editions have been prepared by other authors such as Hugh Beale, and when using the library catalogue you should be able to trace entries under these names as well. In addition, since the book is popularly known as *Chitty on Contracts*, you may find an additional entry in the title catalogue in this form.

Quite a large number of well-known law books are written by *joint authors*, that is, two or more authors are responsible for the text, for example: Hepple and Matthews, *Tort: Cases and Materials*. Usually the library author catalogue will have two entries, one under Hepple, B.A., and the other under Matthews, M.H., so you can successfully search under either name. This is particularly helpful where one of the authors has a very commonly occurring surname, such as Smith, as in Smith and Hogan, *Criminal Law*. Save time and effort and search under Hogan!

Lawyers can be rather lax about giving *the surname and forenames or initials of authors* to whom they are referring; frequently only the surname is given. Tracing Smith, *Casebook on Contract* in a library catalogue will be a very time-consuming task. If, however, the catalogue has a title section, search that instead! Also, why not consider encouraging others to follow a more helpful policy and when *you* write about an author, give the surname *with* initials or forenames.

Some famous law authors have *double barrelled names* such as O. Hood-Phillips. Libraries adopt different practices and it is worth checking the catalogue under Phillips and, if unsuccessful, Hood-Phillips, before declaring the library does not stock his books.

A substantial number of legal publications are prepared by *organisations* rather than individuals, for example: the Law Commission, the Home Office, the Law Society. To find an entry in the library catalogue use the author section and search under the name of the organisation, ignoring 'the' at the beginning of the name.

TSO or *SO*, which stands for The Stationery Office (formerly Her Majesty's Stationery Office, HMSO) is a *publisher* of a very wide range of materials lawyers use (see 8.6). TSO is not the author of law books. You should avoid the common trap of trying to search the library author catalogue under TSO or HMSO for entries on the particular official publication you require. Instead, either search the author catalogue by the name of the organisation which prepared the document (e.g., Home Office, Law Commission), or the title, or name, catalogue by the title of the publication.

1.2.8   What if the library appears not to have the book or periodical you require?

First, make sure you have used the correct section of the catalogue for your search. For example, here are three fairly common errors in catalogue use:

(a)   Picking a word from the title of a book and searching the subject section of the catalogue, then the classified in the hope of finding an entry.

(b)   Searching the author section of the book catalogue for an entry for the author of a periodical article you are trying to trace — no library catalogue indexes the contents of periodicals except where an article has been photocopied and added to stock, and this is not a common occurrence.

(c)   Searching the title section of the catalogue for the title of a periodical. This can be achieved successfully on some computerised catalogues, but if only microform or card catalogues are available, information about the periodicals stocked by the library is kept in a separate periodicals catalogue.

Secondly, make sure you are using the correct spelling of the author's name or the title of the book or periodical. Try some alternatives. If that fails ask library staff for advice.

Thirdly, when you have exhausted the two foregoing possibilities, then the chances are the library probably does not stock what you require. But do not give up! All academic and public libraries in the UK are members of a national inter-library loan service, which enables them to trace and obtain from other libraries copies of books and periodicals which they, themselves, do not possess. The service is also part of an international network. If the information you have about a particular book or periodical article is *full and accurate* — and these are vital requirements — you can make an application through your local library for the item to be obtained for you. If you are preparing a final-year project or dissertation you will probably need to use the inter-library loan service quite often; more details are given in appendix 2.

1.2.9   How to use electronic databases to study law

The skill to successfully search and retrieve relevant information from electronic databases is now as important to a law student as the skill of finding material on the library shelves. There is a wide range of databases available over the internet and on Compact Disc (CD-ROM). Most universities or colleges will either provide tuition in the use of relevant law databases as part of the law course you are following, or provide self-help leaflets covering the basic steps of searching or, both. Appendix 4 gives details of the different types of database you may come across when studying law and some principles of good search technique.

It's worth remembering that although the internet is now an important source of legal information, some of the most useful databases are accessible only to subscribers. Many universities and colleges have institutional subscriptions which will give you access via the passwords assigned to your university or college. The cost of a personal subscription to one of these databases will be such as to put it outside the pocket of a student.

Chapter 2

Effective use of catalogues and indexes

This short chapter describes some techniques for making the most effective use of library catalogues and indexes in all types of legal publication and electronic databases. Law is a subject so dependent on written words and their meaning that having the skill to extract all the required information from a catalogue index or database is one of the basic abilities a lawyer should possess.

When you have analysed a legal topic or problem with which you have to deal, you may have formed a list of words or phrases in your mind which sum the matter up. The challenge before you is to accurately match *your* list with the words provided in library catalogues, publication indexes and databases, so that you can quickly and accurately find the information about the topic or problem you require.

The language of law is particularly rich and you will discover that in many instances no two indexes to publications or databases are likely to use exactly the same words to describe a particular legal concept. There are several reasons for this. First, the authors may be considering the concept from different viewpoints and in different contexts. Secondly, the index compiler, who is normally a different person from the author, will not only echo the author's approach but develop the structure and content of the index in a way which will be most helpful for the intended readership. So a student textbook on industrial relations law, for example, may use different subject headings from a three-volume practitioners' encyclopaedia on the same subject. Thirdly, a good index will use a single word or phrase to describe a fact or concept which, in the text of the book, may have been referred to by several different words and in several different ways — the index will bring all references to the same matter together at the same point. Further, whilst many electronic databases index virtually every word they contain, unless there has been tight control of the vocabulary used, the same legal concept could be mentioned in different ways.

To ensure that when you use an index you refer to all the possible words which might be used to describe the concept in which you are interested, you should master the use of a word association technique, such as cartwheeling.

An example of this technique is given in figure 2.1.

Place the concept in which you are interested at the centre of the page, then cluster in groups around it words which have a broader meaning, closely related terms, synonyms (words with the same meaning), related terms, narrower words and so on.

To help you compile these groups of words use ordinary English dictionaries, such as the *Oxford English Dictionary*, or law dictionaries, or a specialised publication — a legal thesaurus. An example of one published for the law of the United Kingdom is *A Legal Thesaurus*, 3rd edition, edited by Christine Miskin, published by Legal Information Resources Ltd. It is an alphabetical listing of legal terms against each of which are noted broader terms, narrower terms and related terms. So, in the example shown in figure 2.2, for the word

Figure 2.1   Cartwheel for the word 'pollution'. After Statsky (1982).

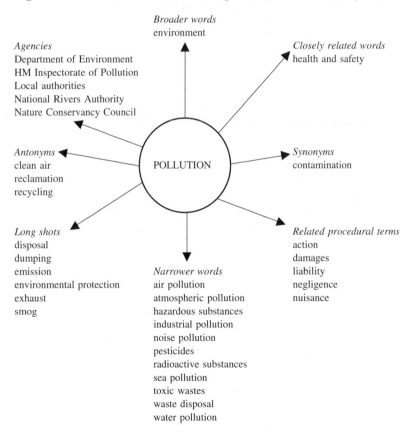

Figure 2.2   Extract from *A Legal Thesaurus* (1997).

> **NEGLIGENCE   (G)**
> NT: CONTRIBUTORY NEGLIGENCE
> NT: DUTY OF CARE
> NT: ECONOMIC LOSS
> NT: FORSEEABILITY
> NT: LATENT DAMAGE
> NT: PERSONAL INJURIES
> NT: PRODUCT LIABILITY
> NT: PROFESSIONAL NEGLIGENCE
> NT: PSYCHIATRIC HARM
> NT: RES IPSA LOQUITUR
> NT: STANDARD OF CARE
> BT: TORTS
> RT: MEDICAL NEGLIGENCE
>
> **NEGOTIABLE INSTRUMENTS   (G)**
> NT: AMERICAN DEPOSITARY RECEIPTS
> NT: BANKERS DRAFTS
> NT: BILLS OF EXCHANGE
> NT: COMMERCIAL CREDITS
> NT: STERLING COMMERCIAL PAPER
> BT: FINANCIAL INSTRUMENTS
> RT: CHOSES IN ACTION
> RT: SHARE WARRANTS
>
> **NEGOTIATION   (G)**
> BT: DISPUTE RESOLUTION
> RT: GRIEVANCE PROCEDURES
>
> **NEIGHBOURHOOD ADVICE CENTRES   (G)**
> BT: LEGAL ADVICE CENTRES
>
> **NEIGHBOURHOOD WATCH   (G)**
> BT: CRIME PREVENTION

'negligence', 11 narrower terms are given ranging in alphabetical order from contributory negligence to standard of care; one broader term (torts), and one related term (medical negligence) complete the list.

Having compiled your cartwheel you can run the list of terms you have discovered against the index entries in the book, encyclopaedia or electronic database you are using, and so be more certain of extracting all the information relevant to your problem. Constructing a cartwheel takes time but in the early stages of your law course you will be trying to understand the relationships between legal concepts and the words used to describe them, so learning the discipline of using a word association technique will be worthwhile.

A final word about the different types of index you are likely to come across in your legal research. Publishers usually group indexes at the back of a book or in the last volume of a multi-volume encyclopaedia, or even as a separate index volume if the main text of the publication is so extensive. Alphabetical lists of the subjects covered by the publication are commonplace. However, you will find in law publications some specialised indexes, and these are frequently placed at the *front*: they include alphabetical lists of the titles of Acts and court cases referred to in the text, or even chronological lists of Acts and other statutory materials referred to, the oldest placed first in the list.

The main points to ask yourself when using indexes are:

(a)   What information is being searched for: a subject, a title, the name of an organisation?

(b)   Which types of index are available in the publication? Check the contents page at the front.

(c)   Where are the indexes placed: at the front, at the back, in a separate volume?

This checklist may seem like 'teaching Grandma to suck eggs' but few students stop to think about these points and so fail to fully benefit from the thoughtful and careful work of the indexer.

PART 2

RESEARCHING THE LAW OF ENGLAND, WALES AND SCOTLAND

Chapter 3

The structure of the literature

'*Where* do I start to look for the answer to this legal problem?' This thought commonly crosses the minds of students, and some practitioners, who, having already expended considerable mental effort to identify to their satisfaction the nature of the problem to be solved, now stand in the library wondering which publications are likely to contain the solution. Two of the most basic research skills are to understand that there is a structure to the literature of law, and to know how the component parts relate to one another so that relevant sources can be matched and applied to information needs.

The literature of English, Welsh and Scots law may be divided into two broad categories: the primary sources and the secondary sources, as shown in figure 3.1.

The basis of this distinction is that the primary sources are the law itself whilst the secondary are commentaries on it.

3.1 PRIMARY SOURCES

The primary sources comprise original and authoritative statements of the law, sub-divided into three: legislation — law made by Parliament; case law — the decisions of the courts; and a minor, frequently overlooked yet valuable, group of sources, which might be collectively referred to as 'extra-legal'.

3.1.1 Legislation

Legislation is itself divided into primary (original) and secondary (delegated or subordinate), the distinction being that primary legislation, in general, becomes law only after detailed debate and scrutiny within Parliament culminating in approval by the Sovereign, whilst secondary legislation is, generally speaking,

Figure 3.1   The literature of the law of the United Kingdom.

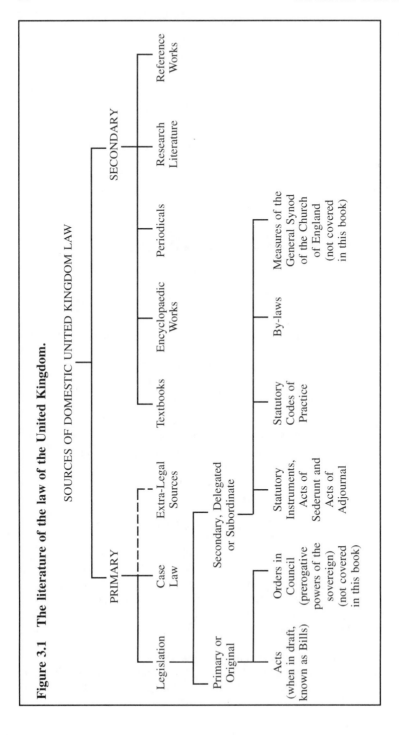

prepared by an authority outside Parliament (usually a Minister of the Crown), under powers given by Parliament through primary legislation. Secondary legislation contains detailed rules and regulations, which it would be impractical to include within primary legislation, in an attempt to cover every contingency the legislation might involve. The usual practice is for primary legislation to contain the broad outlines of a particular scheme and secondary legislation to contain the detail.

Primary or original legislation can take the form of an Act of Parliament or an Order in Council, but since the latter are only infrequently issued and their main application is in relation to the armed forces, the civil service or emergency powers, further discussion of Orders in Council as primary legislation is omitted. However, law students must be aware of how to trace and use draft versions of Acts of Parliament, better known as Bills of Parliament. Bills of Parliament contain proposals which, if enacted, would either introduce new provisions or amend, repeal or consolidate the existing law — a knowledge of such current proposals and their likely effect will impress examiners. Bills of both the current and past sessions of Parliament are valuable to students undertaking final-year projects or higher-degree research. Bills are often heavily amended and revised as they pass through Parliament, and tracing these changes provides insights into the development of the law and the lobby work of pressure groups. The ability to trace Bills which failed to receive Parliamentary support and have never become law is also useful — in recent years, more Public Bills have failed to become Acts than the number which have successfully completed the legislative process. Many will have been contentious, some may have failed through lack of Parliamentary time, but all contain pertinent views on how the law should develop to either cause or reflect change in society. The different types of Bills and Acts are discussed in chapter 4.

Secondary legislation may be split into four categories: statutory instruments, codes of practice, by-laws and Measures of the General Synod of the Church of England. Only the first three will be covered in this book as rarely, if ever, even in legal practice, will a lawyer need access to Church of England Measures. The differences between statutory instruments, statutory codes of practice and by-laws, and how to trace these publications are explained in chapter 5.

The Scotland Act 1998 devolved extensive law-making powers to the Scottish Parliament sitting in Edinburgh. Prior to the 1998 Act, legislation applying to Scotland was made at Westminster and followed the procedures discussed in chapters 4 and 5. Since devolution, Westminster has retained responsibility for legislating on a number of matters including the constitution, defence and treason, and specific powers relating to aspects of trade and industry, transport, social security and employment. A full list is given in chapter 9. Legislation relating to these non-devolved matters will continue to be created at Westminster. Therefore, a student of Scots law will need to be familiar with the procedures and sources of both the new Scottish Parliament (chapters 10 to 12) and Parliament at Westminster (chapters 4 and 5). Strictly speaking, the Acts of the Scottish Parliament are a form of delegated legislation. These Acts, unlike those passed by Westminster, can be challenged in the courts on the grounds that they are ultra vires. In this respect they resemble statutory instruments.

The Government of Wales Act 1998 established a National Assembly for Wales, sitting in Cardiff, and having transferred to it most of the administrative functions of the Secretary of State for Wales. The Assembly does not have powers to make primary legislation (Acts) but can make secondary legislation (statutory instruments) in 18 specific subject areas, mostly concerned with public sector matters, ranging from agriculture and ancient monuments to water and flood defence. The legal documents which the Assembly produces are discussed as part of chapter 5. Westminster will continue to legislate for those matters not devolved to the National Assembly.

3.1.2   Case law

The second subdivision of the primary sources of law comprises case or judge-made law — the decisions of the courts. Built up from over seven centuries of work of the courts, the sheer volume of decisions and number of different source publications available means, that of all the categories of primary legal sources, case law frequently causes students the most research difficulty. However, as with other legal sources, the key to mastering legal research skills lies in recognising and understanding patterns and structures, and for case law they are (a) the historical development of law report publishing and (b) the characteristics and use of a range of case-locating publications such as indexes, digests and *Citators*, available to assist research; see chapter 6. The Scottish dimension in researching case law is discussed in chapter 12.

3.1.3   Extra-legal sources

The third subdivision of the primary sources of law, the extra-legal, comprises what are generally referred to as non-statutory codes of practice. The individual documents may be called either codes of practice, codes of conduct, guidance or standards, but they have two things in common: they are issued without the authority of Parliament by a variety of public and private organisations, and secondly, they are not legally enforceable in their own right. They are not found in all areas of legal study but most frequently in business, commercial and consumer law. They can be difficult to track down in legal research, but chapter 7 provides assistance.

3.2   SECONDARY SOURCES

Standing distinct from the primary sources of the literature of English law are five secondary, an even more extensive and varied group, comprising commentaries, explanations, reviews or guides to the primary sources. They are:

(a)   textbooks comprising books of authority, modern textbooks, casebooks, practice books and precedent books;

(b)   encyclopaedic works;

(c)   periodicals, also referred to as journals;

(d)   research literature, such as postgraduate theses and other research publications;

(e)   and reference works, including dictionaries and directories — see chapter 8.

Commentary on Scots law is discussed in chapter 13.

3.3   THE GOVERNMENT

So far the outline of the structure of legal literature has been based on the type of information or form of publication. However, no guide to legal research skills would be complete without a section devoted to the output of probably the most prolific and diverse publisher in the UK — the government. The government publishes legal information in virtually every one of the forms so far described. Ways of tracking down government publications will be explained in the final section of chapter 8. Researching Scottish official publications is discussed in the final section of chapter 13.

Chapter 4

Primary legislation

4.1 BILLS OF PARLIAMENT

4.1A Description

4.1A1 Definition

A Bill is a draft version of a proposed Act of Parliament, a document containing the text of a piece of legislation. A Bill may be introduced in Parliament in either the House of Lords or the House of Commons but must successfully pass through several stages in both Houses before it can be submitted to the Sovereign for Royal Assent. Once the Sovereign has signified assent the Bill becomes an Act of Parliament.

There are three classes of Bill: Public, Private and Hybrid (see figure 4.1).

Public Bills (which, if successful, will become Public General Acts) relate to matters of *public policy* and are introduced directly by members of Parliament. If a Public Bill is introduced by a member of the government (for example, a Minister) the Bill will be referred to as a Government Bill; if it is introduced by a private member of Parliament (in the Commons an individual Member of Parliament (MP) or in the Lords an individual peer) it is formally referred to as an 'unofficial Member's Bill', or more familiarly as a 'Private Member's Bill'. A Private Member's Bill should not be confused with the second class of Bills, Private Bills. A Private Bill (which, if successful, will become a Private Act, or more correctly a Local or Personal Act) is a Bill which relates to an individual or small group of people, a public company or corporation or a local authority — its application is restricted in scope to particular people, organisations or a geographical location. As a further distinction, a Private Bill is presented to Parliament in the form of a petition, by the parties whom the legislation is intended to benefit, acting through a specialist firm of Parliamentary Agents, and

Figure 4.1   Types of Bill of Parliament.

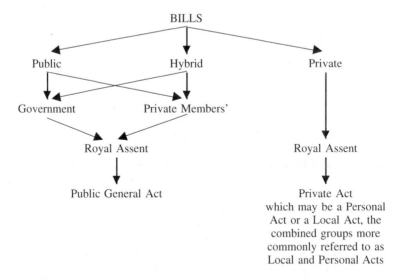

not a member of Parliament. A Private Bill also follows a quite different Parliamentary procedure from a Public Bill. The Greater Manchester (Light Rapid Transit System) Bill, which received the Royal Assent in 1990, is an example. It provides for the construction and operation of a 'tram' system on the public road and rail networks.

The third category of Bill is known as a Hybrid Bill which, as the name suggests, is a Public Bill which may in certain respects affect private rights, and is dealt with by a special procedure. The Channel Tunnel Bill, which received the Royal Assent in 1987, not only provides for the construction and operation of the railway tunnel, but also the compulsory purchase of land around Folkestone for roads and other works.

One type of Bill you will frequently come across is a consolidation Bill, normally found amongst Public Bills. It does not introduce any new law but seeks to tidy up existing legislation by bringing together scattered elements in one Bill. For example, the Companies Act 1985 comprises 747 sections and 25 schedules consolidating legislation from 1948 to 1983.

As a law student you are likely only to use Public Bills, but once in legal practice, especially with a local authority or a statutory undertaker (for example, an electricity, gas or water company), skill in researching private legislation may be required. In the rest of 4.1, therefore, the accent is on the skills and techniques required when researching Public Bills.

4.1A2   Origin

Bills themselves have draft versions. They are prepared by specialist lawyers known as Parliamentary counsel. The draft versions are not normally published but reports of the Law Commission and the Scottish Law Commission (see 8.6) frequently include a draft Public Bill in its entirety or selected clauses, to show how recommendations for the reform of a legal topic should be given effect.

It is important to understand the broad outline of the procedure followed by Parliament when considering Bills because they are reprinted, incorporating amendments, at several stages in the Parliamentary process. It is crucial, when researching, to match the correct version of the Bill to the relevant *Reports of Parliamentary Debates (Hansard)*, in which the arguments put by MPs and peers for and against the Bill's provisions, are reported in full.

The discussion which follows relates to the procedure for Bills at Westminster applying to England and Wales. Special procedures exist for Bills relating exclusively to Scotland which involve referral to the Scottish Grand Committee and a Scottish Committee. In the post-devolution era this is only relevant if the proposals are not within the legislative competence of the Scottish Parliament (see chapters 9 and 10).

The procedures of the House of Commons and House of Lords when considering a Public Bill are quite complex and different. Figure 4.2, kindly supplied by staff at The Stationery Office, highlights the crucial points for legal research purposes, relating each stage through which a Bill may pass to (a) the times when the Bill may be printed or reprinted (marked 'Bill' in the columns headed 'Reported in (publication)', (b) the places where reports of the debates will be printed (*Hansard* and *Reports of Standing Committees of the House*), (c) when amendments will be printed, and (d) where details of the progress of business on the Bill will be found (*Minute, Journal*).

A Bill may be first presented in either the House of Commons or the House of Lords. In the first House it would require support at all stages through to transfer stage when it would go to the other House to follow a similar path again. If amendments have been made in the other House, an exchange of messages occurs between the Houses until the differences are resolved, and finally the Bill is sent for Royal Assent by the Sovereign. A Bill may be printed up to six times during the Parliamentary process, each printing may include agreed amendments to the original document. The timing of these key events is noted in figure 4.2 by the word 'Bill' appearing in the columns headed 'Reported in (publication)'. They are after first reading (both Houses), after committee stage if amended in committee (both Houses), and following report stage, if amended (both Houses, though this does not usually occur in the Commons).

There are a few more points to bear in mind. First, there are several ways in which a Member of Parliament in the House of Commons can introduce a Bill. One is under the so-called 'ten-minute rule', when the Member gives a brief explanatory statement on the objects of the proposed Bill. This statement will be reported in full in *Hansard*. If, as a result of the statement, the Commons do *not* give leave to introduce the Bill, then the Bill will not be published, and the only public statement about it will be the MP's speech. Secondly, a Bill can be defeated at several other stages in the Parliamentary process, notably at the second reading and third reading stages in either House. The second reading normally commences with a speech by the Bill's proposer followed by a debate

Figure 4.2   Legislation procedures and related publications for Parliamentary Bills. Source Hallett (1992).

HOUSE OF COMMONS		HOUSE OF LORDS	
STAGE	REPORTED IN (PUBLICATION)	STAGE	REPORTED IN (PUBLICATION)
Presentation (First Reading)	Bill, Order Paper, Votes and Proceedings, Hansard, Journal	Presentation (First Reading)	Bill, Minute, Hansard, Journal
Second Reading (General Debate) (approval to continue)	Order Paper, Hansard, Votes and Proceedings, Journal	Second Reading (General Debate) (approval to continue)	Minute, Hansard, Journal
Amendments (can now be tabled)	Notices of Amendments	Amendments (can now be tabled)	Peers Amendments, Marshalled Lists
Committee Stage (amends Bill) (usually Standing Committee, can be a whole House Committee)	Amendments, Standing Committee Debate (or Hansard if whole House Committee), Votes and Proceedings, Journal, Minutes of Proceedings, Notices of Amendments, Committee Business, Bill (if amended)	Committee Stage (normally whole House, can be a Public Bill Committee)	Amendments, Marshalled Lists, Hansard, Minute, (or Public Bill Committee Official Report), Journal and Bill (if amended)
Report Stage (Can further amend Bill)	Order Paper, Amendments possible, Hansard, Votes and Proceedings, Journal, Notices of Amendments, Bill (not normally printed)	Report Stage (can further amend Bill)	Amendments, Marshalled Lists, Hansard, Minute, Journal and Bill (if amended)
Third Reading (Can further amend Bill)	Amendments possible, Order Paper, Hansard, Votes and Proceedings, Journal, Notices of Amendments	Third Reading (can further amend Bill)	Amendments possible, Hansard, Minute, Journal
Transfer or Consideration Stage		Transfer or Consideration Stage	
Messages	Lords Reasons and Amendments, Commons Amendments, Votes and Proceedings, Notices of Amendments, Hansard, Journal	Messages	Commons Reasons and Amendments, Lords Amendments, Marshalled Lists, Hansard, Minute, Journal
Royal Assent	Votes and Proceedings, Hansard, Journal	Royal Assent (Notice to Commons)	Hansard, Minute, Journal

on the general principles of the proposed legislation. If the Bill successfully receives a second reading it will go to the committee stage where detailed consideration, line by line, word by word, is given to the Bill's proposals. There is no vote at the end of the committee stage, but at the report stage amendments made in committee and, in the House of Commons only, any new amendments, are considered. Again, there is no vote at the conclusion of this stage but there is following the brief proceedings of the third reading. For legal researchers the committee stage, especially in the House of Commons, has the most interest, for the Bill is here considered by a Standing Committee of, on average, about 20 MPs. The discussions are reported verbatim, not in *Hansard*, but in a separate series: *Reports of Standing Committees of the House*. On a few occasions the Commons sits as a committee of the whole House, and in that case the debate on the Bill is printed in *Hansard* itself.

For further information on Public, Private and Hybrid Bill procedure consult the authoritative source used in Parliament itself: Erskine May's *Treatise on the Law, Privileges, Proceedings and Usage of Parliament* (often referred to as Erskine May's *Parliamentary Practice*), published by Butterworths and frequently revised through new editions.

In general, for a Public Bill to become law it must complete its passage through both Houses within a session of Parliament, which is usually a period of about a year between one Queen's Speech and the next. One exception, recently topical, is where a Bill passes successfully through the House of Commons but is defeated in the House of Lords in two successive Parliamentary sessions. Even without the support of the House of Lords, providing certain procedural details have been followed, the Bill can be sent for Royal Assent. This procedure, laid down in the Parliament Act 1911, as amended by the Parliament Act 1949, has been used on only a few occasions. The length of each Parliamentary session is determined by the government of the day, but the normal pattern is for the State Opening of Parliament, when the Queen's Speech is delivered, to take place in early November, so marking the beginning of a fresh session of Parliament, with no Bills yet introduced. The Queen's Speech itself will set out in general terms the legislation which the government intends to introduce into Parliament during the session. Nearly a year later, just before the next Queen's Speech, the session is brought to an end by prorogation, and any Bills which have yet to complete their passage are lost. This frequently happens with Private Members' Bills, most getting no further than the first reading stage, a few to second reading and an even fewer number beyond. All will fail to become law because the session was brought to a close before all Parliamentary stages were completed. Commonly only around 10 per cent of all Private Members' Bills satisfactorily complete the Parliamentary process and become law (see Drewry 1989 and 1992). Government Bills, however, fare much better, and once introduced into Parliament are highly likely to complete all stages by the end of the session and become law. When a General Election is called Parliament is dissolved and all Public Bills will be lost. The only exception to this general position is that some Private Bills and Hybrid Bills can be carried over from one session of Parliament to the next, provided specific resolutions to that effect are agreed by the House or Houses which have already given them consideration.

4.1A3   Structure

A Public Bill comprises nine different parts, not all of which are essential.

(a)   *Short title* — this is the title under which the eventual Act will be generally known. It is given in three places: at the head of the Bill, in a clause of the Bill (usually the last) and on the outside of the back cover.

(b)   *Arrangement of clauses* — a table at the front of most printings of all but the briefest of Bills sets out in order the parts, chapters and clauses into which the text is divided, with their respective titles (see appendix 3 for further details of the terminology for the divisions of a Bill).

(c)   *Long title* — this sets out in general terms the purposes of the Bill. It appears twice in a Bill, once above the enacting formula, and also on the outside of the back cover.

(d)   *Preamble* — its purpose is to state the reasons for and the expected effects of the proposed legislation. A preamble is rarely incorporated in Public Bills nowadays but still appears in Bills of great constitutional importance or in a Bill giving effect to international conventions.

(e)   *Enacting formula* — this short paragraph summarises the legislative authority of Parliament and precedes the first clause of the Bill.

(f)   *Clauses* — the Bill is divided into a series of numbered clauses, each with a descriptive title, known as a 'side note' or 'marginal note' printed in the margin. The word clause is often abbreviated in writing to 'cl'. When a Bill receives Royal Assent and becomes an Act, the clauses of the Bill become sections of the Act.

Clauses may be divided into subsections, subsections into paragraphs, and paragraphs into subparagraphs — see appendix 3. Towards the end of the Bill, or if appropriate, at the end of one of its parts, formal clauses are placed which contain very important information for the legal researcher:

(i)   Definition clauses, indicated by the marginal note 'interpretation', give the meaning of certain key words used in the text of the Bill.

(ii)   Saving clauses, indicated by the marginal note 'savings' or similar, have the function of saving or preserving rather than altering an existing right or powers; it has been said that they are often included by way of reassurance, for avoidance of doubt or from abundance of caution. They often begin with a phrase: 'Nothing in this section shall be construed as . . .'.

(iii)   The short title clause, indicated by the marginal note 'short title', sets out the title under which the Act will be cited amongst the statutes. This title is also given at the head of the Bill and on the outside of the back cover.

(iv)   Commencement clauses, indicated by the marginal note 'commencement', detail when the Act is to come into force. Since the beginning of the 1982/83 session of Parliament, commencement clauses ought usually to be grouped at the end of a Bill (see Anon (1983)).

(v)   Extent clauses, indicated by the marginal note 'extent', detail the geographical area to which the Bill applies (England and Wales, Scotland, Northern Ireland individually or in any combination, or the United Kingdom as a whole).

(g) *Schedules* — at the end of many Bills will be found one or more schedules (abbreviated to 'Sch.') containing detailed provisions dependent on one or more of the preceding clauses, rather like appendices at the back of a book.

(h) *Explanatory memorandum* — though not technically part of the Bill, an explanatory memorandum is often attached to the first printing of the Bill in each House. If appropriate a financial memorandum is also included, on the Bill's likely effect on public expenditure. The explanatory memorandum sets out the contents and objects of the Bill and briefly describes, clause by clause in non-technical language, the provisions of the Bill. For the legal researcher this provides a very helpful summary. All Government Bills requiring expenditure must include a financial memorandum, setting out the financial effects with estimates, where possible, of the amount of money involved, and also forecasts of any effects on manpower in the public service, expected as a result of the passing of the Bill.

(i) *Back cover information* — printed sideways across the back cover of the Bill, and known as an endorsement, similar to those found on other legal documents, such as court briefs, conveyances, wills, leases etc., are the short and long titles and then several groups of information valuable to the researcher: the name of the MP or peer presenting and the names of up to 11 supporters of the Bill, and details of the stage in the Parliamentary process the particular version of the Bill relates to, the date of the order for the Bill to be printed and the sessional running number for the Bill. The names will indicate whether the Bill is a Government Bill (which will have a high chance of becoming law) or a Private Member's Bill (which will have a greatly reduced chance of becoming law). The stage, printing date and sessional running number assist identification of the version of the Bill to hand.

Since the late 1990s many Public Bills are now accompanied by a separate document called Explanantory Notes. These notes are prepared by the sponsoring Government Department and are intended to assist the reader of the Bill and help inform debate and understanding of it. The notes need to be read in conjunction with the Bill and they are not intended to be a comprehensive description. Consequently, where it is thought that a clause does not seem to require an explanation or comment, none is given. These notes do not form part of the Bill, and have not been endorsed by Parliament. They can either be published at the same time as the Bill or at a later date. If, during the Bill's passage through Parliament, it is heavily amended, the Explanatory Notes may be amended to relate to the altered content of the Bill.

4.1A4 Publication and general availability

Public Bills are published by The Stationery Office (TSO), formerly Her Majesty's Stationery Office (HMSO) and are one of a larger group of publications known as Parliamentary Papers (see 8.6). They can be purchased through TSO Bookshops or private bookshops acting as agents for TSO. Bills are normally printed in small quantities and should be available until three months after the end of the session in which they were presented. If out of print, TSO can arrange for a photocopy of the Bill to be supplied. The Bills themselves are printed on pale green tinted paper, whilst lists of amendments for consideration by Parliament are printed on white paper. Bills and related papers can be ordered from TSO on a short-term standing order, known as the 'all follows system'. This will supply the specific Bill requested, all reprints, related debates and amendments. After the end of each session of Parliament TSO publishes bound volumes of Sessional Papers, the first two or three volumes of which contain all Public Bills in alphabetical order by title, all the amendments and different versions of a Bill brought together at one point. Sessional indexes are also published to assist searching. However, only major, academic law libraries or libraries having comprehensive collections of British official publications are likely to collect all Public Bills.

The full text of all Public Bills before Parliament in the current session, together with any accompanying Explanatory Notes, is available on the Parliament web site at

http://www.parliament.the-stationery-office.co.uk/pa/pabills.htm

Added value information provided at the site and not found on the printed copies includes a note placed at the head of each Bill giving the stage which the Bill has reached in its passage through Parliament. In addition, amendments currently proposed are shown separately from the text of the Bill.

Private Bills, on the other hand, are printed at the expense of the promoters themselves and are available from their Parliamentary Agent (the *Weekly Information Bulletin of the House of Commons* — see 4.1B1 — provides details of names and addresses of agents for Private Bills being considered in the current session of Parliament). Few libraries collect Private Bills — to obtain copies of old Bills contact the local authority, corporation or individuals concerned. The text of Private Bills is not available on the internet, though Committee Reports on the Bills are, at

http://www.parliament.the-stationery-office.co.uk/pa/cm/cmpubns.htm

4.1A5 *Citation*

For Public Bills a serial number appears at the bottom left-hand side of the first page of each Bill. When a Bill is reprinted at any subsequent stage it is given a new number. Traditionally, the number on a Bill originating in the House of Commons appeared in square brackets and those originating in the Lords appeared within curved brackets, but since the mid-1980s, with the change from Royal Octavo to A4 paper size, although Commons Bills continue to be signified in the traditional manner, Lords Bills are now designated 'HL Bill' followed by a number without brackets. Since a new numerical sequence begins with each new session of Parliament, the correct method of citing a Bill should not only include the running number, but also the session, e.g:

HC Bill (1989–90) [51].
HL Bill (1989–90) 57.

4.1B   Finding information

4.1B1   Weekly Information Bulletin of the House of Commons

Weekly Information Bulletin is compiled by the Public Information Office of the House of Commons Library and published each week Parliament is sitting. Amongst the vast amount of information provided in each issue are two lists, one of Public (including Hybrid) Bills, the other of Private Bills, before Parliament this session. The Bills are listed in alphabetical order by title. The Bill number and the dates when each stage of Parliamentary scrutiny has been reached are given. The dates are specially useful for they assist (a) in identifying the most up-to-date printing of a Bill, and (b) in tracing in *Hansard* the reports of debates on the Bill. It is important to note that debates in House of Commons Standing Committees are *not* printed in the same series of *Hansard* as reports of debates on the floor of the House of Commons, but in a separate series. Standing Committee debates are frequently of greatest interest to legal re-searchers because it is in committee, comprising on average only 20 MPs selected for their interest in and knowledge of the subject area, that the most detailed scrutiny of a Bill occurs (see 4.1B6).

The *Bulletin*, from the issue for 19 October 1996 onwards, is also available free on the internet after 12.30 pm on the Monday following the Saturday publication of the paper version. The web address is

http://www.parliament.the-stationery-office.co.uk/pa/cm/cmwib.htm

A partial cumulation of *Weekly Information Bulletin* is published at the end of each Parliamentary session as the *Sessional Information Digest*. The *Digest* is useful for tracing the dates of debates on a Bill from a past session of Parliament. It is available free on the internet from the 1995–96 *Sessional Information Digest* onwards, at

http://www.parliament.the-stationery-office.co.uk/pa/cm/cmsid.htm

4.1B2   JUSTIS Parliament

JUSTIS Parliament comprises six CDs containing an index to (*not* the text of) proceedings in the UK Parliament. Amongst other matters, the index holds references to all Public and Private Bills laid before Parliament from session 1979–80 to the very recent past (the CDs carrying the most recent material are updated twice a year). Some libraries may subscribe to an add-on service, called *JUSTIS Parliament Online*, by which all the files from session 1992 to the present are available from a web site, updated daily and with only a few days delay after the events indexed occured. From session 1987–88 onwards the database has included a Bill Histories section which records for each Bill a complete history of its passage through Parliament. The *JUSTIS* service is authoritative for it is based on the *Parliamentary Online Information System (POLIS)* database, compiled by staff of the House of Commons Library. The

JUSTIS CDs and internet services are far quicker to use than ploughing through many sessional indexes to *Hansard* or Parliamentary Bills and Papers.

4.1B3   Lawtel

Information on the progress of Public Bills through Parliament is included in the Legislation section of this internet database. Links are available to the full text of Bills on the Parliament web site. Private Bills are not included. To obtain this information select 'legislation' from the *Lawtel* Databases index and type in a keyword from the title or the full title of the Bill in which you are interested. *Lawtel* is available to subscribers only; a user code and password are required to access the database. It is at

>   http://www.lawtel.co.uk

4.1B4   Current Law Monthly Digest

Although this popular publication carries tables listing the progress of Bills and references to debates reported in *Hansard*, the content is neither as full nor as up-to-date as the lists in *Weekly Information Bulletin*.

4.1B5   Daily List of Government Publications

In the late afternoon of every working day a list is published of all TSO and some non-TSO official publications issued that day. The first part of the list gives details of Parliamentary publications, which includes Bills. TSO also publishes a *Monthly Catalogue* and an *Annual Catalogue* which also list Bills published. However, all the listings produced by TSO are primarily intended to help booksellers correctly identify a publication, not assist legal researchers. They do not give much detail of the stages and no detail of the dates of progress of Bills. They merely tell you that different printings of a Bill were made! *The Daily List* is also available on the internet at

>   http://www.the-stationery-office.co.uk/daily_list/

4.1B6   Hansard

The series titled *Parliamentary Debates (Official Reports)* is popularly known as *Hansard* after the printer of one of the earliest (but not *the* earliest) reports of Parliamentary debates. It is a full report of what is said in the House of Commons and the House of Lords; it is published in two series, one covering each House. *Hansard* is available the day following the debates reported, with, in addition, a weekly edition, *Weekly Hansard*, merely gathering together the daily parts. Finally, bound volumes are published, a new volume commencing at the start of each session of Parliament. Indexes are available to the weekly and sessional volumes.

There are a number of points to watch when using *Hansard* and its indexes:

(a)   *Hansard* is laid out with two columns of print to a page. References in the indexes refer not to page numbers but column numbers.

(b)   In House of Commons *Hansard* written answers to Parliamentary questions are gathered in a separate section at the end of each volume with column numbering in italics. Take care when looking for the debate on a Bill, that you are not looking in the Parliamentary questions section.

(c)   The indexes are so constructed that references to a debate on a topic are given *after* entries for Parliamentary questions, comments, brief statements etc. on the same topic. Although the debate may occupy the greatest area of text in *Hansard*, the index places the reference to it last in order of priority.

Since 1909 a quite distinct series covering the debates of Standing Committees has also appeared. Parliament may appoint as many Standing Committees as necessary; normally under 10 are appointed each session, designated by the letters 'A', 'B', 'C' etc. Their debates are published only as daily parts and as sessional volumes. Unfortunately, there is no equivalent weekly index to this series and although each individual bound volume has an index, there is no general index to a sessional set. Reference should therefore be made to the *Annual Catalogue of Government Publications* (see note within 4.1B5), which lists alphabetically the Bills considered in Standing Committee, identifying the Committee and the dates of sittings.

The full text of the House of Commons Official Report (*Hansard*), from May 1988 onwards, is available on CD-ROM. *Hansard* for the House of Lords is also available on CD from session 1992–93 onwards. One disc is available for each House for each Parliamentary session, and as each session progresses, discs are issued in April, September and January, cumulating the file to the Easter and Summer recesses, and the end of session, respectively. This means the CD version makes the content of *Hansard* more easily and quickly accessible than printed indexes.

Even more rapidly updated and almost as easy to search as the CD version is the text of *Hansard* placed on the Parliament web site by 9.00 am the day following the debates reported. *Hansard* for the House of Commons and the House of Lords is available on the internet for the same time periods as the CD versions. In addition, the web site has House of Commons Standing Committee Debates on Bills from the beginning of session 1997–98. The web site is free and reached via the UK Parliament Welcome page at

http://www.the-stationery-office.co.uk/pa/cm/stand.htm

4.1B7   *Current Law Statutes*

This publication (formerly called *Current Law Statutes Annotated*), covered in more detail in section 4.2B2.2.2, provides three valuable services. First, it details the progress of both Private and Public Bills before Parliament during the current session, through tables given in the loose-leaf Statutes Service File. Secondly, it reprints the Public General Acts of each session and, since 1992, the Private Acts also, many with additional editorial notes and commentary. Just below the list of contents at the beginning of each Act, the editors include references to the volume and column numbers in *Hansard*, where reports of the debates in the House of Commons (HC) and House of Lords (HL) are printed. Since 1989, references have been given for Standing Committee debates. *Current Law Statutes*, of course, prints only successful Bills which have become law, and is of no use for tracing failed legislation. Thirdly, the loose-leaf Statutes Service File binder carries a Table of Parliamentary Debates covering the years 1950 to the end of the last complete Parliamentary session, listing against every Public General Act references to debates reported in *Hansard* as the Bill passed through Parliament.

A CD, initially containing the statutes and the *Current Law Legislation Citators* for 1998 and 1999, is under development. Future issues of the CD will add to the backrun, but will eventually extend back only as far as 1992.

4.1B8   Law periodicals

The progress of Bills through Parliament may be traced using one of the weekly law journals such as the *Gazette, New Law Journal, Solicitors Journal* and, for Scotland, *Scots Law Times*. Their coverage of Bills is usually selective based on the perceived needs of their readerships.

4.1C   Answering research queries

For background information on using CDs and the internet for legal research, see appendix 4.

4.1C1   Tracing information on Bills of the current session of Parliament

Electronic route
Use one of the following:

(a)   *Weekly Information Bulletin* (see 4.1B1) — the internet version is authoritative;
(b)   *JUSTIS Parliament* (see 4.1B2) preferably with the add-on service *JUSTIS Parliament Online*;
(c)   Lawtel (see 4.1B3) — will provide a link to the full text of the Bill on the Parliament web site.

Paper route
Use one of the following:

(a)   *Weekly Information Bulletin* (see 4.1B1) — follow figure 4.3 from the top;
(b)   *Current Law Statutes* (see 4.1B7) — but updated only at monthly intervals.

Assuming it is a Public Bill you are researching, you will need to match the 'date' and 'stage' information against part of figure 4.3, to clarify what ought

Figure 4.3   Tracing information on Bills of the current session of Parliament using Parliamentary publications.

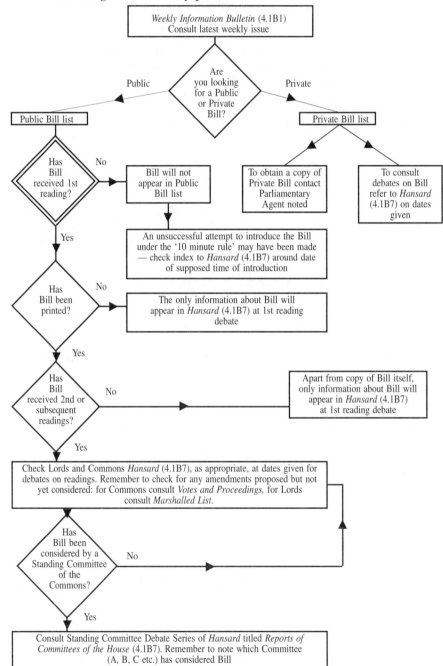

to be available in *Hansard* or elsewhere in Parliamentary publications. For a Public Bill, start at the diamond-shaped 'decision box' with a double border in figure 4.3.

4.1C2   Tracing information on Bills of a past session of Parliament

Quite apart from the historical value of tracing the development of an area of legislation, the House of Lords' decision in the case of *Pepper* v *Hart* [1993] AC 593, has made this type of research query popular with practising lawyers. Before the decision, the 'exclusionary rule' made reference to Parliamentary material as an aid to statutory construction not permissible. The rule was made by the courts in the eighteenth century. *Pepper* v *Hart* concluded (per Lord Browne-Wilkinson at 640) that:

'. . . subject to any question of Parliamentary privilege, . . . the exclusionary rule should be relaxed so as to permit reference to Parliamentary materials where: (a) legislation is ambiguous or obscure, or leads to an absurdity; (b) the material relied upon consists of one or more statements made by a minister or promoter of the Bill together with such other Parliamentary materials as is necessary to understand such statements and their effect; (c) the statements relied upon are clear.'

In these limited circumstances it is now permissible to 'go behind the Act'.

Electronic route
Use one of the following:

(a)   *JUSTIS Parliament* CD or online service (see 4.1B2) — a good starting-point because the index file for Bills goes back to 1979. You can also search by subject, as well as title;

(b)   *Weekly Information Bulletin* or the *Sessional Information Digest* on the internet (both at 4.1B1) — only cover the period from 1996 onwards.

Paper route
Start with (a) and then go to (b):

(a)   If the Bill became a Public General Act and you know the year of the Act try *Current Law Statutes* (see 4.1B7): either, the appropriate annual volume to see if there is a note, immediately following the contents list to the reprint of the Act, detailing where debates on the Bill will be found in *Hansard* or, the Parliamentary Debates Table in the Statutes Service File binder.

(b)   If *Current Law Statutes* does not provide this information or the Bill did not become an Act, *either*, use the final issue of the paper *Weekly Information Bulletin* or the *Sessional Information Digest* (see 4.1B1) for the relevant Parliamentary session and follow the procedure in figure 4.3 *or* consult the sessional index to Parliamentary Papers under the title of the Bill to find copies in the Sessional Papers, and check indexes to *Hansard* (see 4.1B6) for Lords,

Commons and Standing Committees (as appropriate) to find reports of debates; if the sessional index to Parliamentary Papers is not available try the TSO *Annual Catalogue* (discussed within 4.1B5) which at least will tell you about the different printings of the Bill made.

4.1C3   Tracing commentary on Bills of Parliament

The best method of answering this research question is to use one or a number of periodical indexing services, fully described in 8.3 below.

4.2   ACTS OF PARLIAMENT

4.2A   Description

4.2A1   Definition

An Act of Parliament is a Bill of Parliament which has been passed by both Houses of Parliament and then received the Royal Assent. The Parliament Act 1911 (as amended) provides two exceptions to this rule, allowing Bills which have passed the House of Commons to be presented to the Sovereign for Royal Assent without having passed the House of Lords. One exception is for 'Money Bills' and has never been used; the other deals with all other Bills, and has been invoked on only a few occasions. Briefly, the procedure is that the Bill must have been passed by the House of Commons in two successive sessions, have been sent to the House of Lords at least one month before the end of the session and have been rejected by the House of Lords in each of those two sessions. Other, specific, time-limits must be met also. On rejection the second time by the House of Lords, unless the House of Commons directs otherwise, the Bill is presented to the Sovereign and, on receiving the Royal Assent, becomes an Act of Parliament.

Acts of Parliament are sometimes collectively referred to as The Statute Book; an individual Act may be called a Statute.

There are two classes of Act: Public General, and Local and Personal. The distinction is that Public General Acts relate to matters of *public policy* while Local and Personal Acts are restricted in application to a particular geographical location or organisation (such as a local authority area, a harbour or a port) or a group of individuals. As a law student you will be most likely to use only Public General Acts, but once in legal practice, especially with a local authority or public corporation, skill in finding Local and Personal Acts may be required as well. In future, however, as a result of the Transport and Works Act 1992, the authorisation of railway, tramway, canal and other schemes of works will no longer be by means of Local and Personal Acts but by a system of Ministerial orders — statutory instruments (see chapter 5).

Public General Acts may apply to one or all of the jurisdictions of the United Kingdom (England and Wales, Scotland and Northern Ireland). The name of the Act may indicate this by specifying the jurisdiction.

4.2A2 Origin

See 4.1A2.

4.2A3 Structure

Figure 4.4 reproduces the whole of one Act of Parliament — it is unusual for an Act to be so brief; normally they cover many pages.

An Act of Parliament comprises nine parts, not all of which are essential. As might be expected nearly all correspond to the parts of a Bill discussed in 4.1A3, but there are some important differences.

(a) *Short title* — this is the title under which the Act is generally known. It is given in two places: at the head of the Act and in a section of the Act, usually the last. Sometimes in the second or subsequent Act of a series on the same subject, provision is made in the section dealing with the short title for both or all the Acts to be cited together by a short title, for example: the Merchant Shipping Acts 1894 to 1986. Prior to 1845 Acts did not carry clearly defined short titles but the Short Titles Act 1896 and the Statute Law Reform Act 1948 assigned short titles to many of the earlier Acts. This is worth remembering, for if you are searching for an Act of the first half of the 19th century, or earlier, in the indexes to volumes of Acts published at that time, you will have to scan long, rather than short, titles. There is also another difficulty connected with titles of Acts, which is when an Act gains a popular, rather than its correct, title — fortunately, it only rarely occurs with Acts of the 20th century, but can be a problem when studying legal history. Popular titles for Acts most commonly occur when the Act is identified with a personal sponsor or champion of Parliamentary legislation. One of the most notable recent examples is the Butler Act of 1944 (properly, the Education Act 1944), but the period of Georgian and Victorian social reform is littered with popular personal attributions. Another circumstance when popular names occur is when they are used to describe the activity for which the statute legislates: the Ten Hours Act (properly, the Factories Act 1847). More insights into this fascinating problem area are given in an article by Alex Noel-Tod (1989), who has compiled an index (not published) listing close to 1,000 different popular titles. Of published indexes, Noel-Tod identifies three which yield about 250 to 300 popular titles:

(i) University of London, Institute of Advanced Legal Studies, *Manual of Legal Citations*, part 1, The British Isles (London: The University, 1959), pp. 3 and 4.

(ii) *Chitty's Statutes of Practical Utility*, 6th ed. (London: Sweet & Maxwell, 1913) vol. 16, table of short and popular titles, etc.

(iii) Craies, W. F., *Craies on Statute Law*, 7th ed. (London: Sweet & Maxwell, 1971), pp. 593–97: appendix A, some popular titles of statutes.

(b) *Official citation* — this is a shorthand way of referring to the Act, comprising a date and running number. Currently, Acts are numbered sequentially, beginning with 1, throughout the calendar year, in the order in which

Figure 4.4   A Public General Act of Parliament.

① # Explosives (Age of Purchase &c.) Act 1976

② ## 1976 CHAPTER 26

③ An Act to restrict further the sale to young persons of explosive substances, including fireworks, and to increase the penalties provided by sections 31 and 80 of the Explosives Act 1875.   ④ [22nd July, 1976]

⑤ **B**E IT ENACTED by the Queen's most Excellent Majesty, by and with the advice and consent of the Lord Spiritual and Temporal, and Commons, in this present Parliament assembled, and by the authority of the same, as follows:—

⑥   1.—(1)   In section 31 of the Explosives Act 1875 (which, as extended by section 39 of that Act, prohibits the sale to children of explosives, including fireworks, and provides that a person who makes a sale in contravention of the said section 31 shall be liable to a penalty not exceeding £20) for the words "any child apparently under the age of thirteen" there shall be substituted the words "any person apparently under the age of sixteen" and for the word "£20" there shall be substituted the word "£200".

⑦ Increase of age for purchase of fireworks etc and of certain penalties relating to fireworks etc.

1875 c. 17.

   (2)   In section 80 of that Act (which provides that a person who lets fireworks off in a highway or public place shall be liable to a penalty not exceeding £20) for the word "£20" there shall be substituted the word "£200".

⑧   2.—(1)   This Act may be cited as the Explosives (Age of Purchase &c.) Act 1976, and this Act and the Explosives Acts 1875 and 1923 may be cited together as the Explosives Acts 1875 to 1976.

Citation, extent and commencement.

⑨   (2)   This Act shall not extend to Northern Ireland.
⑩   (3)   This Act shall come into force at the expiration of one month beginning with the date of its passing.

---

① Short title   (a)   ⑥ Section and Subsection   (h)
② Official Citation   (b)   ⑦ Marginal note   (h)
③ Long Title   (d)   ⑧ Citation   (h)(iii)
④ Date of Royal Assent   (e)   ⑨ Extent   (h)(v)
⑤ Enacting Formula   (g)   ⑩ Commencement   (h)(iv)

(The letters in parentheses refer to paragraphs in the text where discussion on the element of an Act occur.)

they receive the Royal Assent. Public General Acts are numbered in arabic numerals, Local and Personal Acts are numbered with lower-case roman numerals. So, the example illustrated earlier, the Explosives (Age of Purchase etc.) Act, was the 26th Act to receive the Royal Assent in 1976. In general use the citation may be further abbreviated to 1976, c. 26. ('chapter' may be abbreviated to 'c.', 'ch.' or 'cap.'). The use of the word chapter derives from the medieval period when a single statute emerged from the brief Parliamentary sessions, dealing with many different topics, each constituting a separate chapter of the one statute.

The present system of citation based on the calendar year and a running number was introduced in 1963. Prior to that the official citation was constructed in a far more complex and confusing way, as is explained in 4.2A5.

(c) *Arrangement of sections* — a table at the front of all but the shorter Acts, sets out in order the parts, chapters and sections into which the text is divided, with their respective titles (see appendix 3 for further details of the terminology for the divisions of an Act).

(d) *Long title* — this sets out in general terms the purpose of the Act and, in contrast to its appearance in a Bill, is found only above the enacting formula.

(e) *Date of Royal Assent.*

(f) *Preamble* — its purpose is to state the reasons for and the expected effects of the proposed legislation. It is rarely incorporated in Public General Acts but is a required feature of Local and Personal Acts.

(g) *Enacting formula* — this short paragraph summarises the legislative authority of Parliament and precedes the first section of the Act.

(h) *Sections* — an Act is divided into a series of numbered sections, each with a descriptive title, known as a 'side note' or 'marginal note' printed in the margin. The word section is frequently abbreviated in writing to 's.' or, in the plural, 'ss.'. Sections may be divided into subsections (abbreviated to 'subs.'), subsections into paragraphs (abbreviated to 'para.') and paragraphs into sub-paragraphs (abbreviated to 'subpara.') — see appendix 3 for further details of terminology. Towards the end of the Act or, if appropriate, at the end of one of its parts, formal sections are placed which contain very important information for the legal researcher:

(i) Definition sections, indicated by the marginal note 'interpretation', give the meaning of certain key words in the text of the Act.

(ii) Saving sections, indicated by the marginal note 'savings' or similar, have the function of saving or preserving rather than altering an existing right or powers; it has been said that they are often included by way of reassurance, for avoidance of doubt or from abundance of caution. They often begin with a phrase: 'Nothing in this section shall be construed as . . .'.

(iii) The short title section, indicated by the marginal note 'short title', or sometimes 'citation', sets out the title under which the Act will be cited amongst the statutes. This title is also given at the head of the Act.

(iv) Commencement sections, indicated by the marginal note 'commencement', detail when the Act is to come into force. Since the beginning of the 1982–83 session of Parliament, commencement sections ought usually to be grouped at the end of the Act (see Anon (1983)). It is a commonly held fallacy amongst law students that all Acts come into force on the date they receive the Royal Assent. In fact, only those statutes which contain no express provision as to commencement come into force beginning with the day on which they receive the Royal Assent. The commencement of most modern statutes is expressly postponed. Most Acts include commencement sections which may detail any number of different dates or ways in which the Act will come into force. Sometimes a particular date is named, sometimes commencement is set at the expiry of a fixed period (commonly one or two months after the date of Royal Assent), and sometimes the power to set a date for commencement — an 'appointed day' — is delegated to a government Minister. This Ministerial power is exercised through the issue of a 'commencement order', which is one of the several different types of statutory instrument (see 5.1). It is important to check the commencement section carefully since different sections of an Act may be brought into force at different times. Only where no provision is made for an Act to come into force, will the date of Royal Assent be the commencement date.

It is worth noting that the commencement of an Act may be considerably delayed — for example, not one section of the Easter Act 1928 has, at the time of writing, been brought into force, and substantial parts of the Social Security Act 1989, the Companies Act 1989 and the Merchant Shipping Act 1995 are not yet in force either; much of the Reservoirs Act 1975 was only brought into force in 1986 and 1987 by statutory instruments issued over 10 years after the Act received the Royal Assent.

Since the early 1980s Parliamentary counsel, who have the task of drafting Government Bills, have adopted more clearly standardised practices for the grouping and identification of commencement provisions, and the adoption of specific commencement dates in Acts (see Anon (1983)). Nevertheless, finding, understanding and applying the information about commencement within an Act of Parliament is an important legal research skill to master.

(v)   Extent sections, indicated by the marginal note 'extent', detail the geographical area to which the Act applies (either England and Wales, Scotland, Northern Ireland individually or in any combination, or the United Kingdom as a whole). There is a presumption that statutes passed by the Parliament of the United Kingdom extend to the whole of the United Kingdom unless parts of the United Kingdom are expressly excluded by the 'extent' section.

(i)   *Schedules* — at the end of the Act will be found one or more schedules (abbreviated to 'Sch.') containing detailed provisions dependent on one or more of the preceding sections, rather like appendices at the back of a book.

4.2A4   *Publication and general availability*

Public General Acts are published by the Queen's Printer, currently the Controller of Her Majesty's Stationery Office (HMSO) — following privatisation, a small residual HMSO was retained and is responsible for printing Acts of Parliament. The paper copies on sale to the public are known as Queen's Printer's copies and are accepted as evidence in courts of law. As well as copies of single Acts published separately by HMSO, a number of official and unofficial collected editions are published, which are widely available in both specialist law libraries and many general academic and public libraries.

Acts of Parliament from the first Act of 1996 onwards (and a handful from before that date) can also be found in full text on Her Majesty's Stationery Office web site at

http://www.hmso.gov.uk/acts.htm

Note that the version given on the internet is as originally passed by the UK Parliament and does not include subsequent amendments or information about repeals. A search engine allows users to search the text of all documents on this site.

Most Local and Personal Acts are today published by the Queen's Printer, the one exception being Acts of a very limited, personal character. Local and Personal Acts are published only as individual Acts and are not republished in official collected editions. Print runs are likely to be short so unless copies are purchased shortly after the Act is published, the best means of obtaining a copy is to contact the local authority or organisation which promoted the Act. The major public library or county record office in the area to which the Act refers may be able to assist. A list of libraries in the UK with major collections of local legislation is given near the front of volume 1 of *Chronological Table of Local Legislation* (London: Her Majesty's Stationery Office, 1996). Alternatively, major collections can be identified by consulting Jones, D.L. and Pond, C., *Parliamentary Holdings in Libraries in Britain and Ireland* (London: House of Commons Library, 1993).

For Local and Personal Acts passed since 1997 the position has been eased by HMSO placing the full text of each Act on its web site at

http://www.hmso.gov.uk/acts.htm

The full text of Local and Personal Acts passed from 1992 onwards has been included in *Current Law Statutes* (see 4.2B2.2.2).

4.2A5   Citation

An Act is usually referred to by its short title, e.g., the Explosives (Age of Purchase etc.) Act 1976, though for completeness the chapter number (c. 26 in the example) may be added after the date. Prior to 1 January 1963 when the Acts of Parliament Numbering and Citation Act 1962 came into force, the official citation comprised not the calendar year and chapter number but the regnal year or years of the Parliamentary session in which the Act was passed, followed by the chapter number.

This rather complex system needs some explanation. First, what is meant by 'regnal year'? It refers to the year beginning with the date of the Sovereign's accession to the throne. For Queen Elizabeth II the regnal year commences on 6 February — she came to the throne on that day in 1952 following the death of George VI. Secondly, what is meant by Parliamentary session? It refers to the period from the opening of Parliament by the Sovereign (normally, but not always, in early November) to the ending or prorogation of Parliament, normally, but not always, about a year later (late October). However, the length of each Parliamentary session is determined by the government of the day, and if a General Election is called the session may be considerably shorter than a year.

Now, putting these two cycles, the regnal and Parliamentary, together means that an Act receiving the Royal Assent between early November and 5 February in any year between 1952 and 1962 would fall in one regnal year, whilst an Act receiving the Royal Assent between 6 February and the end of the Parliamentary session would fall in a different regnal year.

There are three further complications with this awkward system of citation. First, when an Act given the Royal Assent was to be first published, the printer might not at that time be sure the monarch would survive until his or her next accession day. So, for example, the Family Allowances and National Insurance Act 1961 received the Royal Assent on 20 December 1961, late in the 10th year of Queen Elizabeth II's reign. The printer was obliged to use the citation 10 Eliz. 2 c. 6, since he could not be sure she would survive to 6 February of the year following. But, when in due course Queen Elizabeth II commenced her 11th regnal year the citation 10 & 11 Eliz. 2 c. 6 was used for the same Act. The latter citation supersedes the first.

Secondly, occasionally a Parliamentary session began and ended within a single regnal year and another started within the same year. This occurred in 1950. The Parliamentary session ran from 11 March to 26 October, wholly within the 14th year of the reign of George VI. The 39 Acts passed during that period bear the citation 14 Geo. 6 whereas the Expiring Law Continuance Act 1950, given the Royal Assent on 15 December 1950, bears the citation 14 & 15 Geo. 6, c. 1.

Thirdly, a Parliamentary session could cover the end of one Sovereign's reign and part of the first regnal year of the next. In this case both Sovereigns' names are included in the citation. For example, the 68 Acts passed in the Parliamentary session 1951–52 are styled 15 & 16 Geo. 6 & 1 Eliz. 2.

This system of citation causes particular difficulties around the year 1936. George V reigned until 20 January 1936, to be followed by Edward VIII whose brief monarchy lasted until 11 December 1936, when George VI took the throne. During 1936, Acts bear the regnal citations of either 26 Geo. 5 & 1 Edw. 8 or 1 Edw. 8 & 1 Geo. 6. The difficulties in finding statutes for this period are further compounded by the fact that up until 1940, official collections and some unofficial collections of Acts were bound in volumes containing those passed within each Parliamentary session, which in the case of 1935–36 ended in October 1936 and for 1936–37 started in November 1936. So, this means that some Acts passed only a few months apart within calendar year 1936, bear different regnal year citations and are published in different volumes based on the Parliamentary session in which they received the Royal Assent. This complicated set of circumstances affects two Acts law students are frequently required to consult: the Public Health Act 1936 (26 Geo. 5 & 1 Edw. 8, c. 49) which received the Royal Assent on 31 July 1936 and the Public Order Act 1936 (1 Edw. 8 & 1 Geo. 6, c. 6) which received the Royal Assent on 18 December 1936. They will be found in 1936 and 1937 volumes of statutes, respectively.

It is easy to see why the old system of citation was abandoned, but you will need to be familiar with it so as to correctly identify and quickly find older Acts of Parliament in the printed volumes of the period. As an aid you will find lists of the monarchs with the dates of their regnal years in the following publications:

(a) *Osborn's Concise Law Dictionary,* 8th ed., edited by Leslie Rutherford and Shelia Bone (London: Sweet & Maxwell, 1993).

(b) Pemberton, John E., *British Official Publications*, 2nd revised ed. (Oxford: Pergamon Press Ltd, 1973), pp. 120–5.

(c) *Guide to Law Reports and Statutes*, 3rd ed. (London: Sweet & Maxwell, 1959), pp. 58–70.

4.2B Finding information

In most of your legal research as a student you will be concerned with Acts which are currently in force. Much of this section of the book deals with the sources and skills required to find 'live' statute law. However, occasionally you may need to look at Acts of Parliament since repealed, to trace the historical development of legislation. Two publications should be noted: first, *Statutes of the Realm*, covering statutes from 1235 (the Statute of Merton) to 1713, and published between 1810 and 1828. The texts are given in the original language of early statutes (Latin or Norman French) with translations into English where necessary. Each of the 11 volumes has a subject index with, in addition, alphabetical and chronological indexes published separately to the whole work. The second publication to note is *Statutes at Large*, containing statutes from Magna Carta (1215) onwards. The most frequently cited edition is Owen Ruffhead's, revised by Charles Runnington, and published between 1786 and 1800 in 14 volumes.

Sources of pre-1707 Scottish legislation are dealt with in section 10.1B.

Publications containing Acts of Parliament may be divided into two groups — those published officially by HMSO and those issued by commercial publishers.

4.2B1 Official versions

4.2B1.1 Public General Acts and General Synod Measures

Sometime after the end of each calendar year all the Acts of the year are published in annual bound volumes entitled *Public General Acts and General Synod Measures*. Prior to 1940 the volumes included Acts passed each Parliamentary session rather than calendar year. From the first year of publication, 1831, until 1870 the publication was titled *Public General Statutes*. Each year's edition currently consists of two or three volumes. Each volume begins

with four tables, listing the Public General Acts alphabetically and chronologically, Local and Personal Acts alphabetically and General Synod Measures
chronologically. Then follow, in chapter number order, the full text of Public
General Acts and General Synod Measures but *not* Local and Personal Acts. At
the back of the final volume for each year, or in a separate volume, are further
tables: first, a concordance, detailing existing legislation against each section of
any new consolidating Act which replaces it and, secondly, the effect of new
Acts on existing legislation — whether repealed, amended or otherwise altered.

The annual volumes of Public General Acts merely reprint Acts in the form
in which they were originally given the Royal Assent. No subsequent repeals or
amendments are included. To overcome this disadvantage HMSO has published
two further editions of the statutes: *Statutes Revised* and *Statutes in Force*. Since
1996, The Statutory Publications Office has set a number of dates for the launch
of *Statute Law Database* (see 4.2B1.6), which will replace *Statutes in Force*,
but it has yet to become available.

4.2B1.2   Statutes revised

Statutes Revised has been published as numerous bound volumes in three
editions, the first completed in 1885, comprising the Public General Acts in
force at the end of 1878. A second edition published between 1888 and 1929
brought the revision down to 1920. Finally, a third edition, published in 1950,
reprinted Acts as they were in force in 1948. Since 1940 an annual volume,
Annotations to Acts, has been published giving instructions for copying in to the
pages of *Statutes Revised* minor amendments, striking out Acts which have been
repealed and sticking in gummed sheets where more substantial textual changes
have occurred. Needless to say this tedious work, even if library staff have time
to undertake it, makes the original publication very difficult to use with
confidence. Pre-1707 Scottish legislation is not included.

4.2B1.3   Statutes in force

To overcome the problems of updating created by a bound-volume format,
HMSO has published in 108 loose-leaf binders, totalling over 60,000 pages, the
currently unrepealed Public General Acts of England and Wales, Scotland, Great
Britain and the United Kingdom, some Acts of the Parliament of Ireland, Church
Assembly and General Synod Measures and selected Local and Personal Acts.
This huge work is arranged in 131 broad subject groups extending from agency
to weights and measures. In theory, the advantage of loose-leaf publication is
that new Acts can be inserted in the appropriate binder for the subject, repealed
Acts can be removed and Cumulative Supplements detailing amendments and
partial repeals can be inserted. In practice, for various reasons, *Statutes in Force*
fell far short of the ideal. In the mid-1990s publication of updates ceased and the
publication has been allowed to become badly out of date. The publication ought
not to be used for legal research. One of the reasons why the publication was
allowed to fall into arrears was to permit time to be devoted to the development
of its electronic successor: *Statute Law Database* (see 4.2B1.6).

4.2B1.4   Index to the Statutes and Chronological Table of Statutes

Both these publications were originally intended to be used in conjunction with *Statutes in Force*. *Index to the Statutes* provided a subject index to *Statutes in Force* but has ceased publication: the last edition covers the period 1235–1990, and is of no use for current research. If the law in Scotland is sufficiently different it is treated separately at the end of the *Index* entry. *Chronological Table of Statutes*, on the other hand, although not up-to-date, is of value. The most recent edition was published in 1999 and covers the period 1235–1996. The compliers intend to catch up by omitting the separate editions for 1997 and 1998 and the next edition will cover the period 1235–1998. *Chronological Table of Statutes* is a list beginning with the Statute of Merton of 1235 of all Acts of Parliament, against each of which there is an entry detailing whether the Act has been repealed or amended. Even though not up-to-date the volume can be very useful for historical research when checking details about Acts repealed long ago.

4.2B1.5   Index to the Local and Personal Acts and Chronological Table of Local Legislation

The *Index* is in six volumes and lists all Private Acts made between 1797 and 1995. The list is alphabetical by title with cross-references to personal names and places. The *Chronological Table* is in four volumes and lists in date order over 26,500 Local Acts made up to the end of 1994, with details of repeals. A separate volume: *Chronological Table of Private and Personal Legislation* lists in date order all Private and Personal Acts passed between 1539 and the end of 1997. Together, the two sets of chronological tables, published between 1996 and 1999, are the first complete listing of all Private, Local and Personal Acts passed since 1539. They are supplemented by the annual publication *Local and Personal Acts Tables and Index*, which contains alphabetical title, chronological, subject and place name indexes. The indexes and tables published between 1996 and 1999 replace earlier attempts to list Private Acts: *Index to Local and Personal Acts 1801–1947*, and a *Supplementary Index to Local and Personal Acts 1948–1966*.

4.2B1.6   Statute Law Database

Eventually, this database will provide the original text of Acts in force and all amendments to those Acts since 1 February 1991. It will allow users to retrieve not just the text of the Act currently in force but also the text at any time since 1 February 1991. This feature will be of use to tax lawyers who need to apply the exact wording of an Act within a particular tax year to the problem in hand. Although work on this database began in the early 1990s, with the intention of making it available to Government Departments and eventually the general public within the second half of the decade, at the time of writing, the database is still not available.

4.2B2   Commercial versions

The commercially published editions of Acts of Parliament reprint Public General Acts only. They fall into five distinct groups:

(a)   Mere reprints of the Queen's Printer's copies of Acts.

(b)   Reprints of the Queen's Printer's copies but with additional commentary or editor's notes on the meaning and effect of each Act.

(c)   Reprints of the Queen's Printer's copies with additional commentary or editor's notes and a regular updating service indicating legal developments affecting earlier legislation.

(d)   Reprints of Queen's Printer's copies with subsequent amendments included but without additional commentary or editor's notes.

(e)   Summaries of Acts.

4.2B2.1   Reprints of Queen's Printer's copies

4.2B2.1.1   Law Reports Statutes   The Incorporated Council of Law Reporting for England and Wales, a non-profit-making organisation responsible for the most authoritative reports of cases available, known as the *Law Reports* (see 6A1), also publishes a reprint of the Queen's Printer's copies of Public General Acts, known as the *Law Reports Statutes*. It appears in several parts each year followed by annual bound volumes of all the parts issued that year. However, the publication has limited value since it is frequently published months behind the Queen's Printer's copies and has no added value in the way of commentary or an updating service. *Law Reports Statutes* includes exclusively Scottish Acts made at Westminster.

4.2B2.2   Reprints of Queen's Printer's copies with commentary

Two publications reprint the Queen's Printer's copies of Public General Acts with additional commentary and notes; these annotations have *no* official standing but can be very helpful in explaining the meaning of words or phrases and state, in relatively simple language, the relationship of the new law to existing legislation and decisions of the courts.

4.2B2.2.1   Butterworths Annotated Legislation Service   This publication was formerly known as *Butterworths Emergency Legislation Service*, since it was first published in 1939 with the intention of assisting practitioners keep track of the large quantity of legislation passed as a result of the outbreak of war. It reprinted *selected* Acts applying to England and Wales of more use to legal practitioners rather than academic students. Since the early 1990's the selection of Acts has become very limited. Acts are reprinted with notes and detailed annotations given in a small typeface following the section to which they refer. Quite a few of the recent volumes have been reprinted by Butterworths as textbooks. If *Current Law Statutes* (see 4.2B2.2.2) is available, use it in

preference, since its coverage and contents are far more comprehensive than the Butterworths publication.

4.2B2.2.2   Current Law Statutes   First published in 1949, *Current Law Statutes* (CLS) (known up to 1993 as *Current Law Statutes Annotated* (CLSA)) is one of the most useful publications available for research on statutes. It is widely available and has the following valuable characteristics:

(a)   It includes all, not just a selection, of Public General Acts and, since 1992, all Private Acts.

(b)   It publishes new Acts as loose-leaf pages which slip into the Service File binder; this means CLS is one of the first commercially-produced versions of an Act to appear after the Queen's Printer's copy. The first release of an Act in CLS is printed on blue paper and is merely a reprint of the Queen's Printer's version, but this is subsequently replaced by a version on white paper which includes extensive annotations and commentary. Several times a year the white paper versions of Acts in the Service File are replaced by bound volumes. This three-stage process: loose-leaf blue paper, loose-leaf white paper, bound-volume white paper, means CLS can publish legislation with annotations rapidly.

(c)   It includes amongst the editorial notes at the head of most Acts, references to where in *Hansard* debates in Parliament on the Bill which preceded the Act may be found.

(d)   It provides a cumulative subject index to the loose issues of Acts and incorporates this index at the back of each bound volume.

(e)   It has included, since 1984, in the bound volumes, a statute *Citator* (see 4.2B2.2.3).

(f)   Tables listing, by title of statute, details of any commencement orders made, which bring the Act into force, and a table of legislation made since 1949 but not yet in force; these are used to trace whether a statute or section of a statute, although passed by Parliament, is in force.

A Scottish edition entitled *Scottish Current Law Statutes* covered all Public General Acts for the years 1949 to 1990, with the addition of Acts of Sederunt and Acts of Adjournal (see section 11.3). The editions merged in 1991.

Finding commentary in Current Law Statutes   Each Act reprinted in CLS on white paper usually includes editorial notes and commentary, printed in small type, in three places. The reprint of most Acts begins with a contents list, and immediately following it under the heading 'Parliamentary debates', details are given of where in *Hansard* (the full reports of debates in Parliament) to find the text of what Members of Parliament said in discussion on the Bill — the draft form of the Act. In this list the HC abbreviation stands for House of Commons, followed by the volume and column number where the debates are reported; HL stands for House of Lords. In some of the early volumes of CLS this information may have been omitted, but in the Service File there is a Table of Parliamentary Debates listing references to *Hansard* for substantive debates in Parliament on all Public General Acts between 1950 and the past year.

The next heading, 'Introduction and general note', is the second place where commentary will be found. Under it is given a description of what led up to the legislation being presented to Parliament — an official report or policy document, for example. These references are very useful, for if you follow them up they enable you to set the legislation in context and understand why the law has developed in a particular way. The remainder of the introduction and general note consists of a summary of the main provisions of the Act.

The third type of annotation is placed at the end of each section of the Act. Details are given of where to find elsewhere in the Act the definition of words used in the section reprinted above, and under the heading 'General note', the authors provide a commentary on the meaning of the section with references to earlier Acts and any court cases which relate to the new provisions.

The commentary is written by expert lawyers in the relevant field of law, not an in-house editorial team, which has implications for the depth, quality and usefulness of the commentary.

Like the Butterworths service, some Acts and their commentary appearing in CLS are published additionally as textbooks.

A CD, initially containing the statutes and the *Current Law Legislation Citators* for 1998 and 1999 is under development. Future issues of the CD will add to the backrun, but will eventually extend back only as far as 1992.

4.2B2.2.3   Current Law Statute Citator and Current Law Legislation Citator

Paper version
Both the Butterworths service and CLS have a major disadvantage: they are published as bound-volume services without a means of updating either the statements of law or the editorial annotations. The information contained in the volumes is 'frozen' at the date of publication whilst the law, in reality, continues to develop. Having said that, the publishers of CLS have tried to overcome this disadvantage in part with the issue of two associated publications: *Current Law Statute Citator* (CLSC) and *Current Law Legislation Citator* (CLLC). There are, in fact, at least five parts to these citators, but first, what does the word '*Citator*' mean? Quite simply it is a listing of original documents, whether they be Acts, statutory instruments or cases, with details of references or 'citations' made in later Acts, statutory instruments or cases to the original documents. The statute and legislation *Citators* are valuable tools for discovering whether a particular Act:

  (a)   has come into force;
  (b)   has been amended;
  (c)   has had detailed rules, orders or regulations made under powers contained in it;
  (d)   is still in force;
  (e)   has been considered by the courts and the meaning of sections interpreted in judgments.

The various volumes forming the set of *Citators* are as follows:

1947–71	Hardback volume entitled *Current Law Statute Citator*
1972–88	Hardback volume entitled *Current Law Legislation Citator*
1989–95	Hardback volume entitled *Current Law Legislation Citators* — it also includes a *Statutory Instrument Citator* for 1993–1995
1996–1999	Hardback volume entitled *Current Law Legislation Citators* — it also includes a *Statutory Instrument Citator*
The current calendar year	Use the loose-leaf *Citator* section of *Current Law Statutes Service File*

A Scottish edition entitled *Scottish Current Law Statute Citator* and *Scottish Current Law Legislation Citator* covered 1948–71 and 1972–88 respectively. The editions merged in the *Current Law Legislation Citators* for 1989–95.

When using the set of *Citators* it is important to bear in mind that each volume gives details of changes to all statutes of any date during the period of time covered by the *Citator*. For example, the first volume (1947–71) includes citations made during that period to all statutes, even back to the Statute of Merton 1235. There is no *Citator* covering citations made before 1947.

If you are checking citations for an Act, start your search with the *Citator* which includes the year given in the title of the Act, and work forward through the various parts of the *Citator* until you reach the loose-leaf update in the *Current Law Statutes Service File*. For a pre-1947 Act search all parts of the *Citator* service. The important point to bear in mind is to search the various parts in a *methodical order* so you pick up *all* relevant citations, rather than only using whichever part comes immediately to hand at the shelves.

How is information presented in the Citators? Both CLSC and CLLC list Public General Acts in chronological order: by year and then by chapter number within the year, and against each Act note, section by section, repeals, amendments, the application of any secondary legislation such as statutory instruments (see 5.1) and citations to cases in which the courts have considered the provisions of the Act judicially.

Figure 4.5, taken from *Current Law Statute Citator 1996–98*, shows part of a page from the sequence of Acts passed in 1994. The page is split into two columns. The chapter numbers of the Acts are given in the left-hand margin of each column. The extract shows the entries for chapter 36, Law of Property (Miscellaneous Provisions) Act 1994 and part of chapter 37, the Drug Trafficking Act 1994. Take a closer look at the wealth of information given for chapter 37. First, there is reference to a law report, *L (Restraint Order: Legal Costs)* 1996, with a citation to where a report of the case can be read in the law reports — the case mentions the Act in general and not any particular section of it. Then follow references to statutory instruments (SI 1996/1299 and

Figure 4.5   Extract from *Current Law Statute Citator 1996–1998*.

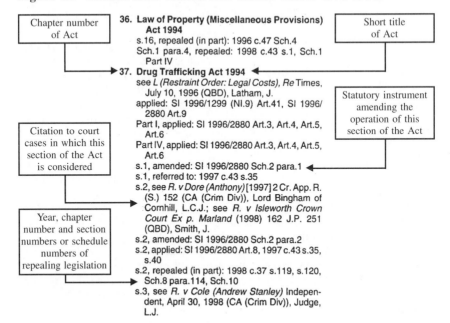

SI 1996/2880) which extend the application of the Act. Next follow the individual sections of the Act, against each of which are noted any decisions of the courts in which the judges have considered the meaning of the section, any statutory instruments comprising detailed legislation made under powers given by that section of the Act and any amendments or repeals made by later Acts — see, for example, that section 2 has been repealed in part by an Act of 1998, chapter 37, sections 119, 120, Schedule 8 paragraph 114 and Schedule 10 (unfortunately, the short title of the repealing Act is not given, but the citation is sufficient for you to find it in volumes of the 1998 Acts).

The *Citator* provides more information about Acts than the *Halsbury's* publication described below (see 4.2B2.3.1). In addition to being able to check whether an Act has been brought into or still is in force, the *Citator* gives details of:

(a)   amendments and repeals;
(b)   all statutory instruments made under powers provided in an Act;
(c)   citations to cases where the courts have interpreted the meaning of a section of an Act.

The value of *Citator*s will become even clearer in section 4.2C, on answering research queries.

Electronic version
The set of statute and legislation citators dating back to 1989 is available in electronic format, either on CD or via the internet, as part of the *Current Legal Information (CLI)* database. Both formats cover Scotland as well as England and Wales. The electronic version is much easier and quicker to search than the paper version because:

(a)   all the separate volumes of the citator have been placed in a single search file;
(b)   it is possible to key in just a single word from the title of the statute (so long as it is not a common word such as 'law' or 'tax', otherwise many statutes will be retrieved) and obtain information relating to it;
(c)   in the CD version only, there are links from the information displayed about subsequent developments such as a case or later, amending or repealing statute, to further details.

The internet version is at

http://193.118.187.160/cli.htm

It is available only to subscribers, though most universities and colleges teaching law have a subscription. You will need a user name and password to get into the site; ask library staff for this information. An online User Guide for Students — intended for trainee solicitors rather than university or college students — is available at

http://www.smlawpub.co.uk/digital/cli/index.cfm#student

4.2B2.3   Reprints of Queen's Printer's copies with commentary and full updating service

4.2B2.3.1   Halsbury's Statutes of England   The first edition of *Halsbury's Statutes* was published in 1930; the work is now in its fourth edition and is one of the key research sources you should learn to use with confidence. Copies of this publication will be found in virtually every academic library where students study law to degree level or beyond. Many large public libraries also subscribe to it, but more importantly, most firms of solicitors and barristers' chambers will contain and use *Halsbury's Statutes* as an everyday research source.

Halsbury's Statutes aims to provide up-to-date versions of *all* Public General Acts (except Consolidated Fund Acts and Appropriation Acts) in force in England and Wales and, in addition, provides copious commentary and notes. As one might expect Scottish Acts are not covered by *Halsbury's Statutes* although specific sections which have an effect in England and Wales or Northern Ireland are reproduced. Indeed, those sections of Public General Acts which affect only Scotland are generally omitted. There are six parts to the publication (summarised in figure 4.6):

Figure 4.6   Structure of *Halsbury's Statutes of England.*

50 MAIN VOLUMES	CURRENT STATUTES SERVICE	CUMULATIVE SUPPLEMENT
Subject arrangement of Public General Acts.	Six loose-leaf volumes containing the Text of recent Acts not yet included in Main Volumes.	Single bound volume issued annually — records changes affecting Main Volumes and Current Statutes Service. Up-to-date to end of year prior to publication.
NOTER-UP	**TABLES OF STATUTES AND GENERAL INDEX**	**IS IT IN FORCE?**
Single loose-leaf volume — records very recent changes to Main Volumes and Current Statutes Service.	Single bound volume issued annually — index to Main Volumes and Current Statutes Service.	Single bound volume issued annually — records exact commencement dates of all Public General Acts over previous 25 years.

(a)   *Main volumes.* Fifty Main Volumes contain an alphabetical subject-by-subject arrangement of the Public General Acts in force at the time of publication in the second half of the 1980s — the whole work was issued volume by volume over several years. Volume 1 contains the Acts relating to the topic of admiralty law and volume 50 ends with those dealing with wills. When the law on a topic has changed considerably since a Main Volume was published, a 'reissue' volume is compiled to replace the original one. Some areas of law change faster than others; for example, the original volume 12 on criminal law was replaced by a reissue volume within just four years. You can identify reissue volumes by the word and the date of publication marked on the spine. It is important to note this, as will be explained later in the section on using *Halsbury's Statutes.*

You will find editorial notes and commentary are provided in two places in the Main Volumes. At the beginning of each group of Acts relevant to a particular subject, there is a review of the development, purpose and effect of the legislation. The review is a very useful synopsis (i) highlighting earlier legislation which may have been replaced by current Acts, (ii) drawing attention to government or other reports which may have shaped the content of legislation, and (iii) placing particular Acts in context. Following after the review, the Acts are reprinted in chronological order, the oldest first, with notes in smaller type, giving details of (i) where to find in this or other statutes definitions of words or phrases, (ii) associated provisions in other Acts, (iii) relevant secondary legislation, and (iv) cases in which the courts have considered the meaning and effect of the text of the statute. These notes are placed after the particular section of an Act to which they apply.

(b)   *Current Statutes Service.* Currently six loose-leaf volumes contain the text of recent Acts not yet included in the Main Volumes.

(c)   *Cumulative Supplement (sometimes referred to as the 'Cum. Supp.').* This single bound volume issued annually and replacing the previous Cumulative Supplement, contains details of changes which affect the information given in the Main Volumes and the Current Statutes Service. The Cumulative Supplement is usually up-to-date to around the turn of the year.

(d)   *Noter-Up Service.* Bridging the gap between the compilation of the Cumulative Supplement and the present is a single loose-leaf volume. Every month the publisher issues loose-leaf pages containing details of very recent developments in the law which are inserted in the binder.

(e)   *Tables of Statutes and General Index.* This single bound volume, issued annually, is the usual starting point for research using *Halsbury's Statutes.* At the front is a list in alphabetical order by title of all the Acts reprinted in *Halsbury's Statutes*, with a subject index to the whole work, at the back.

(f)   *Is it in Force?* Another single bound volume, issued annually, records the exact commencement dates of all Public General Acts over the previous 25 years, with details of the authority (such as a statutory instrument) by which they were brought into force. *Is it in Force?* covers all Public General Acts and is also issued as part of the *Laws of Scotland* (see 12B4.1).

Using Halsbury's Statutes   The key skill to be learnt in searching *Halsbury's Statutes* is to correctly and confidently link together the use of these six parts, to ensure the law you eventually cite is up-to-date.

There are two ways in which *Halsbury's Statutes* can be used for research: to find information about an Act when you know its title, or to find information on a legal subject or topic. Figures 4.7 and 4.8 indicate the steps to be followed for each search.

Here are some points to note when using *Halsbury's Statutes*:

(a)   The references in the Tables of Statutes and General Index are to the volume number (in bold type) and page number (lighter type). Where (S) follows the volume number this means that the Act is to be found in the Current Statutes Service and not the Main Volume. Note the 'subject' given between (S) and the page number since each Current Statutes Service volume contains several subjects.

(b)   Main Volumes are revised and reissued when the law they contain is out of date. However, there can be a gap between the publication of a reissue Main Volume and an up-to-date edition of the Tables of Statutes and General Index to the whole set. So, it is important to check which issue of a Main Volume has been used from which the publishers have compiled the Tables of Statutes and

Fig 4.7   Searching *Halsbury's Statutes* for an Act by its title.

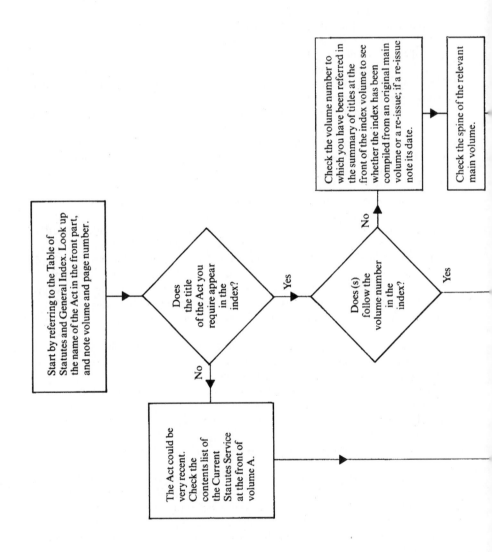

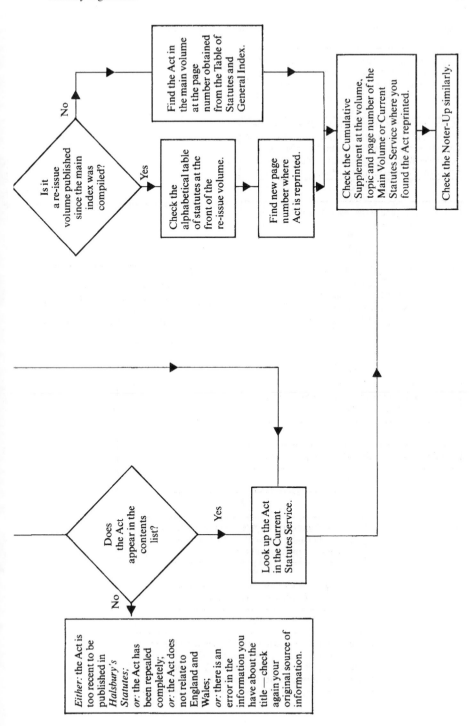

Figure 4.8   Searching *Halsbury's Statutes* for information on a subject.

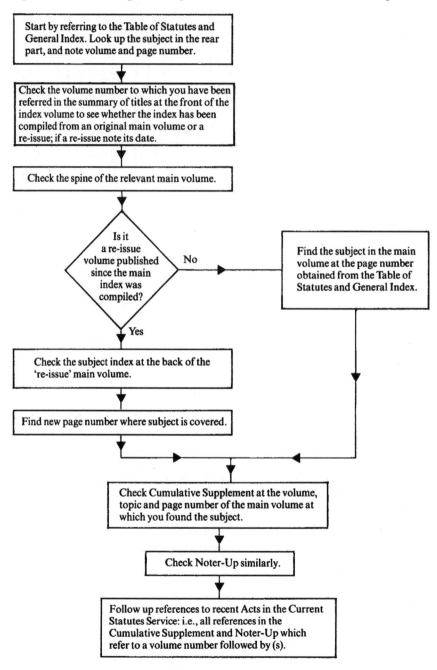

General Index. This can be done quite simply by turning to the summary of titles given at the front of the Tables of Statutes and General Index, and noting which issue of the Main Volume in which you are interested has been used to compile the index entries. Compare this information with that on the spine of the relevant Main Volume itself and if the details match, then so should the entries in the Tables of Statutes and General Index and the Main Volume. If they do not as where, for example, the Tables of Statutes and General Index has been compiled from an original Main Volume but the current Main Volume is now a reissue, then you will need to look up the topic again in the index to that particular reissued Main Volume, to find the new page on which the information you require is given.

(c)   When you have found the statute or information you require in the Main Volume or Current Statutes Service, note down three elements: the *volume, subject* and *page number* of the section in which you are interested, so you can find relevant new information quickly in the Cumulative Supplement and Noter-Up. The subject is given as part of the running head across the tops of pages.

(d)   In the Cumulative Supplement and Noter-Up the volume number and subject are given as running heads across the tops of pages. The page numbers of Main Volumes to which more recent developments relate are given in the left-hand margin. If the page number in which you are interested does not appear in the list you can assume there have been no changes to the law as stated in the Main Volume in which you originally looked. If a page number *is* given but is followed by an 'n', this indicates the change is to an editorial note on that page rather than the text of the Act itself.

The part of *Halsbury's Statutes* called *Is it in Force?* is arranged chronologically; then, within each year, the titles of Acts are printed in alphabetical order and against each is given details of when it came into force and by what authority. If you do not know the year of the Act you wish to check then, so long as you know the correct title, you can find the missing information by using the front part of the Tables of Statutes and General Index to *Halsbury's Statutes*, and afterwards consult *Is it in Force?* The annual softback volume of *Is it in Force?* is updated with information on commencements occurring since it was published, by using a loose-leaf addendum in the Noter-Up service binder, indicated by a guide card with the title *Is it in Force?* printed on it.

4.2B2.3.2 Specialist subject encyclopaedias   An increasing range of loose-leaf encyclopaedias has appeared in recent years, particularly in subjects of interest to practitioners, where the law is developing or changing rapidly. Revenue law was the first area in which these were published since the law is susceptible to frequent and often unpredictable change. Most, but not all, encyclopaedias reprint Acts of Parliament with copious editorial notes and commentary and are kept up-to-date by publishers issuing loose pages containing new developments, which are inserted within the binder by library staff and replace old pages. The coverage of some loose-leaf encyclopaedias extends to Scotland and any relevant legislation may be reproduced. These encyclopaedias are very valuable because of the greater detail given in the notes and commentary and the wide range of reprints of publications other than Acts they often contain. These characteristics are explained further in section 8.2. A number of the most popular encyclopaedias are now issued as CDs, which can mean searching for the use of a particular word or phrase in a statute is easier, and also avoids the frustration felt when the relevant page from the paper version is found to be missing.

To discover if your library has a subject-specific encyclopaedia relevant to your enquiry, use the subject index section of the library catalogue (see 1.2.4) and then the classified section to find entries for books on the general area of law in which you are interested. Note any catalogue entries which have the word 'ency-clopaedia' in the title or any indication after the title information that it is issued in loose-leaf format — unfortunately, not all library catalogues are designed to give this type of information. If in any doubt ask library staff for assistance. It should be emphasised that publishers only produce loose-leaf encyclopaedias in topics where they believe there is a ready market — i.e., where there is sufficient need amongst practising lawyers for a rapidly updated service. Unfortunately for students this means you will *not* find encyclopaedias in some basic legal topics such as jurisprudence, constitutional law and English legal system!

4.2B2.4   Reprints of Queen's Printer's copies with subsequent amendments included but without additional commentary or editor's notes

4.2B2.4.1   LEXIS   The on-line database *LEXIS* contains the *full text* of all Public General Acts currently in force in England and Wales. Access to the database is available only to subscribers, but most university and college libraries take it. However, because use of *LEXIS* is charged for differently from other databases, frequently, students are not given direct access but only through a member of teaching staff or the librarian. The database is updated each week, but it may take several weeks, even months, between the publication of the Queen's Printer's copy of a new Act and its inclusion in the database, especially if it is a major piece of legislation effecting many changes to existing law; nevertheless, the database is reasonably well up-to-date. The text of every Act on *LEXIS* includes amendments made by subsequent legislation; the text is not merely a reprint of the Act in the form in which it received the Royal Assent.

The database is divided into libraries. The ENGGEN Library (*Eng*lish *Gen*eral) contains separate files including one devoted to statutes entitled STAT and also one for statutory instruments entitled SI, which may be combined by using the STATIS file, so that both can be searched together. Other sources, such as that described in 4.2B2.4.2 may be just as useful.

LEXIS is of limited value for Scottish legislation as it includes only those provisions of Scottish Acts which affect British or UK legislation. Even provisions relating to Scotland in Acts of general application prior to 1980 are excluded.

4.2B2.4.2   Legislation Direct   This is an internet database similar to the one on *LEXIS*. It is available at

http://www.butterworths.com

Options leading to a range of Butterworths services are displayed here, but only subscribers will be able to provide the user name and password which will give access to each of the services.

The database reprints Acts applying to the UK as a whole and Acts of the Scottish Parliament. It displays them in the version currently in force, including all amendments. Links within each page enable you to follow references to other parts of the Act or other related pieces of legislation.

The *Halsbury's Statutes Is it in Force?* service is also available online, updated as soon as new commencement orders are received. It is possible to browse *Is it in Force?* by the titles of Acts during each calendar year (as is possible in the paper version) and to search across the whole database using a word or phrase.

4.2B2.4.3   JUSTIS UK Statutes   In contrast to *LEXIS* and *Legislation Direct*, the two CDs which form *JUSTIS UK Statutes* provide the full text of all Public Acts for England, Wales and Scotland, including repealed Acts, from Magna Carta to the present, together with indexes and cross-reference tables compiled from *The Chronological Table of the Statutes 1235–1994* and the latest official *Public General Acts Tables and Index*. There are links to amended and amending legislation. The CDs are updated quarterly.

4.2B2.5   Summaries of Acts

4.2B2.5.1   Lawtel   The internet database, *Lawtel*, is a *digest* of legal information — it does not contain the full text of Acts, only summaries. All Public General Acts, including those applying exclusively to Scotland, passed since 1 January 1984 are provided with summaries. Statutes passed from 1996 onwards contain links to the original version of the full text on the HMSO web site (see 4.2A4). To search for statutes, at the page displaying the *Lawtel* databases select 'legislation'. *Lawtel* also contains a commencements and repeals database which contains details of changes to all statutes since 1986 (Finance Acts since 1997). To use this tracking facility, select 'Commencement and Repeals' at the *Lawtel* Database page. *Lawtel* is available to subscribers only; a user code and password are required to gain access to the database. *Lawtel* is at:

http://www.lawtel.co.uk

4.2C   Answering research queries

For background information on using CDs and the internet for legal research, see appendix 4.

4.2C1   Is this Public General Act in force? Has any section or schedule of the Act been amended or repealed by subsequent legislation?

Electronic route
Use one or more of the following:

(a) *Legislation Citators* on the *Current Legal Information* database (see 4.2B2.2.3) — coverage from 1989 onwards, but does not provide the text of the statute or the amendments themselves.

(b) *Lawtel* (see 4.2B2.5.1) — coverage from 1984 onwards, but does not provide the text of the statute or the amendments themselves.

(c) *LEXIS* (see 4.2.B2.4.1) and *Legislation Direct* (see 4.2B2.4.2) — provide details of changes and the text of the current version of the statute. Using *LEXIS*, to find if all sections of the Marine Insurance Act 1906 are in force go into the STAT or STATIS files, and type the search:

> title (marine insurance w/5 1906)

Again on *LEXIS*, to find if section 8 of the Unfair Contract Terms Act 1977 has been amended go into the STAT or STATIS files, and use the search:

> annotations (unfair contract w/5 1977)

LEXIS is of limited value for Scottish legislation as it includes only those provisions of Scottish Acts which affect British or UK legislation. Even provisions relating to Scotland in Acts of general application prior to 1980 are excluded.

Note that use of the HMSO web site is inappropriate for this research since the site (i) holds only the text of statutes in their original, unamended form, and (ii) only provides information on commencement included within the text of the Act itself.

Paper route
These routes assume you know the year of the Act — if you do not, the Tables of Statutes and General Index to *Halsbury's Statutes*, may provide the information you require.

(a) *Halsbury's Statutes* (see 4.2B2.3.1) and the separate volume entitled *Is it in Force?* Note that *Is it in Force?* excludes statutes more than 25 years old. Depending on the year of the Act, use the softback volume, supplemented by the more up-to-date information in the loose-leaf binder. Since there is a delay in the publication of *Is it in Force?* complete the research by using the *Daily List* of publications issued each day by The Stationery Office, which includes, in its final section, brief details of new statutory instruments. Searching the *Daily List* is possible, but there is no search engine on the site. You need to know the day on which the Act was published to find a reference to it! The site is at:

> http://www.the-stationery-office.co.uk/daily_list/

(b) Use either the *Current Law* publications of Sweet & Maxwell or the full set of *Halsbury's Statutes* published by Butterworths:

Figure 4.9   How to search *Current Law Citators*.

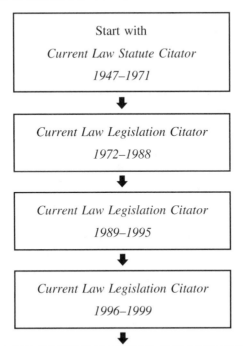

(i)   *Current Law* citators (see 4.2B2.2.3) — Where you start the search depends on the date of the Act of Parliament. Figure 4.9 provides the full path available.

(ii)   *Halsbury's Statutes* — Follow the chart in figure 4.7. When you find the text of the Act you require, check the contents list of the Act itself for mention of a commencement section. Read the section and any notes added in small type by the editors of *Halsbury's Statutes*. For 'commencement' research and especially 'amendment or repeal' research, make sure you follow your search path right through *all* the parts of the *Halsbury's Statutes* publication, ending with the Noter-Up Service.

4.2C2   *Tracing Acts currently in force by subject*

Electronic route
Use one or more of the following:

(a)   *Legislation Direct* (see 4.2B2.4.2);

(b)   *LEXIS* (see 4.2B2.4.1) — take care that your search request comprehensively describes the subject in which you are interested, because the computer will be searching the full text of the Acts, not an index to them;

(c)   *Lawtel* (see 4.2B2.5.1) — but it will only search and retrieve from summaries.

Note that *JUSTIS UK Statutes* (see 4.2B2.4.3) is not appropriate for this search since it contains the text of both repealed and 'live' Acts.

Paper route
Either:

(a)   *Halsbury's Statutes* — follow figure 4.8; or

(b)   if *Halsbury's Statutes* is not available, the next best alternative is to use *Halsbury's Laws* (see 6B5.1). *Halsbury's Laws* does not contain the text of Acts, but is a commentary on the whole law of England and Wales. Follow the research path for *Halsbury's Laws* given in figure 6.7. From the commentary you will be able to identify titles of relevant Acts and follow up the references in any publication to hand which gives the text of Acts.

The *Laws of Scotland*, which provides a comprehensive narrative statement of the law of Scotland, will also direct the researcher to relevant legislation.

4.2C3   *Tracing debates on legislation*

See section 4.1C1 if tracing debates on legislation currently before Parliament, and section 4.1C2 if tracing debates on legislation before Parliament during a past session.

4.2C4   *Tracing historical (i.e., repealed) legislation by subject*

Electronic route
JUSTIS UK Statutes (see 4.2B2.4.3).

Paper route
(a)   *Halsbury's Statutes* — follow figure 4.8. Read the review section at the beginning of the subject group of Acts currently in force.

(b)   If legislation currently in force for the subject was published since 1947, find the text of the current Act in *Current Law Statutes* (see 4.2B2.2.2) and read the introduction and general note at the beginning of the reprint of the Act noting the titles and dates of earlier Acts mentioned.

(c)   For references to statutes up to 1713 check the subject index to *Statutes of the Realm*, described at the beginning of 4.2B.

4.2C5   *Are there any cases on this Act or section of an Act?*

Electronic route
Use one or more of the following:

(a) *LEXIS* (see 4.2B2.4.1) — the richest source since it contains the largest number of cases of any of the electronic databases. However, it will retrieve all cases mentioning the Act or section regardless of how trivial or passing was the comment. Considerable time will need to be spent evaluating the results to identify significant comment. To find cases referring to the Unfair Contract Terms Act 1977 section 11, go into the CASES file, and type:

Unfair Contract Terms w/15 11

If there is more than one Act with the same title in force as, for example, Employment Act, you need to include the year of the Act in which you are interested or you will get references to every Employment Act. So, in LEXIS, to find cases referring to section 20 of the Employment Act 1984, go into the CASES file, and type:

Employment w/4 1984 w/15 20

(b) *Lawtel* (see 4.2B2.5.1) — but the search will be only on the unofficial summaries contained in *Lawtel*, not the full text of the cases;

(c) the *Legislation Citator* on the *Current Legal Information* database (see 4.2B2.2.3) will identify only the significant references to a statute or section of a statute within cases.

Paper route
Experience suggests that the editors of *Halsbury's Statutes* and the *Current Law* publications employ different criteria by which they select cases for inclusion in their publications. This may be due to (a) the subjective judgment required to determine whether a court has judicially considered a particular section of an Act, and (b) whether decisions of courts below the High Court have precedential value. To obtain a full answer to this type of research query it is advisable to check *both* publications rather than rely on one only.

(a) *Halsbury's Statutes* (see 4.2B2.3.1) — follow figure 4.7. Read the editorial notes in small type attached to the section of the Act in which you are interested. Make sure you follow the chart to its end, and finish your research by using the Noter-Up Service.

(b) *Current Law* citators (see 4.2B2.2.3) — where you start the search depends on the date of the Act of Parliament. Figure 4.9 provides the full path available.

4.2C6   Have any statutory instruments been made under this Act?

Electronic route
Use one or more of the following:

(a) The *Legislation Citator* on the *Current Legal Information* database (see 4.2B2.2.3) — but this only goes back to 1989.

(b)   *LEXIS* (see 4.2B2.4.1). To find all statutory instruments made under the Merchant Shipping Act 1983, go into the SI or, preferably, the STATIS file and type:

authority (merchant shipping w/6 1983)

(c)   *Legislation Direct* (see 4.2B2.4.2).
(d)   *Lawtel* (see 4.2B2.5.1) — coverage from 1984 onwards.

Paper route
Use one or more of the following:

(a)   *Halsbury's Statutes* (see 4.2B2.3.1) — follow figure 4.7. Read the editorial notes in small type attached to the section of the Act in which you are interested. Make sure you follow the chart to its conclusion, and finish your research by using the Noter-Up Service.
(b)   *Current Law* citators (see 4.2B2.2.3) — where you start the search depends on the date of the Act of Parliament. Figure 4.9 provides the full path available.

4.2.C7   Have any case notes or articles been written about this Act?

The best method of answering this research question is to use one or a number of periodical indexing services, fully described in section 8.3 below.

Chapter 5

Secondary legislation

The last two hundred years have witnessed great changes in life and society. The continued growth and diversity of industry, commerce and technology, the creation and administration of the welfare state, are just a few of the many developments which have increased the legislative burden on Parliament. However, Parliamentary time is limited and the complexity and detail of legislation have been in conflict with the need for proper debate and scrutiny of proposals. Therefore, by the inclusion of a so-called 'enabling' section in an Act of Parliament, responsibility for drawing up details of the operation of the principles laid down in an Act can be conferred on a body outside Parliament. The bodies involved are Ministers of the Crown, local authorities, public corporations and the General Synod of the Church of England. The secondary legislation made by them falls into four categories: statutory instruments, codes of practice, by-laws and Measures of the General Synod. In addition, from 1 July 1999, the Scottish Parliament (sitting in Edinburgh) and the National Assembly for Wales (sitting in Cardiff), have exercised powers granted them by Parliament at Westminster, to make statutory instruments on a range of topics defined in the Scotland Act 1998 and the Government of Wales Act 1998. All statutory instruments falling outside those delegated to the Scottish Parliament and the National Assembly for Wales, and Measures of the General Synod must be laid before Parliament at Westminster for approval before they can take effect. Most codes of practice must also receive Parliamentary approval, but some codes, along with local authority and public corporation by-laws, are subject only to confirmation by a Minister of the Crown, and not Parliament. Unlike the procedures followed by a Bill passing through Parliament at Westminster, those for secondary legislation are of no direct relevance to the development of legal research skills and are therefore not dealt with here.

As a law student you are likely to use statutory instruments and probably codes of practice during your course, but this will depend largely on the areas of law you study. By-laws have been an important source of local authority law from the Municipal Corporations Act 1835 onwards and impinge on several areas of law affecting the work of solicitors. You are unlikely to be required to use Measures of the General Synod during your course and rarely, if ever, in legal practice. So, the description of research skills and techniques which follows concentrates on statutory instruments, codes of practice and by-laws.

5.1   STATUTORY INSTRUMENTS

5.1A   Description

5.1A1   Definition

The term 'statutory instrument' (often abbreviated to SI) was introduced in the Statutory Instruments Act 1946. It is one of the few instances where the definition, Parliamentary procedure and publication of a legal document are governed by an Act of Parliament. Even so, confusion still arises when undertaking legal research with SIs, because the term is generic and applies to a variety of documents which may contain in their individual titles the words 'regulation' or 'rule' or 'order' or 'scheme'. Lawyers in everyday practice are more likely to refer to these documents by their individual title rather than the collective term, and yet they are published, both officially by HMSO and commercially, in volumes with 'statutory instrument' in the title, not regulation, rule, order or scheme. So, if you are referred by a lecturer or in your reading to one of these individual forms of secondary legislation, you will need to consult volumes of 'statutory instruments' and not a separate collection of, for example, 'regulations'.

Statutory instruments can be made by Ministers or by the Queen in Council — in the latter case they are known as Orders in Council. The most substantial group of Orders in Council relate to Northern Ireland. There appears to be no particular significance in the use of an Order in Council rather than an order made by a Minister, though it obviously indicates the matter is of some importance. These Orders in Council must not be confused with Orders in Council which are a form of primary legislation made by Royal decree, and are usually restricted to the affairs of dependent territories, and not classed as a statutory instrument.

Before the Statutory Instruments Act 1946, the variety of secondary legislation called rules, orders, warrants and schemes was subject to the requirements of the Rules Publication Act 1893 and was collectively known as statutory rules and orders (abbreviated to SR & O). Very occasionally you will need to consult these older documents, for some are still in force.

Although the following statistics are over 10 years old they illustrate the quantity of secondary legislation which forms our law, and the flow has continued unabated since. Over the last 50 years an average of 2,000 SIs have been passed each year. In 1955 the total length of all SIs published by the then HMSO was about 3,240 pages; by 1988 the figure had risen to 9,048 (Bennett, 1990). As at 31 December 1989 some 17,674 SIs published by HMSO were still in force, and the number was rising annually (see Bates, 1986). Concern is sometimes expressed that too much use is made of SIs by Ministers, and the chairman of the Parliamentary Joint Committee on statutory instruments has commented that 'the trouble is that a lot of statutory instruments today no longer deal with means but with principles' (cited in Bates, 1986).

There are two broad classes of SI: local and general. The distinction is analogous to that between a Public General Act and a Local and Personal Act and has implications for publication and general availability (see 5.1A4). Ministers are required to determine whether an SI is local or general before sending it to the Queen's Printer (HMSO).

In legal research one group of general SIs is of particular importance: commencement orders. As their title suggests, they fix the date for the commencement or bringing into force of provisions in an Act of Parliament. They will be noted in 5.1A3, below.

Depending upon the enabling Act, an SI may apply to one or all of the jurisdictions of the UK (England, Wales, Scotland and Northern Ireland). The name of the SI may indicate this by specifying the jurisdiction.

5.1A2   Origin

See 5.1A1, above.

5.1A3   Structure

The structure of SIs made at Westminster, Edinburgh and Cardiff is similar. Figure 5.1 reproduces the whole of one SI, though to make reproduction in this book easier, the explanatory note given on the back of the original has been moved to a space at the front. Only a minority of SIs fit on to a single sheet of paper, some run to hundreds of pages and are thicker than many Acts of Parliament.

An SI comprises nine parts:

(a)   *Citation* — SIs are numbered consecutively by the Statutory Publications Office, roughly in the order in which they are received from Ministers, following Parliamentary approval. The sequence of numbers starts at 1 at the beginning of each calendar year. The citation is composed of the calendar year and the sequence number. Some SIs bear a letter (either C, L or S) and numbers in brackets after the sequence number. Those with a C are commencement orders, bringing an Act or part of an Act into operation, and the number which follows is the sequence number for commencement orders issued during the particular year. The letter L signifies the SI is an instrument relating to fees or procedures in courts in England and Wales, again followed by the sequence number for that series, and SIs bearing the letter S are instruments which apply to Scotland only. These secondary letters and numbers should not be used when citing an SI.

(b)   *Subject-matter* — this word or phrase describes the subject of the SI and is the same word as will be used in the indexes to SIs published by HMSO (see 5.1B1.3 to 5.1B1.5).

Figure 5.1 A statutory instrument.

STATUTORY INSTRUMENTS

---

① **1989 No. 1674**

② **PENSIONS**

③ The Superannuation (Valuation and Community Charge Tribunals) Order 1989

④
Made - - - -	*4th September 1989*
Laid before Parliament	*15th September 1989*
Coming into force	*6th October 1989*

⑤ The Treasury, in exercise of the powers conferred by section 1(5)(c) and section 1(8)(a) of the Superannuation Act 1972(**a**) and now vested in them(**b**), hereby make the following Order:—

⑥ **1.** This Order may be cited as the Superannuation (Valuation and Community Charge Tribunals) Order 1989 and shall come into force on 6th October 1989.

2. Employment by a valuation and community charge tribunal is hereby removed from the employments listed in Schedule 1 to the Superannuation Act 1972 with effect from 1st May 1989.

Kenneth Carlisle
Nigel Lawson
Two of the Lords Commissioners
of Her Majesty's Treasury

⑦ 4th September 1989

⑧ EXPLANATORY NOTE

(This note is not part of the Order)

Employment with a valuation and community charge tribunal was on 1st May 1989 added to the employments listed in Schedule 1 to the Superannuation Act 1972 ("the 1972 Act") by the Local Government Finance Act 1988 (c.41), section 136 and Schedule 11, paragraph 6(6), and so falls within those employments to which the Principal Civil Service Pension Scheme and the Civil Service Additional Voluntary Contribution Scheme (made under section 1 of the 1972 Act) may apply. This Order removes employment by a valuation and community charge tribunal from the employments listed in that Schedule. Under the power conferred by section 1(8)(a) of the 1972 Act the Order takes effect from 1st May 1989.

A valuation and community charge tribunal will be a "scheduled body" for the purposes of the Local Government Superannuation Regulations 1986 (S.I. 1986/24) with effect from 1st May 1989 by virtue of the Local Government Superannuation (Valuation and Community Charge Tribunals) Regulations 1989 (S.I. 1989/1624).

① Citation (a) ② Subject Matter (b) ③ Short Title (c)
④ Statements of Progress (d) ⑤ Preamble and enabling powers (e)
⑥ Main Text (f) ⑦ Signatures (g) ⑧ Explanatory Note (i)

(Letters in parentheses refer to paragraphs in text where discussion on the elements of a SI occur.)

(c)   *Short title* — this is the title by which the SI is generally known.

(d)   *Statements of progress* — section 4(2) of the Statutory Instruments Act 1946 requires that every SI must bear on its face a statement of the date on which it came or will come into operation, and either a statement of the date on which copies were laid before Parliament or a statement that copies are to be laid before Parliament. In addition, it is usual practice for SIs to also bear the date on which they were made.

(e)   *Preamble and enabling powers* — the text of the SI commences with a recital of the statutory authority and powers under which the instrument is made.

(f)   *Main text* — an SI is divided into a series of numbered divisions which may be subdivided. The name given to the divisions is determined by the title given to the SI. If the SI is titled XYZ Order then the divisions are called articles; if it is titled XYZ Regulations then the divisions are called regulations; if the SI is titled XYZ Rules then the divisions are called rules. A subdivision of an article, regulation or rule is called a paragraph. In lengthy SIs the articles, regulations or rules may be grouped into numbered parts but the structure is not as uniform as with Bills or Acts (see appendix 3). There are four special types of articles etc. of which you should be aware; they are indicated by a heading printed in bold type. The 'short title' or 'citation' article etc. sets out the correct title by which you should refer to the SI; the 'commencement' article etc. gives the date on which the SI is to come into force (which should be the same date as given in the statements of progress); the 'extent' article etc. details the geographical area to which the SI applies; and, finally, the 'interpretation' article etc. gives the meaning of particular words or phrases used in the SI. Not all SIs include all these four, and some SIs roll citation and commencement together under one heading, throwing in, for good measure, an article etc. headed 'revocation', which states which earlier SIs are replaced by the new SI.

(g)   *Signatures* — this is the name(s) and title(s) of the Minister(s) making the SI, and the date the SI was made.

(h)   *Schedules* — at the end of many SIs will be found one or more schedules containing detailed provisions dependent on one or more of the preceding paragraphs of text, rather like appendices at the back of a book.

(i)   *Explanatory note* — because of the complexity of many SIs, an explanatory note is added to aid the understanding of the provisions. The note is prefaced by a warning that it does not form part of the instrument. In the example illustrated in figure 5.1 the explanatory note is longer than the text of the SI itself!

5.1A4   Publication and general availability

As was noted in 5.1A1, there are two classes of SI: general or local. General instruments made at Westminster, are published and sold by HMSO, several separate instruments appearing each working day. Between 50 per cent and 60 per cent of all SIs are general. The remainder are local instruments; examples include those relating to a particular local authority area. They are exempt from printing and sale unless the Minister concerned requests otherwise. As a law student you will be concerned with general instruments, but should you eventually practise in local authority law, the difficulties in tracing local instruments will become apparent (see Morris, 1990).

Some Acts of Parliament require a draft SI to be laid before Parliament. Draft instruments for Parliament at Westminster are published by HMSO but lack the citation details (year and running number) and, of course, the date on which they were made. Draft SIs of the National Assembly for Wales are not published by HMSO at present but are only available in electronic format at the Assembly web site at

> http://www.wales.gov.uk/index_e.html

Most law libraries will collect loose, separate SIs as they are published, but some may only subscribe to the bound annual volumes (see 5.1B1.1), and so will not have copies of the most recent instruments in stock. The full text of all general instruments made at Westminster, issued since 1 January 1997, has been placed on the internet by HMSO at

> http://www.hmso.gov.uk/stat.htm

All approved Welsh SIs made by the National Assembly are published in paper form by HMSO and are also available at the HMSO Welcome to Wales Legislation web site at

> http://www.wales-legislation.hmso.gov.uk/

5.1A5   Citation

Statutory instruments, regardless of where they have been made, are cited quite simply: the short title followed by the abbreviation 'SI', the year, followed by a slash '/' and then the running number. If the year and running number are very similar, confusion can be avoided by substituting the abbreviation 'No.' for the slash, but since the calendar year should *always* be cited *before* the running number the confusion is only in the mind of the reader. Here is the correct way of citing the instrument illustrated in figure 5.1:

> Superannuation (Valuation and Community Charge Tribunals) Order 1989 SI 1989/1674.

5.1B   Finding information

There are a number of official and commercially produced publications which reprint SIs or assist your researching them.

5.1B1   Official publications

These may be divided into publications which reprint SIs (see 5.1B1.1) and those which merely list them (see 5.1B1.2 to 5.1B1.5).

5.1B1.1   Statutory Instruments 19—

At the end of each calendar year, annual volumes entitled *Statutory Instruments*, containing reprints of general instruments, are compiled by HMSO. Unfortunately publication is frequently delayed by up to two years.

At the time of writing, the bound volumes for the Welsh Assembly have yet to appear, and it is not clear whether their SIs will be included in this publication or published separately. However, the bound volumes for the first year of the Scottish Parliament are due to be out by the end of 2000, and these volumes will be separate from those of the SIs.

The texts of only those instruments in force at the end of the year are included — this is significant because some instruments have only temporary application. The final volume of each annual set contains a subject index and numerical lists of all the SIs printed and sold by HMSO during the year, whether reprinted in the annual volumes or not. A classified list of all *local* instruments is also given and after 1988 the text of selected local instruments has been printed also.

From 1890 to 1960 the annual volumes of instruments were arranged by subject, but since 1961 they have been printed in numerical order.

Three editions of the official, revised edition of instruments have appeared, giving the text of all general instruments in force at a particular date. The latest edition, *Statutory Rules and Orders and Statutory Instruments Revised to December 31st 1948*, was published in 25 volumes between 1949 and 1952. The arrangement is alphabetical by subject.

5.1B1.2   Daily List of Government Publications from TSO

Every working day The Stationery Office (TSO) publishes a list containing brief details (really little more than the citation) of the documents it and HMSO have issued that day — it is known as the '*Daily List*'. SIs are included and for lawyers the list has two benefits:

(a)   By the Statutory Instruments Act 1946, section 3, the inclusion of an SI in this list is conclusive evidence of publication — there have been one or two court cases which have turned on this point, for if there is not appropriate evidence that a particular SI had been published or published on a particular day, then an action concerned with compliance with the requirements of the instrument can fail.

(b)   Although most HMSO publications are included in the *Monthly* and *Annual Catalogues* of TSO publications, SIs are not. So, the entries in the *Daily List* are the only official means of knowing that an SI has been published, until the separate monthly *List of SIs* (see 5.1B1.3) appears. There is no index to the *Daily List*, so to find the entry for a particular SI it is necessary to scan the copies of the *Daily List* around the time you think the SI you want was published. The *Daily List* is best used as an 'alerting' publication — that is, to give warning, day by day, of the publication of new material. Whenever you can, use the monthly *List of SIs* in preference. The *Daily List* is available on the internet at

http://www.the-stationery-office.co.uk/daily_list

5.1B1.3   List of Statutory Publications (formerly List of Statutory Instruments)

This is a useful index for tracing relatively recent SIs; although published monthly it is usually a few months in arrears. At the year end it is replaced by an annual list which is delayed by several years. The main body of the monthly list arranges brief details about each SI published that month, under the same subject headings as are printed at the top of the SI itself. At the back of the list is an alphabetical subject index, cumulated throughout the calendar year, the December issue acting as an interim annual subject index until the annual list proper is published. There is also a list of SIs issued during the month in question, arranged in order by the sequence running number.

5.1B1.4   Index to Government Orders

In effect, this two-volume publication is a subject index to all SIs in force. It was published every other year up to the early 1990's but the last available edition, published in 1995, was correct only to the end of 1991. The publication is of very little use for current research.

5.1B1.5   Table of Government Orders

This is a chronological listing of all instruments falling within the definition of statutory rules given in the Rules Publication Act 1893 and SIs as defined in the Statutory Instruments Act 1946, and certain Orders in Council made under the Royal Prerogative (i.e., primary legislation). The list starts with an Order in Council of 1671 and gives year by year the serial number for each instrument, its title and an indication of whether it is still in force (noted in bold type) or no longer in force (noted in italic type), with brief details of why it is no longer in force. So if you know the year and serial number of an SI, you can use the *Table* to check whether it is still in force. However, the *Table* does not contain very current information. The latest edition available, published in 1992, covers the period 1671 to 1990. The publication is of very little use for current research.

5.1B2   Commercial publications

Like the official publications noted above, the commercial ones may be divided into those which reprint SIs (see 5.1B2.1 to 5.1B2.7) and those which merely list them (see 5.1B2.8 to 5.1B2.12).

5.1B2.1   JUSTIS UK Statutory Instruments

The *JUSTIS UK Statutory Instruments* CD contains the full text, tables, diagrams and maps of all SIs applying to England, Wales and Scotland from January 1987 onwards. It does *not* include local SIs. The database reproduces SIs in the form in which they were originally published and does *not* indicate where amendments or revocations have occured. Other sources (such as those described in 5.1B2.3 to 5.1B2.5, and 5.1B2.10 or 5.1B2.11) will need to be used to check whether the text of the SI in which you are interested has been altered. The database is updated quarterly, but it is possible to subscribe to the Context Online Service which provides updates every two or three weeks.

5.1B2.2 LEXIS

The on-line database *LEXIS* contains the *full text* of all SIs currently in force in England and Wales, published in the Statutory Instruments series. The following are not included in the database: instruments made by the Welsh Assembly, instruments applying exclusively to Scotland and all local SIs. The database is updated very slowly and can run as much as six months behind the original date of publication of a SI. The text of every SI on *LEXIS* will include any amendments made by subsequent SIs and is not merely a reprint of the SI in the form in which it was originally approved by Parliament.

The database is divided into libraries. The ENGGEN library (*Eng*lish *Gen*eral) contains separate files including one devoted to statutory instruments, with the name SI. Another file named STATIS allows you to search the statutory instruments and statutes (Acts) files together, which is advisable for some research queries since Acts and SIs modify one another.

Since use of *LEXIS* is charged differently from most databases, frequently universities and colleges do not give students direct access to the database. Teaching and library staff will advise you whether use of the database is appropriate for the research you wish to conduct. Other sources, such as those described in 5.1B2.3 to 5.1B2.5 and 5.1B2.10 or 5.1B2.11, may be just as useful and, in some instances, more up-to-date.

5.1B2.3 Legislation Direct

Legislation Direct is an internet database providing the full text of all statutory instruments in force in their amended versions. It includes SIs applying to the whole of the UK and instruments made by the Scottish Parliament. It does not include instruments made by the Welsh Assembly. It is updated on a daily basis but has been found to take a few weeks to include some new SIs. The site is at

http://www.butterworths.com

Buttons leading to a range of Butterworths services are displayed here, but only subscribers will be able to provide the user name and password which will give access to each of the services. Ask library staff if your university or college subscribes.

5.1B2.4 Halsbury's Statutory Instruments

Halsbury's Statutory Instruments reprints a large number, but not all, SIs of general application, currently in force in England and Wales; the remainder are summarised. It does not include SIs made by the National Assembly for Wales nor instruments extending only to Scotland. The decision by the editors of the publication to reprint or merely summarise an SI is based on their assessment of the general importance of an SI, set against the likely requirements of subscribers to the service. This is an occasional, but not major, disadvantage, and is more than compensated for by the superior indexing and the system for keeping the statement of law up-to-date.

Halsbury's Statutory Instruments consists of three parts:

(a) *Main volumes.* These comprise 22 grey-coloured volumes in which reprints or summaries of SIs are arranged under 97 broad subject headings (called 'titles' in the publication). Each title may be subdivided. At the beginning of each title there is a chronological list of instruments and a table of instruments no longer in operation. Then follows a preliminary note describing the scope of the title and, if the title is subdivided, there are introductory notes to each part. Finally there follows the text or a summary of each SI relevant to the title.

When the law stated in a Main Volume becomes considerably out of date, a reissue volume is published to replace the original volume. The word 'reissue' is printed at the foot of the spine and on the title page. On the page following the title page, is given the date to which the law is stated in the volume. This is important information because the Consolidated Index to the whole set is published annually, and there may be short periods when the page information given in the annual index refers to an original volume and not the recently published reissue volume to hand. If that happens it is necessary to check again the subject you want in the index to the reissue volume to find the new page number.

(b) *Service binders.* Two loose-leaf binders contain information which assists you using the Main Volumes and keeps them up-to-date. The Main Service Binder contains a number of indexes: first, a chronological list of instruments (a list in date order of those instruments included in the Main Volumes with references to the volumes in which they will be found); secondly, an alphabetical list of instruments for the current year featured in the Main Volumes, and thirdly, a monthly update and associated index, the equivalent of a noter-up, detailing recent changes to instruments featured in the Main Volumes. The second loose-leaf binder: the Additional Texts binder, contains the full text of selected statutory instruments awaiting inclusion in reissued Main Volumes. These additional texts are arranged in SI number order, not the subject order employed in the Main Volumes.

(c) *Consolidated index and alphabetical index.* The third part of *Halsbury's Statutory Instruments* is a thick paperback index volume, replaced annually, which is in three sections: a list of the Main Volumes and their dates of issue from which the indexes have been compiled; a subject index (called the Consolidated Index) and, lastly, a list of SIs included in the publication in alphabetical order by their title (called the Alphabetical Index). The majority of entries in the subject index will provide references to the volume and page number in the Main Volumes where relevant information on the subject will be found, but where a statutory instrument is still only available in the first loose-leaf binder, a letter S in bold type is given, instead of the volume and page number, followed by the SI citation.

Using Halsbury's Statutory Instruments   If you remember that the general arrangement of the publication is by subject, that where this is not so indexes are provided to help you find the information you require, and that to carry out a fully up-to-date piece of research you must also use the loose-leaf binders, you should not go far wrong.

There are three different ways of using *Halsbury's Statutory Instruments* for research:

(a)   Finding SIs on a subject — follow figure 5.2.
(b)   Finding an SI when all you know is its title — follow figure 5.3.
(c)   Finding an SI when all you know is its citation — follow figure 5.4.

All the research steps outlined suggest using the various indexes to the whole publication as a way of finding information. This is by far the best method to adopt when you are first learning how to use the publication. However, once you have become familiar with the presentation of material in *Halsbury's*, and especially the contents of the subject titles into which it is divided, you may wish to start your research by browsing over the spines and selecting the most appropriate of the 22 Main Volumes from the shelves and using the index and lists in that volume to guide you to the information you require. The danger to the uninitiated is that unless you use the Consolidated Indexes to the whole publication you can never be sure (a) you are checking the correct volumes for the information you require and (b) if you do not find what you are seeking, that it does not appear somewhere else in *Halsbury's*.

5.1B2.5   *Specialist subject encyclopaedias*

Many specialist law encyclopaedias reprint SIs relevant to their topic area. Although the subject coverage of particular encyclopaedias may be narrow, the greater detail included in their subject indexes, together with the rapidity with which they are updated (most are loose-leaf publications), and the fact that SIs are reprinted with explanatory notes and annotations by the encyclopaedia's editorial staff in addition, makes them a very valuable source for SIs. An increasing number of the most popular encyclopaedias are being issued in CD format as well as paper. Encyclopaedias dealing with the law in Scotland are more likely to reproduce SIs which only apply to that jurisdiction.

5.1B2.6   *Knight's Local Government Reports*

First published in 1903 and appearing monthly, this publication included up to 1990 the full text of SIs relevant to the work of local government in England and Wales only. However, there is no subject index, nor are there annotations, and neither are the texts updated as amendments and revocations occur.

5.1B2.7   *Knight's Local Government Legislation*

From 1991 onwards, the SIs which would have been published as part of *Knight's Local Government Reports*, have been issued as loose-leaf pages

Figure 5.2 Searching *Halsbury's Statutory Instruments* by subject.

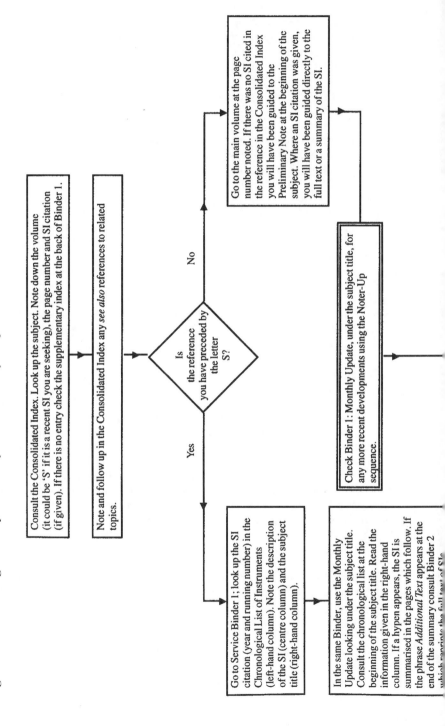

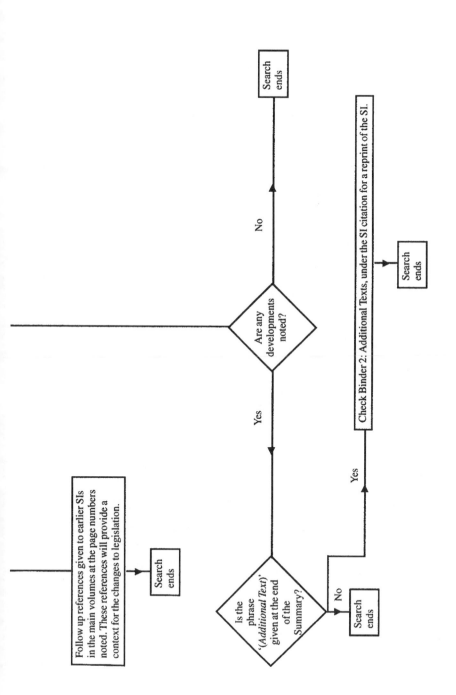

Figure 5.3   Finding a statutory instrument in *Halsbury's Statutory Instruments* when all you know is its title.

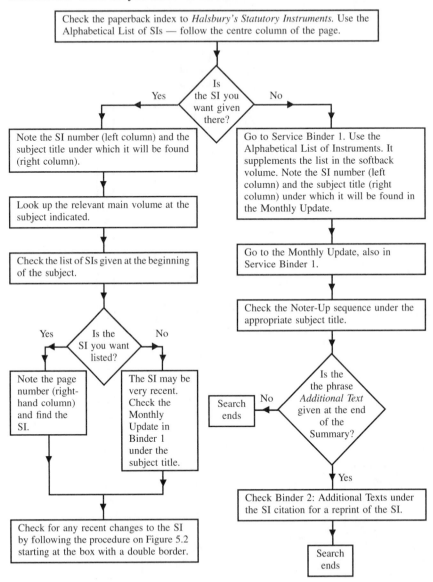

Figure 5.4 Finding a statutory instrument in *Halsbury's Statutory Instruments* when all you know is its citation.

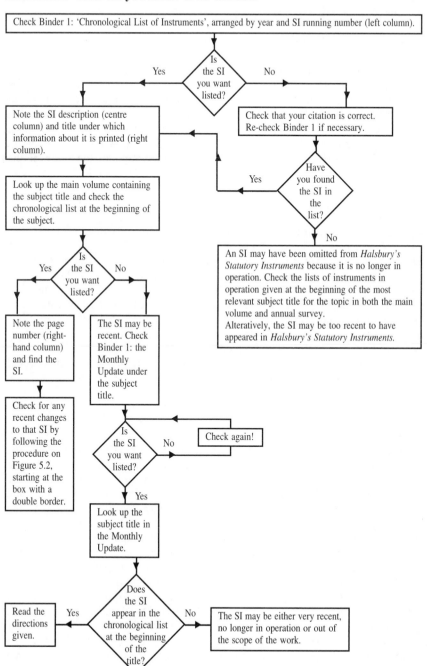

inserted within binders. This innovation means the text of SIs is now updated
when amendments or revocations occur but there is still neither a subject index
nor any annotations.

5.1B2.8   Current Law Monthly Digest

Summaries of a selection of SIs are given in *Current Law Monthly Digest* and
Current Law Yearbook. You can trace where these summaries are printed by
using the Alphabetical Table of Statutory Instruments found in both publications, which lists SIs by title. For SIs of the current calendar year use the list
in the latest issue of *Current Law Monthly Digest* which will provide a reference
to the paragraph number and monthly issue in which the summary is given. In
Current Law Yearbook the reference is to the paragraph in the body of the
Yearbook itself.

5.1B2.9   Current Law Legislation Citator

A table 'Statutory Instruments Affected' at the back of the Citators for 1972–88
and 1989–95 lists all amendments and revocations made by SIs to post-1946
SIs. The table is arranged by year and then numerically by SI number within
each year. So, for example, if you wish to trace changes to SI 1980/541 you
would find the section of the list for 1980 in the 1972–88 Citator, the entry 541
and discover 'amended 81/575; revoked 85/1218', meaning the instrument was
amended by SI 1981/575 but eventually revoked by SI 1985/1218. If the SI had
not been revoked, you would need to bring your research further up-to-date by
consulting the list in the 1989–95 Citator.

A Scottish edition entitled *Scottish Current Law Legislation Citator* covered
1972–88 with a similar table of statutory instruments affected between 1947–88.

5.1B2.10   Current Law Statutory Instrument Citator

Paper version
Checking the status of SIs has improved considerably since 1993 with the
publication of *Current Law Statutory Instrument Citator*, the earliest part of
which is included in the *Legislation Citator* volume for 1989–95, updated by
later volumes. The SI Citator provides details of amendments, revocations and
cases in which the meaning and effect of an SI has been considered by the
courts. Figure 5.5 taken from the *Statutory Instrument Citator 1996–1998*,
shows part of a page from the sequence of SIs passed in 1995.

The page is split into two columns. The SI numbers are given in the left-hand
margin of each column and, in the extract, include the last part of the entry for
SI 1995/416 and the beginning of the entry for SI 1995/418 (there is no entry
for SI 1995/417). Take a closer look at the wealth of information given for SI
1995/418, Town and Country Planning (General Development) Order 1995.
First, there is a reference to a law report, *Thames Heliport Plc v Tower Hamlets*
1997, with a citation to where a report of the case can be read in the law reports
— the case mentions the SI in general and not any particular part of it. Then

Figure 5.5   Extract from *Current Law Statutory Instrument Citator 1996–1998*.

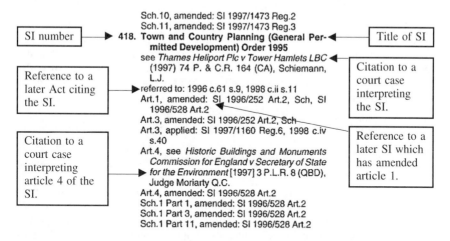

there is a reference to an Act of 1996, chapter 61, and section 9 of that Act which refers to the SI. Another Act is also cited at this point. Then follow references to individual articles within the SI, against which are noted any decisions of the courts in which the judges have considered the meaning of the article and any SIs which have changed the wording of the article or referred to it or revoked it.

A full search of the *Citators* is achieved in three steps: start with the oldest part covering citations made during 1993 to 1995 to SIs of any date, included within the volume: *Current Law Legislation Citators 1989–1995*. Next, use the softback volume: *Current Law Legislation Citators 1996–199—*. Finally, for citations during the current year, consult the loose-leaf Service File to *Current Law Statutes*, which contains monthly updates.

Electronic version

The set of *Statutory Instrument Citators* from 1993 onwards is available in electronic format, either on CD or via the internet, as part of the *Current Legal Information (CLI)* database. The SI Citator database is included within the Statute Citator database — there is not a separate entry on the menu. The electronic version is much easier and quicker to search than the paper version because:

(a)   all the separate volumes of the Citator have been placed in a single search file;

(b)   it is possible to key in just a single word from the title of a statutory instrument (so long as it is not a common word such as Law or Tax, otherwise many SIs will be retrieved) and obtain information relating to it; and

(c)   in the CD version only, there are links from the information displayed about subsequent developments such as a case or a later, amending or revoking SI, to further details.

The internet version is at:

http://193.118.187.160/cli.htm

The site is available only to subscribers, though most universities and colleges teaching law have a subscription. You will need a user name and password to get into the site; ask library staff for this information. An online User Guide for Students — intended for trainee solicitors rather than university or college students — is available at:

http://www.smlawpub.co.uk/digital/cli/index.cfm#student

5.1B2.11   Lawtel

Lawtel is an internet database, updated daily, providing brief details (not the text) of every SI within a day of publication by HMSO. It includes all SIs made at Westminster including those applying exclusively to Scotland. The digest of information commenced in 1984. Details about SIs published after 1 January 1997 include links to the full text of the SI on the HMSO web site. *Lawtel* is available to subscribers only, though many universities and colleges have a subscription. A user code and password are required to gain access to the database. Ask library staff about this. Lawtel is at:

http://www.lawtel.co.uk

5.1B2.12   Welsh Legal Digest Online

Cardiff University launched in February 2000, an internet service which will provide lists, summaries and analysis of all law relating to and issued by the National Assembly for Wales. The service is still under development. Access to the full service is available to subscribers only but 'guests' can view a restricted sample at:

http://www.welsh-legaldigest.co.uk/

5.1B2.13   Practitioners' law periodicals

Each week a summary or list of the most important new SIs is printed in *New Law Journal* and *Solicitors' Journal*. Some specialist law periodicals also note recent changes in the law brought about by SIs.

5.1C   Answering research queries

For background information on using CDs and the internet for legal research, see appendix 4.

5.1C1   You know the title of an SI but not the year or running number. How do you trace a copy of it?

There are several ways of undertaking this research. Given the volume of SIs published each year and the possibility of titles being very similar, care should be taken to ensure any SI you find is the one relevant to your research.

Electronic route
Use one or more of the following:

(a)   *LEXIS* (see 5.1B2.2) — has the text of SIs in force but is not kept well up-to-date. To find the text of the Mental Health Review Tribunal Rules, you would type:

title (Mental Health Review Tribunal)

(b)   *Legislation Direct* (see 5.1B2.3) — has the text of SIs in force.
(c)   *Lawtel* (see 5.1B2.11) — digest coverage from 1984 onwards.
(d)   *JUSTIS UK Statutory Instruments* (see 5.1B2.1) — full text coverage from 1987 onwards.
(e)   Statute Citator on the Current Legal Information database (see 5.1B2.10) — titles and citations only from 1993 onwards.
(f)   The SI web site provided by The Stationery Office (see 5.1A4) — full text from 1997 onwards, but no indication of amendments etc.

Paper route
Using paper sources there are several research routes, but quite a few publications, especially those officially produced, do not include indexes to SI titles but are based on the SI year/running number or the subject. In the circumstances, therefore, the following paths are suggested:

(a)   *Halsbury's Statutory Instruments* (see 5.1B2.4) — use figure 5.3. *Halsbury's* is the only source to comprehensively index SIs in force in this way.
(b)   *Current Law Monthly Digest* (see 5.1B2.8) — use the Alphabetical Table of Statutory Instruments in the latest monthly issue, the December issue of any year for which *Current Law Yearbook* is not available, and each *Current Law Yearbook*. Having found the SI year/running number you should then turn to a full-text source for the SI, such as *Statutory Instruments 19*— (see 5.1B1.1). A tedious task, made more so by the way titles are grouped under subject headings in the *Yearbooks*.
(c)   *Current Law Statutory Instrument Citator* (see 5.1B2.10) — coverage from 1993 onwards. Includes a list of SIs in title order at the front of each volume.
(d)   Specialist subject encyclopaedias (see 5.1B2.5) — another research method would be to select a specialist subject encyclopaedia and search either its subject index or any tables of SIs, for a reference which matches the title you have and, if successful, look up the reprint of the SI in the encyclopaedia.

5.1C2   Is this SI, the title, year and number of which you know, in force?

Electronic route
Use one or more of the following:

    (a)   *Legislation Direct* (see 5.1B2.3).
    (b)   *LEXIS* (see 5.1B2.2) — see 4.2C1 on how to undertake this search.
    (c)   *Lawtel* (see 5.1B2.11).
    (d)   Statute Citator on the Current Legal Information database (see 5.1B2.10) — titles and citations only from 1993 onwards.

Note that the *JUSTIS UK Statutory Instruments* CD is not sufficiently up-to-date to perform this research satisfactorily.

Paper route
Use one of the following:

    (a)   *Current Law Statutory Instrument Citator* (see 5.1B2.10).
    (b)   *Halsbury's Statutory Instruments* (see 5.1B2.4) — use either figure 5.3 or figure 5.5.
    (c)   Specialist subject encyclopaedias (see 5.1B2.5).

5.1C3   Has this SI been amended?

Electronic route
Use one or more of the following:

    (a)   *Legislation Direct* (see 5.1B2.3).
    (b)   *LEXIS* (see 5.1B2.2) incorporates into the text of SIs all amendments made up to the date the file is current (i.e., the date given on the screen displaying the files available). Repealed or spent provisions are not available on *LEXIS*. So, to answer this research query for, say, the Mental Health Review Tribunal Rules, you would type:

    title (Mental Health Review Tribunal)

Within the text of the SI displayed amendments will be represented in three ways:

    (i)   where words have been substituted and new words have been added or new words are to be added, square brackets [   ] will be used;
    (ii)   where words have been repealed or revoked or amend or repeal earlier legislation, three dots . . . will be found;
    (iii)   where words are prospectively repealed or repealed with savings, they will be contained between *R*** and ***R*.

At the end of each of the documents retrieved by your search request, a list headed 'Annotations' will give details of the Acts or SIs under which the amendments have been made.

(c)   *Lawtel* (see 5.1B2.11).

(d)   Statute Citator on the Current Legal Information database (see 5.1B2.10) — titles and citations only from 1993 onwards.

Note that the *JUSTIS UK Statutory Instruments* CD is not an entirely appropriate database to use for this query because its SI texts are in their original and not amended form. Searches could be conducted either under the title of the SI in the heading field to uncover an amending SI with the same title, or under the title of the enabling Act to discover all SIs made under it and note any which amend the particular SI in which you are interested, or, finally, a subject search in the heading field to retrieve SIs on the same topic (though not necessarily with the same title) to see if they amend the SI in question.

Paper route
Use one of the following:

(a)   *Halsbury's Statutory Instruments* (see 5.1B2.4) — use either figure 5.3 or figure 5.5.

(b)   *Current Law Statutory Instrument Citator* (see 5.1B2.10).

5.1C4   Which SIs have been made under this Act?

Electronic route
Use one or more of the following:

(a)   *Legislation Direct* (see 5.1B2.3).

(b)   *LEXIS* (see 5.1B2.2) — select the STATIS file, which combines the statutes and statutory instruments files. The reason for doing this is that Acts and SIs frequently modify one another. Supposing the Act in which you were interested is the Merchant Shipping Act 1995, type:

authority (Merchant Shipping w/6 1995)

(c)   *Lawtel* (see 5.1B2.11).

(d)   Statute Citator on the Current Legal Information database (see 5.1B2.10) — titles and citations only from 1993 onwards.

(e)   *JUSTIS UK Statutory Instruments* (see 5.1B2.1) — full text coverage from 1987 onwards.

Paper route
Use one of the following (note that item (a) is the easiest source to use and the most comprehensive):

(a)   *Current Law Statute Citator* and *Current Law Legislation Citator* (see 4.2B2.2.3).

(b)   *Halsbury's Statutory Instruments* (see 5.1B2.4) following figure 5.4.

(c)   *Halsbury's Statutes* (see 4.2B2.3.1) — follow figure 4.7. When you have found the Act in the Main Volumes or Current Statutes Service, check the editorial notes attached, and follow any recent developments through the Cumulative Supplement and Noter-Up.

(d)   Specialist subject encyclopaedias (see 5.1B2.5) may also be used.

5.1C5   Is this SI still in force?

Electronic route
Use one or more of the following:

(a)   *Legislation Direct* (see 5.1B2.3).

(b)   *Lawtel* (see 5.1B2.11) — will provide an answer if you know the title of the enabling Act under which the SI was made.

(c)   *LEXIS* (see 5.1B2.2) — contains the text of only those SIs currently in force at the date to which the file is current. So, to answer this research query you would undertake a title search, as in 4.2C1, and if the SI is in force, *LEXIS* will trace it. If it is not, *LEXIS* will either declare it has found nothing or if it has been revoked by an SI of the same title it will retrieve the new SI.

(d)   *JUSTIS UK Statutory Instruments* CD (see 5.1B2.1) — full text coverage from 1987 onwards, but in view of the poor currency of the information the answer will not take account of recent developments.

Paper route
Use one or more of the following:

(a)   *Halsbury's Statutory Instruments* (see 5.1B2.4), follow figure 5.3 or 5.5.
(b)   *Current Law Statutory Instrument Citator* (see 5.1B2.10).
(c)   Specialist subject encyclopaedias (5.1B2.5) may also be used.

5.1C6   Has this SI been considered by the courts?

Note that for this research problem the case database of the various electronic sources should be used, *not* the statutory instrument database.

Electronic route
Use one or more of the following:

(a)   *LEXIS* (see 5.1B2.2) — this database will retrieve every citation to an SI, regardless of the importance of the judicial comment. Select the CASES file, and supposing you wished to check for cases on the Social Security Benefits Up-Rating Regulations, you would type:

Social Security Benefits Up-Rating Regulations

If there is any possibility of there having existed several SIs with the same title, the search request could be made more specific by adding the date of the particular SI in which you are interested:

Social Security Benefits Up-Rating Regulations w/4 1981

(b)   *Lawtel* (see 5.1B2.11) — search the cases database. Since *Lawtel* carries only summaries of cases it will retreive only major references to an SI.

(c)   *Current Law Cases* on the Current Legal Information database (see 6B2.4) — will retrieve major references from the summaries of cases held from 1947 onwards.

Paper route
Use one or more of the following (note that item (b) probably notes more cases than the other sources):

(a)   *Halsbury's Statutory Instruments* (see 5.1B2.4) — the editorial notes to instruments included mention cases where the meaning and effect of the SI have been judicially considered.

(b)   *Current Law Statutory Instrument Citator* (see 5.1B2.10).

(c)   *Law Reports* index (see 6B1.1) carries a table of statutory instruments etc. judicially considered, but appears to restrict coverage of cases to those mentioned in the handful of law reports it indexes.

5.1C7   Have any notes or articles been written in periodicals about this SI?

The best method of answering this research question is to use one or a number of periodical indexing services, fully described in 8.3 below.

5.2   STATUTORY CODES OF PRACTICE

5.2A   Description

5.2A1   Definition

There is no official definition, and this is one of the difficulties faced by the researcher and user of statutory codes of practice. Although Parliament, through provisions in an Act, gives a government department, or in some cases an outside body, the power to prepare a code, the code may not be subject to approval by Parliament (as is a statutory instrument) but by a Secretary of State, or a Minister, or even the outside body itself, depending on what the Act stipulates. Further, some codes are intended merely to provide guidance or to be a statement of accepted good practice, whilst others have a legal effect and may be used in civil or criminal proceedings as tending to establish or negate liability. There has been concern amongst lawyers and Parliamentarians at:

(a)   the uncertainty of the legal effect of failure to comply with codes of practice,

(b)   the lack of a standard procedure for the approval of codes of practice, and

(c)   the nature of the content of some codes, which could and should have been included in an Act or in regulations.

These concerns led to a debate in the House of Lords on 15 January 1986 and the subsequent issue, in 1987, by HM Government, of a note: 'Guidance on Codes of Practice and Legislation' (reprinted in [1989] Stat LR 214). The aim of the guidance note is to secure consistency and legal certainty in future legislation. Nevertheless, between 1973 and 1986, 25 statutes have come into force under which 48 codes of practice may be made (per Lord Renton, HL Deb (1985–86) 469 col. 1086), and a considerable number of those which were made during that period are of particular value to law students, and embody the qualities the guidance note seeks to correct. Some statutes confer duties on regulatory authorities, such as the Director General of Fair Trading, to encourage private organisations to prepare and disseminate codes of practice. These 'voluntary' codes are dealt with in chapter 7 on extra-legal sources since they are not legally enforceable in their own right and may rely on non-legal sanctions.

5.2A2   Origin

The oldest and no doubt the best known statutory code of practice is the Highway Code. By the Road Traffic Act 1930, section 45, the Minister of Transport was empowered to issue directions for the guidance of road users. Clearly, the statute could not deal with all the details relating to proper conduct on the road, so the code of practice was created. Similarly, the Industrial Relations Act 1971 provided for the issue of an Industrial Relations Code of Practice by the Secretary of State, covering a wide range of matters such as employment policies, collective bargaining, grievance and disputes procedures. But it was the spate of legislation commencing with the Health and Safety at Work etc. Act 1974, and the Control of Pollution Act 1974, quickly followed by the Employment Protection Act 1975, Sex Discrimination Act 1975 and Race Relations Act 1976 and later, the Employment Act 1980, Child Care Act 1980, Police and Criminal Evidence Act 1985 and Housing Act 1985 which led to the concerns noted in 5.2A1. Codes under many of these Acts are likely to feature in your reading as a law student.

5.2A3   Structure

Since each code may be designed for a different purpose and addressed to a different audience, including the general public as well as local authority officers, trade union representatives, police officers etc., there is no common structure for statutory codes of practice. However, one feature is common: they are meant to be read by lay people, not lawyers, and so frequently use simple, intelligible language rather than the stilted or obscure language of statutes. They are, therefore, much easier to understand!

5.2A4   Publication and general availability

Again, there is no common practice though many, like the Highway Code, are published by The Stationery Office (TSO). Some, like the codes prepared by the

Equal Opportunities Commission for the elimination of discrimination in employment, are published by the organisation which prepared them. The note of guidance on codes of practice (see 5.2A1) suggests authorities should consider arranging for sale through TSO or include the code in a relevant annual report. So, the picture remains rather confused. Many academic law libraries will keep individual copies of the major codes of practice a student will need to consult — the best way to track them down, so long as you know either the correct title or the name of the issuing authority, is through the library's catalogue. If you are not sure of either the title or 'author' try one of the methods outlined in 5.2B.

5.2A5   Citation

There is no standard form of citation but, for clarity, codes of practice should usually be referred to by their full title, the date of publication (especially if more than one edition or a revision has been published) and the name of the authority which has prepared the code.

5.2B   Finding information

Invaluable assistance in tracing codes of practice can be obtained by using law encyclopaedias. A check of a general encyclopaedia like *Halsbury's Statutes*, either by the title of the Act under which the code was made, or by the subject matter, should lead to an editorial footnote at the appropriate section of the Act, which will give details of the title and issuing authority for the code (follow figures 4.7 and 4.8 on how to use *Halsbury's Statutes*). *Halsbury's* will not reprint the code itself and the summary provided may be very brief, but with the correct title and issuing authority you can now try the library catalogue with more confidence. *The Laws of Scotland* (see 12B4.1) will also direct the researcher to relevant codes of practice. However, a better strategy is to consult a specialist law encyclopaedia covering the subject area with which the code deals. Specialist subject encyclopaedias (see 8.2) are a valuable resource for they:

(a)   are frequently well and fully indexed making searching for information easier,

(b)   may even bring similar types of publication, such as codes of practice, together in one section,

(c)   are usually published in loose-leaf format and some as CDs, so the information they contain is updated regularly by the publishers — if a revision to a code of practice has been made, it will be included with very little delay.

So, for example, a number of the codes of practice relating to industrial relations law are reprinted complete, with the addition, in some cases, of footnotes by the encyclopaedia editors, in the specialist title: *Sweet & Maxwell's Encyclopaedia of Employment*.

In addition, some textbooks will reprint codes of practice as appendices, and in the area of industrial relations law, one textbook is published in loose-leaf format and includes several codes: *Harvey on Industrial Relations and Employment Law* (published by Butterworths).

For codes of practice in which local authorities may be interested, covering subjects such as housing or control of pollution, the Local Government Library series of specialist encyclopaedias published by Sweet & Maxwell may be of help. A number of the encyclopaedias in this series are now appearing in CD format.

As to electronic versions of codes of practice, some of the most popular encyclopaedias are issued in CD format. The web site of the relevant Government department may contain the text of codes. To trace a departmental site, use the organisational index on the Government Information Service web site at:

http://www.open.gov.uk/

Apart from these specialised sources, there is no electronic source which includes all codes of practice either in full text or as summaries.

5.2C   Answering research queries

See the discussion under 5.2B.

5.3   BY-LAWS

5.3A   Description

5.3A1   Definition

By-laws are a form of secondary legislation (i.e., detailed rules or regulations) made by a local authority or public authority (such as Britsh Waterways Board or the former British Rail) under powers given by an Act of Parliament. The by-laws have to be confirmed or approved by the Minister of the government department nominated by Parliament in the Act which grants the power to make the by-laws. By-laws differ from other types of secondary legislation in two ways: first, whilst Parliament defines the content, the responsibility for drawing up the by-law rests with an authority outside central government; secondly, by-laws are not approved by Parliament but by a Minister. Specific aspects of by-laws in Scotland are dealt with in section 11.4.

5.3A2   Origin

Although by-laws may be made by local or public authorities, it is those made by local authorities which you are more likely to need to be aware of both as a student and later, particularly if you decide to practise in local government law. The discussion which follows therefore concentrates on local authority by-laws.

By-laws existed long before the period of great municipal reform in the early 19th century, but it was the need to tackle the physical and social problems of the rapid growth and expansion of industrial towns and cities that led Parliament to give local authorities powers to make by-laws which had far-reaching effect for 'good rule and government' (Municipal Corporations Act 1835, section 90) and the 'prevention and suppression of nuisances' (Public Health Act 1875, sections 182 to 188), for example. To assist local authorities, the Local Government Board (set up under the Local Government Board Act 1871) began to issue model by-laws, providing guidance on what was likely to be confirmed by the Board and to ensure some degree of uniformity amongst local authorities. However, during the 20th century, despite these models, it was difficult to achieve adequate uniformity and gradually local by-laws were replaced by Ministerial regulations (i.e., statutory instruments). The Local Government Act 1972, which reorganised local government, provided an opportunity for a thorough review of the accumulated mass of 'local' law. As a result each new local authority was required to submit a Private Bill to Parliament incorporating all the powers under Local Acts and by-laws it had inherited from predecessor authorities, and which it wished to retain. Model clauses for the Private Bill were prepared by government departments to give authorities guidance on what was considered acceptable and desirable. Parliament then had the opportunity to scrutinise each Private Bill and amend it as necessary before it became law as a Local Act. Any legislation not included in these Local Acts ceased to have effect. This review therefore considerably tidied up the 'local' statute book and means that the large number of Local Acts dating from the late 1970s and early 1980s entitled '—shire County Council Act' are the *first* place to look when researching by-laws. However, these recent Local Acts are not the only place to look for by-laws, because Parliament has continued to include within Public General Acts powers for local authorities to make local by-laws on a number of matters, for example, the regulation of pleasure boats (Local Government, Planning and Land Act 1980, section 185), and the regulation of acupuncture, tattooing, ear-piercing and electrolysis (Local Government (Miscellaneous Provisions) Act 1982, sections 14 to 16). A list of principal powers to make by-laws is given in Appendix E of Cross and Bailey (1991).

5.3A3   Structure

There can be variety in the structure of by-laws, but they usually comprise a series of numbered sections, rather similar to an Act.

5.3A4   Publication and general availability

According to the Local Government Act 1972, section 236, copies of local authority by-laws must be available for inspection at the offices of the local authority by whom the by-laws were made, and the by-laws should be available for sale to the public at a cost of not more than 20p per copy. Similar requirements may exist for public authority by-laws; for example, copies of the British Railways Board by-laws are available for inspection at station ticket offices.

Academic law libraries are unlikely to stock by-laws made by either local or public authorities, but the larger public libraries may keep copies of those for the local authority in whose area they are situated, possibly as part of the local history collection, if not as part of the reference library.

5.3A5   Citation

No generally accepted method of citation exists.

5.3B   Finding information

See 5.3A4. By-laws are not included on electronic databases.

5.3C   Answering research queries

See 5.3A2 and 5.3A4.

Chapter 6

Case law

6A   DESCRIPTION

6A1   Definition

There is no official definition of what constitutes a law report, the name given to a single, published decision of the courts. In the plural, the term law reports refers to the publication(s) containing collections of decisions. However, to research this important source of law effectively you need to appreciate two basic characteristics of the system which makes law reports available:

(a)   There is no official series of law reports covering the courts of England and Wales — there is no case-law equivalent of the Queen's Printer's copy of an Act, which forms an official, authentic record of what the courts have determined in every case. The situation is slightly different in Scotland (see section 12A1). Law reporting has traditionally been in private hands and, although The Stationery Office (the government printer) is responsible for publishing reports of cases in revenue law (*Reports of Tax Cases, Value Added Tax Tribunal Reports*), immigration law (*Immigration Appeal Reports*) and social security law (decisions of the Social Security Commissioners), the great majority of reports of cases are published by over 20 different, often competing, private publishers.

(b)   Whilst the courts hear and decide over 200,000 cases each year in England and Wales alone, only about 2,500 (or 1.25 per cent) are published, or as lawyers say, reported. The rest remain either as unpublished (unreported) transcripts or go totally unrecorded.

Keep these two points in your mind whenever you research case law and you will be able to make some order of what, at first sight, appears to be a rather complex and bewildering system. In contrast with the other major sources of law, such as Acts and statutory instruments both of which are published by the authority of Parliament, there is no official, authoritative version of all case decisions.

Let us explore some of the implications of these characteristics a little further.

Since there are so many different law report publications, what constitutes an authoritative report? First, it has been a long established but unwritten rule, that to be accepted by a court as authority, the report must have been prepared by and published under the name of a barrister. Some law report publications, such as *The Times, Current Law* and *Estates Gazette* have been criticised in judicial statements from the 1880s down to the 1950s because it appears that even though the reports were compiled or edited by barristers, their names did not appear against the reports. Secondly, whilst there is no official series of law reports, the courts have accorded greater respect and authority to some publications over others. From about 1785 some report publications became recognised as 'authorised' or 'regular'. Their authority stemmed, in part, from the assistance the judges gave the particular reporters in revising oral judgments and providing copies of written notes before publication. During the early 19th century an 'authorised' reporter was attached to each of the higher courts and their reports published in collected volumes under the personal name(s) of the reporters, for example, Phillips, *Chancery Reports*, Adolphus and Ellis, *King's Bench Reports*. By 1865 there were 16 individual reporters compiling and publishing 'authorised' reports, as well as a considerable number of barristers producing reports which were not authorised, either issued under their own names or in the columns of the increasing number of law journals. In that year the mantle of these 16 authorised reports passed to a new, single series of reports entitled the *Law Reports*. The series is still active today. The judgments published in this title have been checked by the bench before publication, and because of this greater authority, the rule of 'exclusive citation' has developed, whereby should a case be reported in several publications including the *Law Reports*, the version in the *Law Reports* should be cited to the court and no other (see *Practice Direction (Law Reports: Citation)* [1991] 1 WLR 1). For this reason you may find both in your reading and during lectures that the *Law Reports* are cited most frequently.

However, whilst the *Law Reports* possess great authority they only report around 175 or about 7 per cent of the 2,500 cases published annually. Further, it seems the price of accuracy is delay in publication, and the *Law Reports* frequently take nine months from the date of the decision to the date of publication. Those cases not included in the *Law Reports* are scattered through about 50 different titles of lesser authority. Also, some titles aim to publish brief reports of the latest decisions as quickly as possible. For example, about 10 per cent of all cases reported in *The Times* are reported the day after the judgment was given, but the report, when compared with later versions in other publications, is often very much shortened. Unfortunately, not all reports of cases which appear in *The Times* or other 'advance' series such as *Solicitors' Journal* and *New Law Journal* are selected by other law report publications for full reporting. In 1985, for example, nearly one in eight of the cases published in

The Times was never printed as a fuller report in another series of reports (Clinch, 1989). If barristers rely on these brief versions the authority of their argument can be weakened for in 1983, Lord Roskill in a House of Lords judgment in *Export Credits Guarantee Department* v *Universal Oil Products Co.* [1983] 1 WLR 399 considered a case briefly and only reported in *Solicitors' Journal* to be 'virtually unreported'.

This brings us to consider the second implication of the way the law reporting system in England and Wales is organised — who selects the cases to be reported and on what criteria?

As strange as it may seem, whilst the courts make decisions on the law, only with the birth of the internet have they begun to play a part in ensuring those decisions are made available to the profession and public at large. Historically, the process of selecting which of the 200,000 or so cases heard in court each year should be reported, and so formally become part of the law of this jurisdiction, is in the hands of the editors of the 50 or so different law report publications currently active. Different series may employ different selection criteria, dependent on the editor's perception of the needs of the market the particular law report publication is intended to serve. For example, some series of reports (such as the *All England Law Reports* or the *Weekly Law Reports*) set out to serve the needs of general practice, whilst others are aimed at particular groups of lawyers (such as *Justice of the Peace Reports* or *Solicitors' Journal*) or compiled on special subjects (such as *Butterworth's Company Law Cases, Family Law Reports* or *Criminal Appeal Reports*). According to Paul Brown (1989), publishing director of Butterworths, six basic selection criteria are used by the editors of the *All England Law Reports*. A case will be reported if it:

(a)   *makes new law* by dealing with a novel situation or by extending the application of existing principles;
(b)   includes a *modern judicial restatement* of established principles;
(c)   *clarifies conflicting decisions* of lower courts;
(d)   *interprets legislation* likely to have a wide application;
(e)   *interprets a commonly found clause*, for example in a contract or will;
(f)   *clarifies an important point of practice or procedure.*

So, for example, cases of narrow specialist interest, such as decisions in intellectual property or criminal sentencing, might fall outside these criteria, and are in fact rarely reported by the *All England Law Reports*, but left to such specialist titles as *Reports of Patent, Design and Trade Mark Cases* and *Criminal Appeal Reports (Sentencing)*, respectively.

But what of those cases which are *not* selected by any law report publication? Before 1980 and the advent of *LEXIS*, the computer database which includes thousands of reports in its database, most unreported cases would remain largely undisturbed on court files or the shelves of the Supreme Court library or the files of the private firms of shorthand writers whose employees sat in court taking the judgments down. Assiduous textbook or periodical article writers or exceptionally industrious barristers would occasionally unearth an unreported decision and cite it in support of their argument. The *Report of the Law*

Reporting Committee (Lord Chancellor's Department (1940), p. 20) considered that after the law report editors had selected cases for inclusion in their publications, 'What remains is less likely to be a treasure-house than a rubbish heap in which a jewel will rarely, if ever, be discovered'. *LEXIS* made the search of the 'rubbish heap' much easier but in 1983 the courts took fright of being 'bombarded' with cases 'which contained no new law', and 'hoped that a good deal of discretion would be used in citing such cases' (Donaldson MR in *Stanley* v *International Harvester Co. of Great Britain Ltd* (1983) *The Times*, 7 February 1983). Just eight days later the House of Lords, in *Roberts Petroleum Ltd* v *Bernard Kenny Ltd* [1983] 2 AC 192 took a much stronger and unorthodox line in henceforth prohibiting the citation of transcripts of un-reported judgments of the Civil Division of the Court Appeal without special leave having been gained to do so. The rulings gave rise to considerable discussion on the use of both unreported cases and online database services, including a cogent review by Nicolas Harrison, then managing director of Butterworth (Telepublishing) Ltd, the firm which markets *LEXIS* in the United Kingdom (Harrison, 1984). With the advent of the internet more and more unreported cases are becoming accessible. Official organisations such as the House of Lords and the Court Service (part of the Lord Chancellor's Depart-ment) and commercial organisations such as Smith Bernal, Lawtel and New Law Online have placed either the full text or a summary of judgments (with the facility to order a full transcript) on their sites. The information is made available sometimes within hours or a day or two of the judgment being given. Although a proportion of judgments will be published in conventional law reports at a later date, the 'rubbish heap' is now many times more extensive than in 1940 and 1983.

There are two further points to consider: first, do all courts contribute decisions to the body of case law, and secondly, what of those decisions made not in open court, but in the judges' chambers?

Since the operation of the principle of precedent relies on a hierarchical arrangement of courts it might follow that the higher a court is in the structure, the more likely its decisions will be reported. Very little empirical work has been done on this, but the rather limited results available (Clinch, 1989, p. 350) appear in part to support this hypothesis. In practice virtually every decision of the House of Lords is reported, and in the single year (1985) studied, over 70 per cent of the decisions of the Court of Appeal (Civil Division) were also reported. A little over a third of the decisions of the Family Division of the High Court, and 29 per cent and 22 per cent of the Queen's Bench and Chancery Divisions respectively were reported, but under 10 per cent of the decisions of the Court of Appeal (Criminal Division) appeared in law reports. In some areas of law such as social welfare, industrial relations, landlord and tenant, immigra-tion, and VAT, tribunals have been created to resolve disputes. Comparatively few of the cases they hear are reported. One particular group of tribunal decisions must be highlighted for it forms a very important part of the law of a specialised area: the decisions of the Social Security Commissioners. Of the 2,000–3,000 decisions made each year, well under 100 are published — the selection of decisions for reporting is made by the Chief Commissioner after consultation with Commissioners. At Crown Court or county court level only a handful of decisions are reported each year (somewhere around one or two in every 10,000 heard). So broadly speaking, the lower the court in the hierarchy the less chance there is of its decisions being available in law reports.

Some cases are heard and determined not in open court but in judges' private rooms or chambers. This practice is most frequently found in divorce-related cases (Pearson, 1986). It is traditional that only decisions given in open court may be reported, and there are instances where a judge has heard a case in chambers but decided, because issues or concerns have been raised deserving wider dissemination, to give his judgment in open court (see, for example, *Re Y (A Minor)* [1985] FLR 294, *M* v *Lambeth Borough Council (No. 2)* [1985] FLR 371, *Re PB (A Minor) (Application to Free for Adoption)* [1985] FLR 394 and *Re C (Adoption Application: Legal Aid)* [1985] FLR 441).

As the foregoing discussion shows, the courts have been concerned with two matters: the adequacy of the record and the value of the decision as a precedent. Therefore, a definition of a law report must highlight these essential elements, and the following, by a respected law reporter, expresses it succinctly:

> an adequate record of a judicial decision on a point of law, in a case heard in open court, for subsequent citation as a precedent (Moran, 1948, p. 13).

Since there is no official published record of the decisions of the courts, and most law libraries will have access to both reported and, via *LEXIS* and the internet, unreported decisions, when you research case-law sources you will need to ask yourself:

(a)   Is the record of the decision the most authoritative available?

(b)   Is it sufficiently full for the point of law that was decided to be stated clearly and unambiguously?

(c)   Are there alternative and fuller versions of the same case?

(d)   Does the decision, particularly if it is unreported, really extend, clarify or interpret the law, or does it merely restate previously established principles?

6A2   Origin

During your legal studies you will need to refer not only to recent law reports but also decisions made in the 18th and 19th centuries and, perhaps, earlier still. The brief historical survey of the development of law reporting which follows concentrates on those factors which affect the way you research case law of different periods.

6A2.1   The Year Books

The medieval equivalent of the law reports are the *Year Books*. They commence in 1272 and cease in 1535. They were compiled anonymously and were probably intended for the personal use of individual members of the legal profession. They are mainly handwritten in law French, though some were amongst the first books to be available in the new printing technology of the late 15th and early 16th centuries. The individual case reports are very brief and concentrate on the pleadings (the arguments, claims and counter-claims put forward by either side), and often omit all reference to the judgment. Rarely are *Year Books* cited in present-day courts and, unless you are studying English legal history, you are unlikely to need to consult them. Modern reprints with English translations alongside have been made during the 19th and 20th centuries, in the *Rolls Series*, and volumes published by the Selden Society and the Ames Foundation.

6A2.2   The nominate reports

After a short break, the period of the nominate reports commences with the publication in 1571 of Edmund Plowden's *Commentaries*. This formative period in law reporting, with collections of cases published under the name of the individual responsible for compiling them (hence the collective term, 'nominate reports'), lasted until the founding of the *Law Reports* in 1865. The earliest collections were never intended for publication, being notes of cases prepared for personal use, and were frequently published posthumously. Up to 1750 very little in the way of a *system* of law reporting may be traced. But in the second half of the 18th century three developments took place which laid the foundations of the system which has evolved to the present:

(a)   the setting of accepted standards in the technique of reporting;
(b)   the appointment of authorised reporters;
(c)   the publication of reports with the minimum of delay.

Between 1765 and 1786 three reporters, James Burrow, Henry Cowper and Sylvester Douglas, established standards for the technique of law reporting and the layout of reports. During the same period, probably after 1782, judges became willing to revise reports of their judgments or even make written copies of them available to particular reporters. The judges also took part in the appointment of a particular reporter to the court. Thus developed the concept of the 'authorised' report, accurate and authentic. If there were two reports of the same case, that of the 'authorised reporter' was taken as 'the deliberate expression of the judge's opinion' (Pollock, 1896, p. 292). The third break-through was the reduction in the delay with which reports were published. In 1786 two reporters: Charles Durnford and Edward East began publishing their reports of King's Bench cases 'within a short time after each term' (Durnford and East, 1786, preface) — hence the popular name for their publication, '*Term Reports*'. The venture was immediately successful and followed by reporters in other courts. Delay was even further reduced from 1822 onwards with the advent of the monthly publication *Law Journal*, which carried law reports. In 1830 a weekly publication, *The Legal Observer*, commenced, followed in 1837 by *The Jurist* and in 1843, *The Law Times*. This was the age of free trade and the principles also applied in law report publishing: all that was required was a barrister to write the reports of cases he had heard and a publisher willing to print them. The 'authorised reports' accounted for only a small number of the cases reported, and since many of the reporters also carried on business as practising barristers, representing and advising clients, they were often slow to publish and expensive! So a huge industry of competing reports developed — multiple versions of the same case, each trying to undercut the other in terms of the number of cases published and the speed with which they were made available. In 1863 the situation became intolerable and the Bar formed the Council of Law Reporting (later the Incorporated Council of Law Reporting for England and Wales), which began publication of the *Law Reports* in 1865, a series designed to replace the authorised reports, make reports available quickly, and cheaply, but above all, still ensure they were accurate. So, the nominate reports died, but many of the weekly and monthly periodical publications survived; including one to this day: *Solicitors' Journal* (founded 1857).

Over 500 different publications containing law reports were published between 1571 and 1865. Although some libraries will have modest collections of some of these reports in their original, published form, most libraries may have none at all, but either rely on reprint collections, of which there are three, or on a photographically reduced version of the originals. The three reprint series are the *English Reports*, the *Revised Reports* and the *All England Law Reports Reprint*. The *English Reports* are widely found and the most comprehensive set of the three, covering over 170 report titles. They comprise 176 volumes of verbatim reprints of the most significant decisions up to 1865. Two further volumes (177 and 178) are an alphabetical index to the main work, arranged by the names of cases. The whole set of the *English Reports* is also available on two CDs. The *Revised Reports* reprint cases from a selection of about 140 report titles from the period 1785 to 1865 only. Whilst there is quite a large measure of duplication with the *English Reports*, several 19th century report titles are only reprinted in the *Revised Reports*. The third reprint source is the *All England Law Reports Reprint*, quite widely available in law libraries. Published between 1957 and 1968, it reprints a selection of cases from 1558 to 1935, which were considered by the editors still to be of value. The final source for pre-1865 cases is the Readex Microcard Reprint of pre-1865 cases, held by a few libraries. A large number of reports, some not appearing in any of the reprint sources, have been photographically reduced and printed on to thick card. The photographic image can only be read through special viewing equipment which requires some patience and good eyesight to use, and it is virtually impossible to take copies from the images; consequently it is not popular!

6A2.3   Modern reports

Two trends evident before 1865 have become more marked since. First, the division of law report publications into the 'general' series, attempting to report cases on points of law of wide interest, and the 'specialist' series, selecting cases of particular interest to lawyers in a discrete practice area. Secondly, the division of law report publications into those which report cases in a brief, edited form, but as rapidly as possible, referred to by some lawyers as 'advance

Figure 6.1   A typology of modern law reports.

	Advance	Full-text
General	All subjects. Edited reports.	All subjects. Full reports.
Specialist	Selected subjects. Edited reports.	Selected subjects. Full reports.

reports' (using terminology from the United States), and those publications which report judgments verbatim but are subject to some delay. The relationship between these two categories is illustrated in figure 6.1.

Amongst the 'general' series will be found those like *The Times* newspaper, which publishes brief reports of a very large number of cases, about 10 per cent of which appear the day following the judgment was given. Two other generalist publications, the *Weekly Law Reports* and the *All England Law Reports*, normally publish full-text reports but, on average, about five months after the judgments were handed down. The most highly respected series of law reports, the *Law Reports*, the text of which is checked by the judges before publication and also includes summaries of the arguments of counsel, takes between 10 and 14 months, on average, to report cases. A similar pattern will be found amongst the specialist reports: in criminal law, for example, *Criminal Law Review* publishes brief reports of cases but with a delay of about four and a half months on average, whilst *Criminal Appeal Reports* prints the full text but takes nearly nine months on average.

The problem for the legal researcher is that because law reporting is presently in the hands of over 20 different publishers, each employing different criteria for the selection of cases (see 6A1), it does *not* follow that every briefly reported case will be reported eventually in one of the full-text services. In one study of law reporting (Clinch, 1989) about a third of all cases reported during a selected year were reported only once, and 129 or 16 per cent of these appeared in *The Times*. On the other hand, there is also a very high degree of duplication of reports between the 50 or more titles currently published: in the same study nearly 25 per cent of all cases were reported in between five and 10 different law report titles, and one case had the dubious distinction of being printed in 15 different publications!

Add to these difficulties the question of unreported decisions available on electronic databases, such as *LEXIS* (explored in 6A1), and it becomes even more apparent why case law research causes students so much difficulty, and why it is important to ask yourself the questions posed at the end of 6A1 when you are gathering material to answer a legal problem.

6A3   Structure

Since there are so many law report publishers attempting to serve the differing needs of the profession, it is not surprising that there is a variety in both the different pieces of information (or elements) each publication includes in its reports of cases, and the order in which they are presented. Fifteen different elements are found in law reports of the English jurisdiction but no report publication includes them all. The basic elements found in virtually all modern law reports are marked * in the list which follows. The illustration in figure 6.2 is an extract from a case taken from the *All England Law Reports*.

(a)   *Names of parties.** Individual cases are identified and referred to by the names of the parties involved. In civil actions the name of the person bringing the case (the claimant or, prior to 1999, the plaintiff) is given first, followed by the name of the defendant; for example, *Smith v Jones*. The 'v' separating the parties means 'versus' but when spoken becomes 'and': 'Smith and Jones'. In criminal actions, the single letter '*R*' (standing for the Latin words *Rex* or *Regina* (King or Queen)) comes first, indicating the State's role as prosecutor; the accused person, the defendant, is named after the 'v', for example, '*R v Smith*'. However, when spoken, a criminal case name becomes 'the Crown against Smith'. Unfortunately, there are differences in the practice of citing criminal cases, and you may find cases referred to in law reports and textbooks with the '*R v*' omitted, and cited merely as, for example, '*Smith*'.

These simple, straightforward rules are subject, however, to a number of variations:

(i)   In shipping cases the case name is frequently subtitled with the name of the ship involved and this shorthand case title is sufficient on most occasions to find the case in textbooks and *Citators*. So, for example, *Overseas Tankship (UK) Ltd v Morts Dock and Engineering Co. Ltd (The Wagon Mound)* [1961] AC 388 may be referred to simply as: *The Wagon Mound*.

(ii)   In some property and family cases the report may be headed either '*In re Smith*' or in modern cases '*Re Smith*'. *Re* means 'in the matter of' or 'concerning'. Similarly, some cases may be titled '*Ex parte Smith*' meaning that Smith is the name of the party on whose application the case is heard. In some actions the identity of the people involved is protected by using only the initial letters: '*In re S*', '*Ex parte S*' or '*S v J*'.

(iii)   Where the court is being asked to judicially review the administrative actions of, for example, a government department, or a lower court, the case title is usually in the form, '*R v Secretary of State for the Environment, ex parte Jones*'.

(iv)   Some criminal prosecutions may be commenced by one of the government's law officers: the Attorney-General or the Director of Public Prosecutions. Where this occurs the official's title (sometimes abbreviated to A-G or DPP) appears in place of the Crown as prosecutor, for example:

Attorney-General v British Broadcasting Corporation
Director of Public Prosecutions v Goodchild

Occasionally, the Attorney-General may obtain the opinion of the Court of Appeal on a point of law. The title in such cases is given as, for example, *Attorney-General's Reference (No. 2 of 1983)*.

Figure 6.2   A law report.

① a **Bentley-Stevens v Jones and others**

② CHANCERY DIVISION

③ PLOWMAN J

④ 15th, 18th MARCH 1974

b   *Company — Director — Removal — Resolution to remove director — Interlocutory*
⑤   *injunction to restrain company acting on resolution — Quasi-partnership — Irregularity*
in convening meeting — Irregularity capable of being cured by going through proper
processes — Whether director entitled to interlocutory injunction.

The defendant company was a wholly-owned subsidiary of another company, H
c   Ltd, of which the plaintiff and the first and second defendants, J and H, were the three
directors. They were also three of the four directors of the defendant company. J and H
⑥   held between them 58 per cent of the issued share capital of H Ltd. They wished to remove
the plaintiff from the board of the defendant company, under s 184 of the Companies Act
1948, and on 27th January 1974 J sent the plaintiff a letter notifying him of a board
meeting of H Ltd to be held the next morning at which it was to be resolved
d   that H Ltd should convene an extraordinary general meeting of the defendant company for
the purpose of removing the plaintiff from the board. The plaintiff did not receive the letter
until after (i) J and H had met and passed the resolution, (ii) H Ltd had requisitioned the
extraordinary general meeting and (iii) J, as a director of the defendant company, had
called an extraordinary general meeting of that company for 26th February. The notice
convening that meeting purported to be given by order of the board but no board
e   meeting of the company was held. The extraordinary general meeting was held on 26th
February and the votes of H Ltd were cast in favour of removing the plaintiff from the
board. The plaintiff brought an action against the defendants and applied for an interlocutory injunction restraining them from acting on the resolution on 26th February.

f   **Held** — The plaintiff was not entitled to an interlocutory injunction for the following
reasons—
(i)   The court would not grant an interlocutory injunction in respect of irregularities
which could be cured by going through the proper processes. If, for example, the
⑥   proceedings that followed the board meeting of 28th January were invalid because proper
notice had not been given, the invalidity could be cured by the giving of a valid
g   notice (see p 655 *f* to *h*, post); dictum of Lindley LJ in *Browne v La Trinidad* (1887) 37
Ch D at 17 applied.
(ii)   Assuming that the plaintiff was a quasi-partner he could still be expelled; the
defendant company had a statutory right to remove him from its board and his only remedy
was to apply for a winding-up order on the ground that it was just and equitable for the
court to make such an order (see p 655 *f* and *j*, post); *Ebrahimi v Westbourne*
h   *Galleries Ltd* [1972] 2 All ER 492 explained.

Notes
For convening of meetings of a company, see 7 Halsbury's Laws (4th Edn) 330-334,
⑦   paras 560-566; and for cases on the validation and waiver or irregular notice, see 9 Digest
(Repl) 604, 4000-4004.
j   For the Companies Act 1948, s 184, see 5 Halsbury's Statutes (3rd Edn) 255.

⑧   **Cases referred to in judgment**
Browne v La Trinidad (1887) 37 Ch D 1, 57 LJCh 292, 58 LT 137, CA, 9 Digest (Repl)
604, 4003.
Ebrahimi v Westbourne Galleries Ltd [1972] 2 All ER 492, [1973] AC 360, [1972] 2 WLR
1289, HL.

⑨ **Case also cited**   *a*
Bainbridge v Smith (1889) 41 Ch D 462, CA.

⑩ **Motion**
By notice of motion dated 26th February 1974 Charles Edward Bentley-Stevens, the
plaintiff in an action commenced by writ issued on 26th February 1974 against the
defendants, (1) D Gareth Jones, (2) Gerald S J Hyam and (3) Sloane Nursing Home *b*
Ltd, sought an order restraining the defendants and each of them until the trial of the action
or further order from acting on the resolution purported to have been passed by the
defendant company at a purported extraordinary general meeting thereof held at 9.30 am
on 26th February 1974 removing the plaintiff as a director of the defendant company. The
facts are set out in the judgment.
                                                                            c
⑪ *Allan Heyman QC* and *M K I Kennedy* for the plaintiff.
Ralph Instone for the defendants.

⑫ **PLOWMAN J**. The notice of motion which is before me asks for an order on behalf of
the plaintiff—
                                                                            d
        'restraining the Defendants and each of them until the trial of the action or further
        order from acting upon the resolution purported to have been passed by the Defendant
        Company at a purported Extraordinary General Meeting thereof held at 9.30 a.m. on the
        26th February 1974 removing the Plaintiff as a Director of the Defendant Company.'

        . . .

        For these reasons the plaintiff is not, in my judgment, entitled to the relief which he
seeks on this motion, and I must dismiss it.
                                                                            e
⑬ *Motion dismissed.*

⑭ Solicitors: *A Kramer & Co* (for the plaintiff); *Norton, Rose, Botterell & Roche* (for the
defendants).
⑮   Jacqueline Metcalfe Barrister.

① Names of Parties (a) ② Name of Court (c) ③ Name of Judge (d)
④ Date/s of hearing and judgment (e)   ⑤ Catchwords (f)
⑥ Headnote (g) ⑦ Commentary or notes (h) ⑧ List of cases cited in
judgment (i) ⑨ List of other cases cited in argument (j) ⑩ Details of
proceedings (k) ⑪ Names of counsel (l) ⑫ Judgment (n) ⑬ Formal
order ⑭ Names of solicitors (l) ⑮ Name of law reporter (p)

(Letters in parentheses refer to paragraphs in the text where the elements of a
report are discussed.)

Further details of these and some archaic forms of case title you may come across in *Year Books* and other older reports are given in: University of London, Institute of Advanced Legal Studies, *Manual of Legal Citations*, part 1, The British Isles (London: The University, 1959), pp. 14–24.

It might be thought that the names of parties to an action would be a good enough identifier for the researcher trying to trace a case in indexes. Unfortunately this is not always so, because there appear to be wide variations in the practice of law reporters identifying parties to an action or, more technically speaking, formulating the style of cause to an action. The House of Lords recognised the problem as long ago as 1974, and issued a *Practice Direction* [1974] 1 WLR 305, requiring the title of cases brought before it to carry the same title as that used in the court which first heard the case. Other courts have not made any similar ruling. Actual examples of some of the most common difficulties encountered are noted below, but a fuller list, based on a large-scale study is given in Clinch (1990).

   (i)   Local authority names:

          Westminster City Council v *British Waterways Board*
          also styled as
          City of Westminster v *British Waterways Board*

          Newham London Borough v *Ward*
          also styled as
          London Borough of Newham v *Ward*

          Cahalne v *London Borough of Croydon*
          also styled as
          Cahalne v *Croydon LBC*

   (ii)   Rotation of names of parties:

      (1)   Single actions:
            Cornish v *Midland Bank*
            also styled as
            Midland Bank plc v *Cornish*
            (This was an appeal in an action in which Cornish was the claimant, reported under different styles.)

      (2)   Consolidated appeals:
            Carver v *Duncan* and *Bosanquet* v *Allen*
            (Consolidated appeals, also reported with *Bosanquet* v *Allen* first.)

   (iii) Anonymity lost!

          L v *K*
          also styled as
          Kane v *Littlefair*

        AR v *Avon County Council*
    also styled as
        Ashley-Rogers v *Avon County Council*

(iv)   Entirely different names!

        Re C
    also styled as
        Re a Baby

        Council of Civil Service Unions v *Minister for the Civil Service*
    also styled as
        R v *Secretary of State for the Foreign and Commonwealth Office,*
    ex parte the Council for Civil Service Unions

        *Frampton and another (Trustees of Worthing Rugby Football
    Club)* v *Inland Revenue Commissioners*
    also styled as
        Worthing Rugby Football Club v *Commissioners of Inland Revenue*

        Fox v *Chief Constable of Gwent*
    also styled as
        R v *Fox*

        Anderton v *Ryan*
    also styled as
        Chief Constable for Greater Manchester v *Ryan*

In every instance the variations in styles of cause would result in the entries for these cases in an index falling at quite different parts of the alphabetical sequence. In a few cases the form of an alternative style of cause can be guessed from elements in the one available, but in most cases, unless the index is well constructed and includes entries under both styles, a researcher could draw a blank. If you are unsure whether the case you have found under an alternative style of cause is the same as the one you require, check whether the court in which it was heard and the dates of hearing and/or judgment accord with information you may have.

(b) *Official court roll or docket number.* Only a few of the publications of the Incorporated Council of Law Reporting provide this information: *Chancery, Queen's Bench* and *Weekly Law Reports*, for example.

(c) *Name of the court in which the case was heard.** This is now a universal and very important feature of case reports, for without this information a system of precedent, which depends on a hierarchical court structure, cannot exist.

(d) *Names of the judges, with abbreviations for their rank.** Early law reports omit this detail. The status and rank of judges can influence the weight of the decision.

(e) *Date(s) of hearing and judgment.** Without this information, often lacking in early law reports, it is virtually impossible for a system of precedent to develop.

(f) *Catchwords.* They provide a succinct summary of the subject of the decision. There can be several paragraphs of catchwords, each dealing with a different issue considered in the case. The catchwords are compiled by the law reporter and have no official standing with the court. Some law reports, such as *Housing Law Reports, New Law Journal* and *Trading Law Reports*, do not provide them.

(g) *Headnote.* The headnote is a summary of the facts of the case, the questions of law and finally, after the word 'Held' frequently printed in a bold type, the decision of the court. In the USA a headnote is called a 'syllabus'. Like the catchwords, it is compiled by the law reporter and although it is a useful guide to the main issues, it should not be relied on as a sole source of information about the case. Read the whole report. Some law reports, such as *Building Law Reports, Criminal Law Review* and *Estates Gazette*, do not provide headnotes.

(h) *Commentary or notes.* A minority of law reports, all specialist, provide a commentary to place a particular case in context. *All England Law Reports* provide notes referring to Butterworths' other publications, *Halsbury's Laws* and *Halsbury's Statutes of England*, and *The Digest*, where further information on the subject may be found.

(i) *List of cases cited in judgment.* Quite a few law reports provide this list, and helpfully provide a number of alternative citations for each case, so that finding reports of these cases is made much easier.

(j) *List of other cases cited in argument.* This is used to check that relevant cases were cited to the court even if they were not referred to in the judgment.

(k) *Details of the proceedings.* This note, compiled by the law reporter, gives a short history of the case.

(l) *Names of counsel and solicitors.* Omitted from many specialist reports, such as *Criminal Appeal Reports (Sentencing), Housing Law Reports.*

(m) *Argument.* Only the *Law Reports* and, in a minority of cases, *Reports of Tax Cases*, give a résumé of the arguments of counsel.

(n) *Judgment.** All law reports give details of the judgment of the court (called in the House of Lords, individual 'opinions'), but the fullness of the report varies considerably between different law report publications. As a student learning the law you should, whenever possible, use full-text reports rather than brief-note versions. The list below shows the general-coverage law reports divided into full-text and brief note categories.

Full-text	*Brief-note*
All England Law Reports	All newspaper law reports
Appeal Cases	*Gazette*
Chancery	*New Law Journal*
Family	*Solicitors' Journal*
Queen's Bench	
Weekly Law Reports	

(o) *Formal Order**. Indicates the result of the litigation, for example, in criminal cases it might read 'Appeal against conviction allowed' and in a civil action 'Application dismissed'.

(p) *Name of reporter*. May be given as a full name or just initials, most frequently at the end of the individual case report.

The foregoing description of the structure of a law report does not apply to the specialised decisions of the Social Security Commissioners. Initially, these decisions are published as *individual* case reports, not collections, by The Stationery Office. They do not carry the names of parties. In most other respects, however, there are similarities in the structure of the report.

6A4 Publication and general availability

Most academic libraries where law is taught to degree level will have at least one set of each of the full-text general-coverage modern law reports, and some, if not all, of the brief-note general reports. They will subscribe to a selection of the 40 or more specialist law report publications, depending on the subjects taught.

As for older law reports, you should find academic law libraries will keep a set of the *English Reports* (1220–1865) or at least the *All England Law Reports Reprint* (major cases 1558–1935). Some of the larger academic libraries will also have a selection of the nominate reports in their original form, and copies of some of the defunct Victorian weekly periodicals which published law reports, such as *Law Journal Reports* and *Law Times Reports*.

Some series of law reports are now available on CD. The range of titles is ever widening and includes CD versions of the *English Reports*, the *Law Reports*, the *All England Law Reports*, *Weekly Law Reports* and specialist series such as *Criminal Appeal Reports* and *Family Law Reports*. Some of these publications are also available on the internet but from subscriber access only sites — ask law library staff if your university or college has a subscription to internet versions of any of the major series of law reports and, if so, for the passwords to enter the sites.

The internet has made it easier to obtain the transcript or a summary of a unreported case, whether it is of a case decided this week or in the last few years. One of the first web sites set up by a UK court was the House of Lords site, which holds the full text of all its decisions made from 14 November 1996 onwards. Transcripts are placed on the internet within two hours of delivery. The free site is at

http://www.parliament.the-stationery-office.co.uk/pa/ld/ldjudinf.htm

The Court Service, an agency of the Lord Chancellor's Department, has a free web site, still developing, which carries the full text of a selection of High Court and Court of Appeal judgments from the late 1990s onwards. It is at

http://www.courtservice.gov.uk/judgments/judg_home.htm

During 2000, Privy Council Decisions from 1999 onwards became available on the British and Irish Legal Information Institute web site:

http://www.bailii.org/uk/cases/UKPC/

The BAILII site permits free searching across a large number of databases of cases for the UK; see

http://www.bailii.org/

Smith Bernal, a firm of court reporters, has developed a free site called Casebase which contains the full text of all Court of Appeal and Crown Office (Queen's Bench Division) decisions from 1996 to the end of last year. The database is updated annually. The site is at

http://www.casetrack.com/casebase

An associated part of the Smith Bernal site, Casetrack, includes the latest transcripts from the day judgment is handed down. Access to the site is available only to subscribers and is password protected.

LEXIS contains, since 1 January 1980, the transcripts of English unreported cases from the House of Lords, Privy Council and Court of Appeal (Civil Division), along with selected decisions of the High Court and some tribunals. Although *LEXIS* is not as up-to-date as the web sites it holds a longer backrun of unreported decisions and offers sophisticated search possibilities.

Some libraries may have purchased the set of over 2,000 microfiche of the transcripts of 13,613 Court of Appeal (Civil Division) judgments (1951–80), published by TSO. The set is indexed by claimant (or plaintiff), defendant and judge. Unfortunately there is no subject index to this huge collection.

Help in tracing whether transcripts of decisions of a particular court are usually made and how they might be obtained other than via the internet, is available in a useful booklet: *Transcripts of judicial proceedings: how to obtain them (1996)*.

Public libraries do not normally keep or subscribe to law report publications, but it is worth checking at the central public library of your nearest city.

6A5   Citation

The majority of the information given in this subsection applies to all reports of cases. However, the decisions of Social Security Commissioners are cited quite differently and a note on this is provided in 6A5.2.

6A5.1   General practice

Cases are referred to by the names of parties to the action (see 6A3). In addition, because there may be several versions of a case reported, the case name is followed by a sequence of numbers and letters which identify where the report is published. Here is how the case illustrated in figure 6.2 would be cited:

Bentley-Stevens v *Jones* [1974] 2 All ER 653

The citation comprises four elements: a date, a volume number, an abbreviation for the title of the publication in which the case is published, and the page number. This apparently simple system of reference is qualified by a number of conventions:

(a)   *The date* is the year in which the case was *reported* and is given in square brackets. If, however, the publication in which the case is reported is identified by volume numbers running sequentially from the first volume to the present, then the date will be the year the judgment was *given* and will be printed in round brackets (parentheses). For example:

(1986) 130 *SJ* 785
(1986) 83 *LSGaz* 2919

(b)   *The volume number:* if the date preceding is given in square brackets and the publication is issued in more than one volume during that year, then a volume number will be given. Some law reports are published in only one volume each year so the volume number is omitted. If the date preceding is given in round brackets, the volume number — not the date — is what you should be looking for on the spine or on the cover of the law report publication. A case may have been judged one year but reported the next; a date in round brackets indicates this is information *not* relevant to finding the case in the particular law report publication cited.

(c)   *Abbreviations* for the names of many law publications abound. Although many publishers of modern law reports give details of the preferred style of citing their law reports (a note will usually be found on the title page or introductory pages near to it), hybrid abbreviations are in common use. For example, the *All England Law Reports*, properly abbreviated by All ER may be found cited as AELR or AER or All Eng. The problem is even worse with old reports: *Railway and Canal Cases* (published 1840–55) has 24 different citation abbreviations attributed to it! Confusion can also arise amongst the nominate reports where reporters with commonly occurring surnames are cited without the inclusion of forenames or initials. Sometimes an abbreviation may be too concise to distinguish between different series, for example, B & A could refer to Barnewell & Adolphus or Barnewell & Alderson or Barron & Arnold or Barron & Austin. Sometimes references to pre-1865 cases do not include the abbreviation of the original series of reports in which they were published, but the abbreviation to the reprint collection, such as the *English Reports* (ER) instead (see 6A2.2).

However, help in expanding fully the abbreviation of the title of the law report, is available in the following publications (note that item (i) is the most comprehensive of all the indexes here listed):

(i)   Raistrick, D., *Index to Legal Citations and Abbreviations*, 2nd ed., (London: Bowker-Saur, 1993).
(ii)   *Guide to Law Reports and Statutes*, 3rd ed. (London: Sweet & Maxwell, 1959).

(iii)   *Osborn's Concise Law Dictionary*, 8th ed., edited by Leslie Rutherford and Shelia Bone (London: Sweet & Maxwell, 1993).

(iv)   French, D., *How to Cite Legal Authorities* (London: Blackstone Press, 1996).

(v)   University of London, Institute of Advanced Legal Studies, *Manual of Legal Citations*, part 1, The British Isles (London: The University, 1959).

(vi)   *Halsbury's Laws of England*, vol. 1 (London: Butterworths).

(vii)   *The Digest*, vol. 1(1) (London: Butterworths).

(viii)   *Current Law Case Citator* (London: Sweet & Maxwell), any issue.

(d)   *The page number* refers to the page on which the case begins. Sometimes in periodicals and textbooks, authors wish to draw attention to a later section of the report whilst still giving the proper form of citation for the case. This is achieved by giving the number of the first page of the report followed by the word 'at' and then the page number of the particular section to which attention is drawn, for example:

Fox v *P.G. Wellfair Ltd* [1981] 1 Lloyd's Rep 514 at p. 521

This citation practice is peculiar to law; in other subjects references would be given to the page where the particular text of interest is given, and would not include the number of the first page in the chapter.

6A5.2   Decisions of the Social Security Commissioners

The decisions of the Social Security Commissioners differ from all other series of law reports in the form of citation they use. The names of parties are not given in the report at all. Anonymity is preserved as far as possible. The decisions are referred to by a system of letters and numbers. Reported decisions carry the letter R followed, in brackets, by letters indicating within which of the benefit series of commissioners' decisions the case falls. The full list of series (as presently published) is as follows:

R (A)   Attendance allowance
R (CR)   Compensation recovery
R (CS)   Child support appeals
R (DLA)   Disability living allowance
R (DWA)   Disability working allowance
R (F)   Child benefit and formerly family allowances
R (FC)   Family credit
R (G)   General — miscellaneous: maternity benefit, widow's benefit, death
           grant etc.
R (I)   Industrial injuries benefits
R (IB)   Incapacity benefit
R (IS)   Income support
R (M)   Mobility allowance
R (P)   Retirement pensions

R (S)   Sickness and invalidity benefit
R (SSP)   Statutory sick pay
R (U)   Unemployment benefit.

The citation of unpublished decisions is prefaced by C rather than R, followed by letters not in brackets, indicating the benefit series. Within each series, whether reported or not, decisions are cited by the report number and the year. So, for example, R (S) 2/82 Incapacity for work, is the second reported decision in the sickness and invalidity benefit series for 1982, while CS 69/58 Incapacity for work, is the 69th unreported decision in the sickness and invalidity benefit series for 1958. This system of citation operates for all reported decisions since the beginning of 1951. Prior to that date decisions which become reported retained their original decision number on publication with the addition of the suffix 'KL' (Key Law). As a result reported decisions for the years 1948 to 1950 are not consecutively numbered. In addition some decisions given up to the end of January 1950 bear the suffix 'K' which indicates that the decision was of limited value and did not establish any new principle of law.

Since the beginning of 1987, revisions have been made to the way in which the commissioners make decisions available. Decisions which are of more general significance are 'starred' — these are the decisions the commissioners think should be published. Decisions which are not starred should remain unreported. A starred case prior to publication is cited in the same manner as illustrated above, except that the year is given in full, e.g., CS 2/1982. On being published this decision would become R (S) 2/82. If, however, it was not starred then it would be cited as CS 2/82.

Starred and unreported decisions can be inspected, and copies made on payment, at the London and Edinburgh offices of the Social Security Commissioners. Reported decisions are published individually and then reissued in bound volumes every two or three years.

6B   FINDING INFORMATION

There are five different types of publication which will help you find cases:

(a) indexes to law reports;
(b) indexes with brief summaries of cases;
(c) *Citators*;
(d) full-text databases;
(e) commentaries.

6B1   Indexes

6B1.1   Individual law report publications

Some individual law report publications publish not only annual indexes but also indexes to the cases they have reported over much longer periods of time. The *All England Law Reports* publishes a *Consolidated Tables and Index* covering the period from 1936 to the present, but it only indexes the 300 to 400 cases reported each year in the *All England Law Reports*. The *Law Reports* has published an index since it commenced in 1865, but it is the set of 'red books' published since 1951, each covering up to a ten-year period, supplemented by 'pink books' published quarterly, which is of the most use in present-day research. Not only do these volumes index the *Law Reports* themselves but also a number of other law report publications such as the *Weekly Law Reports, All England Law Reports, Industrial Cases Reports, Knight's Local Government Reports, Tax Cases, Lloyd's Law Reports, Criminal Appeal Reports* and *Road Traffic Reports*. Each red or pink book includes up to nine separate indexes, the main ones being an alphabetical list by the name of the case, to all those cases reported in these publications, with citations to where the report may be found. An alphabetical subject index with a paragraph of catchwords for each case, and indexes of statutes and cases considered by the courts in these cases, are also included.

The index to the *Law Reports* is a valuable starting-point for research on cases in the absence of the more sophisticated publications (see later parts of this sub-section) which are updated regularly and contain more substantial summaries of cases or commentary.

Many textbooks include, at the beginning of the publication, tables of cases discussed in the work and can be a valuable starting-point for research on a subject.

6B1.2   Legal Journals Index

Legal Journals Index (LJI) is an index to the contents of over 400 legal periodicals published in the UK, including journals such as *New Law Journal, Solicitors' Journal* and the *Gazette*, which include brief reports of cases on a wide range of subjects, and *Criminal Law Review, Family Law* and *Construction Law Journal* which carry brief reports of cases of specialist interest. The paper version of this index commenced in 1986 and is to be phased out during 2000. The CD and internet versions of LJI are part of the *Current Legal Information* database and will continue to be available. The electronic versions contain a separate and better database for finding case law, called *Current Law Cases* (see 6B2.4).

6B2   Indexes with summaries

6B2.1   Daily Law Notes

This free internet service comprises summaries of cases which have been selected for inclusion in full text in *The Weekly Law Reports*, to be published at a later date. The site has limited use when compared with the full transcripts made available on the sites mentioned in 6A4 and the coverage of *Lawtel* (see 6B2.3) and *Current Law Cases* (see 6B2.4). The site is at

http://www.lawreports.co.uk/indexdln.htm

6B2.2   New Law Online

This internet database is available to subscribers only. The service is primarily intended for use by law firms rather than universities and colleges so, as a result, few academic libraries subscribe. The database provides a Daily Digest of case decisions from the higher courts. The summaries are extremely brief. Subscribers are able to order for delivery by fax or e-mail, the full text of those decisions.

6B2.3   Lawtel

Lawtel is an on-line *digest* of legal information — it does not contain the full text of cases, only summaries. Cases have been added to the database since 1 January 1980 and new cases are added as soon as *Lawtel*'s own team of reporters at the Royal Courts of Justice, London have prepared a digest of a case (often only hours after judgment is given), or a newspaper law report or the transcript of the case is to hand. When a fuller report of a case is published in the printed law reports *Lawtel* provides citations to these reports. *Lawtel*'s court coverage is extremely wide: it provides comprehensive coverage of the decisions of the House of Lords, Privy Council and Court of Appeal (Civil Division), selected coverage of the Court of Appeal (Criminal Division) and the High Court, all decisions of the Lands Tribunal and selected, important judgments of a number of other tribunals and courts. The database is at

> http://www.lawtel.co.uk

It is available only to subscribers. To access it you will need a user code and password. Once you have entered *Lawtel*, select the case law database and type in either the name of the case or the subject in which you are interested.

6B2.4   Current Law Monthly Digest and Current Law Cases

Current Law commenced in 1947 and provides a monthly digest or summary of changes in the law. *Current Law Cases* is the electronic equivalent of summaries of cases found in *Current Law Monthly Digest* and forms part of the *Current Legal Information* database available on CD and over the internet to subscribers only. The electronic versions are far easier and quicker to search then the paper version.

Paper version
In the paper version, the case summaries are arranged under broad subject headings and include details of recent cases as well as many other sources of legal information. *Current Law* digests cases from most series of law reports and the quality newspapers. Towards the back of each monthly issue are two indexes, one a cumulative table of cases summarised in the publication so far during the calendar year, arranged alphabetically by case name; the other index is a cumulative index to subjects. In both indexes the reference against each entry refers to the monthly issue and paragraph at which a brief summary of the case will be found.

During the summer of each year, the *Current Law Yearbook* for the previous calendar year is published, and cumulates the monthly parts into a single sequence. The case summaries are edited in the light of events which may have occurred since the case was noted in a monthly issue. The table of cases summarised is given at the *front* and the index to subjects at the *back* of the *Yearbook*. The references in both indexes against each entry refer to the paragraph in the *Yearbook* where the case summary is to be found.

Scottish material was excluded from the *Yearbook* until 1991, a separate edition entitled *Scottish Current Law Yearbook* being published for the years 1948 to 1990.

The organisation of *Current Law Yearbook* is not entirely straightforward. The summaries for the first five years, the period 1947–51, are reprinted in a very thick single volume entitled *Current Law Consolidation* volume. At five-year intervals since then, up to and including the *Yearbook* for 1971, individual issues have been designated 'Master Volume', and are marked as such on the spine. These thicker volumes for 1956, 1961, 1966 and 1971 cumulate, in a single sequence, all the summaries for the preceeding four *Yearbooks* and the monthly parts of the fifth year. However, by 1976 so much material was being summarised in *Current Law* that only the subject index at the back of the *Yearbook* was cumulated, and this covers the period 1947–76. The 1986 *Yearbook* index covers the period 1972 to 1986 and the 1989 volume, 1987–89. The advent of an electronic version has made the creation of further 'Master Volumes' unnecessary.

This arrangement means that to carry out a thorough search of *Current Law Yearbook* from 1947 to date requires the use of the indexes at the back of the volumes for 1976, 1986, 1989 and all the annual volumes since. The lack of a single, cumulated index covering the whole period is a handicap, and use of *Current Law Yearbook* for case research over long periods of time can be laborious.

There are two further drawbacks to using *Current Law Monthly Digest* and *Current Law Yearbook* to research cases:

(a)   The subject terms used are frequently rather broad so it is possible to end up looking at a large number of references to cases which do not cover the specific topic in which you are interested.

(b)   The subject index refers not only to summaries of cases, but also all the summaries of Acts and statutory instruments as well. References to cases are not specially or separately indicated in the subject index so, again, you can be led to summaries which are irrelevant to your research needs.

Current Law Monthly Digest's strength, however, is in keeping regular readers of the monthly issues up-to-date with new legal developments, a technique covered in more detail in chapter 18.

References in the indexes of *Current Law Yearbook* are of two types. Volumes which cover the period 1947–51 may contain against index entries a series of numbers without a slash dividing them, such as 3588 or 11062. These are references to the paragraph numbers of summaries in the very thick *Current Law Consolidation* volume. Most references, however, will be of the second form, a series of numbers separated by a slash such as 56/2302 or 61/5914 or 71/7837. The two numbers in front of the slash indicate the year of the *Current Law Yearbook* referred to (1956, 1961, 1971), followed by the paragraph number where relevant information within that *Yearbook* will be found.

Electronic versions

The CD and internet versions possess few of the drawbacks of the paper version. The 'look' and search possibilities of the two electronic versions are quite different because, for technical reasons, the different formats cannot use the same software. In both electronic versions the case summaries included in *Current Law* and *Current Law Yearbooks* are merged into a single database, called *Current Law Cases*. The internet version covers the period 1986 to the the present only, but the CD version includes a complete file from 1947. On the internet version the file can be searched in one go, but on the CD version it is split over two CDs, according to date: a Current Disc and an Archive Disc. So, to search the whole period from 1947 to the present means switching fom one disc to another and repeating the search. The split between the two discs occurs in the early 1990s. This is not really a problem, just something important to remember if you are undertaking a search for information on pre-1990 cases. In most universities and colleges the two discs are networked and, to switch between discs, the user simply clicks on the Archive Disc button on the menu screen, to reach the historical file. To return to the latest disc, click on the Current Disc button on the archive disc menu screen.

The CD version is updated monthly but the internet version is updated daily. The internet version is obviously the best to use for information about the latest cases. However, the CD version has five advantages over the internet version:

(a)   The CD version offers the possibility of restricting your search to any field into which a case record is divided. This is especially useful if the only information you have about a case is the name of one of the parties and it is a commonly occuring name, and also one that is an adjective, such as Black. By selecting the case name field and typing in Black, the search will retrieve only those cases where one of the names of parties is Black. In the internet version, it is not possible to search by field and a search on the word Black will retrieve not only cases with the name appearing in the case title but also as counsel or solicitors or any other person of this name mentioned in the summaries, as well as use of the word in the summaries as an adjective ('black smoke', 'black person').

(b)   The CD version displays the results of a search in a single sequence complete with summaries. It is easy to scroll down the information to identify relevant material. In contrast, the internet version displays the results in two steps. First, the results of a search are displayed as a list with only a single line of information about each item retreived. To view the summary of any case to check whether it is relevant, it is necessary to take a second step and click on the relevant line of information to open the individual case summary.

(c)   As a result of the way in which information is presented on screen, it is far easier to print or download information from the CD version than the internet version, especially if you have undertaken a subject search and found many relevant cases.

(d)   The CLI web site in which the *Current Law Cases* database resides is subscribed to by many practising lawyers as well as universities and colleges. Sometimes, especially during normal office hours, the site can run slowly or even 'freeze'. There is nothing you or your university or college can do when this happens, except be patient and try again in the evening or at weekends, when traffic is lighter. On the other hand, the CD version runs on a computer in your university or college, which will be faster to access and usually more stable.

(e)   The CD version includes a link from each case summary to the *Case Citator*, where information on the judicial history of the case and how the courts have viewed the decision subsequently, in later cases, can be found.

If both electronic versions are available to you, the relative advantages and disadvantages of the two mediums suggest that, if you are seeking information on the latest cases, use the internet version, otherwise your first search should be on the CD version, to find the bulk of the information required, followed by the internet version, to sweep up the latest developments.

6B2.5   *Halsbury's Laws Monthly Review and Law Online*

Halsbury's Laws Monthly Review is a paper booklet published as part of the up-dating service to *Halsbury's Laws* encyclopedia (see 6B5.1). It is usually filed in Binder 1. It digests recent developments in the law and can be read independently of the encyclopedia. Short summaries of cases are arranged under the same broad subject headings as are employed in the encyclopedia. The electronic equivalent of the *Monthly Review* is *Law Online* (part of the *Law Direct* database). It is a daily alerting service available on the Butterworths Direct web site at

> http://www.butterworths.com

Access to the site is available only to subscribers. *Law Online* contains short digests of a wide variety of legal information, including cases, cumulated at the end of each day into a three-month archive. Experience indicates that the coverage of cases in the Butterworths products is probably not quite so comprehensive as in *Lawtel* and the *Current Law* products.

6B2.6   *The Digest*

The Digest has three main purposes:

(a)   To summarise over 250,000 cases drawn from over 1,000 different series of law reports covering the whole case law of England and Wales (from the 16th century onwards), together with a selection of cases from the courts of Scotland, Ireland, Canada, Australia, New Zealand and other Commonwealth countries. Cases dealing with the law of the European Community are also included.

(b)   To act a case citator — for every entry it lists subsequent citations to that case (see 6B3.1 for a definition of 'citator').

(c)   To act as a finding tool for the correct citation of cases not included in *Current Law Case Citator* (see 6B3.1) by reason of date (i.e. pre-1947 cases not cited since 1947) or the jurisdiction of the decision.

The first edition of *The Digest* (it was known until recently as *The English and Empire Digest*) was published in 47 volumes between 1919 and 1932. Since then it has been replaced by a second edition, known as the blue band edition because of the coloured band on the spine, and is now into a third edition, known as the green band edition. The current edition is in about 60 volumes which divide into five parts, see figure 6.3.

(a)   *Main Volumes*. The largest part of *The Digest* comprises over 50 Main Volumes which provide short summaries of cases arranged under a similar subject arrangement as found in *Halsbury's Laws* (see 6B5.1). Each subject title, and several may appear in a single volume, begins with a table of contents or a synopsis showing how the cases are arranged. Then follow case summaries arranged under each subject heading and subheading in chronological order. Immediately following each major heading, cross-references are provided to *Halsbury's Statutes of England* (see 4.2B2.3.1) and *Halsbury's Laws of England* (see 6B5.1). English cases are summarised first under each heading and are printed in ordinary size type, cases from other jurisdictions are printed in a smaller type following the English ones. Each individual case summary ends with a citation to where the case was originally published in law reports. Where appropriate, following the case summary and citation, details are provided of subsequent decisions of the courts in which an opinion on the earlier case has been given. This concise history of judicial comment on the original decision is a valuable feature of *The Digest*.

Figure 6.3   Structure of *The Digest* (formerly *The English & Empire Digest*).

MAIN VOLUMES	QUARTERLY SURVEY	CUMULATIVE SUPPLEMENT
Over 50 volumes containing summaries of over 250,000 cases drawn from over 1,000 different series of law reports.	Summarises reported cases published since the current Cumulative Supplement.	Annual bound volume containing summaries of recent cases not included in the Main Continuation Volumes.
CONSOLIDATED TABLE OF CASES	**INDEX**	
Alphabetical list of cases summarised in Main and Continuation Volumes.	Subject index.	

When the law on a subject has changed considerably since the Main Volume was originally published, the publishers produce a so-called reissue volume which replaces the out-of-date original volume. The 'reissue volume' incorporates summaries of new cases as well as retaining relevant older cases. In some subjects, so many changes have occurred since the original Main Volumes began to appear from 1971 onwards, that even the first reissue volumes have been replaced by second reissue volumes. If a volume has been reissued the word 'reissue' appears on the spine, and if it is a second or subsequent reissue, the word 'reissue' is preceded by 2nd, 3rd etc.

(b) *Cumulative Supplement.* Two bound volumes, published annually, contains summaries of recent cases and indicates where amendments to the text of the Main Volumes have occurred. The Cumulative Supplement is usually up-to-date to 1 January of the year of publication.

(c) *Quarterly Survey.* This softback volume updates the Cumulative Supplement and Main Volumes. The arrangement is by title corresponding to the Main Volumes. Within each title information is arranged in three sections: section 1 lists new cases; section 2 updates the case histories and section 3 digests the new cases. It is very important to remember that the Quarterly Survey is *not* cumulative and that the contents are usually up-to-date to between four and six months before the month of publication.

(d) *Consolidated Table of Cases.* These volumes, updated and replaced annually, are a list of cases included in *The Digest*, arranged in alphabetical order by the names of parties. The reference given against each entry is to the Main Volume number and subject heading (given in an abbreviated form) within that volume where the case will be found. To find the precise location of the summary for the case in which you are interested you will need to look up the case name again in the list of cases at the front of that particular Main Volume. Depending on the age of that Main Volume, you will be referred either to a page number, or in more recently published volumes, a case summary number.

(e) *Index.* This single volume, updated and replaced annually, is a subject index to the whole of *The Digest*. It is probably the most frequent point at which to start research using *The Digest*. It is an alphabetical list of subjects against each of which is the Main Volume number, the subject heading (in abbreviated form) and the relevant case summary numbers. Because of the frequency with which Main Volumes are reissued with extra, new case summaries, there are always times when some of the summary numbers in the Index refer to superseded Main Volumes and the index and summary numbers do not match. If this occurs, carefully follow the instructions given below on using *The Digest*.

Using The Digest   Since the Quarterly Survey is usually published four to six months after the decisions it contains, *The Digest* is inappropriate for tracing the latest developments in the law.

There are three different ways in which research can be carried out using *The Digest*; the steps to follow are given in figure 6.4: (a) search by subject, a general review of a wide subject area; (b) search by subject, a highly specific subject enquiry; (c) search by case name. The last search method should be used when you have an incomplete or incorrect citation to a case, and you have been unable to trace the case in the *Current Law Case Citators* (see 6B3.1). *Current Law Case Citators* contain references to English cases reported from 1947 onwards and major pre-1947 cases cited since then. *The Digest*, on the other hand, is valuable for tracing citations to less well-known, pre-1947 English cases and cases from outside the English jurisdiction.

Here are examples, with explanations, of how information in the Index and the Consolidated Table of Cases is arranged:

Index   Information is arranged alphabetically by subject and references to the Main Volumes are given as follows:

> Formation of contract
> telephone communication   **12(1)** *Contr* 938

The reference means Volume 12, part 1, the section on Contract, at page 938. A list of the abbreviations for the subjects into which the Main Volumes are divided is reproduced in the front of the Index volume.

Consolidated Table of Cases   Case names are given alphabetically with references to the Main Volume as follows:

> Cooper v Bill (1865) **32(2)** Lien; **39(2)** Sale of Goods

This means the case of Cooper v Bill (1865) is summarised in Main Volume 32, part 2, in the section on Liens and also in Main Volume 39, part 2 in the section on Sale of Goods.

Figure 6.4   Step-by-step research using *The Digest*.

(a)   *Search by Subject* — a general review of a wide subject area.

```
┌─────────────────────────────────────────┐
│   Consult list of Main Volume titles at front  │
│        of Cumulative Supplement.                │
└─────────────────────────────────────────┘
```

```
┌─────────────────────────────────────────┐
│  Consult Main Volume indicated; use contents   │
│   pages of that volume to discover subject      │
│       arrangement and page numbers.             │
└─────────────────────────────────────────┘
```

```
┌─────────────────────────────────────────┐
│   Consult Cumulative Supplement and            │
│  check all parts of the Quarterly Survey        │
│         for up-dating material.                 │
└─────────────────────────────────────────┘
```

(b)   *Search by Subject* — a highly specific subject enquiry.

> Consult the Index for relevant
> Main Volume number, subject and case numbers.

> Consult contents pages at the front of
> the Index to see from which issue of the
> Main Volume the index you require has been compiled.

> Consult Main Volume, check spine to see it is same
> issue as used to compile the Consolidated Index. If it is,
> look up subject and case numbers. If it is not, use
> Reference Adaptor at back of Main Volume to
> convert old case numbers to reissue case numbers.
> Take care to use the correct Reference Adaptor —
> there are often two: one for English cases, one for
> other jurisdictions. Look up subject and case numbers
> in body of Main Volume.

> Consult Cumulative Supplement and check all parts
> of the Quarterly Survey for up-dating material.

(c)   *Search by case name*

> Consult Consolidated Table of Cases
> for volume number and subject.

> Consult case name index at front of
> relevant Main Volume.

> Consult Cumulative Supplement and
> check all parts of the Quarterly Survey
> for up-dating material.

There is an important point to note about the reissue volumes and use of the Index to *The Digest*:

Main volumes are revised and reissued when the law they contain is out-of-date. However, there can be a gap between the publication of a reissue Main Volume and an up-to-date Consolidated Index to the whole set. So it is important to check which issue of the Main Volume has been used from which to compile the index. This can be done by comparing (a) the information given in the contents pages at the front of the Consolidated Index under the volume you wish to consult, to see whether the word 'reissue' is given against it, with (b) the 'reissue' information on the spine of the Main Volume itself or its publication date. If the index was published *after* the Main Volume, then the references it contains should match the case numbers in the Main Volume. If the index was published *before* the Main Volume, then the references it contains may not match the case numbers in the reissued Main Volume; in this instance you will need to use the reference adaptor printed at the back of the reissued Main Volume, to convert the case numbers given in the Consolidated Index to their new equivalents in the latest reissue volume.

6B2.7   Social Security Case Law; Digest of Commissioners' Decisions

This two-volume loose-leaf work compiled by Desmond Neligan, and frequently referred to as *'Neligan's Digest'*, contains brief summaries of a large number of the reported and some unreported decisions of the Social Security Commissioners. The two volumes are divided into 31 chapters (though, currently, chapters 20 to 29 are not yet used). Each chapter commences with a contents list of the subjects covered and then follow case summaries under each subject heading in chronological order. At the back of volume 2 is a general index — an alphabetical subject index to both volumes — with references to where in the body of the Digest the appropriate decision summaries will be found. The Digest is useful for identifying relevant decisions through its subject indexing and arrangement, but the summaries should not be relied on solely, since references ought be followed up in the full versions of commissioners' decisions.

6B3   Citators

6B.3.1   Current Law Case Citator

Current Law Case Citator is a unique and valuable service. It is available in paper, CD and internet formats. The information provided is identical, though the layout is different.

The *Citator* is an alphabetical list by case name of cases reported between 1947 and the present with:

(a)   A comprehensive list of references to where the case was originally reported in the law reports.

(b)   A judicial history of each case detailing reported appeals to a higher court.

(c)   Details of whether courts in later cases have applied, considered, approved, disapproved, followed or referred to the original decision.

(d)   Details of where the case is summarised in the sister publication of *Current Law Yearbooks*.

These four characteristics are illustrated in figure 6.5, which is taken from the paper version of the *Citator*.

Figure 6.5   Extract from *Current Law Case Citator 1977–1997*.

GIL   CASE CITATOR 1977–97

Gillenden Development Co Ltd v. Surrey CC (1997) 74 P. & C.R. 119; [1997] J.P.L. 944;
     [1997] E.G.C.S. 4, CA . . . .   *Digested, 97/4069*
Gillespie (t/a Gillespie Transport) v. Anglo Irish Beef Processors Ltd [1994] N.I. 65, QBD
     (NI)
Gillespie v. Northern Health and Social Services Board (C342/93) [1996] All E.R.
     (EC) 284; [1996] I.C.R. 498; [1996] I.R.L.R. 214; (1996) 31 B.M.L.R. 65; *Times,*
     February 22, 1996, ECJ . . . .   *Digested, 96/2570:*
                                                                                                               Applied, 97/2241, 97/2239
Gillespie v. Northern Health and Social Services Board (No.2); Todd v. Eastern Health
     and Social Services Board [1997] I.R.L.R. 410; [1997] Eu L.R. 566; [1997] N.I.
     190, CA (NI) . . . .   *Digested, 97/5227*
Gillespie v. Secretary of State [1990] N.I. 392 . . . .   *Digested, 94/5060*
Gillespie v. Trustees of Portadown Masonic Hall (R/18/1991) . . . .   *Digested, 92/4903*

Gillespie

Citation to Appeal Cases, followed by citations to 6 other reports of House of Lords (HL) decision.

efence (The Angel Bell) see Iraqi Ministry of
     and Gillespie Bros & Co Ltd
     Transport [1973] Q.B. 400; [1972] 3 W.L.R.
     ] 1 Lloyd's Rep. 10; [1973] R.T.R. 95, CA;
     [1972] R.T.R. 65, QBD . . . .
          Considered, 74/1222, 88/461:
               Not followed, 96/12
     don Communal Mikvah [1983] J.P.L.
     °.C. 271 . . . .

Details of where case is summarised in Current Law Yearbook: 1985 volume at paragraph 2230

Gillett (\
Gillette I
Gillette :

Trading Ltd (1913) 30 R.P.C. 465 . . .

Names of parties to the action

AW Gamage (1907) 24 R.P.C. 1. . . . .
1994] R.P.C. 279; *Times,* March 9, 1994, Ch D . . . . . .
.M.L.R. 267; *Times,* October 20, 1995; *Independent, C*

Gillick v. Di Chemicals Ltd [1993] I.R.L.R. 437, EAT . . . .   *Digested, 94/1990:*
                                                                                                               Applied, 95/2114

Gillick v. West Norfolk and Wisbech AHA and Department of Health and Social
     Security [1986] A.C. 112; [1985] 3 W.L.R. 830; [1985] 3 All E.R. 402; [1986]
     Crim. L.R. 113; (1985) 135 N.L.J. 1055; (1985) 82 L.S.G. 3531; (1985) 129 S.J.
     738, HL; reversing [1985] 2 W.L.R. 413; [1985] 1 All E.R. 533; (1985) 15 Fam.
     Law 165; (1985) 135 N.L.J. 81; (1985) 82 L.S.G. 762; (1985) 129 S.J. 42, CA;
     reversing [1984] Q.B. 581; [1983] 3 W.L.R. 859; [1984] 1 All E.R. 365; (1983)
     147 J.P. 888; (1984) 14 Fam. Law 207; (1983) 80 L.S.G. 2678; (1983) 127
     S.J. 596; (1983) 133 N.L.J. 888, QBD . . . .   *Digested, 85/2230:*
          Applied, 87/2483, 92/35, 93/2845: Cited, 92/2919, 93/2730:
          Considered, 86/19, 87/21, 90/1571, 91/2512, 94/3234, 95/4105:
                              inguished, 92/3135: Referred to, 94/3229 }

Court of Appeal (CA) decision reverses the decision of Queen's Bench Division (High Court) reported in 8 publications.	‑td 19) [197 al Ban 's App i C.O.l hatha ‑. 923 J.P.L. oer 20) 3 P/ ; sub i	House of Lords (HL) decision reverses decision of Court of Appeal (CA), and citations to 6 reports of this decision are given.

. . . .   *Digested, 77/2048*
. . . .   *Digested, 80/884*
. . . .   *Applied, 78/2025*

[1992] 3 W.L.R.
.R. 160; [1992] 1
391] N.P.C. 97;   *Digested, 94/4309*
) . . . .
959] Ch. 62, CA
‑ollowed, 60/372: Nc

Details of where decision in Gillick v West Norfolk and Wisbech AHA has been applied, cited, considered, distinguished and referred to in other cases, with references to where summaries of these later cases may be found in Current Law Yearbook.

Gilmartin (A Bankrupt), Re [1989] 1 W.L.R. 513; [1989] 2 All E.R. 835; (1989) 133 S.J. 877;
     (1989) 86(23) L.S.G. 36, Ch D . . . .
Gillow v. United Kingdom, *Times,* November 29, 1986, ECHR . . . .

Gilmartin v. West Sussex CC (1976) 242 E.G. 203, CA . . . .
Gilmore (Valuation Officer) v. Baker-Carr (1962) [1962] 1 W.L.R. 1165; [1962] 3 All
     E.R. 230; 60 L.G.R. 443; [1962] R.V.R. 486; 9 R.R.C. 240; [1962] R.A. 379;
     (1962) 126 J.P. 476; 106 S.J. 569, CA; affirming 179 E.G. 475; [1961] R.V.R.
     598; [1961] J.P.L. 689, Lands Tr . . . .
                                   Applied, 68/3317, 68/3318: Considered
Gilmore (Valuation Officer) v. Baker-Carr (1964) 188 E.G. 977; [1964] J.P.L. 287;
     [1964] R.V.R. 7; 10 R.R.C. 205; 114 L.J. 60; [1963] R.A. 458, Lands Tr . . . .
Gilmore v. Secretary of State for Northern Ireland [1995] N.I. 46, QBD (NI)
Gilmore's Application, Re see R. v. Medical Appeal Tribunal Ex p. Gilmore
Gilmour v. Coates; *sub nom* Coates' Trust, in re; Coates v. Gilmour [1949] A.C. 426,
     HL [1948] Ch 340, CA . . . .   Di
                                   Applied, 53/455: Considered, 81/22
                                                                               Distinguishe
Gilmour Caterers v. St Bartholomew's Hospital Governors [1956] 1 Q.B. 387, CA . . . . .
Gilmurray v. Corr [1978] N.I. 99. . . . .
Gilmurray v. Secretary of State [1976] N.I. 28, CA . . . .   *Digested, 78/2117*

Some points to note when using the *Citator*:

(a)   It lists not only cases *reported* since 1947, but also major pre-1947 cases *cited* since 1947 with, usually, a single citation to where the original case might be found in law reports, and a reference to where in the relevant *Current Law Yearbook* the summary of the case in which it was cited, will be found.

(b)   It includes not only English cases but also those from the courts of Northern Ireland, Scotland and the European Communities which have been summarised in *Current Law Monthly Digest*.

Although at first sight you may think the *Citator* a tool to be used only in the most detailed research on a case, you will find it invaluable in day-to-day use of the law library because:

(a)   There will be occasions, especially during lectures, when you will be given the name of a case without its citation. Using *Current Law Case Citator* you can check:

(i)   whether it has been reported since 1947, and if so, where;
(ii)   if it was reported before 1947 but has been cited since, one citation will be given to where it was originally reported.

(b)   You may be competing frequently with other students for the same volume of law reports. Using *Current Law Case Citator* you can check whether the case has been reported in any other series of law reports and use that alternative version for your reading, unless the lecturer has made a special point of recommending a particular version, which won't often happen.

(c)   You may be referred in lectures and your reading to cases in law reports which your law library does not possess. Using *Current Law Case Citator* you can find the reference to the summary of the case in the appropriate *Current Law Yearbook* and read that as an alternative. It should be emphasised that whilst reading case summaries is a valuable 'safety net' when the full reports are not available in the library, it can be a recipe for disaster in essays, assignments, projects and examinations if undertaken as the sole method of reading case law.

Paper version
It is published in several volumes:

Period covered	Title of publication
1947–1976	*Current Law Case Citator 1947–1976*: a bound volume covering cases reported or cited between those dates;
then either:	
1977–1997	*Current Law Case Citator 1977–1997*: a bound volume supplementing the above and consolidating the next two volumes;

Period covered	Title of publication

or, if the consolidated volume is not available:

1977–1988	*Current Law Case Citator 1988*: a bound volume covering 1977–1988, supplementing 1947–1976;
1989–1995	*Current Law Case Citator 1989–1995*: a bound volume supplementing 1947–1976 and 1977–1988;
1996–1997	*Current Law Case Citator 1996–97*: a softback volume;

followed by:

1998–	*Current Law Case Citator 1998–;* a softback volume which will be replaced each year by an updated volume;
Current year	*Current Law Monthly Digest:* the cumulative table of cases at the back of the current issue lists, in ordinary type, new cases which have been summarised in *Current Law Monthly Digest* during the current year, and in italic type, cases which have been judicially considered, overruled by statute, or been the subject of an article or case note.

A Scottish edition entitled *Scottish Current Law Case Citator* was published until 1991, adding coverage of cases reported in Scotland and judicially considered in the Scottish courts. This material was not included in the English edition and first became generally available in the *Current Law Case Citator 1989–1995*. However, the consolidated and corrected *Current Law Case Citator 1977–1997* may be in your library and this covers both jurisdictions. Since 1991, *Scottish Current Law Case Citator* and *Current Law Case Citator* have been merged and cases arranged in two parts: part I contains the English *Citator* and part II contains cases digested or referred to in the Scottish section of *Current Law Yearbook*. Make sure you are referring to the correct part in the *Citator*!

Using the Citator: Select the single most appropriate route of the four according to the information you have about the case:

(a)   if the case you are checking is reliably referred to as 'recent' or you are looking for the 'latest' information, start your search with the latest issue of *Current Law Monthly Digest*, and work backwards in time through the set of *Citators*;

(b)   if you know the date of the case you are checking, begin with the volume which embraces the date and work forwards through the set;

(c)   if you do not know the date of the case you are checking, either work methodically forwards in time from the 1947–1976 volume (the recommended technique, as the history and subsequent judicial comment about the case will unfold in the correct chronological sequence) or backwards from the latest issue of *Current Law Monthly Digest* (not the recommended technique, since judicial comment and appeals against the decision may appear in several volumes and you will come upon them in reverse chronological order);

(d) if you are trying to check for citations made before 1947 (a very rare research need), use *The Digest* (see 6B2.6).

It is essential when researching the history of a particular case to use *all* the appropriate volumes of the *Citator* and not, as some students do, rely on a dip into whichever of the volumes is immediately to hand at the time, otherwise the result is likely to be an incomplete piece of research.

Electronic versions

The *Citator* is available on CD and via the internet. It covers English, Welsh and Scottish cases. Both formats are considerably easier to use than the paper version. To search either it is only necessary to enter the name of the case (in many instances just one of the names of parties will be sufficient) in the search box, and the computer will respond with the same four pieces of information listed at the beginning of 6B3.1. The CD version has an advantage over the internet version, in that it is possible to click on the reference to where the case is summarised in the sister database: *Current Law Cases*, and read the summary given there. The internet version does not offer any possibility of cross-linking within the *Current Legal Information* family of databases. The site is at

http://193.118.187.160/cli.htm

It is available only to subscribers, though most universities and colleges teaching law have subscriptions. You will need a user name and password to get into the site; ask library staff for this information.

6B3.2   The Law Reports Index

This publication, sometimes referred to as the Red Book owing to the colour of its cover, contains a list of cases considered. The list is compiled from the dozen or so series of law reports it indexes (see 6B1.1). Whilst it will act as a case citator, the limited coverage of law reports means it should be used only if you do not have access to *Current Law Case Citator* (see 6B3.1).

6B4   Full-text databases

6B4.1   CDs

A wide range of the most popular law reports is now available on CD. The list includes the *All England Law Reports*, *Weekly Law Reports*, *Criminal Appeal Reports*, *Family Law Reports* and *The Times Electronic Law Reports*. Rather than providing here descriptions which will go rapidly out-of-date, instead, here are some questions worth asking yourself before you use a CD version of a series of law reports for research:

(a)   Most CD versions of paper law reports include the full text of the whole set of reports. A few cover a more limited period of time. Check that the period covered by the CD is appropriate for your research.

(b)   How up-to-date is the CD? Many are updated quarterly. If you are looking for recent cases try internet services, either those descibed in (c) and (d) below, or the summary services such as *Lawtel* (see 6B2.3) and *Current Law Cases* (see 6B2.4) or even the paper equivalent of the title.

(c)   Does the CD I wish to use have the benefit of an add-on service with access via the internet to files updated more frequently than the CD? For example, some of the JUSTIS CDs have access to JUSTIS 5 Online, which contains updates to the data contained on the disc. The updating information is added to the internet service at intervals which vary from every few days to weeks. Libraries have to pay an extra subscription for this internet add-on service — does your library have this service?

(d)   The complete files (rather than only the updates) of a very small number of commercially published law reports are being made available over the internet. For example, the *All England Law Reports* are now available in three formats: traditional paper, CD and, as All England Direct, via the Butterworths Direct subscriber only web site. Which services does your library provide and which is the most appropriate for your particular research needs?

6B4.2   Internet databases

Apart from those CD services which provide internet add-on services, there are a number of important case law databases available only on the internet (these have been mentioned in detail already, please see section 6A4):

*   The House of Lords:

    http://www.parliament.the-stationery-office.co.uk/pa/ld/ldjudinf.htm

*   The Court Service:

    http://www.courtservice.gov.uk/judgments/judg_home.htm

*   The Privy Council:

    http://www.bailii.org/uk/cases/UKPC

*   The British and Irish Legal Information Institute:

    http://www.bailii.org/

*   Smith Bernal:

    http://www.casetrack.com/casebase

6B4.3   LEXIS

The on-line database *LEXIS* contains the *full text* of virtually all reported cases since 1945, plus *Tax Cases* reports since 1875 and, since 1 January 1980, transcripts of a large number of unreported cases of the Court of Appeal (Civil Division), some from the High Court and selected tribunals. The database is updated each week, but it frequently takes several weeks between a judgment being given and its inclusion in the database, for only the fullest version of the decision is carried, not the brief or edited report.

The database is divided into libraries. The ENGGEN Library (*Eng*lish *Gen*eral) contains separate files including one devoted to law reports entitled CASES.

Since use of *LEXIS* is charged differently from most databases, frequently universities and colleges do not give students direct access to the database. Teaching and library staff will advise you whether use of the database is appropriate for the research you wish to conduct. Other sources, such as those described in 6B4.1, 6B4.2 and 6B5.1, may be just as useful and, in some instances, more up-to-date.

6B5   Commentary

6B5.1   Halsbury's Laws of England

Paper version
Halsbury's Laws of England was first published in 1907 and is now in its fourth edition. It is a key research publication and copies will be found in virtually every academic library where students study law to degree level or beyond. Many large public libraries also subscribe to it, but more importantly, most firms of solicitors and barristers' chambers will use *Halsbury's Laws* as an everyday research source. *Halsbury's Laws* is a commentary, written by editorial staff, on the whole law of England and Wales. Unlike its sister publication *Halsbury's Statutes*, with which it should not be confused, *Halsbury's Laws* does not reprint original legal materials.

There are seven parts to the publication, as summarised in figure 6.6.

(a)   *Main Volumes*. Fifty-two Main Volumes contain a narrative statement, arranged by subject, of the whole law of England and Wales, derived from statutes, rules, regulations and cases. The volumes were originally published at a variety of dates between 1973 and 1986, when the fourth edition was completed. Volume 1 contains the law relating to the topic of administrative law and volume 50 ends with that on wills. Two further volumes (51 and 52) cover European Communities law. When the law on a topic has changed considerably since a Main Volume was published, a 'reissue' volume is published to replace the original one. Some areas of law change faster than others. You can identify reissue volumes by the word appearing near the top of the spine of these particular volumes and also on the title page. It is important to note this, as will be explained later in the section on using *Halsbury's Laws*.

Figure 6.6   Structure of *Halsbury's Laws of England*.

Main Volumes	Annual Abridgements	Cumulative Supplement	Current Service
Narrative statement, arranged by subject, of whole law of England and Wales derived from statutes, rules, regulations and cases.	Annual bound volumes recording changes to law not yet included in Main Volumes.	Two bound volumes issued annually — record changes affecting Main Volumes and Annual Abridgements. Up-to-date to end of previous year.	Two loose-leaf binders: **Binder 1: Monthly Review:** details very recent changes to Main Volumes and Annual Abridgements. **Binder 2: Noter Up:** brief annotations to Main Volumes and Annual Abridgements.

Consolidated Table of Statutes	Consolidated Table of Cases	Consolidated Index
Alphabetical list over two volumes, of Statutes (Acts) occupying both volumes, and Statutory Instruments (towards back of second volume).	Alphabetical list of cases noted in Main Volumes only, not the Annual Abridgements.	Two volume subject index.

(b)   *Annual Abridgements.* These volumes record changes to the law in any one year not yet included in the Main Volumes and provide brief summaries of cases and legislation.

(c)   *Cumulative Supplement* (sometimes referred to as the 'Cum. Sup.'). Two bound volumes, issued annually and replacing the previous Cumulative Supplement, record changes affecting the Main and Annual Abridgements, and are up-to-date to late in the year prior to publication.

(d)   *Current Service.* Two loose-leaf binders contain the Monthly Review, a booklet published monthly which provides brief summaries of recent cases and legislation, and in the second binder, the Noter-Up Service, which includes citations to new court decisions and legislation arranged under subjects in the same order as in the Main Volumes and Cumulative Supplement.

(e)   *Consolidated Index.* A two-volume alphabetical list of references to subjects included in the Main Volumes.

(f)   *Consolidated Table of Statutes.* Alphabetical list by title of the statutes referred to.

(g)   *Consolidated Table of Cases.* Alphabetical list by title of the cases referred to.

Figure 6.7   Step-by-step research using *Halsbury's Laws of England.*

Four step search: Index ➡ Main Volume ➡ Cumulative Supplement ➡ Current Service

INDEX
Look up the statute, case or subject in the appropriate volume of the consolidated indexes. Note the volume and paragraph number to which you are referred. If the statute, case or subject is too recent to be included in the main work index, consult the index at the back of the Cumulative Supplement and the index at the back of the Current Service volume. These will guide you to the appropriate part of the work for the latest information.

MAIN VOLUME
Compare the date of issue of the Consolidated Index with the date at which the Main Volume states the law — this is given a couple of pages after the title page. If the Main Volume pre-dates the index find the relevant paragraph number noted from the Consolidated Index. If Main Volume has been published after the Consolidated Index look up statute, case or subject in the index to the reissued Main Volume itself. Then find relevant paragraph number.

CUMULATIVE SUPPLEMENT
If you have not been guided by the indexes to the Cumulative Supplement volume refer to it under the relevant Main Volume, subject and paragraph numbers.

CURRENT SERVICE
Check the Noter-Up in Binder 2 under the appropriate volume, subject and paragraph number to trace latest developments. Short summaries of these developments can be read in the Monthly Review in Binder 1. Use the Key to Monthly Reviews, set out at the beginning of Binder 1, to trace where the summaries are located.

Using Halsbury's Laws   The key skill to learn in searching *Halsbury's Laws* is to correctly and confidently link together the use of the seven parts to ensure the law you eventually cite is up-to-date.

There are four steps in research using *Halsbury's Laws*, as figure 6.7 shows. Here are some points to note when using *Halsbury's Laws*:

(a)   Research should normally start with one of the consolidated indexes, which one will be determined by the information sought: about a subject, a particular statute or a case. Each reference in the index consists of two groups of figures: a bold number indicating the volume, followed by a number in a lighter type indicating the paragraph number — note: not the page number. An alternative approach, not recommended, is to browse over the spines of the Main Volumes or glance through the list printed towards the back of the

Halsbury's Laws of England User's Guide booklet, and select the title volume most relevant to the subject of enquiry. Then look up the topic in the index to that particular volume. The danger of this procedure is that there can be several possible titles relevant and you will not take advantage of the work of the indexer in bringing mention of them together in the consolidated index.

(b)   Main volumes are revised and reissued when the law they contain is out-of-date. However, there can be a gap between the publication of a reissue Main Volume and an up-to-date edition of the consolidated tables or consolidated index to the whole set. So it is important to check which issue of the Main Volume has been used to compile the tables and index. This can be done by comparing the date given on the title pages of the tables and index with the date up to which the law is stated in a Main Volume. If the tables and index were published *after* the Main Volume then the references they contain should match the paragraphs in the Main Volume. If the tables and index were published *before* the Main Volume then the references they contain may not match the paragraphs in the reissued Main Volume; in this case you should look up the topic you require again in the index to the particular reissued Main Volume to discover the new paragraph number at which it is discussed.

(c)   When you have found the information you require in the Main Volume, note three elements: the *volume, subject* and *paragraph number* of the section in which you are interested, so you can find relevant new information quickly in the Cumulative Supplement and Noter-Up. The subject is given as part of the running head across the tops of pages.

(d)   In the Cumulative Supplement and Noter-Up the volume number and subject are given as running heads across the tops of pages. The paragraph numbers of Main Volumes to which more recent developments relate are given in the left margin. If the paragraph number in which you are interested does not appear in the list you can assume there have been no changes to the commentary in the Main Volume in which you originally looked.

(e)   Research using *Halsbury's Laws* may be completed by using the relevant Annual Abridgement volumes to trace summaries of the cases and legislation to which you have been referred by the Main Volumes. This is a useful step for a busy solicitor or barrister, but as a law student you should try to avoid depending on case summaries until you are fully conversant with the structure and principles of a legal topic, otherwise, you may have difficulty relating one case decision effectively to another. Whenever possible consult full-text versions of cases, as originally published.

Electronic version

Halsbury's Laws Direct is the electronic version of *Halsbury's Laws of England.* It is available to subscribers to the Butterworths Direct web site at

    http://www.butterworths.com

The electronic version comprises the full text of the Main volumes with, in a separate window of the screen, the Current Service which is the updating text of the Cumulative Supplement and Noter-Up merged together. New material is added to *Halsbury's Laws Direct* at the same monthly interval as the paper version. Apart from presenting the text and updating material in two steps, rather than three as with the paper version, *Halsbury's Laws Direct* provides:

(a)   conventional word and phrase search software which will trace the occurence in the encyclopaedia of the precise words or phrases typed in;

(b)   an advanced natural language search software called Eureka!, into which it is possible to type a request in plain English (for example: 'What are my duties when I leave a builders' skip in the road outside my house?') and which the software will analyse into legal concepts, match against the text of the encyclopaedia and report the findings as paragraph numbers;

(c)   links to cases available in the related *All England Law Reports* database — but the link only works if this extra service has been included within the subscription; and

(d)   links to other parts of *Halsbury's Laws Direct*.

These features mean using the electronic version is preferable to the paper version.

6C   ANSWERING RESEARCH QUERIES

For background information on using CDs and the internet for legal research, see appendix 4.

6C1   Tracing a report of a case where only the names of parties are known

This is one of the most frequently occurring research tasks facing a law student.

Electronic route
Use one of the following:

(a)   Case Citator in *Current Legal Information* database (see 6B3.1) — coverage from 1947 onwards.

(b)   *Lawtel* (see 6B2.3) — coverage from 1980 onwards, but updated daily.

(c)   *LEXIS* (see 6B4.3) — updated less rapidly than either *Lawtel* or the Case Citator but contains the full-text versions of cases. To find the case of *Candler* v *Crane, Christmas & Co.* type:

name (Candler w/4 Crane)

If one party's name is very common then, to avoid being inundated with references to cases which are not relevant, you could request the computer to look for another name, phrase, word or number in close proximity to the common name, to narrow the number of cases found and improve the chances of a hit. For example: to find *R* v *Smith*, assuming you know the subject-matter of the case, type:

name (Smith) and burglary

If you do not have a complete case name, for example, only the popular name for a case, and the popular name actually appears in the case title, such as '*High Trees*', then you should type:

    name (High Trees)

The computer should retrieve *Central London Property Trust Ltd* v *High Trees House Ltd* [1947] KB 130.

(d)   *Halsbury's Law Direct* (see 6B5.1) — coverage of report titles not as wide as any of the above, and weak on unreported decisions.

Use of a CD or web site restricted to covering a single law report title is not advised. There is no guarrantee that the case you want was reported by the particular title.

Paper route
Research using paper sources is a little more laborious; figure 6.8 illustrates the preferred sequence.

An alternative strategy, if *Current Law Case Citator* is not available, would be to substitute the *Law Reports Index* (the 'red' and 'pink' books, see 6B1.1) or the *All England Law Reports* consolidated tables and index (see 6B1.1). Where *The Digest* is not available, substitute the *English Reports* index (see 6A2.2) or the *All England Law Reports Reprint* index (see 6A2.2), but note that neither indexes cases from outside the English jurisdiction. Where the case is thought to be recent but *Current Law Monthly Digest* is not available, substitute the latest index to the *Law Reports* (see 6B1.1), the list of cases printed in the latest issue of the *Weekly Law Reports*, and the most recent tables and index to the *All England Law Reports*.

6C2   Has this case been considered by the courts on a subsequent occasion?

Electronic route
Use one of the following:

(a)   Case Citator in *Current Legal Information* database (see 6B3.1) — retrieves significant references to a case.

(b)   *LEXIS* (see 6B4.3) — will retrieve all references to a case, regardless of significance of the citation. To find subsequent citations to cases citing *United Scientific Holdings Ltd* v *Burnley Borough Council* [1978] AC 904 type:

    United Scientific w/8 Burnley

If the name of one of the parties to the case you are searching for is very common, such as *R* v *Smith*, to avoid retrieving from the database citations to all cases titled *R* v *Smith*, you will need to include a word, phrase or number which will uniquely identify the case to which you wish to find later citations; type:

    Smith w/15 burglary

If the only information you have about the case is its popular name, such as '*High Trees*', to find cases citing this decision you would type:

High Trees

This should retrieve all cases citing *Central London Property Trust Ltd* v *High Trees House Ltd* [1947] KB 130.

Paper route
Research using paper sources is given in figure 6.9.

An alternative strategy, if *Current Law Case Citator* and *The Digest* are not available, is to substitute either the *Law Reports Index* (see 6B1.1) and check in the table of cases judicially considered, or the *All England Law Reports* consolidated tables and index (see 6B1.1) and check in the tables of cases reported and considered.

6C3   Tracing cases on a subject

Electronic route
Use one or more of the following:

(a)   Current Law Cases in the *Current Legal Information* database (see 6B3.1) — preferably the CD version, covering cases from 1947 onwards.

(b)   *Lawtel* (see 6B2.3) — coverage from 1980 onwards, but updated daily.

(c)   *Halsbury's Laws Direct* (see 6B5.1) but updated monthly.

(d)   *LEXIS* (see 6B4.3) — updated with some delay; searching the full text of case reports for the occurrence of the words, and *only* the words, you specify, requires skill and practice.

Use of a CD or web site restricted to covering a single law report title is not advised. Your search results will be very restricted and may not include the key decisions.

Paper route
Use one or more of the following:

(a)   *The Digest* (see 6B2.6) is arranged by subject and figure 6.4 shows how a search by subject can be carried out. *The Digest* will provide case summaries and covers non-English case law as well as English. However, because there is no loose-leaf updating service it does not feature the very latest decisions.

(b)   *Halsbury's Laws of England* is also arranged by subject and figure 6.7 shows how to search for information by subject. Whilst *Halsbury's* does not contain case summaries, nor does it include cases from outside the English jurisdiction, it does provide a commentary on the law and, through its loose-leaf service, include the latest decisions.

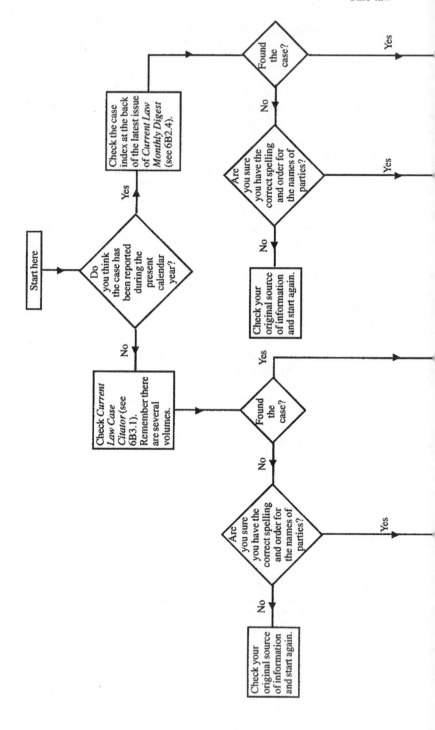

Figure 6.8   Tracing in printed sources a report of a case when only the names of parties are known.

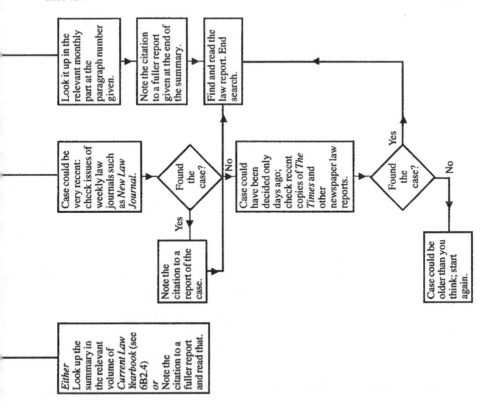

Look it up in the relevant monthly part at the paragraph number given.

Note the citation to a fuller report given at the end of the summary.

Find and read the law report. End search.

Case could be very recent: check issues of weekly law journals such as *New Law Journal*.

Found the case?

Yes — Note the citation to a report of the case.

No

Case could have been decided only days ago; check recent copies of *The Times* and other newspaper law reports.

Found the case?

Yes

No

Case could be older than you think; start again.

Either
Look up the summary in the relevant volume of *Current Law Yearbook* (see 6B2.4)
or
Note the citation to a fuller report and read that.

Either
Case could be pre-1947 and not cited since, *or*
Case could be from outside English jurisdiction.
In both instances check *The Digest*, following the procedure given in Figure 6.5.

(The letter and numbers after publication names refer to the sub-section where they are discussed.)

Figure 6.9   Tracing judicial comment on a case using printed sources.

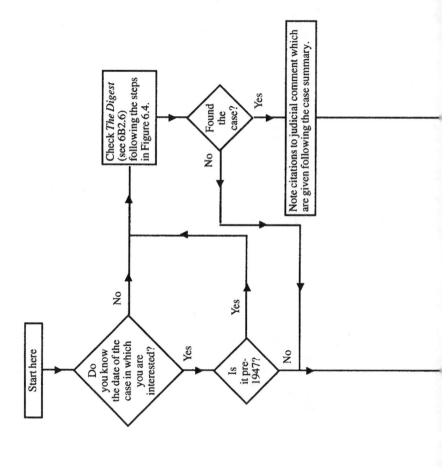

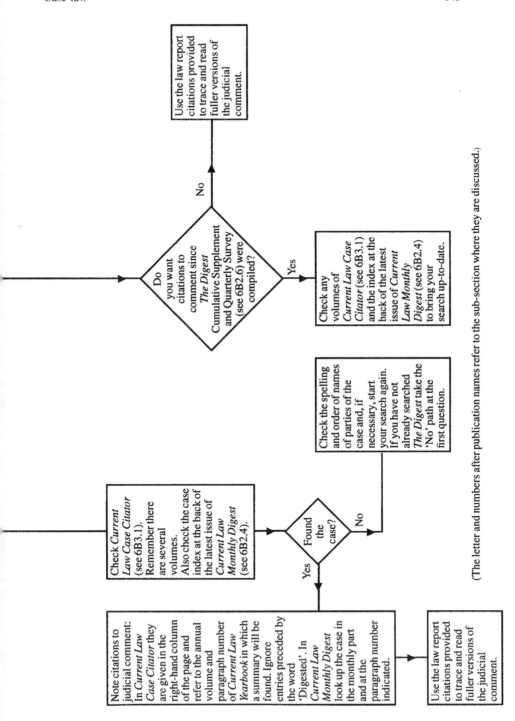

Use the law report citations provided to trace and read fuller versions of the judicial comment.

Do you want citations to comment since *The Digest* Cumulative Supplement and Quarterly Survey (see 6B2.6) were compiled?

No

Yes

Check any volumes of *Current Law Case Citator* (see 6B3.1) and the index at the back of the latest issue of *Current Law Monthly Digest* (see 6B2.4) to bring your search up-to-date.

Check the spelling and order of names of parties of the case and, if necessary, start your search again. If you have not already searched *The Digest* take the 'No' path at the first question.

Check *Current Law Case Citator* (see 6B3.1). Remember there are several volumes. Also check the case index at the back of the latest issue of *Current Law Monthly Digest* (see 6B2.4).

Found the case?

No

Yes

Note citations to judicial comment: In *Current Law Case Citator* they are given in the right-hand column of the page and refer to the annual volume and paragraph number of *Current Law Yearbook* in which a summary will be found. Ignore entries preceded by the word 'Digested'. In *Current Law Monthly Digest* look up the case in the monthly part and at the paragraph number indicated.

Use the law report citations provided to trace and read fuller versions of the judicial comment.

(The letter and numbers after publication names refer to the sub-section where they are discussed.)

(c)   *Current Law Yearbook* is not easy to use for this type of research, especially if you need decisions on a very specific point of law or wish to carry out in-depth subject research over a considerable period of years — the reasons are noted in 6B2.4.

(d)   The *Law Reports* indexes (see 6B1.1) are useful if other sources are not available, but since the number of different law report publications indexed is restricted — specialist subject law reports are particularly under-represented — your research results are unlikely to be comprehensive.

(e)   Least satisfactory is a search of the library catalogue by subject which should retrieve details of relevant textbooks which will contain references to and commentary on the leading decisions on a topic.

6C4   Have there been any case notes or articles on this case?

The best method of answering this research question is to use one or a number of periodical indexing services, fully described in 8.3 below.

Chapter 7

Extra-legal sources

7A DESCRIPTION

7A1 Definition

The term 'extra-legal sources' covers a variety of documents variously called codes of practice, codes of conduct, guidance or standards. The codes of practice described here differ from those discussed in 5.2 (collectively known as statutory codes of practice) in two ways. First, any organisation can issue them, whereas statutory codes of practice can only be issued under powers conferred by legislation, and some must be presented to Parliament for approval before they can take effect. Secondly, extra-legal sources are not legally enforceable in their own right, but either seek to influence behaviour or advise, and may rely on non-legal sanctions, such as loss of membership of a professional or trade association, to ensure conformity amongst those whose activities they are designed to influence.

7A2 Origin

Since 'any Tom, Dick or Harry' (Ferguson, 1988, p. 12) can issue one of these extra-legal sources, it is difficult to trace an historic origin for this type of publication. Ferguson's article makes a major contribution to a better understanding of this frequently neglected type of legal literature, and has formed the basis for the discussion in this section of the book. However, some areas where extra-legal sources occur *can* be identified.

The British Standards Institution, with origins dating back to 1901, was the first national standards body in the world, and has a current catalogue of over 10,000 British Standard publications with more than 700 new or revised standards issued each year. The aim of the publications is to set generally

recognised standards of quality for industry and commerce. The familiar
'kitemark' on a product, followed by a British Standard number (normally
abbreviated to BS followed by a running number), indicates that the product or
service satisfies the requirements of that standard. Some safety legislation,
notably dealing with clothing (e.g., the Nightwear (Safety) Regulations 1985 SI
1985/2043), specifies tests for quality, included in particular British Standards,
to which products should conform.

In consumer law, the Fair Trading Act 1973 placed a duty on the Director
General of Fair Trading to encourage the preparation of Codes of Practice by
trade associations. Nearly 50 have been introduced. They are 'designed to state
the legal responsibilities of the traders supporting them and in addition
consumers receive benefits in excess of the strict legal requirements' (Parry and
Rowell, 1999, division 1, para. 5065). Many codes contain conciliation and
arbitration schemes. Examples include the *Association of British Travel Agents
Ltd (ABTA) Tour Operators' Code of Conduct* and *ABTA's Travel Agent's Code
of Conduct* as well as the *Code of Practice for the Motor Industry* covering
advertising, sales, repair and servicing of both new and used cars, prepared
jointly by three trade associations including the Society of Motor Manufacturers
and Traders Ltd.

Similarly, the Data Protection Act 1993 places a duty on the Data Protection
Commissioner to encourage trade associations to prepare and disseminate codes
on compliance with data protection principles enshrined in the Act.

In business law, the Accounting Standards Committee, formed of representatives of a number of professional bodies in accountancy, has developed a
number of Statements of Standard Accounting Practice (SSAP) to codify
generally accepted best practice in financial accounting and financial statements
in, for example, company accounts. A final area where extra-legal sources may
be found is in the codes of practice or codes of ethics of professional bodies,
such as the British Medical Association, as set out in its *Handbook*, and the
Pharmaceutical Society of Great Britain, in its *Statement upon Matters of
Professional Conduct*.

7A3 Structure

The variety of types of extra-legal source and issuing organisation means there
is no common structure to these documents.

7A4 Publication and general availability

The lack of central control of the publication of extra-legal sources means that
each organisation responsible for a code or standard etc. will adopt its own
policy on publication. Whilst many academic and the larger public libraries will
have complete sets of the British Standards Institution publications, and the
libraries of universities or colleges teaching accountancy will collect Accounting Standards Committee documents, very few will include either the codes of
practice of trade associations or codes of ethics of professional bodies as
original documents. But codes of practice are one type of material which some

of the specialist loose-leaf encyclopaedias described in 8.2, below, provide and so prove their value. For example, Parry, D.L., and Rowell, R., (eds.), *Butterworths Trading and Consumer Law* (London: Butterworths, loose-leaf) gives details of where all the codes of practice made under the encouragement of the Director General of Fair Trading can be obtained; Goode, R.M., *Consumer Credit Legislation* (London: Butterworths, loose-leaf) reprints the *Finance Houses Association Code of Practice* and the *Consumer Credit Trade Association Code of Practice*; and Chalton, S.N.L. and Gaskill, S.J., *Encyclopedia of Data Protection* (London: Sweet & Maxwell, loose-leaf) provides information on trade codes of practice. Alternatively, see the web site of the appropriate organisation. In the examples given, these will be the Office of Fair Trading and the Data Protection Commissioner, respectively:

http://www.oft.gov.uk/

http://www.dataprotection.gov.uk/

The organisational index on the Government Information Service web site may prove helpful in identifying the web site of a relevant organisation:

http://www.open.gov.uk/

7A5 Citation

The variety of types of extra-legal source means there is no standard way in which they should be cited. However, good practice would dictate that a reference should include the name of the issuing organisation, the full title of the document, the edition number or date of publication and any reference number which uniquely identifies it.

Chapter 8

Commentary on the law

8.1 TEXTBOOKS

8.1A Description

A law textbook may be defined as a systematic, narrative explanation of and commentary on the law. Five different types may be identified:

(a) Books of authority: a few, older works written between the late-12th and mid-18th centuries, before the system of law reporting was fully developed, which are accepted as reliable statements of the law of their time. Examples include Sir Edward Coke's *Institutes of the Laws of England* (1628–44), and William Blackstone's *Commentaries on the Laws of England* (1765–69).

(b) Modern textbooks: books which collect, synthesise and critically evaluate the law.

(c) Casebooks: books which reprint or summarise a selection of judgments on a subject, sometimes with editorial commentary — in recent times these publications have also included material from statutes, government reports and periodical articles, with questions and points for discussion highlighted. They are frequently published under the title: *Cases and Materials on [subject]*.

(d) Practice books: guides to practice and procedure in the courts, primarily for the use of practitioners, rather than law students. Examples include: *Supreme Court Practice* (otherwise known as the 'White Book') and its supplement: *Civil Procedure*, *Civil Court Practice* (sometimes referred to as the 'Green Book'), and *Stone's Justices' Manual* (it has blue covers, but is not yet known by its colour).

(e) Precedent books: collections of forms and documents which have been found valid, effective and useful in the past, and provide lawyers with a general layout and wording accepted as standard. They are most frequently used for the preparation of documents in connection with a court action, or in conveyancing.

Much of this section on textbooks applies to Scotland as well as England and Wales. However, a short note on the Scottish equivalents to books of authority and precedent books is given in section 13.1.

8.1A1   Individual categories

8.1A1.1   Books of authority

Textbooks of all types are frequently cited in court, but although they are treated with great respect, their authority is merely persuasive. However, the small group of 'books of authority' are accorded greater respect and in the absence of any conflicting cases their statements of the law may be followed. As well as the works by Coke and Blackstone already noted, those of Glanvill, *Tractatus de legibus et consuetudinibus regni Angliae* (written between 1187 and 1189); Bracton, *De legibus et consuetudinibus Angliae* (written between 1250 and 1258); Littleton's *Tenures* (written in the late-15th century and one of the first, major legal works to be printed in England by Lettou or Machlinia in 1481 or 1482); Hawkins, *A Treatise of the Pleas of the Crown* (1716); Hale, *Pleas of the Crown* (1678); and Foster, *Discourses upon a Few Branches of the Crown Law* (1762) are generally regarded as books of authority. A detailed, yet readable account of these and many other pre-19th century books is given in chapter 9 of *The Chief Sources of English Legal History* by Percy Winfield (1925).

8.1A1.2   Modern textbooks

A customary distinction is made between practitioners' books, mostly written by and for practising lawyers, and students' textbooks, mainly written by academics, but the boundaries are blurred.

Practitioners' books, often in the past though now rarely referred to as treatises, provide a detailed treatment of a subject and are usually read selectively, and used more in the way of a work of reference. The emphasis is on an up-to-date statement and commentary on the law, its practice and procedure. However, because they are such extensive publications, often in several volumes, new editions are expensive to produce and do not appear at very frequent intervals. It is always important to check the statement of the date up to which the law is stated; this is usually printed either on the title page or in or near the preface. Where Cumulative Supplements are issued to keep the Main Volume up-to-date (sometimes the preface will indicate this to be the method of future updating), check that you are about to use the most up-to-date available, because out-of-date ones can sometimes be left on library shelves through an oversight by library staff. Some practitioners' books are now published as loose-leaf works, so that individual pages containing out-of-date law can be replaced with little delay, by pages giving the latest information. Examples of wholly loose-leaf works include: *Woodfall's Law of Landlord and Tenant*; *Emmet on Title*; and *Palmer's Company Law*. The original authors of some practitioners' texts may be long dead but their work has become an established publication and, although subsequently revised by others, the original author's name becomes part of the title; for example: *Chitty on Contracts*, *Rayden on Divorce*. Sometimes, in informal conversation or writing reference to such well-known titles is even further shortened to just *'Chitty'* or *'Rayden'*.

Student textbooks, on the other hand, are less concerned with detail but more with describing general principles of law and identifying and commenting on areas of doubt or conflict in statute or case law. They may also provide background information establishing the social or political context within which the law has developed and note possibilities for future law reform. Some of the more established student texts such as Smith and Hogan, *Criminal Law* and Trietel, *Law of Contract* have become standard works on their subject and are occasionally cited in court. In a study of the law reports for 1985 Clinch (1989, p. 475) found that well over 100 different textbooks, both practitioner and student titles, were cited in judgments. New editions of student textbooks appear at frequent intervals and you should check, when using a library copy, that you are consulting the latest edition available, as many libraries retain superseded editions on the open shelves.

Also, avoid the temptation to save money by buying a student textbook secondhand, when the only edition on sale is other than the latest. It will be a false economy, for citation from out-of-date sources, unless to provide an historical perspective, will be marked down by lecturing staff.

8.1A1.3   Casebooks

At first sight the reprints or summaries of key cases and other materials contained in these publications may seem a great boon to the student faced with a heavy reading list. Eminent lawyers have gathered together in the space of a single volume the essential sources relevant to a subject. However, although this portable library may appear convenient, it does contain only extracts and is no substitute for reading the original statutes, cases and other materials. A casebook is best used as a guide to further research rather than an end in itself.

8.1A1.4   Practice books

Practice books are specialised manuals, including statutes and court rules, with copious notes of guidance on their interpretation and application to the practice and procedure of the courts. Usually, new editions are published annually, and some publishers update the bound volumes with softback cumulative supplements and newsletters to ensure the information provided is as up-to-date as possible. When using practice books it is vital to not only consult the main, hardback volume but also check for supplements and/or newsletters carrying information on the latest developments. An increasing number of practice books are now available as CDs, making searching and use easier.

8.1A1.5   Precedent books

Three different types may be identified:

(a)   Some practitioners' books include standard forms and documents as an appendix, for example, *Rayden on Divorce*.

(b) Separate collections of forms and precedents for particular courts or topics have been published, for example, the loose-leaf series, *Precedents for the Conveyancer*. This latter title is updated six times a year in association with the journal, *Conveyancer and Property Lawyer*.

(c) Two major encyclopaedic collections, *Atkin's Encyclopaedia of Court Forms in Civil Proceedings* (known as '*Atkin's Court Forms*' or more simply still as '*Atkin*'), and *The Encyclopaedia of Forms and Precedents* (often referred to as '*EFP*').

Atkin reprints court forms and procedural documents used in civil proceedings. It also provides commentary and checklists for practice and procedure. It is published in four units: the main work, 51 volumes of forms and precedents, is arranged in 148 subject groups. Within each title there are two or three parts as appropriate: Practice, an explanation of the courts and their practice and procedure on the topic; Procedural Tables, setting out step-by-step procedures to be followed in an action (only printed in titles devoted to a particular course of proceedings); and Forms, reprints of forms and precedents relevant to those proceedings. The second unit of *Atkin* is a Looseleaf Service which records changes to the Main Volumes through updating pages issued four times a year, concerned with forms, documents and proceedings not related to the Civil Procedure Rules. The third unit is a set of volumes giving the text of the Civil Procedure Rules (CPR) and accompanying Practice Directions, forms and commentary, updated through softback supplements issued regularly. The fourth unit is a consolidated index to the whole set, issued in revised form twice a year. The current, second edition was begun in 1961 and is kept up-to-date by the frequent issue of replacement volumes in the main work. Since the revised index is published twice a year, revisions provided in replacement volumes are quickly included. *Atkin* is normally used in four steps: look up the topic in the consolidated index, refer to the Main Volume, consult the Looseleaf Service for the latest developments since the Main Volume was published and, finally, if the research involves the Civil Procedure Rules, consult the CPR volumes and supplements. *Atkin's* is also available in CD format, in which the information in the Looseleaf Service is merged into the main work, making use easier. The CD also allows the user to fill in any form for a particular action and print it out as a word-processed document.

The Encyclopaedia of Forms and Precedents provides a wide range of non-litigious forms and precedents (i.e. forms and precedents used in legal transactions outside the courts) and is an authoritative guide to the drafting of legal documents. It is now in its fifth edition and comprises three units. The first unit comprises 42 Main Volumes, which provide a subject-by-subject presentation of forms and documents for nearly 100 different subjects. Each subject section is in two parts: first, Preliminary Notes, detailing the relevant law and, second, Precedents, with annotations to explain the purpose of particular clauses. The second unit is a loose-leaf updating service, and the final unit is an annual consolidated index to the whole work. The research sequence is in three steps: index, Main Volume, loose-leaf updating volume. *EFP* is also available in CD format with similar advantages to the user as described above for the CD version of *Atkin's*.

The very practical nature of precedent books means few undergraduate students will be likely to use these publications. However, the increasing accent on skills acquisition during all types of law course has resulted in more students practising how to draw up different types of document for transactions, using some of these sources.

8.1B   Finding information

Information sources which help you identify if relevant textbooks exist to assist your research may be divided into two classes: sources which restrict themselves to law; and general sources. Each class again divides into sources which cover new or recently published material, and those which include titles regardless of whether or not they are still in print. The boundary of the division does become rather blurred, so below publications are arranged in a very general sequence starting with in-print sources and gradually moving towards historical listings. As a result of using some of the sources noted you may discover details of books your library does not stock — see appendix 2 for information on the inter-library loans service.

8.1B1   Sources

8.1B1.1   Publishers' or bookshop catalogues

Each of the major law textbook publishers, Butterworths, Sweet & Maxwell, Blackstone Press etc., produces a list of current publications, with summaries of contents. Some issue lists of student textbooks specifically. Two of the largest law booksellers, Hammick's Bookshop and Law Notes Bookshop, publish annual catalogues listing thousands of titles arranged under broad subject headings. Hammick's Bookshop also produces for subscribers only, a CD version of its catalogue, regularly updated. But the research value of these publications is rather limited since they only cover what is in print at the time.

8.1B1.2   Current Law Monthly Digest

Towards the end of the subject entries in each issue of *Current Law Monthly Digest*, brief details of new books are given. Up to and including *Current Law Yearbook 1995* these references are consolidated into a single list near the back of each *Current Law Yearbook*. Since the *Yearbook* for 1996, entries for textbooks are given both at the end of the volume and at the end of each relevant subject section in the body of the volume. Perseverance is required when checking for new or recent publications in a particular subject over a period of years, because the subject headings used are quite broad, and the list does not cumulate year on year.

8.1B1.3   Lawyers' Law Books (3rd ed., 1997)

Subtitled 'a practical index to legal literature' this is a quite detailed subject-by-subject listing of encyclopaedias, periodicals and textbooks. There is no evaluation of the sources. Most texts listed were published after 1980 but a few older and still useful titles are also included. The combination of an arrangement by quite specific subject categories and the inclusion of both in-print, and out-of-print, titles makes this a valuable research source. It includes references to some CDs of practice and precedent books, but excludes CD versions of law reports and all internet sources.

8.1B1.4   Catalogues of major law libraries

The catalogues of two of the most important academic law libraries in the United Kingdom were published in the 1970s as one-off ventures. No volumes of more recent acquisitions have been published. The two libraries are the Squire Law Library, University of Cambridge, and the Institute of Advanced Legal Studies, University of London.

The advantage of these listings lay in the wealth of historical, obscure and long out-of-print material they include. Of course, they are not very helpful for current topics.

An increasing number of university libraries have made their library catalogues available on the internet. Often there are links to the library and the catalogue from the 'home page' of the university. Links to the web addresses of over 200 UK universities, higher education colleges and research sites are given on the University of Wolverhampton UK Sensitive Map at

> http://scitsc.wlv.ac.uk/ukinfo/uk.map.html

Most universities have access to JANET (Joint Academic Network), a network linking UK universities which pre-dates the internet. Many university catalaogues are accessible over JANET, so making it possible to search for material not in your own, home library, and then once you have identified a library with useful material, either visiting the library or using the inter-library loan service to bring the items to you (see appendix 2).

The catalogues of the Inns of Court Libraries, the libraries which serve barristers who practise in London, are available on the *Current Legal Information* (CLI) database, available as a CD or, to subscribers only, on the internet at

> http://193.118.187.160/cli.htm

The Inns are very old foundations and their libraries are especially rich in historical publications and those relevant to the practice of law. Although access in person to the libraries is restricted, the value of the database lies in identifying publications which might be sought in other libraries or by using the inter-library loan service (see appendix 2).

8.1B1.5   Law Books in Print

This is an American publication published every three years, which aims to list all law books in the English language from around the world in print at the time it is published.

8.1B1.6   Law Books Published

Another American publication, but issued twice a year, to act as a supplement
to *Law Books in Print* (see 8.1B1.5).

8.1B1.7   Law Books 1876–1981 plus supplements

A third American publication listing about 130,000 books published in English
(mainly in the United States) from 1876 onwards — supplements have been
issued since the original four volumes appeared, bringing the work more
up-to-date.

8.1B1.8   Current Publications in Legal and Related Fields

This American publication is issued nine times a year and lists English language
law books published in the United States, including many printed originally in
the UK. Its value lies in the short descriptions of the contents of books added
to many of the entries in the lists.

8.1B1.9   International Legal Books in Print

Published in two editions only (1990 and 1992), this two-volume work indexes
over 20,000 English-language legal texts and treatises in print published or
distributed within the UK, Western Europe and current or former Commonwealth countries. Entries are arranged by subject and some carry a brief
annotation describing the content of individual publications. There are separate
indexes for authors and titles.

8.1B2   General sources

8.1B2.1   Whitaker's Books in Print and BookBank CD

Formerly known as *British Books in Print, Whitaker's Books in Print*, lists titles
published in the UK with the addition of some English language titles published in
continental Europe. The paper version is published annually whilst a microfiche
edition is updated monthly. It lists over three quarters of a million titles in a single
alphabetical sequence of authors and titles. The disadvantage for research purposes
is that there is no subject listing — if you look up 'tax', for example, all books in
print with the word 'tax' appearing in the title will be listed, regardless, of whether
they deal with law, accountancy, economics, politics etc. But if the word 'tax' does
not appear in the title yet the book is about the topic, there will be no entry under
'tax'. This problem can be overcome by using the CD-ROM version, *BookBank*,
which will search on book titles, but also subtitles and series titles. In addition it is
possible to undertake very basic subject searches using the 'classification' search
key, but the publisher advises using this in combination with title or author. The
three quarters of a million books detailed in the database are assigned to only 53
subjects, one being 'law and public administration', so searching solely on this key

is likely to produce a long list of titles, very few of which may be relevant to your particular search enquiry. An enhanced version: *BookBank Global*, includes two million entries, including English language titles from the United States, Australasia, Southern Africa and Europe.

8.1B2.2   *British National Bibliography (BNB)*

BNB lists new works published in the British Isles and received under the Copyright Act 1911 by the Legal Deposit Office of the British Library. Unfortunately for lawyers the listing is not comprehensive, for it excludes some publications of The Stationery Office including Bills of Parliament, Local and Personal Acts, House of Commons and House of Lords Parliamentary debates, government circulars, regulations etc. *BNB* is in three sections: the subject index, which is an alphabetical index of subjects appearing in the classified subject catalogue; the classified subject catalogue itself, which lists publications according to the Dewey decimal classification scheme (as employed by the majority of libraries to arrange their stock), and finally, an alphabetical arrangement by author. Weekly lists are published, cumulated quarterly and, finally, into annual bound volumes. The usual way to research the publication is to look up the subject in which you are interested in the subject index, note the classification number and then consult the classified subject catalogue under that number. This laborious process can pay dividends since this is the most comprehensive listing of British publications. Considerable time and effort can be saved if you can gain access to either of the electronic versions: *BNB on CD-ROM* or the online version: *BNBMARC*.

8.1B2.3   *BookFind CD-ROM*

This is the general name for a database which libraries can purchase in several different versions. As *BookWise-CD*, it lists only UK published books and with minimum descriptions. In other versions, *Premier-CD*, for example, the coverage of English language publications is international, with full descriptions of the books listed. The decriptive notes to each entry make *BookFind* more useful than *BookBank* (see 8.1B2.1).

8.1C   Answering research queries

For background information on using CDs and the internet for legal research, see appendix 4.

Since there is such variety amongst the sources noted in 8.1B, you should read the descriptions given and select the titles most appropriate to your research needs.

8.2   ENCYCLOPAEDIAS

One definition of an encyclopaedia is 'an elaborate and exhaustive repertory of information on all the branches of some particular art or department of knowledge; especially one arranged in alphabetical order' (*Oxford English Dictionary*).

In the literature of English law there is one encyclopaedia which attempts to provide information on the whole extent of the law of England and Wales, in an alphabetical subject arrangement — *Halsbury's Laws of England* (see 6.1B5.1). Several others provide information on law and procedure as contained in particular types of publication — *Halsbury's Statutes of England* (see 4.2B2.3.1), *Halsbury's Statutory Instruments* (see 5.1B2.4), *Atkin's Court Forms* (see 8.1) and *The Encyclopaedia of Forms and Precedents* (see 8.1 also). The *Halsbury's Laws* publication is available in electronic form over the internet to subscribers to the Butterworths Direct service. *Atkin's* and *The Encyclopaedia of Forms and Precedents* are available in both paper and CD formats. The most important Scottish title in this category is *Laws of Scotland* (see 12B4.1).

A third category takes a closely defined area of law and provides either, a commentary arranged alphabetically by topic, or reproduces all the relevant statutes, secondary legislation and extra-legal sources on the topic, with footnotes on relevant cases and additional editorial comment. Most, if not all, of the examples of this type of encyclopaedia are published entirely in loose-leaf format, which means publishers can issue 'releases' of pages containing updated information at frequent intervals, for subscribers to insert in the binders and also remove superseded material. These publications are valuable in legal research because (a) they cover a discrete legal topic in depth; (b) they include a wide range of legal source publications, including extra-legal sources which can be difficult to track down otherwise; and (c) they are regularly kept up-to-date. An increasing number are becoming available in CD format.

The range of legal topics covered in encyclopaedic loose-leaf format grows every year. Tax law, for example, which changes frequently, is served by several encyclopaedias. Butterworths, Sweet & Maxwell, CCH Editions, and other major law publishers all produce encyclopaedias. Sweet & Maxwell group together a number in a series entitled 'Local Government Library', covering such topics as planning, compulsory purchase, rating, housing, environmental health, road traffic and local government law in general.

How do you discover if there is an encyclopedia available on the subject in which you are interested? First, check your law library's catalogue by subject, and watch for any entries with the word 'encyclopaedia' (which some publishers like to spell without the 'a') in the title. Secondly, if you cannot spot any from the catalogue ask the library staff for assistance or, alternatively, look in either *Lawyers' Law Books* (see 8.1B1.3) or one of the major law bookshop catalogues (see 8.1B1.1).

Before using one of these specialist encyclopaedias in their paper format, check the pages at the beginning of the volume which tell you how recently the information given has been updated. If the last 'release' was more than a year ago, it is a clear indication that the updating of the work has lapsed and you should enquire with library staff. It could be dangerous to cite from a loose-leaf work which is badly out-of-date. Even when using the electronic version, check that it is up-to-date — many CDs carry 'issue information' in the introductory screens or sometimes it is necessary to click on 'Help' or 'About this CD'.

8.3   PERIODICALS

8.3A   Description

8.3A1   Definition

Periodicals, also referred to as journals or magazines, have been a feature of legal literature since the 1760s. They are normally published as individual *issues*, which at predetermined intervals are gathered together to form a *volume* with a title page and/or index. Each issue is characterised by a variety of contents: *articles, news, notes* and *digests* of information; and a variety of contributors. The law periodicals you may need to use during your studies can be divided into five types:

(a)   Those of primarily academic interest, such as *Cambridge Law Journal, Law Quarterly Review, Modern Law Review* and the *Oxford Journal of Legal Studies*. They generally contain lengthy, analytical articles, often the product of considerable research. Notes of recent cases and legal developments are included by most, and since the periodicals are published quarterly or even less frequently, what they may lack in currency they make up for in thoroughness.

(b)   Practitioners' periodicals, for example, *Solicitors' Journal, New Law Journal* and the *Gazette*. Published approximately weekly, they contain short articles on a wide range of legal topics of interest to practising lawyers, including staff and office management, marketing and promotion, computer and information technology applications for lawyers. Case notes, digests of recent developments, practice notes, book reviews, professional news and advertisements for vacancies and services are also included.

(c)   Specialist periodicals covering particular areas of law, for example, *Criminal Law Review, Journal of Business Law, Family Law, Civil Justice Quarterly*. This is one of the growth areas in legal publishing. These titles usually include articles, case notes, notes on practice and procedure and comment on recent legal developments.

(d)   Newsletters: a recent development in law publishing, newsletters are often only a few pages long, but published frequently. They tend to contain topical information and comment rather than the more comprehensive analysis found in other types of periodical. Most are intended for use by practitioners, and include titles such as *Lloyd's Maritime Law Newsletter, Business Law Brief* or *Simon's Tax Intelligence*. A few are produced by the larger law firms, primarily for client companies and organisations, but are also made more widely available. Yet others are published by pressure groups, such as the Howard League for Penal Reform (*Criminal Justice*).

(e)   Law periodicals published abroad, particularly in other common law jurisdictions, such as the United States, Canada, Australia and New Zealand. They are the overseas equivalents of those given as examples in (a) above. Most academic law libraries will subscribe to a selection.

As well as these publications designed specifically for lawyers, useful information, particularly on the impact of law on a particular section of business, commerce or society, will be carried by non-law periodicals, e.g., titles such as *Economist, New Statesman and Society, Spectator, British Journal of Criminology* and *Town and Country Planning*.

The quality newspapers also carry regular features on legal topics.

So, the number of sources in which useful information for your essay, assignment or project might be found is vast. But as 8.3B shows, there are ways of methodically and efficiently, exploring and exploiting this literature.

8.3A2   Publication and general availability

Most academic law libraries are likely to subscribe to a wide range of academic and practitioner periodicals. The range of specialist periodicals will depend on the particular interests of the teaching department. Some newsletters may be taken, but again the titles purchased will reflect the interests of the law department. The quality newspapers should be available and some of the non-law specialist periodicals, again depending on the teaching interests of the particular university or college.

Public libraries, on the other hand, are likely to take only a very limited number of law titles, such as *New Law Journal* and *Solicitors' Journal*, the quality newspapers and a few of the major non-law specialist periodicals.

The recent issues of a small number of British law journals, mainly those which have a large readership such as the practitioner periodicals, are available on the internet. For example, the *Gazette*, and *New Law Journal* will be found at:

http://www.lawgazette.co.uk

http://www.butterworths.com/nlj/index.htm

At the time of writing there are just three Britsh electronic law journals — that is, journals published initially if not solely on the internet, and not by conventional means. *Web Journal of Current Legal Issues* started in 1995 and covers topics of general interest. It will be found at

http://webjcli.ncl.ac.uk/

Journal of Information, Law and Technology (often referred to as JILT), specialises in law with an IT context. It is at

http://elj.warwick.ac.uk/jilt/

The third electronic journal, *Mountbatten Journal of Legal Studies*, is rather different. It is managed and edited by students of the Law Faculty at Southampton Institute, but carries articles written by eminent lawyers. It is at

http://www.solent.ac.uk/law/silrd.html

A large number of journals published in the United States and a few European titles also, are published on the internet either in full text or in summary. The best site to view this array of electronic publishing is at Washburn University School of Law:

http://www.washlaw.edu/lawjournal.html

8.3A3   Citation

Lawyers frequently abbreviate the title of a journal in which an article they are quoting appears. There are no generally accepted standards for abbreviating titles and a wide variety of practices occur. You may frequently need to use one of the following lists of abbreviations to sort out the journal to which you are being referred:

(a)   Raistrick D., *Index to Legal Citations and Abbreviations* (London: Bowker-Saur, 2nd ed., 1993).

(b)   *Current Law Case Citator* (London: Sweet & Maxwell), any issue.

(c)   French, D., *How to Cite Legal Authorities* (London: Blackstone Press, 1996).

(d)   The compilers of *Legal Journals Index* (Hebden Bridge: Legal Information Resources Ltd) occasionally issue a list of abbreviations used within the database, with an online version at

http://www.smlawpub.co.uk/product/abbrevs/abbrevs.cfm

Ignore the first screen; the list starts lower down the file.

8.3B   Finding information

Many students make the mistake, when looking for periodical articles to assist preparation of an essay or assignment, of browsing through the contents pages or annual indexes of one or two of the major periodicals, in the hope of stumbling over relevant, valuable information. This method is not always productive and costs considerable time and effort. The most efficient way of finding relevant periodical articles is to use an indexing publication: a commercially produced index to the contents of tens if not hundreds of periodicals, with references to each article arranged under appropriate subject headings. *Legal Journals Index, Lawtel, Current Law* and *Index to Legal Periodicals* are the four indexing services relevant to the law of England and Wales. But, as a law student, you may occasionally need to research subjects related to law, such as criminology or social control, so publications including *Criminology, Penology and Police Science Abstracts* and *Sociological Abstracts* are briefly noted below. Finally, newspapers often contain useful background articles on recent legal developments, or publish journalistic reports of notable court cases, which may never appear as authentic law reports. Examples include instances where sentencing policy or the level of awards of damages are in question or where the reliability of original forensic evidence is now doubted. Therefore a description of newspaper indexes, including *The Times Index*, and the *Clover Newspaper Index* is also provided.

8.3B1   Legal Journals Index

Legal Journals Index or *LJI* was first published in September 1986 and has appeared in paper form at monthly intervals ever since. During 2000, the paper version will be withdrawn and users will rely on the well-established CD and internet versions. It quickly established itself as the foremost law periodical indexing service for the United Kingdom for two reasons:

(a)   It indexes a very large number of periodicals — over 400 different titles published throughout the United Kingdom, including over 85 English language legal journals published in European Union countries.

(b)   Its subject coverage is very wide, including not only law as such but also topics such as the legal profession, education, training, computers and information technology generally.

The 'look' and search possibilities of the two electronic versions are quite different because, for technical reasons, the different formats cannot use the same software. In the internet version the complete file of entries from 1986 onwards can be searched in one go, but the CD version splits the database according to date, over two CDs: a Current Disc and an Archive Disc. So, to search the whole period from 1986 to the present means switching fom one disc to another and repeating the search. The split between the two discs occurs in the early 1990s. This is not really a problem, just something important to remember if you are undertaking a search for information on pre-1990 articles. In most universities and colleges the two discs are networked and, to switch between discs, the user simply clicks on the Archive Disc button on the menu screen, to reach the historical file. To return to the latest disc, click on the Current Disc button on the archive disc menu screen.

The CD version is updated monthly but the internet version is updated daily. The internet version is obviously the best to use for information about the latest articles. However, the CD version has five advantages over the internet version:

(a)   The CD version offers the possibility of restricting your search to any field into which a record of a journal article has been divided. This is especially useful if the words on which you are searching could be the names of an author (Banks) as well as a subject, for example: banks. In the internet version there is only a single box into which you type a request and no way to restrict the search.

(b)   The CD version displays a word wheel which, when you type in a request, displays words of similar spelling found in the database. This device is very useful for identifying when the use of a wild card will retrieve an increased number of relevant items. For example, typing in the word negligence will restrict the search to the occurence of this word alone. Using the stem of the word and adding a symbol called a wild card, will retreive more items: negligen*. This search will retrieve items containing the words negligence, negligent, negligently.

(c)   The CD version displays the results of a search in a single sequence complete with summaries. It is easy to scroll down the information to identify relevant material. In contrast, the internet version displays the results in two steps. First, the results of a search are displayed as a list with only a single line of information about each item retreived. To view the summary of any article to check whether it is relevant, it is necessary to take a second step and click on the relevant line of information to open the individual summary.

(d)   As a result of the way in which information is presented on screen, it is far easier to print or download information from the CD version than the internet version, especially if you have undertaken a subject search and found many relevant articles.

(e)   The *CLI* web site in which the *LJI* database resides is subscribed to by many practising lawyers as well as universities and colleges. Sometimes, especially during normal office hours, the site can run slowly or even 'freeze'. There is nothing you or your university or college can do when this happens, except be patient and try again in the evening or at weekends, when traffic is lighter. On the other hand, the CD version runs on a computer in your university or college, which will be faster to access and usually more stable.

An online index to the abbreviations used in the index is available on the internet at

  http://www.smlawpub.co.uk/product/abbrevs/abbrevs.cfm

Ignore the first screen; the list starts lower down the file.

8.3B2   *Financial Journals Index*

This index started in 1992 as a sister to *LJI* and is available only on CD or via the internet. It indexes about 90 journals specific to insurance, pensions, banking and financial services law generally. It is of most use to students studying specialist subjects in the final years of their undergraduate studies or undertaking postgraduate work. The web site address is the same as for *LJI* and a list of journals it indexes and the abbreviations it uses for them is also given at the same web address as given in section 8.3B1.

8.3B3   *Lawtel*

Like *LJI*, *Lawtel* provides an index of journal articles and short abstracts. However the coverage of journal titles and dates is considerably restricted. It indexes only around 50 journals and most of these from only January 1998 onwards. In contrast, *Lawtel* does posses a minor advantage over *LJI*, in that it contains the full text of three journals: *The Lawyer* (1994–), *The Legal Executive* (1996–98) and *The Builder* (June 1998–). Lawtel is available to subscribers at

  http://www.lawtel.co.uk

If a you have a choice between using *LJI* and *Lawtel*, *LJI* is to be preferred for the reasons noted.

8.3B4   Current Law Monthly Digest

Current Law Monthly Digest or *CL* has been published monthly since 1947. It indexes law periodicals published throughout the United Kingdom. At the end of each year index entries are cumulated into a single, bound volume, *Current Law Yearbook* (*CLY*). *CL*, in contrast to *LJI*, indexes a more restricted range of periodicals since it is concerned only with the law as such. As a paper publication it lacks the speed and flexibility of searching that the electronic *LJI* possesses.

Information is arranged in *CL* under very broad subject headings. Where an article is noticed by the compilers it is mentioned in one of the final entries under each subject heading.

The presentation of the same information in *Current Law Yearbook*, the annual cumulation, is different. Up to and including the *Yearbook* for 1995, references to articles were removed from the main sequence in the body of the *Yearbook* and arranged in a separate sequence towards the back of the volume, but still under broad subject headings. References to individual periodical articles were arranged under each subject heading in alphabetical order by the first word in the title. From the *Yearbook* for 1996 onwards the arrangement is the same as in *CL*, simply a list of articles under the headings in the body, and no list at the back of the volume.

The arrangement of entries in the lists is not very helpful for three reasons: the subject headings under which the references are arranged are very broad, for example, environmental law, public health; second, the individual references are arranged alphabetically by the first word in the title rather than by more specific subject categories; and third, some of the titles of the articles are enigmatic or too brief to give much idea of the content of the article itself — there are no helpful summaries. The references in *CL* and *CLY* to periodical titles are abbreviated, so you will need to use the list of abbreviations, printed elsewhere in the publication, to expand the title fully, before you can check your library's periodical holdings list to see if the original periodical is in stock.

CL and *CLY* do not include case or legislation indexes, so it is difficult to find articles about a specific case or Act.

8.3B5   Index to Legal Periodicals

Index to Legal Periodicals or *ILP* has been published since 1908. It is an American publication, issued 11 times a year, with quarterly and annual cumulations. It indexes over 750 periodical titles and, as you might expect, they are mainly United States publications but it also includes major titles published in Canada, Australia, New Zealand, Ireland and Great Britain. It is valuable for the references it contains to overseas writing on UK law, and on occasions when you need to compare practice and procedure in UK law with that in another common law jurisdiction (when you are studying comparative law).

There are four separate indexes in each issue: a combined subject and author index, which is the one you will probably find most useful, a Table of Cases, which is an index to periodical articles or notes on cases (the majority are to non-UK cases), a Table of Statutes, which is an index to articles on statutes (again, mainly non-UK) and, finally, an index to book reviews.

The layout of the combined subject and author index is helpful, as figure 8.1 shows. Just beneath some subject headings a 'see' reference guides you to the preferred heading used by the indexer for a topic. Some subject headings have lists of 'see also' reference which guide you to entries on related subjects, elsewhere in the publication. These 'see' and 'see also' references are especially useful because, being an American publication, it uses transatlantic terminology. For example, there are no entries under 'murder' but the index will guide you to the preferred term 'homicide'.

As with the other periodical indexing services discussed above, the titles of individual periodicals indexed are much abbreviated and to expand the title you will need to consult the list printed at the front of each issue.

For a periodical article to appear in *ILP* it must be at least five 'ordinary' pages or two folio pages in length. This means the short articles in practitioners' periodicals are not included. So, coupled with its distinctive American bias, *ILP* is not the first periodical indexing service to consult when undertaking legal research, except if you specifically require material for comparative law.

CD and internet versions of *ILP* contain the index entries from August 1981 onwards. They are quick and easy to use.

8.3B6   *Halsbury's Laws of England — Noter-Up and Annual Abridgements*

Since 1990, articles from a limited number of the leading practice and academic periodicals have been indexed in the Noter-Up and Annual Abridgements under broad subject headings, which correspond to those used in the arrangement of information in the Main Volumes of this encyclopaedic work. The most recent articles are listed in the loose-leaf Noter-Up binder. At the end of the year they are incorporated in the Annual Abridgement volume. The arrangement of individual articles under a subject heading is by the first word in the title chosen by the author, so searching can be tedious. There are no cross-references to ensure readers are guided to the most appropriate heading for their query. However, since *Halsbury's Laws* is so widely available in libraries it is a valuable stand-by, but not the first publication to consider using for research on the periodical literature.

8.3B7   *LEXIS*

LEXIS contains the full text of only a handful of English law periodicals. Issues of two are included from 1986 onwards, the remainder from more recent dates. To search the periodicals select the ENGGEN library and the UK journal file, entitled UKJNL, and then select whether you wish to search all the files in that library (i.e., all the periodical titles) or just an individual title. Your search request could be either for a subject, or an author, or mention of an Act or case by name, which you should type in the form you believe it would be mentioned in the text of the periodical. Because of its restricted coverage of journal titles, *LEXIS* compares very unfavourably with *LJI* and *Lawtel*.

Figure 8.1 Extract from subject and author index of *Index to Legal Periodicals 1989–90*.

SUBJECT AND AUTHOR INDEX 419

L

Subjects and authors inter-filed in a single alphabetical sequence

Subject heading under which references on labor arbitration will be found

Note American spelling

Subject heading

Kapperman, Joel J.
Relations between the sexes ti ...
25 *San Diego L. Rev.* 1C

Karoda, Kenji
Beware of Japanese negotiation style: how to ...
with Japanese companies; by D. Zhang, K. ...
10 *Nw. J. Int'l L. & Bus.* 195-212 Fall '89

Kurt, Maxine
Report of the public employee relations committee.
M. Kurtz, S. Levian, J. Toole. 21 *Urb. Law.* 94:
Fall '89

Karucza, Robert M.
Securities and investment advisory activities of banks;
by R. M. Kurucza, R. G. Ballen, N. H. Diana. 45
Bus. Law. 1919-29 Je '90
Securities and investment advisory activities of banks;
by R M Kurucza, R. G. Ballen, T. R. McTaggart.

Controls on technology transfer: an analysis of the
Southern response to Northern technological protec-
tionism. 13 *Md. J. Int'l L. & Trade* 301-29 Spr '89
Performance of electric utilities in developing countries:
the Ghanaian and Nigerian experience. 11 *Loy. L.A.*
Int'l & Comp. LJ. 515

Kurzban, Ira J.
Employer sanctions—two y ...
Ja '90

Kushner, James A.
An unfinished agenda: the ...
ment effort. 6 *Yale L. & Pol'y Rev.* 348-60 '88

Kushner, Joseph
... risk, and size in Canadian banks and trust

Ketler, Stanley I.
A sword for a scabbard: reflections on the making of
the Judiciary Act of 1789. 14 *Nova L. Rev.* 97-110
Fall '89

La Fleur, Catherine A.
Duty to defend: does a four corners approach cover
all the bases? by D. H. Piper, C. A. La Fleur. 62
Wis. Law. 19-20+ Jl '89

La Fond, John Q.
Washington's diminished capacity defense under attack;
by J. Q. La Fond, K. A. Gaddis. 13 *U. Puget Sound*
L. Rev. 1-39 Fall '89

Laberge, Danielle
Femmes et criminalité: le contrôle social est-il sexué?
Une analyse des données statistiques québécoises; by
D. Laberge, S. Roy. 3 *Can. J. Women & L.* 457-64
'89/'90

LaBerge, Robert A.
Some of the more exotic risks associated with drug
and alcohol testing; by L. P. DiLorenzo, R. A. LaBerge,
W. M. Burke. 42 *N.Y.U. Conf. Lab.* 6.1-.38 '89

Labor, Migrant *See* Migrant labor
Labor arbitration *See* Industrial arbitration
Labor boycotts

Picketir ...

Handbill ... and the first amendment a symbiotic rela-
tio ...? The impact of DeBartolo v. Florida Building
...s Council [108 S. Ct. 1392] J. P. Tietborg. 41
...ab. LJ. 235-48 Ap '90

industrial protection: a new advance—the use of "employer injunctions" by trade unions. M. L. Worsnop.
63 *Law Inst. J.* 1046-8 N '89

Secondary boycotts after DeBartolo [Edward J. DeBartolo
Corp. v. Florida Gulf Coast Building & Construction
Trades Council, 108 S. Ct. 1392]: has the Supreme
Court handed unions a powerful new weapon? 75
Iowa L. Rev. 217-34 O '89

Labor disputes
See also
Collective bargaining
Industrial arbitration
Labor boycotts
Unfair labor practices

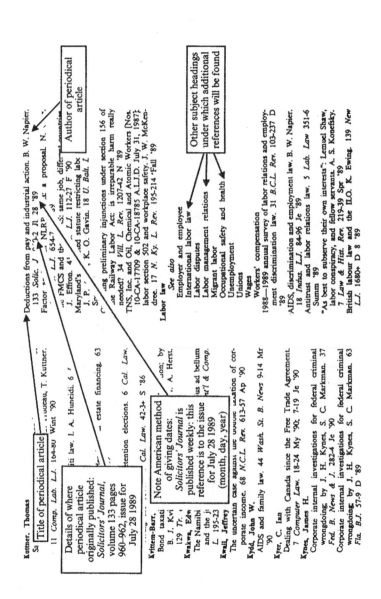

Author of periodical article

Deductions from pay and industrial action. B. W. Napier.
133 *Solic. J* __-2 Jl 28 '89
Factor ~ __ LJ __ NLRP ___ __r a proposal N. __ __

__ FMCS and th__ __S: same job, differ__ __ __
J. Effron. 4' __ __. LJ. 112-27 F '90
Maryland's __ __ __d statute restricting labo
J. P. __ __, K. O. Gavin. 18 *U. Balt. I*
S__

__ __ __ung preliminary injunctions under section 156 of
__ __e Railway Labor Act: is irreparable harm really
needed? 34 *Vill. L. Rev.* 1207-42 N '89
TNS, Inc. and Oil, Chemical and Atomic Workers [Nos.
10-CA-17709 & 10-CA-18785 A.L.J.D. July 31, 1987]
labor section 502 and workplace safety. J. W. McKen-
dree. 17 *N. Ky. L. Rev.* 195-214 'Fall '89

Labor law

Other subject headings under which additional references will be found

See also
Employer and employee
International labor law
Labor disputes
Labor management relations
Migrant labor
Occupational safety and health
Unemployment
Unions
Wages
Workers' compensation
1988—1989 annual survey of labor relations and employ-
ment discrimination law. 31 *B.C.L. Rev.* 103-237 D
'89
AIDS, discrimination and employment law. B. W. Napier.
18 *Indus. LJ.* 84-96 Je '89
Antitrust and labor relations law. 5 *Lab. Law* 351-6
Summ '89
"As best to subserve their own interests": Lemuel Shaw,
labor conspiracy, and fellow servants. A. S. Konefsky.
7 *Law & Hist. Rev.* 219-39 Spr '89
British labour law and the ILO. K. O. Ewing. 139 *New
LJ.* 1680+ D 8 '89

Kuttner, Thomas
Se **Title of periodical article**
11 *Comp. Lab. LJ.* 104-80 Wint '90

Details of where periodical article originally published: *Solicitors' Journal*, volume 133 pages 960-962, issue for July 28 1989

iti law. I. A. Huneidi. 6 __ __ __
__state financing. 63

__tention elections. 6 *Cal. Law.*

Cal. Law. 42-3+ S '86

Kritem-Barr,
Bond taxati __
B. J. Kvi
129 *Tr.* __
Kwakwa, Edw
The Namibi __
and the ji __
L 195-23

Krall, Jeffrey
The uncertain case against __.e __usoble __xation of corporate income. 68 *N.C.L. Rev.* 613-57 Ap '90

Kydd, John W.
AIDS and family law. 44 *Wash. St. B. News* 9-14 Mr
'90

Note American method of giving dates: *Solicitors' Journal* is published weekly: this reference is to the issue for July 28 1989 (month, day, year)

__ion; by
__. A. Herst

__us ad bellum
__n'l & Comp.

Kyer, C. Ian
Dealing with Canada since the Free Trade Agreement.
7 *Computer Law.* 18-24 My '90; 7-19 Je '90
Kynes, James H.
Corporate internal investigations for federal criminal
wrongdoing, by J. H. Kynes, S. C. Markman. 37
Fed. B. News & J. 282-4 Je '90
Corporate internal investigations for federal criminal
wrongdoing, by J. H. Kynes, S. C. Markman. 63
Fla. BJ. 57-9 D '89

8.3B8 LegalTrac

Formerly known as *Legal Resource Index*, this database is available on CD and by subscription on the internet. The database is updated monthly and covers the period 1980 onwards. It indexes over 850 English-language periodicals, most of which are published in America. Some English titles are included. It specialises in indexing law reviews, legal newspapers, bar association journals and special subject publications often in law-related subjects, such as criminology.

8.3B9 Criminology, Penology and Police Science Abstracts

This publication has undergone several changes of title. It commenced publication as *Excerpta Criminologica* (1961–68), then *Abstracts on Criminology and Penology* (1969–79), followed by *Criminology and Penology Abstracts* (1980–93). Although a Dutch publication, it is an international abstracting service which includes references to articles on criminal procedure and the administration of justice. Over 350 periodicals covering sociology, criminology, medicine, psychology as well as law are included in the quarterly issues. *Criminology , Penology and Police Science Abstracts* is an *abstracting* service so each entry includes more information than that appearing in an *indexing* service. In addition to the details of where to find the original article, the compilers provide a brief, descriptive summary of each article ('the abstract') which helps you to decide whether the article is relevant to your research, before spending time tracing the original in the library.

8.3B10 Sociological Abstracts

Sociological Abstracts (or *SA*) an American publication, began in 1953 and is published six times a year. Its coverage is international and entries are compiled from over 2,500 periodicals. Details of articles, with abstracts, are arranged under over 30 broad subject headings, one of which: social control, includes references to articles on the sociology of law, police, penology and correctional problems. Each entry not only includes details of where an article was originally published but also a brief summary of its contents. A CD version contains entries from 1963 to the present. Its advantage over the paper version is that it is possible to search on all the words used in the database.

8.3B11 Applied Social Science Index and Abstracts

ASSIA, as it is commonly called, indexes English language social science journals from 1987 onwards. Like the publication in the next entry, *British Humanities Index*, its value stems from the wide subject coverage — the two publications might be termed 'umbrella' services. *ASSIA* provides references to and summaries of articles on topics such as employment, race relations, health, education, politics, women's studies and criminology. The CD is updated four times a year.

8.3B12   British Humanities Index

BHI covers the whole field of the humanities including the arts, economics, history, philosophy, politics and society, as well as non-specialist articles in science and technology. It indexes major newspaper articles as well as journals. This width of subject coverage is valuable when researching the impact of law on society; for example, articles in non-legal journals on housing law or reform of the law on homelessness will feature in *BHI*. Over 200 journals are indexed. *BHI* is published quarterly with a cumulated, annual bound volume published at the year end. The layout and presentation of index entries is good; 'see' and 'see also' references are amply provided and brief, descriptive notes of the content of articles where the title of the original article is not very informative, are available.

Because of its wide subject coverage *BHI* is one of the few indexing services mentioned in this section of the book which will be found in most academic *and* public libraries.

The CD version, BHIPlus, includes over 100,000 indexed articles from over 320 key humanities journals and daily newspapers from 1985 to the present. The disc is updated with the same frequency as the paper version.

8.3B13   BIDS

BIDS was launched in 1991 and use is free to staff and students of universities and colleges which subscribe. A *BIDS* username and password are required to get into this internet service. *BIDS* is a service which hosts a number of commercial databases, the most useful of which for lawyers are the ISI Citation Indexes (in particular *Social Sciences Citation Index*) and *International Bibliography of the Social Sciences* (*IBSS*). The Citation Indexes not only index journal articles from a huge number of international journals, in a wide range of subjects including law, but also enable users to extend their searches considerably since the list of references given at the end of each original journal article is also displayed. It is possible, therefore, to trace the most frequently cited or key articles and authors for any topic. The *Social Science Citation Index* covers the period 1981 onwards. *IBSS*, on the other hand, is more specialised, indexing over 2,400 selected international social science journals and around 7,000 books published from 1951 onwards. Its subject coverage focuses on economics, sociology, politics and anthropology. *IBSS* is updated weekly. Both *IBSS* and *BIDS* are services not normally used to gather information for your law coursework but for the preparation of extended studies such as projects, dissertations or theses, particularly on topics which border the study of law.

8.3B14   The Times Index and newspaper CDs

The Times Index is compiled from *The Times,* the *Sunday Times* and the various *Times* literary and educational supplements. It is an exhaustive monthly index (cumulated each year) to the entire contents of these publications. The individual index entries are so detailed as to include the date, page and column reference (lettered a to h from the left of the page) to where original articles will be found! The major problem with *The Times Index* is that it takes time to compile and publish, so the most recent issue is always at least three months behind the latest issue of the newspaper itself. Virtually every academic and major public library will take *The Times Index.*

The disadvantages of the paper version have been overcome by the CD and internet versions. A number of newspapers are now available on CD-ROM. The list includes *The Times, Sunday Times, Guardian, Independent* and the *Financial Times.* Each individual disc contains the full text of one of the newspapers, but generally only for 1990 onwards. Usually, the CDs are updated quarterly, so they are no use for research into very recent legal comment. Many of the daily newspapers have web sites. However, the *Independent* does not include law reports on its web site and it is possible only to search by date (not subject) across *The Times* site. New developments occur quickly in electronic publishing; your library staff will be able to advise on current availability and coverage.

8.3B15   *Clover Newspaper Index*

This index is available in paper form, as a CD and over the internet. The internet version is available only to subscribers; a user name and password are required to use it. The database commenced in 1986 and indexes all the quality newspapers (in alphabetical order: *Daily Telegraph, Financial Times, Guardian, Independent, Observer, Sunday Times* and *The Times*) and their 'colour supplements'. The internet version is updated fortnightly, but an unedited version for the latest week is usually placed on the site within 24 hours of the end of the week. Although the subject indexing is basic and the only information given about each article is its title (in its original, attenuated journalese), the index is, nonetheless, very useful because of its good currency. The CD version carries additional keywords and key phrases.

8.3B16   *British Newspaper Index (BNI)*

This CD contains the indexes to nine quality newspapers including *The Times* and its literary and education supplements (1990–), *Sunday Times* (1990–), *Financial Times* (1990–), *Guardian* and *Observer* (1995–), *Independent* and *Independent on Sunday* (both 1991–) and *Sunday Telegraph* (1997–). There are two discs in the set, one covering 1990–94, the other 1995 to date. The discs have to be searched separately. The current disc is up-dated cumulatively every three months.

8.3C   Answering research queries

For background information on using CDs and the internet for legal research, see appendix 4.

The sources you should use and exploit will depend on the type of information you require and how current the topic. If the subject is of very recent origin then you may find that only the most rapidly updated electronic databases such as the internet version of *Legal Journals Index* or *Lawtel* will be of value.

To help you match appropriate paper and/or electronic sources to the subject you want to research, a few general suggestions of titles to search are listed below; it will be profitable if, before you start your research, you talk over your precise information needs with library staff, who will be best able to advise on the most relevant sources and, more importantly, those readily available.

For English law use either the electronic databases: *Legal Journals Index* (see 8.3B1) or *Lawtel* (see 8.3B3), or the paper sources *Current Law* (see 8.3B4) or *Halsbury's Laws* (see 8.3B6).

For English law compared with other common law jurisdictions use one or more of: *Legal Journals Index* (see 8.3B1), *Index to Legal Periodicals* (see 8.3B5), *LegalTrac* (see 8.3B8).

For information on the profession of law and topics related to law use: *Legal Journals Index* (see 8.3B1) or *Lawtel* (see 8.3B3).

For information on related topics select from: *Financial Journals Index* (see 8.3B2), *LegalTrac* (see 8.3B8), *Criminology, Penology and Police Science Abstracts* (see 8.3B9), *Sociological Abstracts* (see 8.3B10), *ASSIA* (see 8.3B11), *British Humanities Index* (see 8.3B12), *BIDS* (see 8.3B13).

For information which might have appeared in newspapers select from: *The Times Index* and newspaper CDs (see 8.3B14), *Clover Newspaper Index* (see 8.3B15), *British Newspaper Index* (see 8.3B16).

8.4   RESEARCH LITERATURE

8.4A   Description

Particularly when you are undertaking a final-year project, dissertation or longer piece of investigative writing, you may wish to check whether anyone else has completed, or is currently undertaking, postgraduate (e.g., masters or doctorate) or other advanced research into the precise topic or a related area in which you are interested. A number of lists or indexes of research are published and will be collected by academic libraries; you are unlikely to find public libraries keeping them. Usually under six copies of higher degree dissertations or theses are produced by the author, and one will be deposited in the library of the university or polytechnic at which the degree was awarded. It is necessary, therefore, to use the lists or indexes as a means of identifying relevant work and then ask your own library to obtain a copy of the thesis or dissertation via the inter-library loan service (see appendix 2 on how to use this service). The written product of research undertaken other than for a higher degree, for example, by a group of staff in a university, college or other institution, may be even more difficult to trace. It could be a research paper or memorandum published by the teaching department, or one or a series of periodical articles. One of the lists of ongoing research, *Current Research in Britain*, is valuable because it gives the names of the researchers and their departmental address, so you will be able to write to them seeking information about their research project and any published results.

However, before you decide to write, ensure you have checked sources of information about books (see 8.1) and periodical articles (see 8.3), so you are already aware of any material published by the researcher(s) and can decide whether your enquiry with them is going to be a worthwhile use of both your, and their, time and effort.

8.4B   Finding information

8.4B1   Legal Research in the United Kingdom 1905–1984

Information for this list of completed research was collected by a survey, conducted by one of the leading academic legal research organisations, the Institute of Advanced Legal Studies (IALS), London, of over 40 universities and colleges throughout the UK. The list is arranged in alphabetical order by subject and within each subject chronologically. The only information given about the content and subject-matter of each thesis is its title. Author and geographical indexes (i.e., by jurisdiction) are also provided. This publication was updated for a few years by an annual publication: *List of Current Legal Research Topics.* It ceased in October 1988 and has never been revived, so it is necessary to rely on the databases and publications listed below, which cover a wide range of subjects, of which law is just one.

8.4B2   Index to Theses

Index to Theses is the only comprehensive listing of British theses (regardless of subject). Unfortunately, the theses awarded at some Scottish universities are not included. It commenced in 1950. From 1986 onwards the *Index* has appeared in four parts each year, listing over 9,000 theses annually, each entry including a substantial abstract or summary of the contents of the thesis. This publication is useful because it includes theses in subjects related to law as well as law itself. It is available as a CD under the title: *Index to Theses Online* and, to subscribers only, on the internet. Both electronic versions cover the period 1970 to the present only. Ask your library staff to which electronic format the library subscribes.

8.4B3   Current Research in Britain

This is a national register of current research being carried out in universities, colleges and other institutions (e.g., government departments) within the UK. It is published in four sections, the volume for social sciences, revised annually, being most relevant to law. Each entry in the list includes details of the name of the principal investigator, and a brief description of the research topic and any publications. The entries are arranged by institution and department where the research is being undertaken, but helpfully constructed subject and keyword indexes at the back of the volume, allow information to be found by other routes. A CD version of this source is available under the title *CRIB*.

8.4B4   Dissertation Abstracts International

First published in 1938, this is now a monthly compilation of abstracts of doctoral dissertations submitted to over 400 educational institutions in the United States and Canada. *Dis. Abs.*, as it is commonly known, is divided into two sections, law dissertations featuring in section A, which covers the humanities and social sciences (section B is not relevant to law). The considerable interest in UK law shown by overseas researchers is apparent, even from the most cursory glance over the subject indexes. *Dis. Abs.* can be searched electronically either by subscribers to a number of on-line host organisations or from a CD — ask your library staff for details of which service is available.

8.4C   Answering research queries

For background information on using CDs and the internet for legal research, see appendix 4.

Are you searching for the products of research, i.e., theses and research publications? If so, use: *Legal Research in the United Kingdom 1905–1984* (see 8.4B1), *Index to Theses* (see 8.4B2), *Dissertation Abstracts* (see 8.4B4).

Are you searching for the names of people currently engaged in research? If so use *Current Research in Britain* (see 8.4B3).

8.5   REFERENCE WORKS

8.5A   Description

The catch-all term 'reference works' embraces three distinct types of publication: dictionaries: which usually explain the meaning of legal terms and phrases; directories: which provide names and addresses of individuals and organisations; compendia: which provide a concise introduction to law.

The range of individual titles available is enormous and what follows is but a brief guide to the wide selection you will find in most law libraries. Scottish reference works are discussed in section 13.4.

8.5A1   Dictionaries

These fall into four groups:

(a)   Conventional dictionaries, which provide an explanation of a word or phrase to varying degrees of detail.

(b)   Judicial dictionaries of words and phrases, which provide details of and quotations from statutes and cases where the courts have considered the meaning of each word or phrase.

(c)   Indexes, or lists of legal abbreviations and citations, with explanations of their meaning.

(d)   Biographical dictionaries — 'who was who' in the legal profession.

8.5A1.1   Conventional dictionaries

A study of reported judgments (Clinch, 1989, p. 481) found that the *Shorter Oxford English Dictionary* was the most frequently cited of all types of dictionary, with the *Oxford English Dictionary* placed second. These two accounted for over half the citations to all dictionaries.

Mozley and Whiteley's Law Dictionary (10th ed., 1988) provides definitions of legal terms across the whole field of law, including legal history. *A Dictionary of Law* (3rd ed., 1993), on the other hand, is primarily intended for those without a qualification in law but who, like surveyors, accountants, civil servants, local government officers, social workers, probation officers, business people and legal secretaries, require some knowledge of the precise meaning and spelling of legal terms in their work. The entries therefore contain quite lengthy explanations but are chosen with modern-day practice in mind. *Osborn's Concise Law Dictionary* (8th ed., 1993) is intended for use by lawyers, and has the added bonuses of a list of law reports, with their abbreviations, and a table of the regnal years of English sovereigns (see section 4.2 for the purpose and value of this). A number of dictionaries have been compiled which restrict entries to words found in a specialised area of law: *Dictionary of Insurance Law* (1981), *Dictionary of Employment Law* (1985), *Dictionary of Shipping Law* (1984), *Dictionary of Commercial Law* (1983), *Dictionary of Company Law* (2nd ed., 1985). So far all the dictionaries mentioned have been compact, single volume works, the sort of publication you might buy for yourself! *Jowitt's Dictionary of English Law* (2nd ed., 1977) is in two large volumes and is kept up-to-date by the publication of supplements every few years. It aims to be comprehensive, giving a definition and explanation of every legal term old and new.

8.5A1.2   Judicial dictionaries

Stroud's Judicial Dictionary of Words and Phrases (5th ed., 1986) published in six volumes and kept up-to-date by annual supplements, provides details of the interpretations by judges of words and phrases, as well as references to definitions included in statutes. Two innovations in this edition are tables of cases and statutes in the sixth volume which enable you to look up the interpretation of a word or phrase from the case name or statute title. *Words and Phrases Legally Defined* (3rd ed., 1988–89), in four volumes with annual Cumulative Supplements, is similar but provides verbatim extracts from speeches and judgments, as well as a selection of statutory definitions.

Definitions of words and phrases can also be found by using the index to *Halsbury's Laws of England*, which will guide you to the appropriate Main Volume of the encyclopaedia. Recent interpretations by the courts are listed in the Noter-Up binder. The same type of search can be undertaken using the internet version of *Halsbury's Laws*: Halsbury's Direct. The service is available to subscribers only — ask your library staff if a subscription is taken. *Current Law Monthly Digest* and *Current Law Yearbooks* provide similar listings, but lack the consolidated index which makes *Halsbury's* so much easier to use.

8.5A1.3   Indexes or lists of legal citations and abbreviations

A glance at the 'citation' sections of the discussions on law reports and law periodicals earlier in this book (sections 6A5.1 and 8.3A3, respectively) will reveal how little standardisation there is in the abbreviations used by authors to identify the material they cite. Many publications are commonly referred to by several abbreviations and many abbreviations have more than one meaning. The most comprehensive index available is Donald Raistrick's *Index to Legal Citations and Abbreviations* (2nd ed., 1993) which includes not only abbreviations used in the United Kingdom, but also the Commonwealth, USA and European Community. A word of warning, though; some students are baffled when, on checking an abbreviation for a law report or periodical title cited in their reading, they learn that it is a rather obscure overseas publication. The chances are that the citation abbreviation is a new concoction of the author, and really relates to a more well-known publication in the English jurisdiction. So, a little guesswork, as well as delving into *Raistrick*, is required.

Much smaller lists of abbreviations will be found in Sweet & Maxwell's *Guide to Law Reports and Statutes* (3rd ed., 1959) and the University of London, Institute of Advanced Legal Studies, *Manual of Legal Citations*, part 1, The British Isles (1959). Lists will also be found in *Current Law Monthly Digest* and *Current Law Yearbooks, Index to Legal Periodicals*, the first volume of *The Digest* and the first volume of *Halsbury's Laws*. The compliers of the *Legal Journals Index* database occasionally issue a list of abbreviations to the 400 or more titles it indexes — this is particularly useful because of *LJI*'s comprehensive coverage of the periodical literature. A list of the journals indexed in *LJI* is at the Sweet & Maxwell web site at

http://www.smlawpubs.co.uk/product/abbrevs/abbrevs.cfm

Ignore the first screen; the list starts lower down the page.

8.5A1.4   Biographical dictionaries

Occasionally you may want to go behind the law itself and learn something of notable people in the legal profession. For those still alive the best sources are *Who's Who in the Law* (1991) or *Who's Who* (annual) or *Havers' Companion to the Bar* (annual).

For details of names from the past, the *Biographical Dictionary of the Common Law* (1984) edited by A.W.B. Simpson will prove invaluable. The more famous lawyers noted in Professor Simpson's work will also have entries in *Who Was Who* (published each decade) and the *Dictionary of National Biography* (originally published between 1885 and 1901 and updated every 10 years, and more recently by a new volume every five years).

8.5A2   Directories

These may be divided into three groups:

(a)   those specific to law and the law profession;
(b)   titles of general coverage; and
(c)   compendia.

8.5A2.1   Directories for law

There are many; here is a selective list.

One of the most authoritative listings of solicitors and barristers is the *Law Society Directory of Solicitors' and Barristers'*, published annually. It includes a list of solicitors and, in addition, official lists of barristers, Fellows of the Institute of Legal Executives and licensed conveyancers. The list of solicitors' firms and individuals is arranged geographically with details of the work they will undertake — very useful when you are seeking a placement or trainee post! *The Bar Directory: The General Council of the Bar*, is the official listing of barristers. *Chambers and Partners' Directory*, is an annual guide to the top 1,000 law firms and all barristers' chambers in England, Wales and Scotland, with useful specialist lists indicating which firms and chambers are best known for particular areas of expertise, and also includes regional listings. Indexes at the back of the volume enable you to identify those firms or sets of chambers handling particular types of business. *Havers' Companion to the Bar* is different yet again; as well as a conventional listing of barristers and their chambers it provides biographies of 4,000 individual lawyers, including details of leading cases in which they have appeared.

The Solicitors' and Barristers' Diary, a companion volume to the *Law Society Directory*, lists the courts and tribunals of England and Wales, their addresses and telephone numbers, and the names of judges, recorders and clerks. In addition it provides names and addresses for the members of the government legal service. *Shaw's Directory of Courts in the United Kingdom* (annual) provides similar information but includes Scotland and Northern Ireland. A similar title is *Hazell's Guide to the Judiciary and the Courts* (annual).

Finally, a volume you will find useful when wishing to study in vacations, or when you wish to find a law library with a more comprehensive collection than is available locally. *The Directory of British and Irish Law Libraries* (6th ed., 1998) provides details of the names, addresses and telephone numbers, and in most instances a named contact, with brief details of collections and services for hundreds of law libraries in all types of organisation. Many are private, so if you are contemplating using them, it is essential to contact the librarian beforehand to discover whether you can gain admission and on what conditions. Discuss your need to use other libraries with your 'local' law librarian, who may be able to assist and advise on the best approach.

8.5A2.2   General directories

Again, there is a vast number, but here is a selection you should find invaluable, particularly when researching your final-year project or dissertation.

The Civil Service Year-book (annual) is a comprehensive listing of government departments and organisations, with brief details of the responsibilities of each right down to quite specific operational levels, names of key civil servants and enquiry point telephone numbers. It lists staff in government serving not just Westminster but also the Scottish Parliament and the Welsh Assembly. It is available as a CD, and on the internet (by subscription) at

http://www.civil-service.co.uk/

Municipal Yearbook is in two volumes: the first, reviewing one by one the functions of local government, the second, comprising entries for every local authority in the United Kingdom including the names, addresses and telephone numbers of individual offices and departments. *Councils, Committees and Boards* (10th ed., 1998) is a directory of advisory, consultative and executive organisations working at national or regional level — very useful for tracing the names and addresses of obscure government advisory committees or public authorities. A companion volume, *Directory of British Associations* (14th ed., 1998), is even more valuable, for you can trace the existence of pressure groups, professional and trade associations, societies and similar organisations with voluntary membership. Details of their names, addresses, contact person, sphere of interest etc. are provided.

8.5A2.3   *Compendia*

I mention two, quite different in their aims and content. The *Oxford Companion to Law* (1980) contains thousands of dictionary-like entries on the principal legal institutions, courts, judges, jurists, systems of law, branches of law, legal ideas, concepts, doctrines and principles of law. References at the end of some articles and in one of the appendices provide leads to major sources of information. In complete contrast, *The New Penguin Guide to the Law* (2nd ed., 1992) is a highly readable, lay person's guide to the law and the legal system in England and Wales. However, in using this particular publication you should remember it is a highly condensed view of the law, and the law changes fast, so parts of the book will be out-of-date. Little skill is needed to open and read a text such as the *New Penguin Guide* but, as a law student, you should be honing your research skills on some of the sources noted much earlier in this chapter!

8.6   OFFICIAL PUBLICATIONS

8.6A   Description

8.6A1   *Definition*

There is no agreed definition of what constitutes an 'official publication'. The Stationery Office (TSO) is the publisher for Parliament, government departments and other organisations funded or controlled by government. A small 'rump' of the organisation which preceded TSO, Her Majesty's Stationery Office (HMSO) still exists to publish Acts and statutory instruments (see sections 4.2 and 5.1). All the publications required by Parliament to carry out its business (Parliamentary publications) are published by TSO and comprise about half the 8,000 to 9,000 titles issued by TSO each year. The other half are termed non-Parliamentary, and are published by TSO on behalf of government departments and other 'official' organisations. However, in addition, as many titles again as are published by TSO in total are issued direct to the public by government departments and other organisations, and not through TSO at all.

Included in this huge output is a wealth of material relevant to the study of law. It is essential that you gain a basic grasp of the sources devised to help you find your way around this publishing maze and develop skills in using them.

What follows is a sketch of the main types of TSO and non-TSO official publications you are likely to come across in law or legal studies. They fall into three groups: Parliamentary publications; TSO non-Parliamentary publications, and, finally, non-TSO official publications.

Scottish official publications are quite distinctive and dealt with in section 13.5.

8.6A1.1   Parliamentary publications

8.6A1.1.1   Parliamentary proceedings and debates   Both Houses of Parliament produce records of what was done rather than what was said; they are, respectively, the *House of Commons Votes and Proceedings* and *House of Lords Minutes of Proceedings*. They are of limited legal research value, save that the *House of Commons Votes and Proceedings* records amendments to Bills at committee stage submitted *before* the committee has met.

Of considerably greater research value are the *Official Reports of Parliamentary Debates*, which since 1943 have been officially known as *Hansard*, after the person most closely linked with the reports when they were published privately in the early 19th century. There are two series, one for Commons and one for Lords, and they are a full report of what was said in Parliament (see 4.1B6 for further details). Part of the process of scrutiny of Public Bills in the Commons requires that they be considered by a Standing Committee of between 16 and 50 members. A separate publication from Hansard, *Official Report of Standing Committee Debates*, reports verbatim the deliberations of the Committees. These reports are of considerable research value because of the detailed scrutiny of the meaning, and effect, of the provisions of a Bill (see 4.1B6 for further detail).

There appear to be several different ways of citing a reference in the *Official Reports of Parliamentary Debates*, but the method recommended here is adapted from the one used in Erskine May's *Parliamentary Practice*, the authoritative guide to Parliamentary procedure:

> House Deb (Parliamentary session) volume number abbreviation col. followed by column number.

The following are examples of a reference to a House of Commons debate, a House of Commons written answer to a question and a House of Lords debate:

> HC Deb (1990–91) 195 col. 311
> HC Deb (1990–91) 195, written answers col. 41
> HL Deb (1990–91) 529 col. 111

Official Reports of Parliamentary Debates in Standing Committees are published in a separate series. Each Standing Committee may scrutinise several different pieces of legislation each session, and the column numbering of the reports begins afresh with each new legislative title. It is essential, therefore, not only to cite the House, the Standing Committee identifying letter, Parliamentary session dates, and column number, but also the title of the legislation under discussion. The manner of citing from debates in Standing Committees is rather different from debates on the floor of the House, as the example shows:

Stg Co Deb (1980–81) Co E Finance Bill col. 46

title of series (Parliamentary Session) Committee letter Bill title abbreviation col., followed by column number.

Most academic and many of the major public libraries will subscribe to *Official Reports of Parliamentary Debates* for the House of Commons, fewer will subscribe to those of the House of Lords, and fewer still to the *Official Reports of Standing Committee Debates*. As was noted in section 4.1, *Hansard* is available on CD and the internet.

The work of a quite different type of committee, the Select Committee, can provide unique background material when looking at the administrative and social context of government policy and legislation. Select Committees, as their title suggests, are composed of members selected by the House who are best qualified for the specialised, essentially investigative work of the Committee. Their main purpose is to review the work of government, especially in the financial field, and examine aspects of public life. A Select Committee is given a specific remit by the House and usually empowered to summon people (witnesses), and require papers and records to be presented to it. These witnesses are not only Ministers and officials of government departments, but also representatives of private organisations and pressure groups. Following its investigations and deliberations the Select Committee will issue a report, with appendices containing the verbal and written evidence given to it. The report and appendices are published as part of a much more extensive series of Parliamentary publications known as House of Commons Papers, or, for the Lords, House of Lords Papers. If the matter investigated touches on the actions of a government department it is usual for the department to respond to the committee's recommendations and observations. The response is frequently in the form of a Command Paper (see 8.6A1.1.3).

The House of Lords, with two exceptions, has a system of *ad hoc* Select Committees which are convened as the need arises. The House of Commons Select Committees number 25 at present, and 14 directly relate to the areas of responsibility of the principal departments of government. These are of the greatest interest to law students, and of the 14 the Home Affairs Select Committee is probably the most relevant. The reports of this Committee have influenced the nature of subsequent legislation, notably its criticism in 1980 of the use of the Vagrancy Act 1824 to arrest a person suspected of loitering with criminal intent — the 'sus' law — and its effect on race relations. In the following Parliamentary session the government introduced the Criminal Attempts Bill which repealed the 'sus' law.

A House of Commons Paper is identified by a serial number printed without brackets at the bottom left of the title page. Since a new sequence of numbers begins each session, it is essential to include details of the session. Variations can be found in the order in which the elements in the citation are given but the citation must include an abbreviation for the House, dates of the session of Parliament and the paper number as in the following example:

HC (1990–91) 7

House of Lords Papers were, up to the Parliamentary session 1988–89, issued in a numerical sequence which included House of Lords Bills as well. Since then they have been separated. The serial number of each item is printed in round brackets at the foot of the front cover. Again, variation can be found in the order with which the elements in the citation are given but the reference must include an abbreviation for the House, dates of the session and the paper number, in round brackets, as in the following example:

HL (1984–85) (244)

Very occasionally Joint Committees of the House of Lords and the House of Commons issue reports. Citations to a Paper of *both* Houses are usually given in the form:

HL paper number, HC paper number (session)

as in the following example:

HL 40, HC 15-viii (1981–82)

House of Commons Papers are likely to be held by most academic libraries and the larger public libaries, but House of Lords Papers are not widely collected.

8.6A1.1.2 Primary legislation   Bills and Acts of Parliament are fully described in sections 4.1 and 4.2.

8.6A1.1.3 Command Papers   These are documents which originate outside Parliament and are presented to Parliament 'by command of Her Majesty' usually by the Minister responsible. The Sovereign, in fact, is never personally involved, for the procedure is merely a technical device used by Ministers to place documents before Parliament which have not been created through the business of Parliament. About 300 to 400 are presented each year and, for lawyers, are one of the most frequently sought Parliamentary publications. There are several different types:

(a)   Statements of government policy on a topic, which may indicate the broad lines of future legislation — these are often referred to as 'White Papers', a historical term for a Parliamentary Paper not thick enough to require a protective cover. A recent example is *Modernising Parliament: Reforming the House of Lords* (Cm 4183, 1999).

(b)   Reports of Royal Commissions: prestigious, investigative bodies set up under Royal Warrant to examine a topic of public concern where legislation seems desirable. The use of this type of investigation has diminished considerably during the last decade; an example of one of the most recent reports published is the Report of the *Royal Commission on Criminal Justice* (Cm 2263, 1993).

(c)   Reports of Departmental Committees, set up by a Minister to carry out investigations into a matter of public concern, such as the *Departmental Committee on Section 2 of the Official Secrets Act 1911* (Cmnd 5104, 1972).

(d)   Reports of tribunals or commissions of inquiry set up to inquire into a matter of urgent, public importance such as *The Stephen Lawrence Inquiry: Report of an Inquiry by Sir William MacPherson of Cluny (Chairman)* (Cm 4262, 1999).

(e)   Reports of a number of permanent investigatory bodies such as the Competition Commission (formerly the Monopolies and Mergers Commission) and the Law Commission. In the case of the Law Commission, and pre-devolution, the Scottish Law Commission, the reports may be published either as Command Papers or House of Commons Papers. Joint reports of the two Commissions are still published as Command Papers. In addition to bearing a Command Paper number or a House of Commons Paper number, the reports of the Law Commission are individually numbered in a single sequence. The citation is officially abbreviated, as in this example: Law Com. No. 196 or even just L.C. 196. If, as sometimes happens, this is all the information you have about the report, check the Law Commission's web site which carries a complete list of the titles of the publications which usually precede a Report: Consultation Papers, with the full title and ensuing Report number. The web site is at

http://www.lawcom.gov.uk/library/library.htm

The Commission's consultation papers are published as non-Parliamentary papers (see 8.6A1.2.1).

(f)   Treaties and agreements with other countries and with international organisations — these form the largest single group of Command Papers.

(g)   Annual accounts and statistics, such as the annual report of the Commissioner of Metropolitan Police, or the Home Office compilation published each year, *Criminal Statistics, England and Wales.*

So far, this categorisation of Command Papers appears logical and reasonably clear cut, but in 1967 a new type of publication began to appear: the 'Green Paper'. In a House of Commons debate (HC Deb (1966–67) 747 col. 651), the Minister credited with having coined the term defined a Green Paper as 'a statement by the government not of policy determined but of propositions put before the whole nation for discussion'. Individual Green Papers are sometimes subtitled: 'a consultative document'. The choice of the collective title 'Green

Paper' is the result of the colour chosen for the cover of the first one. At first
these documents were published either by TSO's predecessor, HMSO as non-
Parliamentary papers or by government departments themselves. However, an
increasing number are now published as Command Papers, yet according to the
original, and frequently repeated intention behind their production, they are *not*
statements of government policy but are published to stimulate discussion and
enable the government to obtain the views of interested parties before making
a policy statement (a White Paper). A recent example is *Legislation against
terrorism: a consultation paper* (Cm 4178, 1998).

Individual Command Papers are numbered sequentially in long series regardless of Parliamentary session. The running number, with a prefix, is printed at
the bottom left-hand corner of the cover and title page. The prefix is very
important, for it indicates which of the six series (the first began in 1833) the
running number refers to. It is an abbreviation of the word 'Command'. The six
series are as follows:

1st series	4th series
[1] — [4222] 1833–69	[Cmd 1] — Cmd 9889 1919–56
2nd series	5th series
[C 1] — [C 9550] 1870–99	Cmnd 1 — Cmnd 9927 1956–86
3rd series	6th series
[Cd 1] — [Cd 9239] 1900–18	Cm 1 — 1986–

Most academic and large public libraries will have collections of Command
Papers usually running back, complete, over several series. Smaller libraries
may have collections either much more restricted in the time period covered or
composed of selected titles only. In some academic libraries you may find they
subscribe to every Command Paper published, and so build up a 'reference
only' set, and additionally purchase selected titles of particular relevance to the
course taught. These selected copies may be available for you to borrow. Some
of the less well-researched reading lists and books you read may refer to a
Command Paper merely by its running number and prefix, with no indication
of the title, Minister or government department responsible — some of the
publications noted in section 8.6B1 will provide assistance in tracing the
publication from such a poor reference. In addition you may find that in some
libraries, particularly those with a computer catalogue, it is possible to search
for and locate a Command Paper solely from the prefix and running number.
Ask the library staff if this is possible, and if it is, ask them to show you how
it can be achieved.

Some Command Papers are available on the internet usually located on the
site of the government department responsible for the preparation of the paper.
The functional index for law and the organisational index, both on the UK
Government Information Service site, will help you locate government departments. The indexes are at

http://www.open.gov.uk/

TSO has a web site which provides access to the full text or summaries of selected TSO publications organised according to government department. The site is at

http://www.official-documents.co.uk/menu/bydept.htm

8.6A1.2   HMSO non-Parliamentary publications

As their name suggests these are publications other than those required for the conduct of the business of Parliament. The range is huge but three broad categories have been identified (see Ollé, 1973, p. 50): (a) statutory instruments (considered in detail in section 5.1 of this book); (b) reports; and (c) information publications.

8.6A1.2.1   Reports   Two types may be noted: annual reports of government institutions, and the reports of some permanent, and many *ad hoc* investigating committees and working parties. The Law Commission is a permanent body and its consultation papers (formerly called working papers) fall into this category. They are very valuable sources of information because they provide an account of the criticisms and supposed defects of the law, with a statement of the options for change, and the Commission's view of the preferred option. Because Law Commission consultation papers are an authoritative distillation and analysis of the law on a topic, they can be a very useful starting-point when researching why the law has developed in a particular way, and the alternatives for change. Following this consultation the Law Commission will issue a report which sometimes includes a draft Bill of Parliament (see 8.6A1.1.3 and also in 4.1A2). Law Commission consultation papers are numbered sequentially and over 200 have been issued since the Law Commission was set up in 1965. They are sometimes referred to solely by their number, without the title of the individual paper, as in Law Comm. C.P. 175 or just LCCP 175. A list of all consultation papers and reports published by the Law Commission is available free at

http://www.lawcom.gov.uk/library/library.htm

The full text of all consultation papers published since March 1997 is available from the library pages of the Law Commission's web site.

Many law libraries have a set of Law Commission consultation papers bound in sequence number order, as well as copies of individual titles which will appear on the library catalogue.

8.6A1.2.2   Information publications   A wide variety of books, pamphlets, leaflets and periodicals fall into this category. They provide the public with information and advice, most of which is derived from experts in government departments and institutions. They range from codes of practice, such as those issued by the Home Secretary under the Police and Criminal Evidence Act 1984 and approved by Parliament (see 5.2), to guides on the practical application of particular legislation: for example, *A Guide to the HSW Act* prepared by the Health and Safety Executive (HSW stands for Health and Safety at Work).

Some information publications may be available on the internet at the departmental site. The indexes to departmental web sites, mentioned at the end of section 8.6A1.1.3, will help you trace the location of the appropriate site.

Non-Parliamentary publications have no overall numbering sequence or system of citation. The publishing output is very large and although some academic and large public libraries will attempt to purchase all non-Parliamentary publications most libraries may be more selective in what they stock. You will probably find that although academic law libraries will take, for example, all the Law Commission working papers, public libraries may not, but instead, collect non-Parliamentary publications of wider public interest.

8.6A1.3   Non-HMSO official publications

This category embraces those documents published by government departments direct to the public, not through TSO, and the publications of over 500 organisations controlled or funded by the government. Of these 500 or so organisations the most important in legal research are the *qu*asi-*a*utonomous *n*on-*g*overnmental *o*rganisations (quangos), for example, the Equal Opportunities Commission, the Health and Safety Commission etc. One difficulty which has faced researchers in the past has been that few government departments and quangos have issued catalogues of their publications, so it has been very difficult to trace what has been published and by whom. It is worth emphasising that a publication prepared by a government department or quango could be published by TSO, or it could be published by the organisation itself — and this has had considerable implications when trying to trace information about it in indexes, explained in section 8.6B.

8.6B   Finding information

8.6B1   TSO catalogues

8.6B1.1   Daily List

Each afternoon, Monday to Friday, TSO issues a list of the publications made available that day. The *Daily List* usually extends to three or four pages of entries, with publications grouped under four headings: Parliamentary publications, non-Parliamentary publications, agency publications (items sold through TSO for British, European and international organisations), Scottish official publications (including those of the Scottish Parliament and the Scottish Executive) and statutory instruments. The purpose of the *Daily List* is to alert booksellers and the public to the very latest material. No subject or title indexes to the *Daily List* are produced, so it is an inappropriate source to search for more than recent publications. For research covering longer periods of time you should use the *Monthly Catalogue* and/or *Annual Catalogue*.

Issues of *Daily List* for approximately the last 12 months are on the internet but there are no search facilities at the site, so you need to know the date when the publication you require was issued. The web site is at

http://www.the-stationery-office.co.uk/daily_list/

8.6B1.2 *Monthly Catalogue*

This contains entries for publications noted in the *Daily List* except for statutory instruments. It is published about four to six weeks after the end of the month to which it relates. During 1999–2000 it suffered very severe publication delays. Currently, it is divided into five parts: Parliamentary publications; a classified section, including all non-Parliamentary publications and Parliamentary publications (excluding Bills, Acts, debates and Measures) listed under the responsible department or body; Northern Ireland publications; Scottish official publications; and, lastly, other agency publications. In addition there is an alphabetical index with entries for subjects, authors, chairmen and editors all in a single sequence. Prior to 1976 there were just two sections, Parliamentary publications; non-Parliamentary and agency publications. The alphabetical index cumulates through the year so it is best to start your search with that in the latest monthly issue. A note at the bottom of each page of the alphabetical index tells you to which monthly issue the page numbers refer.

8.6B1.3 *Annual Catalogue*

As you might expect this is an annual cumulation of the *Monthly Catalogue* but the contents are not quite identical. There are three parts: Parliamentary publications, a classified section and, finally, a list of Northern Ireland TSO publications. Presumably, Scottish official publications, including those of the Scottish Parliament and the Scottish Executive will be listed separately. Publications from British, European and international organisations for which TSO is the UK agent appear in a separate, annual TSO *Agency Catalogue*. Towards the back of the TSO *Annual Catalogue* there is an alphabetical index including subjects, authors, chairmen and editors in a single sequence. Since the mid-1970s there have been marked improvements in the layout and helpfulness of the alphabetical index and it is now relatively easy to track down publications through it. However, should you need to consult *Annual Catalogues* from before that period, you will find the indexing rather rudimentary and you would be advised to ask for help from library staff.

At the front of recent issues of the *Annual Catalogue* there is a list of libraries which take a subscription to one copy of most TSO publications. Before visiting one of these libraries you should telephone or write to find out whether the library does in fact keep the materials you want, since some libraries do not retain all the publications they receive from TSO.

8.6B1.4 *Sectional lists*

The sectional lists were 20 or 30 individual booklets giving details of items in print, published by TSO for certain departments or subjects. They have not been updated for some years. The latest available for law were published in 1996, so using the web site of a government department is now a better way of discovering what it publishes. Use the Government Information Service web site at

http://www.open.gov.uk/

The Stationery Office has created an internet equivalent (sort of!) of the sectional lists. It provides access to the full text or summaries of a selection of Stationery Office publications arranged by government department. The Crown Prosecution Service, Home Office, Scottish Office and Welsh Office feature in the list. The site is at

http://www.official-documents.co.uk/menu/bydept.htm

8.6B1.5   Index to Chairmen: reports of official committees (formerly, Committee Reports Published by HMSO Indexed by Chairman)

Since 1983 an index listing the chairmen of all committee reports has been published. Entries are arranged alphabetically by the name of the chairman. This is a very useful index which, in extended historical research, can be used in conjunction with those noted in section 8.6B2.5. Very often a major official report becomes known colloquially by the name of the chairman of the committee or investigator, for example, the Woolf Report (on access to justice), the Scott Inquiry (export of defence equipment to Iran). This index will help in tracing the correct title, full name of the chairman and other publication details, so that you will have a better chance of tracing the material in a library catalogue.

8.6B1.6   Guide to Official Statistics

The government is the leading collector of statistics and publisher of the results of surveys. Some statistics are collected as a matter of routine and are published at regular intervals. Others are only collected as the result of a particular study of investigation. The most comprehensive guide to the government's published statistics, and to major non-official sources of statistics in the UK, is the *Guide to Official Statistics*. The latest edition of 1996 concentrates on current data sources with historical references included in some cases. The subject index at the back of the *Guide* will lead you to the appropriate section in the body of the work, where the content of each statistical publication is briefly summarised. For a law student, chapter 4 of the *Guide* describing social statistics will probably prove the most relevant, for it includes references to statistical publications on the operation of the civil and criminal justice systems, crime statistics, the police and treatment of offenders. The three major series of statistics you are likely to consult as a law student are *Judicial Statistics England and Wales, Criminal Statistics England and Wales* and *Civil Judicial Statistics, Scotland* (all published annually). There are also a number of occasional series of statistics relevant to your studies issued in the series, *Home Office Statistical Bulletins*, published by the Home Office itself and the Scottish Executive's *Statistical Bulletin: Criminal Statistics* series. The Guide is also available as a CD.

8.6B2   Non-TSO catalogues and indexes

8.6B2.1   Departmental catalogues

Some, but by no means all, government departments and agencies used to publish catalogues or lists of their publications. Most appear not to have been published since the early 1990s. These were not fully comprehensive (for example, they frequently excluded such items as press releases). BOPCAS (see 8.6B2.2) or the *Catalogue of British Official Publications Not Published by TSO* (see 8.6B2.3) are to be preferred.

8.6B2.2   British Official Publications Current Awareness Service (BOPCAS)

BOPCAS is a web site based at the University of Southampton which indexes most items published by The Stationery Office (TSO) and a large number of publications of government departments. The site is in two parts: the free part of the site contains indexes to publications received during the previous six months; the subscriber only part of the site contains the archive files back to July 1995. The site is updated approximately weekly and is easy to use. It is possible to search the indexes by date, publication type (e.g. command papers) and policy area (subject). It is also possible to join a Policy Awareness Electronic Mail Group to be automatically alerted to new publications within a broad subject area, such as law or environment or Wales. The web site is at

http://www.soton.ac.uk/~bopcas/

8.6B2.3   Catalogue of British Official Publications Not Published by TSO and UKOP

First issued in 1980 by a private publisher Chadwyck-Healey, and now published bimonthly with an annual bound volume, this catalogue gives details of the vast publishing output of over 500 official organisations including government departments, nationalised industries, research institutes, quangos and other official bodies. The catalogue is as comprehensive as the compilers can make it, covering periodicals, newspapers, serials, single-sheet publications, leaflets and publicity material of value, as well as more weighty policy documents. The alphabetical index includes subjects, authors, chairmen etc. in a single sequence. Each reference in the catalogue to a publication carries a code number which appears in italics at the end of the entry and an index to these codes provides the names and addresses of the sources from which the publications may be obtained. This catalogue is now available on CD called: *United Kingdom Official Publications (UKOP)*, incorporating the TSO publications catalogue from 1980. It is an extremely valuable database permitting author, title and keyword searching, and so making it much easier to find relevant material than through the paper indexes.

8.6B2.4   Badger

Badger was launched in 1994 and is an index of official publications, press comment and 'grey paper' (that is, documents which have been published for limited circulation), covering topics of interest to the legal profession. The database is available as part of the Current Legal Information database, either on CD or via the internet.

8.6B2.5   British Government Publications: an Index to Chairmen of Committees and Commissions of Inquiry

Currently in four volumes covering the period 1800 to 1982, the index is arranged in alphabetical order by the surnames of the chairmen, with details of the reports for which they were responsible. More recent publications are listed in Index to Chairmen (see 8.6B1.5).

8.6C   Answering research queries

For background information on using CDs and the internet for legal research, see appendix 4.

8.6C1   How to find details of official publications on a subject

Electronic route
Use the service which best covers the period you are searching:

UKOP (see 8.6B2.3) — comprehensive coverage and back to 1980.
BOPCAS (see 8.6B2.2) — comprehensive coverage but only goes back to 1995.
Badger (see 8.6B2.4) — is selective and only goes back to 1994.

Paper route
Daily List (see 8.6B1.1) — trace back to latest TSO *Monthly Catalogue.*
Then:
Monthly Catalogue (see 8.6B1.2) — trace back to latest TSO *Annual Catalogue.*
Then:
Annual Catalogue (see 8.6B1.3) — trace back as far as necessary.
Or:
Catalogue of British Official Publications Not Published by TSO (see 8.6B2.3) — comprehensive coverage back to 1980.

8.6C2   How to find details of Law Commission publications

Electronic route
Use the Law Commission web site (see 8.6A1.2.1).

Paper route
Use the Annual Reports of the Law Commission, themselves published as Law Commission Reports. The recent ones give details of the work in hand and accomplished, pre-1992 Annual Reports also list all the Law Commission publications as an appendix.

8.6C3   How to trace details of an official publication when all you know is the name of the chairman

Electronic route
UKOP (see 8.6B2.3) — comprehensive coverage and back to 1980.
BOPCAS (see 8.6B2.2) — comprehensive coverage but only goes back to 1995.

Paper route

Index to Chairmen (see 8.6B1.5) — goes back to 1983.
British Government Publications: Index to Chairman of Committees (see 8.6B2.5) — covers period 1800 to 1982.

Chapter 9

Researching the law of Scotland: introduction

'There shall be a Scottish Parliament.' With a single sentence the Scotland Act 1998 altered the constitutional structure of the United Kingdom and introduced a new dimension to researching the law of Scotland. Chapters 9 to 13 seek to highlight the effect of legislative devolution, and to draw attention to native sources and Scottish aspects of sources mentioned in the main body of the book.

Scotland had its own legal system when it was an independent kingdom and this was preserved by the 1707 Act of Union which created Great Britain. Although a single legislature now served the United Kingdom, Scots law and Scottish institutions remained sufficiently distinctive to require separate treatment either by separate legislation or by provisions which applied exclusively to Scotland. The Scottish courts continued to apply and develop the law and a parallel system of law reporting gradually evolved. Nevertheless by the 20th century the Scottish legal tradition was widely seen as under threat from the increasing dominance of statutory law and the influence of the law of England.

In the 1960s increased electoral support for nationalist parties persuaded the government to reconsider the constitutional position of Scotland and Wales and a Royal Commission chaired by Lord Kilbrandon was appointed in 1969 and reported in 1973. Proposals to devolve legislative powers to a directly elected Scottish Assembly and executive powers to a Scottish Executive led to a referendum in March 1979. The terms of the referendum required that not less than 40% of those eligible to vote should vote 'Yes' and, though a small majority was in favour of devolution, this requirement was not fulfilled and the Scotland Act 1978 was repealed. The issue of self-government was revived in the 1990s and this led to changes in the arrangements for handling Scottish business in Parliament and the transfer of certain functions from departments in Whitehall to the Scottish Office. The Labour Party came to power in 1997 on a platform which included fundamental constitutional reform and a further referendum was held in September of that year. On this occasion a large majority were in favour of the creation of a Scottish Parliament with tax-varying powers and within three months a Bill had been introduced. Elections were held in May 1999 and the Parliament assumed its powers on 1 July.

The Scotland Act 1998 devolved extensive law-making powers to the Scottish Parliament. However Westminster retains general powers and responsibilities for the constitution, political parties, foreign affairs, the civil service, defence and treason, and specific powers in relation to aspects of central economic policies, home affairs, trade and industry, energy, transport, social security, employment, health and the media. These are set out in full in Schedule 5 of the Act and are referred to as 'reserved matters'. The powers of the Scottish Parliament are not unlimited but they are more significant than might at first appear. Indeed the ability of the Parliament to enact primary legislation on a wide range of issues affecting Scotland is one of the features which distinguish it from other devolved assemblies.

The 1998 Act also established a 'Scottish Administration' which constitutes the government of Scotland in respect of devolved matters. It assumed the functions of the former Scottish Office and associated departments. The Administration is under the direction and control of the Scottish Executive which comprises the First Minister, the Scottish Ministers appointed by the First Minister, and the Scottish Law Officers. The Scotland Office in Whitehall, headed by the Secretary of State, is charged with representing Scottish interests within the UK government on reserved matters and encouraging cooperation between Edinburgh and London.

The student of the law of Scotland must come to grips with this brave new world, with the new legislation which will be made, and with the new research sources which will be developed. However it will still be very important to understand the legislative and judicial processes described elsewhere in this book and to be adept at researching the law on a broader stage. It is hoped that the explanation which follows will be of some assistance.

Chapter 10

Scotland: primary legislation

Primary legislation affecting Scotland can date from three periods in its history. Before 1707 Scotland was an independent kingdom with its own Parliament enacting laws (see 10.1). On ratification of the Treaty of Union the new state of Great Britain came into being and the Parliament at Westminster became the supreme legislative authority (see 10.2). Nonetheless Scotland retained its distinctive legal system. On 1 July 1999 the Scottish Parliament assumed its powers and now legislates for Scotland on most of its internal affairs (see 10.3 and 10.4). It is however important to remember that Westminster can still make legislation which is effective in Scotland.

10.1   PRE-1707 LEGISLATION

10.1A   Description

10.1A1   Definition

The Acts of the Parliaments of Scotland from before the Union with England in 1707 are known as Scots Acts and some of these are still in force. A convenient listing for the period 1424 to 1707 will be found in the *Chronological Table of the Statutes*. Subsequent amendments or repeals may be traced through the *Current Law Legislation Citators* which list the Scots Acts in a separate sequence in the statute citator. Both before and after the Union pre-1707 legislation could be held to be 'in desuetude' if it had been long neglected and there was a clear indication that it was out of keeping with present-day conditions. Whether the repeal of a Scots Act could still be implied in this manner was the subject of *McSkimming* v *Royal Bank of Scotland* 1996 SCLR 547.

10.1A2   Origin

The serious researcher will find information on the history and legislative procedure of the pre-1707 Scottish Parliaments in Rait (1924). Also of value are the relevant volumes of Walker (1988–).

10.1A3   Structure

As might be expected there is less consistency in the appearance and structure of the Scots Acts than in legislation of the modern era. Many are extremely short being little more than a paragraph of text.

10.1A4   Publication and general availability

There are several readily available sources of Scots Acts (see 10.1B). It is worth noting that no matter how modern the publication the Acts themselves are written in Scots.

10.1A5   Citation

Short titles for the Scots Acts still in force at the time were provided by the Statute Law Revision (Scotland) Act 1964. Thus the correct form of citation is to use the short title, e.g.:

Breach of Arrestment Act 1581

or the calendar year and chapter number, e.g.:

1581 c.23

though citation by reference to the volume, page and chapter number of the authoritative *Acts of the Parliaments of Scotland 1124–1707* (see 10.1B1) may still be encountered, e.g.:

APS III, 223, c.23

Regnal years are never used to cite Scots Acts.

10.1B   Finding information

10.1B1   Acts of the Parliaments of Scotland 1124–1707

This 19th century compilation is known as the 'Record Edition' because it was published by the Commissioners on the Public Records and is widely regarded as authoritative. Scots Acts which were repealed prior to and by the Statute Law Revision (Scotland) Act 1964 are generally cited by reference to the volume and page number in the Record Edition. The final volume contains a general index. The first volume covers the Acts prior to 1424 but the doubtful reliability of the sources from which they are derived has led more recent collections to omit them. Unless one is researching historically and in depth the 12 large volumes of the Record Edition are probably a little unwieldy in use.

10.1B2   Statutes in Force

Scots Acts were included in this official collection and it remains a useful source of texts in those libraries in which it is still available. The Acts are distributed throughout the loose-leaf volumes according to subject matter but may be located through either the chronological or alphabetical lists.

10.1B3   Acts of the Parliaments of Scotland 1424–1707

Following the repeal of many Scots Acts by the Statute Law Revision (Scotland) Act 1964, Her Majesty's Stationery Office (HMSO) published the remaining legislation in a convenient single volume in 1966. There is an index of short titles, a chronological table and a subject index.

10.1B4   Scots Statutes Revised

A volume of this unofficial collection published by W. Green covered the Scots Acts of 1424 to 1707 still in force in 1908 with a chronological table and a brief subject index.

10.1C   Answering research queries

Encounters with Scots Acts will be rare for most law students. References may be made in textbooks and subject research in the *Laws of Scotland* will point to those still in force or of particular historical interest. The *Chronological Table of the Statutes* can be used to trace amendments and repeals, and this information is updated by the table of effects of legislation in the annual volumes of *Public General Acts* or more conveniently by the *Current Law Legislation Citators*. The *Citators* can be used to trace cases involving Scots Acts. The *JUSTIS UK Statutes* CD includes those Scots Acts from 1424 to 1707 still in force and an equivalent online database is available by subscription at

http://www.justis.com/navigate/main.html

10.2   POST-1707 LEGISLATION

From the time of the Union down to the present day the Parliament at Westminster has had the power to make laws for Scotland. No matter how the Scotland Act 1998 and the opening of the Scottish Parliament in 1999 may have affected the constitutional position of Scotland within the United Kingdom, Westminster remains the supreme legislative authority. For some considerable time to come the student of the law of Scotland will be working with the legislation described fully in chapter 4 and wherever possible any Scottish dimension has been noted in that text. Section 10.2 therefore confines itself to additional information which may not be of general interest.

10.2A Description

10.2A1 Definition

Given that Scotland retained its own legal system and that Scots law had developed in distinctive ways, it often proved necessary for Westminster to legislate for the jurisdiction separately or by means of provisions in an Act of general application which applied to Scotland alone. If an Act does not stipulate territorial extent it is taken to apply throughout the United Kingdom, although apparently 'Acts containing no express words limiting their extent are often held inapplicable . . . by reason of the phraseology used' (Craies, 1971, p. 470).

10.2A2 Origin

Generally, as described in section 4.1. The Private Legislation Procedure (Scotland) Act 1936 delegates power to issue a Provisional Order to the Secretary of State for Scotland. If necessary parliamentary commissioners sitting in Scotland may hold an inquiry into the need for such legislation. If the petition is successful, formal proceedings in Parliament will result in an Order Confirmation Act. This simplified procedure remains relevant for matters not within the legislative competence of the Scottish Parliament.

10.2A3 Structure

Generally, as described in section 4.2A3. The short title may include the name of the jurisdiction to indicate that the Act applies exclusively to Scotland. In an Act of general application the sections indicating territorial extent are obviously of particular significance. In addition there may be a section specifying application to Scotland in which reference is made to Scottish institutions and Scottish legal terminology is employed.

10.2A4 Publication and general availability

See section 4.2A4.

10.2A5 Citation

See section 4.2A5.

10.2B Finding information

In addition to the commercial versions of Acts of Parliament noted in section 4.2B there are a couple of Scottish collections which may be encountered in some libraries. Both have been moribund for many years and require updating in the usual way. It is also worth repeating that Scottish editions of *Current Law Statutes* and the *Current Law* statute and legislation citators were published, and that to all intents and purposes these are identical to their English counterparts.

10.2B1   Public General Statutes Affecting Scotland

Acts with provisions which related to Scotland were published annually from 1848 to 1947 by the publisher William Blackwood, and are hence referred to as 'Blackwood's *Acts*'. Legislation from the period 1707–1847 and still in force in 1876 was published in three complementary volumes.

10.2B2   Scots Statutes Revised

A 10-volume compilation of statutes affecting Scotland for the period 1707–1900 was published by W. Green at the turn of the century. Annual volumes entitled *Scots Statutes* covered the period 1901–48.

10.2C   Answering research queries

See section 4.2C. However remember that in this context *LEXIS* is of limited value and that *Halsbury's Statutes* does not include exclusively Scottish legislation.

10.3   BILLS OF THE SCOTTISH PARLIAMENT

10.3A   Description

10.3A1   Definition

A Scottish Parliament Bill (SP Bill) is a version of a proposed Act of the Scottish Parliament (ASP). As Acts of the Scottish Parliament must be compatible with the statute law enacted by the United Kingdom Parliament prior to devolution, SP Bills are broadly similar in structure to their Westminster counterparts. However Scottish Bills look very different because the opportunity has been taken to modernise the presentation.

As is the case at Westminster, Bills are either Public or Private, though some Public Bills may be hybrid in that they adversely affect certain private individuals. Hybridity is an issue to be addressed by the Parliament's Legal Adviser before a Bill is introduced.

A Public Bill is introduced directly by a Member of the Scottish Parliament (MSP). If they are acting in their capacity as a member of the Scottish Executive the Bill is known as an Executive Bill. If, on the other hand, they are acting as a member of a particular committee of the Parliament or as an individual, the Bill is known as a Committee Bill or a Member's Bill respectively. The terminology will perhaps avoid the confusion between Private Members' Bills and Private Bills from Westminster.

A Private Bill is introduced by a promoter for the same purposes and with the same outcome as its Westminster equivalent. The promoter may be an individual, a corporate body or an unincorporated association, but there are only two opportunities a year to introduce such a Bill. Detailed procedures for private legislation on devolved matters had not been finalised at the time of writing, but it will be subject to the same level of scrutiny in the Parliament. Private legislation relating to matters not within the legislative competence of the Scottish Parliament are still to be dealt with under the Private Legislation Procedure (Scotland) Act 1936.

There are also special categories of Public Bill such as a Budget Bill, a Consolidation Bill, a Statute Law Repeals Bill, a Statute Law Revision Bill, and an Emergency Bill. The latter is an Executive Bill which needs to be enacted as rapidly as possible and the very first Act of the Scottish Parliament (1999 asp 1) resulted from just such an Emergency Bill.

Law students are most likely to encounter Public Bills and therefore the remainder of section 10.3 concentrates upon researching those.

10.3A2   Origin

An Executive Bill is prepared on behalf of the Executive by draftsmen in the Office of the Scottish Parliamentary Counsel. Public consultation takes place before the Bill is presented to the Parliament, with the draft Bill being published either as part of a consultation paper or as a separate document. This process is regarded as being very important given the unicameral nature of the Scottish Parliament and there is a clear requirement for the Executive to demonstrate the nature and outcome of the consultative process. Drafts of Members' and Committee Bills may not be so readily available. The reports of the Scottish Law Commission frequently include a draft Bill to demonstrate how the reforms proposed may be given effect.

Although the procedure followed by the Parliament when considering Bills is less complex than that at Westminster, it is important to understand at least the broad outline.

An Executive Bill is introduced to give effect to the policy of the Scottish Executive on a particular matter. It must be submitted for introduction with various accompanying documents: statements from the Presiding Officer (the equivalent of the Speaker of the House of Commons) and the member of the Executive in charge of the Bill stating that its provisions would be within the legislative competence of the Parliament; a financial memorandum estimating the costs to which its provisions would give rise; explanatory notes summarising what each of its provisions does and explaining its overall effect; a policy memorandum setting out its policy objectives, justifying the approach taken to meet those objectives, detailing the consultation which took place, and assessing the overall effect; and an Auditor General's report if it contains any provision charging expenditure on the Scottish Consolidated Fund, setting out an opinion on whether the charge is appropriate. Three stages in the consideration of the Bill follow.

At Stage 1 the Bill's general principles are considered in committee, then debated in the Parliament before a decision is made on their acceptability. The

Scottish Parliament has 16 all-purpose subject committees which combine the functions of Standing and Select Committees at Westminster with certain unique functions. The Parliamentary Bureau refers the Bill to a 'lead committee' but other relevant committees may consider the Bill if this is appropriate and report to the lead committee. In addition, if the Bill contains powers to make subordinate legislation the relevant provisions will be referred to the Subordinate Legislation Committee. The committee discussions and subsequent plenary debate appear in the *Official Report*. Separate reports of committee proceedings are published in the *SP Papers* series, with any report by the Subordinate Legislation Committee incorporated in the lead committee's report. This stage is very much concerned with taking an overview of the Bill rather than scrutinising its provisions in detail. If the decision at Stage 1 is in favour of the Bill, it proceeds to Stage 2 and it is open to members to lodge amendments. If the decision is not in favour, the Bill falls.

At Stage 2 the details of the Bill are considered in committee. The committee or committees to which it is referred may differ from those involved at Stage 1. Unless it is a Budget or an Emergency Bill, at least two weeks must have elapsed since the completion of Stage 1. Amendments are printed in the *Business Bulletin* as they are lodged and marshalled lists draw the amendments together before they are considered. The committee discussions appear in the *Official Report* but there are not normally separate reports of Stage 2 committee proceedings in the *SP Papers* series. If any amendment is agreed to, the Bill is reprinted in amended form (recorded in the *Business Bulletin*). In certain circumstances revised explanatory notes may also be issued. Once Stage 2 is completed it is open to members to lodge further amendments.

At Stage 3 there is final consideration of the Bill at a meeting of the Parliament and a decision whether it is passed or rejected. Unless it is a Budget or an Emergency Bill, or a Bill which was not amended, at least two weeks must have elapsed since the completion of Stage 2. Amendments are printed in the *Business Bulletin* as they are lodged and marshalled lists draw the amendments together before they are considered. The debate (published in the *Official Report*) concludes with a vote on whether to pass the Bill. If any amendment is agreed to, the Bill is reprinted in amended form (recorded in the *Business Bulletin*). The requirements of the devolution legislation make this innovation necessary as there can be a lengthy period between the passing of a Bill and its appearance as a published Act.

Once the Bill has been passed, the Advocate General for Scotland, the Lord Advocate and the Attorney General have a four-week period within which to refer issues of legislative competence to the Judicial Committee of the Privy Council. In addition the Secretary of State for Scotland may mount a legal challenge on certain statutory grounds during this period. In the event of a decision in favour of one of the Law Officers or a successful challenge by the Secretary of State, the Parliament may resolve to reconsider the contested provisions of the Bill. Proceedings at the Reconsideration Stage are similar to those at Stage 3. If no challenge is forthcoming, the Presiding Officer submits the Bill for Royal Assent.

A Member's Bill is introduced by an MSP who is not a member of the Scottish Executive on a matter of concern. A proposal for a Member's Bill is published in the *Business Bulletin* for one month. If it attracts 11 supporters during that period, the MSP has the right to have a Bill drafted and introduced at any point in the four-year parliamentary session. Such a Bill must be submitted for introduction together with various accompanying documents (fewer than in the case of an Executive Bill): a statement from the Presiding Officer on legislative competence; a financial memorandum; and an Auditor General's Report if relevant. The procedures for the consideration of a Member's Bill are the same as those for the consideration of an Executive Bill.

A Committee Bill is introduced by a committee on its own initiative or as the result of an approach by an MSP who is not a member of that committee. The committee reports to the Parliament on the perceived need for such a Bill and a debate on the proposal follows. If the proposal is accepted, and if the Scottish Executive does not commit itself to introducing an appropriate Executive Bill, a draft Bill is prepared. The accompanying documents required are as for a Member's Bill. Apart from the fact that once introduced the Bill proceeds directly to the Stage 1 debate, the procedures for the consideration of a Committee Bill are the same as those for the consideration of an Executive Bill.

Further information on procedure may be found in *Guidance on Public Bills* prepared by the Parliament's Clerking Services Directorate and published by The Stationery Office.

10.3A3 Structure

Most of the elements found in a United Kingdom Parliament Bill are to be found in a Scottish Parliament Bill (see 4.1A3). There are however certain important changes in presentation and terminology.

(a) *Short title* — it is set out in a large font and bold type at the top of the Bill, in bold type on the back sheet (the outside of the back cover), and also in italics in the running header on each page. The name of the Bill reflects the name of the proposed Act which is cited in the text, usually in the final section; note that this anticipates the year in which it is expected to receive Royal Assent. If this citation provision were to be amended the short title of the Bill would be changed as a consequence. As the Scottish Parliament cannot make laws which apply beyond Scotland the title always includes the territorial designation, usually in round brackets, e.g.:

Public Finance and Accountability (Scotland) Bill

(b) *Status entry* — gives an indication of the version of the Bill in hand, presented in upper-case characters and square brackets after the short title at the top of the Bill, e.g.:

[AS INTRODUCED]

and repeated on the back sheet.

(c) *Contents* — the table, separately paginated in lower-case roman numerals, does not form part of the legislative text of the Bill. It appears at the front of Bills comprising six sections or more and sets out in order the Parts, Chapters and sections into which the text is divided with their respective titles. This is the equivalent of the arrangement of clauses in a Westminster Bill. As in effect it forms the first page of the document, the short title and status entry are repeated at the top.

(d)   *Long title* — describes the purpose or purposes of the Bill in a single sentence but begins 'An Act of the Scottish Parliament to . . .'. This sentence may be lengthy and complicated, with semi-colons separating the principal purposes.

(e)   *Sections* — the Bill is divided into consecutively numbered sections rather than clauses. The section number appears in bold type followed by the section title also in bold. The title is positioned immediately above the text of the section; there are no side notes in the margin. The method of subdivision into subsections, paragraphs and subparagraphs is unaltered. Sections may be grouped into Parts which may in turn be divided into Chapters. Both Parts and Chapters are numbered in arabic rather than roman numerals and have a brief descriptive title. The number and title of the relevant Part and Chapter appear in italics in the running header on each page which is a useful aid in longer Bills. As a guide to the structure of the Bill, sections may also be grouped under italic cross-headings.

(f)   *Schedules* — set out supplementary or consequential provisions dependent on one or more of the preceding sections. The word is spelt with a lower-case 's' and abbreviated to 'sch.'. Schedules are usually divided into untitled paragraphs consecutively numbered within each schedule. An individual schedule may be divided into Parts which may in turn be divided into Chapters, both with brief descriptive titles. Italic headings may also be employed within schedules to aid comprehension. The number and title of the relevant schedule, Part and Chapter appear in italics in the running header on each page which is a useful aid in longer Bills.

(g)   *Back sheet* — repeats the short title, the status entry and the long title, and sets out the name of the MSP who introduced the Bill, the date of its introduction, the names of supporting MSPs, and an indication of the Bill type.

Commencement provisions, schedules amending or repealing existing Acts, and subordinate legislation provisions will be found in most or all Bills.

10.3A4   Publication and general availability

Scottish Parliament Bills are printed by The Stationery Office (TSO) on purple-tinted paper and are available through the usual suppliers of official publications. Notification of publication appears in TSO's *Daily List* and *Weekly List*, and in the Parliament's *Business Bulletin* and *Minutes of Proceedings*. The policy memorandum (Executive Bills only) is published separately but the other accompanying documents usually form a single publication. These will be published on the same day as the Bill itself. Marshalled lists of amendments for Stages 2 and 3 are printed as necessary, and the Bill will be reprinted if any of those amendments are accepted. Changes since the previous version are highlighted by sidelining in the right-hand margin. The status entry on the reprint will clearly indicate whether the text is as introduced, as amended at Stage 2, or as passed. It is intended that bound volumes including all versions of Bills and other relevant documentation should be published.

The Scottish Parliament web site provides ready access to Bills and associated material. It is at

http://www.scottish.parliament.uk/

10.3A5   Citation

A serial number appears at the bottom left-hand side of the first page of the Bill, repeated on the back sheet and on the contents page if any. There is also an indication of the session and calendar year in which that version of the Bill was published. Unlike Westminster Bills, SP Bills retain their original numbering with subsequent revisions indicated by an alphabetical suffix, e.g.:

SP Bill 2	for the Bill as introduced
SP Bill 2A	for the Bill as amended at Stage 2

Serial numbers of accompanying documents and marshalled lists of amendments are linked to the Bill number, e.g.:

SP Bill 2-PM	for the policy memorandum
SP Bill 2-EN	for the explanatory notes and other accompanying documents
SP Bill 2-ML1	for the first marshalled list of amendments for Stage 2
SP Bill 2A-ML	for the marshalled list of amendments selected for Stage 3

The official form of citation is SP Bill number title [printing] session (year), e.g.:

SP Bill 2 Public Finance and Accountability (Scotland) Bill [as introduced] Session 1 (1999)

10.3B   Finding information

10.3B1   What's Happening in the Scottish Parliament

WHISP is compiled by the Scottish Parliament Information Centre (SPICe) and published each week that the Parliament is sitting. One section of this useful publication lists the short and long titles of Bills, indicates the respective lead committees, and provides a full timetable of their progress to date. The dates given allow committee discussions and plenary debates in the *Official Report* to be traced with ease. The current version of a Bill can be traced through the bibliography section. WHISP is also available on the Scottish Parliament web site.

10.3B2   Current Law Monthly Digest

A table indicates only the latest Stage in the parliamentary progress of Scottish Bills. Although the dates of committee discussions are given, the committees themselves are not named. Useful only for a broad overview.

10.3B3   Daily List and Weekly List

The publication of the various versions of Scottish Parliament Bills, the marshalled lists of amendments, explanatory notes, and other accompanying documents is noted with bibliographic details and occasional helpful notes. The *Daily List* is also available on TSO's web site:

> http://www.ukstate.com/

10.3B4   Official Report

The Scottish equivalent of *Hansard* is a substantially verbatim report of proceedings in the Parliament. It is published in three parts, covering the plenary debates, the committee discussions held in public, and written answers respectively. An unrevised report of a full meeting of the Parliament is published on the following working day. The report of a committee meeting may not be quite so prompt but is always available before the next meeting of the committee in question. The written answers report appears weekly. It is intended that revised and indexed bound volumes should be published. Like *Hansard* the *Official Report* is laid out with two columns of print to a page. References are to column numbers and not to page numbers, e.g.:

> SP OR 3(11) 1 December 1999, col 1060

A reference to the committee series incorporates the official abbreviation for that committee, e.g.:

> SP FI OR 2 November 1999, col 87

The *Official Report* is also available on the Scottish Parliament web site.

10.3B5   Current Law Statutes

This publication, described in more detail in section 4.2.B2.2.2, has a separate sequence for Scotland which reprints the Acts of the Scottish Parliament, many with additional editorial notes and commentary. *Official Report* references are given for the plenary debates but not to committee discussions. *Current Law Statutes*, of course, prints only successful Bills which have become law, and is of no use for tracing failed legislation.

10.3B6   Lawtel

Information on the progress of SP Bills is included in the Parliamentary Bills database. Hypertext links to the full text of the various versions and accompanying documents are provided.

10.3B7   Current Legal Information

Information on the progress of SP Bills is included in the *Badger Grey Paper Index* database in both the CD and internet formats of *Current Legal Information*. Abstracts of Scottish Parliament Papers, Scottish Executive press releases and publications, and newspaper articles provide useful additional information.

10.3B8   Periodicals

Periodicals, especially those directed at practitioners, often draw attention to proposed legislation. *Scots Law Times* for example carries a brief Parliamentary news (Scotland) section which notes the introduction and progress of Bills. A monthly 'alerter' in *Scottish Parliament Law Review* performs a similar function though there is little detail; information is updated for subscribers on its web site at

> http://www.splr.co.uk/

10.3C   Answering research queries

The Parliamentary Business section of the Scottish Parliament web site provides the most up-to-date information on the progress of SP Bills and easy access to the full text. There is also a general search engine which can retrieve additional documentation. *WHISP* is undoubtedly the most comprehensive printed source. The services offered by commercial publishers may provide added value as they develop. The web site is at

> http://www.scottish.parliament.uk/

10.4   ACTS OF THE SCOTTISH PARLIAMENT

10.4A   Description

10.4A1   Definition

An Act of the Scottish Parliament (ASP) is a Scottish Parliament Bill (SP Bill) which has been passed by the Parliament and has received Royal Assent. The majority of Acts will be Public Acts, that is to say Acts which are general in application. Private or local legislation pertaining to devolved matters will result from the introduction of Private Bills (see 10.3A1). The Private Legislation Procedure (Scotland) Act 1936 will continue to govern procedure in relation to matters not within the competence of the Scottish Parliament, and such Acts will of course be Westminster Acts. Law students are most likely to encounter Public Acts and therefore the remainder of section 10.4 concentrates upon researching those.

10.4A2   Origin

See section 10.3.

10.4A3   Structure

Figure 10.1 reproduces part of an Act of the Scottish Parliament.

As a Bill is drawn up on the premise that the legislative text as passed by the Parliament should require no changes of substance for it to become an Act, there are few differences in structure. There are however some differences in the presentation of the document, one of the most immediately noticeable being that it bears the Scottish Royal Arms.

(a)   *Short title* — is the name by which the Act is generally known. This is set out in a large font and bold type at the top of the Act, and also in italics in the running header on each page. A specific provision, usually in the final section, formally states how the Act may be cited. As the Scottish Parliament cannot make laws which apply beyond Scotland the title always includes the territorial designation, usually in round brackets, e.g.:

Public Finance and Accountability (Scotland) Act 2000

(b)   *Official citation* — is a shorthand way of referring to the Act. This comprises a date, a lower-case abbreviation indicating that it is an Act of the Scottish Parliament, and a running number, e.g.:

2000 asp 1

and appears in bold type immediately below the short title. This is of course the equivalent of the chapter number of a Westminster Act. The abbreviation and number are repeated in italics and round brackets in the running header on each page, e.g.:

Public Finance and Accountability (Scotland) Act 2000 (asp 1)

At the time of writing it appears that Public and Private Acts will be numbered in a single sequence.

(c)   *Contents* — the table, separately paginated in lower-case roman numerals, does not form part of the legislative text of the Act. It appears at the front of the longer Acts and sets out in order the Parts, Chapters and sections into which the text is divided with their respective titles. This is the equivalent of the arrangement of sections in a Westminster Act. As in effect it forms the first page of the document, the Scottish Royal Arms, short title and official citation are repeated at the top.

Figure 10.1   An Act of the Scottish Parliament.

(1) *Public Finance and Accountability (Scotland) Act 2000 (asp 1)*
Part 1 — Public Resources and Finances

---

(2) # Public Finance and Accountability (Scotland) Act 2000
(3) # 2000 asp 1

(4) **The Bill for this Act of the Scottish Parliament was passed by the Parliament on 1st December 1999 and received Royal Assent on 17th January 2000**

(5) An Act of the Scottish Parliament to make provision about public resources and finances and, for the purposes of section 70 of the Scotland Act 1998, about accountability for their use; and for connected purposes.

(6) ## PART 1

PUBLIC RESOURCES AND FINANCES

(7) *Use of resources*

(8) **1   Use of resources**

(1)   The use of resources by—

(a)   the Scottish Administration, and

(b)   each body or office-holder (other than an office-holder in the Scottish Administation) whose expenditure is payable out of the Scottish Consolidated Fund ('the Fund') under any enactment,

for any purpose in any financial year must be authorised for that year by Budget Act and must not exceed any amount so authorised in relation to that purpose.

(2)   The use of resources accruing to the Scottish Administration or any such body or office-holder in a financial year ('accruing resources') for any purpose in that financial year must be so authorised separately from the use of other resources.

(3)   In this Act a reference to the use of resources is a reference to their expenditure, consumption or reduction in value.

2   Emergency arrangements

(1)   This section applies where, at the beginning of any financial year ('the current financial year'), the use of resources mentioned in section 1(1) has not been authorised for that year by Budget Act.

. . .

30   Commencement and short title

⑨   (1)   The preceding provisions of this Act (including the schedules) are to come into force on such day as the Scottish Ministers may by order appoint.

(2)   Different days may be appointed under this section for different purposes.

⑩   (3)   This Act may be cited as the Public Finance and Accountability (Scotland) Act 2000.

Crown copyright 2000 with the permission of the Queen's Printer for Scotland

---

① Running header   ⑥ Number and title of Part   (f)
② Short title   (a)   ⑦ Cross-heading   (f)
③ Official citation   (b)   ⑧ Section number and title   (f)
④ Enactment formula   (d)   ⑨ Commencement   (f)
⑤ Long title   (e)   ⑩ Citation   (a)

(The letters in parentheses refer to paragraphs in the text where discussion on the element of an Act of the Scottish Parliament occur.)

(d) *Enactment formula* — is added in bold type to the text of the Bill as passed and includes the date of Royal Assent, e.g.:

> The Bill for this Act of the Scottish Parliament was passed by the Parliament on 1st December 1999 and received Royal Assent on 17th January 2000

(e) *Long title* — describes the purpose or purposes of the Act in a single sentence. This sentence may be lengthy and complicated, with semi-colons separating the principal purposes.

(f) *Sections* — the Act is divided into consecutively numbered sections. The section number appears in bold type followed by the section title also in bold. The title is positioned immediately above the text of the section; there are no side notes in the margin. Sections may be subdivided into subsections, subsections into paragraphs, and paragraphs into subparagraphs. Sections may be grouped into Parts which may in turn be divided into Chapters. Both Parts and Chapters are numbered in arabic rather than roman numerals and have a brief descriptive title. The number and title of the relevant Part and Chapter appear in italics in the running header on each page which is a useful aid in longer Acts, e.g.:

Part 1 — Public Resources and Finances

As a guide to the structure of the Act, sections may also be grouped under italic cross-headings.

As is the case with a Westminster Act a very important section in an Act of the Scottish Parliament is the section dealing with commencement provisions, that is to say the arrangements for bringing the Act into force. This is usually one of the final sections. An Act may be brought into force on a specified date, after a specified period of time, or by subordinate legislation. Given the challenges which may be mounted to Scottish legislation under the devolution process (see 10.3A2) it is likely that most Acts will be brought into force by commencement orders published as Scottish statutory instruments (see 11.2). When such power to determine the commencement of legislation is delegated to the Scottish Executive an ASP will use the phrase 'the Scottish Ministers' rather than specifying a particular Minister. Section 52(1) and (3) of the Scotland Act 1998 gave expression to the convention of collective Cabinet responsibility. If there is no specific provision for commencement the Act comes into force immediately it receives Royal Assent.

(g) *Schedules* — set out supplementary or consequential provisions dependent on one or more of the preceding sections. The word is spelt with a lower-case 's' and abbreviated to 'sch.'. Schedules are usually divided into untitled paragraphs consecutively numbered within each schedule. An individual schedule may be divided into Parts which may in turn be divided into Chapters, both with brief descriptive titles. Italic headings may also be employed within schedules to aid comprehension. The number and title of the relevant schedule, Part and Chapter appear in italics in the running header on each page which is a useful aid in longer Acts, e.g.:

Schedule 1 — Capital Expenditure of, and Borrowing by, Certain Statutory Bodies

10.4A4   Publication and general availability

Acts of the Scottish Parliament are published by The Stationery Office (TSO) on behalf of the Queen's Printer for Scotland. They appear individually soon after receiving Royal Assent and eventually in annual bound compilations. Notification of publication appears in TSO's *Daily List* and *Weekly List*. Her Majesty's Stationery Office (HMSO) has a *Scotland Legislation* web site which provides ready access. It is at

    http://www.scotland-legislation.hmso.gov.uk/

ASPs are also included in the official *Statute Law Database*. In addition unofficial collected or annotated editions may be issued by other publishers.

Acts which originated as Executive Bills are accompanied by explanatory notes separately published by TSO.

10.4A5   Citation

An Act of the Scottish Parliament is usually referred to by its short title, e.g. the Public Finance and Accountability (Scotland) Act 2000, though for completeness the asp number (asp 1 in the example) may be added after the date. At the time of writing it appears that Public and Private Acts will be numbered in a single sequence.

10.4B   Finding information

At the time of writing the pattern of publication of ASPs in both official and unofficial editions is still developing. This is particularly true of bound editions, with any associated finding tools, which have yet to appear. It is clear that commercial considerations will determine how publishers initiate and maintain their coverage of Scottish legislation.

10.4B1   Acts of the Scottish Parliament

Annual bound compilations of Acts will be issued by The Stationery Office with tables and indexes similar to those produced for the UK *Public General Acts and General Synod Measures*. These compilations will merely reprint ASPs in the form in which they were originally given Royal Assent. At the time of writing it appears that Public and Private Acts will be numbered and published in a single sequence.

10.4B2   Current Law Statutes

This long-established publication, described in more detail in section 4.2B2.2.2, now has a separate section for Scotland which reprints the Acts of the Scottish Parliament with brief explanatory introductions, and in many cases with valuable annotations by appropriate experts. *Official Report* references are given for the plenary debates but not to committee discussions. ASPs are issued first as part of a release for the loose-leaf service volumes and are subsequently included in the annual bound volumes, appearing immediately after UK Private Acts. The consolidated index covers ASPs but there is a separate Scottish commencement diary. As time passes ASPs may be integrated more fully into the *Current Law* service, or separate finding tools may be provided to mirror those available for UK legislation. The best advice which can be given to the aspiring researcher is that the preliminaries in the loose-leaf service should be read carefully. The CD version of *Current Law Statutes* also includes ASPs.

10.4B3   Current Law Legislation Citators

The editions of the *Legislation Citators* covering the post-devolution era will allow the researcher to discover whether a particular Act of the Scottish Parliament has come into force or been amended or repealed. It will also be possible to determine whether subordinate legislation has been made under powers conferred by the Act and whether the meaning of specific sections has been considered in the courts. ASPs are listed in a separate sequence by year and then by number. The loose-leaf service volumes of *Current Law Statutes* contain a statute citator which is updated monthly and supplements the relevant part of the *Legislation Citators* between editions. For a fuller description of the use of the *Legislation Citators* see section 4.2B2.2.3.

10.4B4   Is It in force?

Although this Butterworths publication is usually associated with *Halsbury's Statutes of England*, it is also issued in conjunction with the *Laws of Scotland (Stair Memorial Encyclopaedia)* and therefore covers UK Acts which apply to Scotland and Acts of the Scottish Parliament. It is worth noting however that the loose-leaf updating through *Halsbury* is more frequent than the updating through *Stair*. An online version is also available through *Butterworths Scotland Direct* (see 10.4B6).

10.4B5   Butterworths Scottish Legislation Service

This loose-leaf publication aims to be 'a clear and easy to use source of up-to-date statutory materials'. The full text of Acts of the Scottish Parliament is presented with a citator and a version of *Is It in Force?*. Scottish statutory instruments (see 11.2) are summarised. The Scotland Act 1998 is also reproduced with its own citator of amendments to and by the Act. Secondary legislation made under the authority of the Act is presented in summary form with alphabetical and chronological lists as finding aids. The text is annotated but stops short of commentary.

10.4B6   Butterworths Scotland Direct

This developing internet subscription service includes an online version of *Butterworths Scottish Legislation Service* called *Scottish Legislation Direct*.

Acts of the Scottish Parliament are listed by year and asp number with the full text broken down into sections and schedules. Hypertext links to other legislation are provided, although these may not work if the documents are held in other *Butterworths Direct* databases to which the user does not subscribe. An online *Is It in Force?* lists ASPs and UK Acts in a single sequence chronologically and then alphabetically. Commencement information is given for each section with hypertext links to the full text of the commencement order. The site is at

> http://www.butterworths.com/

10.4B7   Lawtel

Acts of the Scottish Parliament are included in the Statute Summaries and Commencements and Repeals databases. Hypertext links to the full text are provided.

10.4B8   JUSTIS UK Statutes

Acts of the Scottish Parliament are included in this CD and in the equivalent online database available by subscription. Links are provided to amended and amending legislation. The web site is at

> http://www.justis.com/navigate/main.html

10.4B9   Current Legal Information

Acts of the Scottish Parliament are included in the *Current Law Legislation Citator* database in both the CD and internet formats of *Current Legal Information.*

10.4B10   Periodicals

Periodicals, especially those directed at practitioners, often draw attention to recent legislation. The *Scottish Parliament Law Review* has a monthly 'alerter' updated for subscribers on its web site at

> http://www.splr.co.uk/

10.4C   Answering research queries

At the time of writing, Acts of the Scottish Parliament are too recent to have appeared in certain research tools. The *Chronological Table of the Statutes* for instance will eventually include a new table of ASPs. The researcher will have to adapt and develop new strategies as the body of legislation grows and publishers extend their coverage of it.

10.4C1 Is this Act of the Scottish Parliament in force? Has any section or schedule of the ASP been amended or repealed by subsequent legislation?

Electronic route

The online version of *Is It in Force?* and *Lawtel* will presumably provide the most up-to-date information on commencement. Her Majesty's Stationery Office *Scotland Legislation* web site has a search engine but, as this operates across the whole HMSO site, a search on 'commencement' and keywords from the title of the ASP will probably retrieve a great deal of irrelevant material. Adding 'asp' as a search term improves matters but this is still rather a hit-and-miss approach. The printed version of *Is It in Force?*, as updated either through *Halsbury* or *Stair*, may be supplemented by consulting *Current Law Monthly Digest* which provides a table of statutory commencement dates.

Consulting the text of the ASP on either *Butterworths Scotland Direct* or *Justis UK Statutes*, or the Commencements and Repeals database on *Lawtel*, should highlight amendments and repeals.

Paper route

Using the *Current Law Legislation Citator* and the monthly statute citator in *Current Law Statutes* is a proven method using printed sources. *Butterworths Scottish Legislation Service* also makes provision for a citator.

10.4C2 Tracing Acts of the Scottish Parliament by subject

Electronic route

Both *Butterworths Scotland Direct* and *Lawtel* provide search engines although the latter only searches summaries of the ASPs. The HMSO web site may be of use if internet subscription services are not available. The *Current Law Statutes*, *Justis UK Statutes*, and *Current Legal Information* CDs have keyword searching facilities although the latter only searches the digest entries.

Paper route

Researching the subject in the *Laws of Scotland* (see 12B4.1), *Current Law Yearbook*, or *Current Law Monthly Digest* will highlight relevant legislation. As time passes textbooks on Scots law will also prove useful.

10.4C3 Are there any cases on this Act of the Scottish Parliament or section of an ASP?

Electronic route

LEXIS has a good file of Scottish cases (see 12B5.1) and searches may be performed as for a UK Act. *Lawtel* only covers Scottish cases reported in certain 'English' series of law reports and these are probably unlikely to be concerned with exclusively Scottish legislation. The *Current Legal Information* database *Current Law Cases* has a legislation field to which searches can be limited but *Scots Law Times Reports on CD-ROM* does not. Legislation considered in a case is often detailed in the headnote and searches may be limited to such a field although this will not retrieve everything of potential interest.

Paper route

The *Current Law Legislation Citator* and the monthly statute citator in *Current Law Statutes* will draw attention to case law. The *Laws of Scotland* and the indexes and tables printed in law reports and in textbooks are another source of information.

10.4C4   Have any Scottish statutory instruments been made under this Act of the Scottish Parliament?

Electronic route

A specific search on the enabling Act can be carried out in the Statutory Instruments database on *Lawtel* and in *Scottish Legislation Direct*. This is also possible in both the CD and internet formats of *Justis UK Statutory Instruments* (see 11.2B12). The HMSO web site is rather hit-and-miss.

Paper route

The *Current Law Legislation Citator* and the monthly statute citator in *Current Law Statutes* will draw attention to secondary legislation.

10.4C5   Have any case notes or articles been written about this Act of the Scottish Parliament?

See section 8.3 for information on periodical indexing publications.

Chapter 11

Scotland: secondary legislation

It should be obvious from what has gone before that secondary legislation affecting Scotland can be pre- or post-devolution in origin. The power to make such legislation may derive from a Westminster Act or from an Act of the Scottish Parliament but the basic principles described in section 5.1 remain the same.

Since 1999 it has been possible for secondary legislation pertaining to devolved matters to be made under powers delegated by an Act of the Scottish Parliament. Such legislative powers may be exercised by the Scottish Executive as the government of Scotland, by local authorities, by the courts, and by certain statutory bodies. Secondary legislation in relation to matters not within the competence of the Scottish Parliament will continue to be made under powers delegated by a Westminster Act. The Scotland Act 1998 itself gave rise to important secondary legislation most of which was designed to deal with implementation of the devolution process. In Scotland as in the rest of the United Kingdom statutory instruments are the most commonly encountered form of secondary legislation.

11.1 STATUTORY INSTRUMENTS

For some considerable time to come the student of the law of Scotland will be working with the legislation described fully in chapter 5 and wherever possible any Scottish dimension has been noted in that text. Section 11.1 therefore confines itself to additional information which may not be of general interest.

11.1A Description

It has already been noted that statutory instruments exclusively affecting Scotland had an S number in addition to the standard citation. However it is important to remember that any SI of more general application might have had an effect on the law of Scotland.

11.1B   Finding information

Generally, as described in section 5.1B. Statutory instruments made under the authority of the Scotland Act 1998 are conveniently brought together on Her Majesty's Stationery Office *Scotland Legislation* web site at

http://www.scotland-legislation.hmso.gov.uk/

Butterworths Scottish Legislation Service provides summaries with alphabetical and chronological lists as finding aids. They are also available in full text on the *Butterworths Scotland Direct* version of the service.

11.1C   Answering research queries

Generally, as described in section 5.1C. The *Laws of Scotland* which provides a comprehensive narrative statement of the law of Scotland (see 12B4.1) will also direct the researcher to relevant secondary legislation.

11.2   SCOTTISH STATUTORY INSTRUMENTS

11.2A   Description

11.2A1   Definition

A statutory instrument pertaining to a devolved matter is designated a Scottish statutory instrument (SSI) and forms part of a separate series of secondary legislation. The power to make such legislation may have been conferred either by an Act of the Scottish Parliament or by a pre-devolution Westminster Act, and that power may be exercised by the Scottish Ministers, by the Queen in Council, or by a Scottish public authority. Power conferred on the Scottish Ministers may be exercised by any member of the Scottish Executive. The provisions of the parent Act also determine to what extent an SSI is subject to scrutiny by the Scottish Parliament (see 11.2A2).

   Like their Westminster counterparts SSIs may be classified as local or general according to the subject matter and commencement orders form an important group of instruments. Until such time as an Act of the Scottish Parliament may address the issue, SSIs are governed by the Scotland Act 1998 (Transitory and Transitional Provisions) (Statutory Instruments) Order 1999 SI 1999/1096.

11.2A2   Origin

The majority of SSIs are prepared on behalf of the Scottish Executive by civil servants. As the Parliament does not wish its primary legislative role to be usurped through the excessive delegation of powers, relevant provisions of the parent Act will have been scrutinised at Stage 1 of the Bill's passage. In addition there are two procedures which may bring any statutory instrument which results under further scrutiny. Under affirmative procedure a statutory instrument is laid before the Parliament for approval by resolution. Most such instruments are laid in draft and cannot be made or come into force until the Parliament has approved them. Under negative procedure a statutory instrument is laid before the Parliament and is subject to annulment. Most such instruments are laid as made instruments and come into force unless the Parliament annuls them within a period of 40 days. The researcher thus may encounter the terms affirmative instrument and negative instrument. Not all statutory instruments are subject to parliamentary control however and some are not even laid before the Parliament.

While all committees have a role to play in this process the Subordinate Legislation Committee is pre-eminent. Reports of the committee are published in the *SP Papers* series. The *Business Bulletin* (see 13.5A1.1) notes the progress of instruments laid before the Parliament.

11.2A3 Structure

There are few differences between Scottish statutory instruments and their Westminster counterparts (see 5.1A3).

(a) *Citation* — SSIs are numbered consecutively by the Queen's Printer for Scotland. The citation comprises the calendar year and a sequence number. Commencement orders bear a supplementary sequence number preceded by the letter C.

(b) *Subject matter* — the same words and phrases are used to describe the subject of the SSI. These are added by the lawyer drafting the instrument and are the same as those used to describe the enabling power in the *Index to Government Orders* (see 5.1B1.4).

(c) *Short title* — is the name by which the SSI is generally known. This is set out in a large font at the top of the instrument and formally stated in one of the provisions. Titles follow the familiar format with the terms regulations and rules recurring.

(d) *Dates* — depending upon the nature of the SSI and the procedure to which it was subject, it will bear a statement of the date on which it was made, the date it was laid before the Scottish Parliament, and the date on which it enters into force.

(e) *Preamble and enabling powers* — the enabling power may derive from an Act of the Scottish Parliament or from a pre-devolution Westminster Act.

(f) *Main text* — is arranged into consecutively numbered divisions known variously as articles, regulations or rules.

(g) *Signature* — this is usually the name of the member of the Scottish Executive making the SSI.

(h) *Schedules* — set out detailed provisions dependent on one or more of the numbered divisions of the main text.

(i) *Explanatory note* — this does not form part of the instrument.

11.2A4   Publication and general availability

Scottish statutory instruments classified as general are published by The
Stationery Office (TSO) on behalf of the Queen's Printer for Scotland. They
appear individually and eventually in annual bound compilations. Notification
of publication appears in TSO's *Daily List* and *Weekly List*. Her Majesty's
Stationery Office (HMSO) has a *Scotland Legislation* web site which provides
ready access. The web site is at

> http://www.scotland-legislation.hmso.gov.uk/

SSIs are also included in the official *Statute Law Database*. In addition,
unofficial collected or annotated editions may be issued by other publishers. SSIs
classified as local are not published unless the Presiding Officer of the Scottish
Parliament directs otherwise or the responsible authority specifically requests it.

11.2A5   Citation

A Scottish statutory instrument is usually cited by the short title followed by the
abbreviation SSI, the year, followed by a slash and then the running number, e.g.:

> Census (Scotland) Order 2000 SSI 2000/68

11.2B   Finding information

At the time of writing the pattern of publication of SSIs in both official and
unofficial editions is still developing. This is particularly true of bound editions,
with any associated finding tools, which have yet to appear. As with the Acts
it is clear that commercial considerations will determine how publishers initiate
and maintain their coverage of Scottish secondary legislation.

11.2B1   Scottish Statutory Instruments

Annual bound compilations of SSIs will be issued by The Stationery Office with
tables and indexes similar to those produced for the UK *Statutory Instruments*
(see 5.1B1.1). These compilations will merely reprint SSIs in the form in which
they were made, excluding those which have ceased to be in force.

11.2B2   List of Statutory Instruments

The monthly lists contain a separate section detailing SSIs and this will no doubt
be mirrored in the annual edition. In the absence of sufficiently up-to-date issues
the *Daily List* and *Weekly List* may be used to trace SSIs.

11.2B3   Index to Government Orders

SSIs may be included in a future edition of the *Index* or there may be a separate
publication.

11.2B4   Table of Government Orders

SSIs may be included in a future edition of the *Table* or there may be a separate publication.

11.2B5   Current Law Statutes

Commencement orders are reproduced as part of this service and a numerical table of all general SSIs is included.

11.2B6   Current Law Monthly Digest

Summaries of SSIs appear in the section covering Scotland and may be traced through a table which lists them in alphabetical order. This information will later appear in the *Current Law Yearbook*.

11.2B7   Current Law Legislation Citators

The editions of the *Legislation Citators* covering the post-devolution era will allow the researcher to discover whether a particular SSI has been amended or revoked. SSIs are listed in a separate sequence by year and then by number. The loose-leaf service volumes of *Current Law Statutes* contain a statutory instrument citator which is updated monthly and supplements the relevant part of the *Legislation Citators* between editions. It is also possible to trace SSIs made under powers conferred by a given Act.

11.2B8   Greens Scottish Statutory Instruments Service

As this developing loose-leaf service is described as 'from *Current Law*' it may in time replace the coverage of exclusively Scottish secondary legislation in *Current Law Statutes* and related titles. It reproduces the summaries of SSIs from *Current Law Monthly Digest* arranged under the same broad subject headings. Alphabetical and numerical lists are provided as finding aids.

11.2B9   Butterworths Scottish Legislation Service

This loose-leaf publication includes summaries of SSIs with alphabetical and numerical lists as finding aids.

11.2B10   Butterworths Scotland Direct

This developing internet subscription service includes an online version of *Butterworths Scottish Legislation Service* called *Scottish Legislation Direct*. All Scottish statutory instruments of general application are listed by year and number with the full text broken down into sections and schedules. Hypertext links to amended and amending legislation are provided, although these may not work if the documents are held in other *Butterworths Direct* databases to which the user does not subscribe. The web site is at

http://www.butterworths.com/

11.2B11   Lawtel

SSIs are included in the Statutory Instruments database with amendments and revocations highlighted. Hypertext links to the full text are provided.

11.2B12   JUSTIS UK Statutory Instruments

SSIs are included in this CD and in the equivalent online database available by subscription. Links are provided to amended and amending legislation. The web site is at

http://www.justis.com/navigate/main.html

11.2B13   Current Legal Information

SSIs are included in the *Current Law Legislation Citator* database in both the CD and internet formats of *Current Legal Information*. SSIs are summarised in the *Badger Grey Paper Index* database.

11.2C   Answering research queries

At the time of writing SSIs are too recent to have appeared in certain research tools. Future editions of the *Index to Government Orders* and *Table of Government Orders* for instance may include SSIs. The researcher will have to adapt and develop new strategies as the body of secondary legislation grows and publishers extend their coverage of it.

11.2C1   You know the title of an SSI but not the year or running number. How do you trace a copy of it?

Electronic route
A title search in *Lawtel* will produce a list of SSIs in reverse chronological order (i.e. the most recent first). It will be important to distinguish the correct instrument from those with similar titles. Follow the hypertext link to see the full text. A similar search in *Justis UK Statutory Instruments* will produce similar results. Her Majesty's Stationery Office *Scotland Legislation* web site has a search engine but, as this operates across the whole HMSO site, a search on keywords from the title of the SSI will probably retrieve a great deal of irrelevant material.

Paper route
Alphabetical lists will be found in *Current Law Yearbook*, *Current Law Monthly Digest*, *Greens Scottish Statutory Instruments Service* and *Butterworths Scottish*

Legislation Service. A summary will be available but the full text will have to be located elsewhere.

11.2C2   Is this SSI, the title, year and number of which you know, in force?

Electronic route
A search in *Lawtel* will provide a record for the SSI and the relevant field will display the date of coming into force. This of course can be confirmed by following the hypertext link to the full text. *Justis UK Statutory Instruments, Butterworths Scotland Direct* and the HMSO web site provide this information by retrieving the document itself while *Current Legal Information* includes it in a summary.

Paper route
The summaries in *Current Law Yearbook, Current Law Monthly Digest, Greens Scottish Statutory Instrument Service,* and *Butterworths Scottish Legislation Service* also include the date of coming into force. The summary of a particular SSI can be located by consulting the alphabetical table provided in each publication.

11.2C3   Has this SSI been amended?

Electronic route
A search in *Lawtel* will provide a record for the SSI and the status field will record whether it has been amended. Follow the hypertext link to see the full text of the amending instrument. On *Justis UK Statutory Instruments* locate the text of the SSI and click on the Crossref button to see a list of amending legislation. The full text of any amending instrument can be easily retrieved. The text of the SSI displayed by *Butterworths Scotland Direct* should be as amended, but links to the amending instrument are also provided. The legislation citator on *Current Legal Information* will record amending legislation but the full text will have to be located elsewhere.

Paper route
At the time of writing the *Current Law Legislation Citators* provide the only convenient means of tracing amendments through printed sources.

11.2C4   Which SSIs have been made under this Act?

Electronic route
A search in *Lawtel* on the enabling Act will produce a list of SSIs in reverse chronological order (i.e. the most recent first). Follow the hypertext link to see the full text. *Justis UK Statutory Instruments* and *Butterworths Scotland Direct* also facilitate retrieval in this manner. Locating the information through the legislation citator on *Current Legal Information* is not so straightforward.

Paper route
At the time of writing the *Current Law Legislation Citators* provide the only convenient means of tracing SSIs by enabling legislation through printed sources.

11.2C5   Is this SSI still in force?

Electronic route
A search in *Lawtel* will provide a record for the SSI and the status field will
record whether it has been revoked. Follow the hypertext link to see the full
text of the revoking instrument. On *Justis UK Statutory Instruments* locate the
text of the SSI and click on the Crossref button to see a list of amending
legislation. The full text of any amending instrument will have to be examined
for its effect which may include revocation. *Butterworths Scotland Direct*
clearly indicates whether an instrument has been revoked and provides a link to
the relevant instrument. The legislation citator on *Current Legal Information*
records revocations but the full text will have to be located elsewhere.

Paper route
At the time of writing the *Current Law Legislation Citators* provide the only
convenient means of tracing revocations through printed sources.

11.2C6   Has this SSI been considered by the courts?

Electronic route
LEXIS has a good file of Scottish cases (see 12B5.1) and searches may be
performed as for a UK statutory instrument. *Lawtel* only covers Scottish cases
reported in certain 'English' series of law reports and these are probably unlikely to
be concerned with exclusively Scottish secondary legislation. The *Current Legal
Information* database *Current Law Cases* has a legislation field to which searches
can be limited but *Scots Law Times Reports on CD-ROM* does not. Secondary
legislation considered in a case is often detailed in the headnote and searches may
be limited to such a field although this will not retrieve everything of potential
interest.

Paper route
The *Current Law Legislation Citator* and the monthly statutory instrument
citator in *Current Law Statutes* will draw attention to case law. The *Laws of
Scotland* and the indexes and tables printed in law reports and in textbooks are
another source of information.

11.2C7   Have any notes or articles been written in periodicals about this SSI?

See section 8.3 for information on periodical indexing publications.

11.3   ACTS OF SEDERUNT AND ACTS OF ADJOURNAL

11.3A   Description

11.3A1   Definition

Acts of Sederunt which govern procedure in the civil courts of Scotland and
Acts of Adjournal which govern procedure in the criminal courts are enacted
by the Court of Session and the High Court of Justiciary respectively.

11.3A2 Origin

Although the power to make Acts of Sederunt dates from the Court of Session's foundation in 1532, the modern sources of its general rule-making powers are the Court of Session Act 1988 and the Sheriff Courts (Scotland) Act 1971. Specific rule-making powers are conferred by many other Acts. In a similar fashion the High Court of Justiciary is empowered by the Criminal Procedure (Scotland) Act 1995. Scotland's most senior judge, who holds the offices of Lord President of the Court of Session and Lord Justice-General, has overall responsibility for secondary legislation emanating from the courts.

Unless the enabling Act provides otherwise, Acts of Sederunt and Acts of Adjournal take the form of statutory instruments and more recently Scottish statutory instruments.

11.3A3 Structure

The structure resembles that of other SIs and SSIs (see 5.1A3 and 11.2A3). The short title will indicate whether it is an Act of Sederunt or an Act of Adjournal and the first subject heading will be 'Court of Session', 'Sheriff Court' or 'High Court of Justiciary' accordingly.

11.3A4 Publication and general availability

Generally as described in sections 5.1A4 and 11.2A4. In addition Acts of Sederunt may be reproduced in the *Parliament House Book* and Acts of Adjournal in *Renton & Brown's Criminal Procedure Legislation*. Both appear in *Scots Law Times*.

11.3A5 Citation

As with other SIs and SSIs citation is by short title, year and running number, e.g.:

> Act of Sederunt (Rules of the Court of Session Amendment) (Miscellaneous) 2000 SSI 2000/66

In some sources the abbreviations 'AS' and 'Act of Adj' are employed.

11.3B Finding information

Generally, as described in sections 5.1B and 11.2B. The *Index to Government Orders*, the *List of Statutory Instruments*, and the indexes to the annual bound compilations of *Statutory Instruments* list most of them under the subject headings for the courts. The alphabetical subject index to the *List of Statutory Instruments* also brings them together conveniently under 'Act of Adjournal' and 'Act of Sederunt'. Summaries in *Current Law Monthly Digest* may be traced through the alphabetical table of Scottish statutory instruments and the cumulative index which employs both terms.

11.3B1   Parliament House Book

Essentially a loose-leaf collection of primary and secondary legislation intended for practising lawyers, *Parliament House Book* concentrates on aspects of private law and court procedure. It is arranged in several 'divisions' and legislation is distributed throughout the publication accordingly, but the chronological list of statutory instruments will indicate whether and where a particular Act of Sederunt is reproduced. Legislation is not necessarily reproduced in its entirety and what there is may be split between divisions.

11.3B2   Renton & Brown's Criminal Procedure Legislation

Legislation is distributed throughout this loose-leaf publication according to subject but the chronological list of statutory instruments will indicate whether and where a particular Act of Adjournal is reproduced.

11.3B3   Scots Law Times

The index to the News section allows the researcher to trace exactly where an Act of Sederunt or an Act of Adjournal is reproduced. It is published on blue paper as part of each issue, cumulates every ten issues into an issue on its own, and appears in the annual bound volume. Note that the separate *Scots Law Times Index* does not index the News section.

11.3B4   Scottish Current Law Statutes

Until it merged with the English edition in 1991 Acts of Sederunt and Acts of Adjournal were reproduced in *Scottish Current Law Statutes*.

11.3C   Answering research queries

Generally as described in sections 5.1C and 11.2C.

11.4   BY-LAWS AND MANAGEMENT RULES

11.4A   Description

11.4A1   Definition

A local authority may make by-laws 'for the good rule and government' of its area and 'for the prevention and suppression of nuisances therein' under powers conferred by the Local Government (Scotland) Act 1973 and other primary legislation. Despite this broad grant of powers for local government, central government retains overall control by requiring that new by-laws must meet with the approval of a confirming authority. Insofar as it is within devolved competence, this function has been transferred to the Scottish Ministers.

Management rules were introduced by the Civic Government (Scotland) Act 1982 as an additional form of secondary legislation and are employed to regulate the use of land or premises under local authority control. Unless criminal sanctions are deemed appropriate for contravention, local authorities are expected to use management rules rather than by-laws. There is no external confirming authority.

11.4A2 Origin

There are 32 local authority areas in Scotland established in 1996 as a consequence of the Local Government etc. (Scotland) Act 1994. By-laws result from a resolution of the appropriate council after which there is an opportunity for public consultation. The confirming authority will consider any objections and may arrange for a public inquiry to be held. The confirming authority has the power to modify any proposed by-law or to refuse confirmation. A by-law comes into operation one month after confirmation unless the confirming authority fixes a date. Local authorities are required to review by-laws regularly and at least every 10 years.

The intention to make management rules must be publicised and members of the public given an opportunity to object. The rules come into force on the day they are signed on behalf of the authority and may remain in force for up to 10 years.

11.4A3 Structure

The structure may vary but numbered sections and paragraphs are a common feature, with a recital of the enabling power and usually information on commencement and interpretation. The Scottish Executive is promoting the use of model by-laws which would standardise such legislation. For instance the majority of local authorities have a by-law banning the consumption of alcohol in public places and most use a standard format approved by the Executive.

11.4A4 Publication and general availability

Local authorities are required to publish, make available and sell copies of their by-laws. Few libraries collect these but they are available for public inspection without payment at the offices of the local authority. A descriptive register of all the authority's by-laws will also be available.

Management rules must be prominently displayed at the entrance to the land or premises to which they apply and copies are also made available for public inspection.

11.4A5 Citation

In the absence of a standardised method of citation the title of the instrument will usually suffice, e.g.:

City of Dundee District Council By-laws for the Cleansing of Common Property 1992

11.4B   Finding information

See section 11.4A4.

11.4C   Answering research queries

See section 11.4A4.

Chapter 12

Scotland: case law

Much of what is described fully in chapter 6 applies in Scotland and wherever possible any Scottish dimension has been noted in that text. Cases reported in 'English' series of reports are used in Scotland and some of the research sources described may also be used to trace Scottish cases. This section attempts to avoid unnecessary duplication and draws attention to sources specific to the jurisdiction.

12A   DESCRIPTION

12A1   Definition

As in England there is no official series of law reports. However *Session Cases*, which reports decisions in the supreme courts of Scotland and the House of Lords, is regarded as having an authority beyond that of any alternative source. The convention is that, when more than one report of a decision is available, *Session Cases* should be preferred to *Scots Law Times*, which in its turn should be preferred to *Scottish Civil Law Reports* or *Scottish Criminal Case Reports* or any other source. In Scotland there seems never to have been a requirement for a report to be prepared and published under the name of a member of the Scottish Bar. The criteria for selection for publication in *Scots Law Times* are broadly similar to those for the *All England Law Reports* outlined in section 6A1. Although there has been an increase in recent years the number of specialist titles in Scotland remains modest compared to the proliferation in England. Unreported cases also seem to be less contentious, the position that the authority of a case 'depends not upon whether it is to be found in a series of reports but upon the fact that it is a judicial decision' having been stated in *Leighton* v *Harland & Wolff Ltd* 1953 SLT (Notes) 34.

12A2   Origin

Although the modern period is dominated by *Session Cases* and *Scots Law Times* it will often be necessary to refer to older decisions and so a grasp of how law reporting developed is valuable. For various reasons the early case law of Scotland is far more fragmentary than that of England. Sources either never existed or have not survived. Although the decisions in some disputes are recorded in contemporary sources, there are no systematic collections of decisions before the 16th century. In 1532 a central royal court known as the College of Justice was established and to this day the judges of the Court of Session are styled Senators of the College of Justice. A journal of the decisions of the court was to be kept and both judges and practitioners began to compile volumes of notes for their own use. These are known as 'practicks' and those which consist of notes of decisions may be regarded as the earliest form of law report in Scotland.

12A2.1   Practicks

Although compiled principally for personal use, practicks began to circulate in manuscript form within the legal profession and were still being produced in the late 17th century. As well as those which comprised notes of decisions in chronological order (nowadays referred to as 'decision practicks') some collected abstracts of statutes, decisions and other legal materials in an alphabetical subject sequence. These 'digest practicks' are therefore an early form of legal encyclopaedia. Some practicks were subsequently published and an important example is Balfour's *Practicks* which was compiled between 1574 and 1579 and published in 1754. A more accessible edition is probably the two-volume Stair Society reprint of 1962–63. The researcher with an interest in early Scots law reports would do well to consult *An Introductory Survey of the Sources and Literature of Scots Law*, Edinburgh: Stair Society, 1936 and the relevant volumes of Walker (1988–). Digest practicks such as Balfour's were superseded by the works of the institutional writers (see 13.1A) while decision practicks were superseded by the early printed reports.

12A2.2   Early printed reports

The first volume of decisions to be printed was Stair's *Decisions* of 1683 although Durie's *Decisions* of 1690, which covered the period 1621–42, is often described as the first of the law reports. These and similar published collections, while displaying a renewed interest in the sources of the law, still relied upon the private individual. In 1705 the Faculty of Advocates approved a proposal from William Forbes to collect the decisions of the Court of Session on their behalf. Although this first attempt resulted in a noteworthy volume covering the period 1705 to 1713 and published in 1714, Forbes' successors were less successful. The Faculty relaunched the venture in 1752 and 21 volumes of what is now known as the *Faculty Collection* were published between 1760 and 1828. Private individuals such as Kames, Elchies and Hume continued to publish on their own initiative throughout this period. Robert Bell, who published collections in 1794 and 1796, claimed to be the first to give the actual opinions of the judges, much to their Lordships' displeasure.

12A2.3   Dictionaries of decisions

Lord Kames' *Decisions of the Court of Session abridged in the Form of a Dictionary* of 1741 was the first attempt to bring together decisions from previous collections and to arrange them under subject to make it easier to find cases on particular points of law. However William Maxwell Morison's *Decisions of the Court of Session Digested under Proper Heads in the Form of A Dictionary*, published between 1801 and 1807 (and continued by him and others), has proved the most popular single source for older reports. 'Morison's *Dictionary*' as it is invariably known is not an easy work to navigate with 38 volumes in the main work, 2 appendices, a synopsis and a supplemental volume. To complicate matters further the *Dictionary* may have been bound up in different ways in different libraries and the researcher will need to examine the set in hand very carefully. Morison is supplemented by Mungo Brown's *Supplement to the Dictionary of the Decisions of the Court of Session* (1826) and *General Synopsis of the Decisions of the Court of Session* (1829). W. Tait's *Index to the Decisions of the Court of Session* (1823) is an invaluable aid to using Morison and the early printed reports.

12A2.4   19th century developments

After the Union it had become possible to appeal from the Court of Session to the House of Lords. However it took a hundred years for such appeals to be systematically reported, a series of 19th century private reporters publishing decisions covering the period 1707 to 1873 with the later volumes running in parallel with coverage in *Session Cases*. The High Court of Justiciary had been founded in 1672 to try serious crimes from throughout Scotland but again collections of decisions in criminal cases did not appear until the 1800s. A series of private reporters of *Justiciary Cases* published opinions covering the period 1819 to 1916, the later volumes also running in parallel with coverage in *Session Cases*. Records for the earlier period such as Robert Pitcairn's *Ancient Criminal Trials* published in 1833 are of most interest to the legal historian. Reporters appointed by the Faculty of Advocates continued to report decisions of the Court of Session and 16 volumes of *Faculty Decisions* were published between 1826 and 1841. These and other 19th century collections are often described as collateral reports because they are contemporaneous with *Session Cases*, but they contain cases not reported in that series. Annual volumes of *Session Cases* cover decisions of the Court of Session from 1821 to the present day. House of Lords' decisions were added from 1850 and Justiciary cases from 1874. Until 1907 when the Faculty of Advocates took over they were known and cited by the names of five editors: Shaw (1821–38), Dunlop (1838–62), Macpherson (1863–73), Rettie (1873–98), and Fraser (1898–1906). The Faculty subsequently relinquished responsibility to the Scottish Council of Law Reporting which was formed in 1957.

12A2.5 Modern reports

Session Cases soon evolved into the most authoritative source for decisions in the supreme courts. *Scots Law Times* began in 1893 and is published weekly during session, combining news and articles with reports from the Court of Session, the High Court of Justiciary, the House of Lords, the Sheriff Court, and courts of special jurisdiction. Other general series which emerged in the 19th century such as the *Scottish Law Reporter* and *Sheriff Court Reports* fell by the wayside. *Scottish Criminal Case Reports*, *Scottish Civil Law Reports* and *Greens Weekly Digest* commenced publication in the 1980s and more specialist series such as *Greens Family Law Reports* appeared in the following decade. Some decisions are reported in more than one Scottish series and may of course also be reported in publications primarily English in scope.

12A3 Structure

As noted in section 6A3 different series of law reports present cases in slightly different ways. The most important elements are:

(a) *Names of parties* — individual cases are identified and referred to by the names of those involved. In civil actions the name of the person bringing the case (the pursuer) is given first, followed by the name of the defender; for example *Gray* v *Gillespie*. The 'v' separating the parties means 'versus' but when spoken becomes 'against': 'Gray against Gillespie'. Criminal actions are usually brought on behalf of the Crown. In cases tried by solemn procedure the abbreviation 'HMA' or 'HM Advocate' comes first followed by the name of the accused (the pannel). In cases tried by summary procedure (without a jury) a procurator fiscal represents the Crown and their surname will be given first. The 'v' separating the parties also becomes 'against' when spoken. If the case goes to appeal the order is reversed and the name of the appellant precedes that of the respondent. Variations will be encountered, where reporting restrictions require anonymity for example.

(b) *Date* — is the date when the case was heard in court. The opinion of the court may have been delivered at a later date.

(c) *Name of the court in which the case was heard* — this may be self-evident from the series of reports in which the decision is published. The Outer House of the Court of Session determines cases at first instance while the Inner House is mainly a court of appeal so this information, often abbreviated to 'OH' and 'IH', is important. The Divisions of the Inner House are of equal authority.

(d) *Names of judges* — the value of a decision as a precedent may be enhanced by the eminence of those on the bench.

(e) *Catchwords* — are key words and phrases selected by the editor of the report to summarise the case, mostly for indexing purposes. Usually presented in italics or bold type.

(f) *Headnote or rubric* — is also prepared by the editor as a summary of material facts, legal issues arising, and the decision of the court.

(g) *Judicial history* — indicates the progress of the action through various stages of litigation.

(h) *Authorities cited* — lists cases, legislation, or textbooks referred to in argument or the opinion.

(i) *Opinion* — presents, in the judge's own words, the reasoning used in reaching the decision of the court. If more than one judge was sitting more than one opinion may have been delivered. However it is common for one judge to deliver an opinion and for the others to state that they concur. Dissenting opinions are always given.

(j) *Disposal* — the outcome of the case which may be incorporated in the opinion or recorded separately.

(k) *Names of agents* — the names of the solicitors and counsel acting for the parties.

12A4   Publication and general availability

While many academic law libraries will have *Session Cases* and *Scots Law Times*, few will be in a position to subscribe to all the other series. Even in Scottish law libraries the availability of the specialist series may vary. Between 1898 and 1909 *Scots Revised Reports* reprinted cases from Morison's *Dictionary*, the *Faculty Collection*, the House of Lords series, early volumes of *Session Cases*, and the *Scottish Jurist*. Those reproduced were selected for their 'practical utility' and this may prove sufficient in those collections which lack the early printed reports. Scottish cases of significance for the law of England and Wales may appear in *Appeal Cases*, *Weekly Law Reports*, or the *All England Law Reports*. Specialist series such as *Industrial Relations Law Reports* will also include cases from Scotland if appropriate. On the electronic front *LEXIS* includes the full text of both reported and unreported Scottish cases and there is a CD version of *Scots Law Times* (see 12B5). The Scottish Courts web site is at

http://www.scotcourts.gov.uk/

This provides access to full text opinions of the Court of Session and High Court of Justiciary and selected Sheriff Court decisions, with coverage beginning in 1998. Scottish appeals to the House of Lords appear on the Houses of Parliament web site at

http://www.parliament.uk/

with coverage beginning in 1996.

12A5   Citation

Cases are referred to by the names of parties to the action (see 12A3). A published report of the case is further identified by a unique reference known as its citation. However as a case may be reported in more than one series of law reports, a case may have more than one citation. The conventions of citing Scottish cases are broadly similar to those for citing English cases.

(a)   *Date* — being the year in which the case was reported. Brackets are not employed when citing modern Scottish reports. However if, as is the case with the first five series of *Session Cases* and the early volumes of *Scots Law Times*, the date is not essential because each volume has a unique number, it is either put in round brackets or not given at all. Square brackets are never used in Scottish citations (cf. 6A5.1).

(b)   *Abbreviation* — representing the title of the series of law reports. The fact that both *Session Cases* and *Scots Law Times* contain separately paginated sequences of reports from different courts makes it vital to be certain which sequence is meant. This too is handled by the abbreviation, e.g.:

SC   for Court of Session cases in *Session Cases*
SC (HL)   for House of Lords cases in *Session Cases*
JC   for Justiciary cases in *Session Cases*
SLT   for any of the above cases in *Scots Law Times*
SLT (Sh Ct)   for Sheriff Court cases in *Scots Law Times*

The publications listed in section 6A5.1 and the tables in the *Laws of Scotland* provide help with deciphering the abbreviations.

(c)   *Page number* — being the page on which the report of the case begins.

12B   FINDING INFORMATION

Remember that some of the publications described in section 6B may also be used to trace Scottish cases.

12B1   Indexes

Indexes are included in the annual volumes of the law reports. In addition there are consolidated indexes to *Scots Law Times* (1961–90 updated annually), *Scottish Criminal Case Reports* (1981–90), *Scottish Civil Law Reports* (1987–96), and *Greens Weekly Digest* (1986–95). There is no consolidated index to *Session Cases*.

12B2   Indexes with summaries

12B2.1   *Current Law Monthly Digest*

Each issue has a separate Scottish section which summarises cases as well as legislation and secondary materials. There is a single subject index and cumulative table of cases. A *Scottish Current Law Yearbook* was published for the years 1948 to 1990 containing material not to be found in the English edition. That publication superseded the *Scots Digest* which covered decisions of the supreme courts from 1800 and the House of Lords from 1707.

12B2.2   Faculty Digest

Prepared for the Faculty of Advocates and latterly for the Scottish Council of Law Reporting, the *Faculty Digest* summarises decisions of the supreme courts and the House of Lords from 1868 to 1990 in six original volumes and a series of permanent supplements. Searches may be made by subject, by names of the parties, by legislation judicially commented on, by cases judicially referred to, and by words judicially defined. It is a continuation of Patrick Shaw's *Digest of Cases Decided in the Supreme Courts of Scotland* the second edition of which (1869) covered the years 1800 to 1868.

12B3   Citators

12B3.1   Current Law Case Citator

A Scottish edition existed until 1991. *Scottish Current Law Case Citator 1948–1976* covers cases reported in Scotland or judicially considered in the Scottish courts during that period, with the greater part of the volume covering English material from 1947. A *Scottish Current Law Case Citator 1988* extended the coverage from 1977 to 1988 and the *Current Law Case Citator 1989–1995* covered both jurisdictions. A consolidated and corrected *Current Law Case Citator 1977–1997* may be available in your library and this also covers both jurisdictions. As Scottish cases judicially considered in the English courts or published in an English series of law reports are listed in the English section, both parts must be thoroughly checked when researching the law of Scotland.

12B4   Commentary

12B4.1   Laws of Scotland

The *Laws of Scotland*, subtitled and also referred to as the *Stair Memorial Encyclopaedia*, is the most recent attempt to produce a comprehensive statement of the law of Scotland. It is an essential research source and a highly-recommended starting point for ascertaining the law on any subject. There are seven parts to the publication, summarised as follows:

(a)   *Main volumes* — the annotated narrative is divided into 136 titles dealing with broad areas of law. The titles are organised alphabetically and were published in 25 volumes between 1987 and 1996. Each title has its own index and each volume has its own tables of legislation and cases. The paragraphs are numbered consecutively throughout each volume. When the law has changed sufficiently to necessitate revision, a title will be reissued.

(b)   *Reissue binders* — the programme of publishing revised titles began in 1999. Individual titles are published as separate booklets to be filed in loose-leaf binders. Each title has its own tables and index. The paragraphs are numbered consecutively within each title. A reissue title supersedes the title in the original volume.

(c)   *Cumulative Supplement* — published annually and updating the individual titles and the various tables to the end of a calendar year. It may exclude titles scheduled for imminent reissue. The supplement is organised by reference to the paragraphs in the original volumes or (if appropriate) in the reissued titles. If the subject matter cannot be dealt with by reference to existing paragraphs new paragraphs are created. Updated by the *Service* volume.

(d)   *Service volume* — two loose-leaf issues per annum updating the *Cumulative Supplement*. The effect of new legislation and case law is noted but there is no commentary. The tables are updated to include the material contained in the noter-up. In addition the *Service* updates the current edition of *Is It in Force?* (although less frequently than *Halsbury's Statutes*) and contains a glossary of Scots legal terms which has also been published separately.

(e)   *Consolidated Index* — merging the title indexes published in the original volumes, with some revision. Not updated.

(f)   *Consolidated Tables of Statutes etc.* — separate tables for statutes; orders, rules and regulations; European Community legislation; treaties and conventions; and other enactments. Updated by the *Cumulative Supplement* and the *Service* volume.

(g)   *Consolidated Table of Cases* — updated by the *Cumulative Supplement* and the *Service* volume.

It is important to note that as part of the *Reissue* programme some reorganisation of the original title scheme took place. Some titles have been dropped and will not be updated or reissued.

When researching a particular subject the *Consolidated Index* should be used to identify the relevant title or titles in the work. Carefully check the *Reissue* binders to see if a revised version of the title has been published; if so that will supersede the version in the original volume. Check the current *Cumulative Supplement* to see if there has been any further updating of the title. Finally check the *Service* volume to see if there has been any legislation or case law which may have had an effect. Throughout your research remember that references are to paragraph numbers and not to page numbers.

When researching a particular case the *Consolidated Table of Cases* should be used to identify references made in the work. The version of the table in the *Cumulative Supplement* and the *Service* volume will point to further references or serve for cases heard since the original volumes were published.

When researching a particular piece of legislation the *Consolidated Table of Statutes etc.* should be used to identify references made in the work. The version of the table in the *Cumulative Supplement* and the *Service* volume will point to further references or serve for legislation passed since the original volumes were published.

An online version of the encyclopaedia will be available through the *Butterworths Scotland Direct* service. The predecessors of *Stair*, the three editions of the *Encyclopaedia of the Laws of Scotland* edited by Chisholm (1896–1904 and 1909–14) and Dunedin (1926–35) are still of occasional use.

12B5   Electronic sources

12B5.1   LEXIS

The SCOT library on *LEXIS* contains a single CASES file which allows searching of full text decisions reported since 1944 in *Session Cases*, *Scots Law Times*, *Scottish Criminal Case Reports* and *Scottish Civil Law Reports*. Unreported cases from the Court of Session are also available beginning in 1982 (Inner House) or 1985 (Outer House).

12B5.2   Scots Law Times Reports on CD-ROM

This service contains all the reports published in *Scots Law Times* since 1893 with additional material from the *Poor Law Reports*. Folio software is employed and permits various approaches to searching. A *User Manual* is available on screen and in print form. The disc is updated monthly.

12B5.3   Current Legal Information

Available on CD and by subscription on the internet at

   http://www.smlawpub.co.uk/

although it is important to note that the coverage is not identical. One of the constituent databases is *Current Law Cases* based upon material drawn from the *Current Law* monthly and annual publications. The online version includes summaries of Scottish cases from 1986 but coverage on the CD extends back to 1948. The online version is updated daily and the disc is updated monthly. A case citator with similar coverage is included.

12B5.4   Lawtel

Only Scottish cases which are reported in the 'English' series of law reports are covered.

12C   ANSWERING RESEARCH QUERIES

Generally, as described in section 6C.

12C1   Tracing a report of a case where only the names of parties are known

Scottish cases from 1948 onwards may be traced through the *Current Law Case Citator*, brought up-to-date by the cumulative table of cases in the most recent issue of *Current Law Monthly Digest*. The citator is arranged alphabetically by the name of the first party and a comprehensive search will involve checking both the English and Scottish sections. Pre-1948 cases may also be located by this method but it depends upon them having been judicially considered in the period covered; a more reliable method is to search the indexes to the *Faculty Digest*, Shaw's *Digest*, or the *Scots Digest*. *Current Legal Information* includes an electronic version of the citators. Indexes to the individual series of law reports and the tables of cases published as part of the *Laws of Scotland* may also prove useful. Very recent decisions may be found by searching *LEXIS* or the Scottish Court's web site.

12C2 Has this case been considered by the courts on a subsequent occasion?

Current Law Case Citator, *Current Legal Information* and *LEXIS* may again be used. For the pre-1948 period the *Faculty Digest* and *Scots Digest* have tables of cases judicially referred to as well as the indexes to cases digested.

12C3   Tracing cases on a subject

The *Laws of Scotland* is an obvious starting point. Check the *Consolidated Index* and the indexes to any reissued titles which may be relevant. Case summaries in the *Current Law Yearbook* and *Current Law Monthly Digest* are grouped under broad subject headings although the subject index facilitates more detailed searching. The subject index was not a regular feature of *Scottish Current Law Yearbook* until 1976; the indexes in the 1986 and 1990 volumes are cumulative and cover 1972–86 and 1987–90 respectively. 'Master volumes' published in 1956, 1961, 1966 and 1971 are a useful shortcut but it is still necessary to refer to the relevant annual volume for fuller information. Electronic sources such as *LEXIS*, *Current Legal Information*, and *Scots Law Times Reports on CD-ROM* are better if you wish to be very specific in your search terms.

12C4   Have there been any case notes or articles on this case?

Legal Journals Index and the equivalent database in *Current Legal Information* cover the Scottish law periodicals and it is possible to search for references by the name of a case.

Chapter 13

Scotland: commentary on the law

13.1 TEXTBOOKS

Section 8.1 fully describes the nature and exploitation of legal textbooks. Bearing in mind that Scottish law publishing is on a more modest scale, most of what is written there applies equally to books dealing with the law of Scotland. Some care needs to be exercised when dealing with textbooks which purport to describe UK law; such publications may have Scottish editors or contributors and can be used with some confidence, but others are in fact books on the law of England and Wales. Most areas of Scots law are served by a relatively modern textbook and not all of these are produced by publishers with a Scottish base. Unfortunately, because the market is small, textbooks are often beyond the means of many students and in that case there is no substitute for a good academic law library.

13.1A Description

The Scottish equivalent of the 'books of authority' described in section 8.1A1.1 are the 'Institutional writings' dating from the mid-17th to the early-19th centuries. These include Stair, J.D., *Institutions of the Law of Scotland* (1681); Erskine, J., *Institute of the Law of Scotland* (1773); Hume, D., *Commentaries on the Law of Scotland Respecting Crimes* (1797); and Bell, G.J., *Commentaries on the Mercantile Law of Scotland* (1800). These may be regarded as potentially decisive in the absence of higher authority, but only in those areas of law where social change over the intervening period has not diminished their persuasiveness. There is some debate as to which works are to be included in the canon, their actual persuasiveness, and even whether they should properly be referred to as authoritative rather than Institutional writings. An appraisal of their current standing and a listing of those works generally accepted as Institutional will be found in White and Willock (1999) pp. 105–108.

The Scottish equivalent of the 'precedent books' described in section 8.1A1.5 are the publications which provide 'styles' for various legal documents. Styles may appear in textbooks, as loose-leaf works, or indeed as software packages and are likely to be of most interest to students on the Diploma in Legal Practice course. Notable examples are *Greens Litigation Styles* and *Greens Practice Styles*.

13.1B   Finding information

See section 8.1B.

13.1C   Answering research queries

See section 8.1C.

13.2   ENCYCLOPAEDIAS

The most important Scottish title in this category is the *Laws of Scotland* (see 12B4.1) and the plan to make it available online is of great interest. Loose-leaf encyclopaedias on well-defined areas of the law of Scotland are growing in number but these are usually expensive and consequently not available in all academic law libraries.

13.3   PERIODICALS

Although boundaries tend to break down somewhat in the smaller jurisdiction, Scotland has its own legal periodicals serving the academic and the practitioner. They range from *Juridical Review* which is closely associated with the faculties of law in the Scottish universities, through the *Journal of the Law Society of Scotland* and *Scottish Law Gazette*, to current awareness publications such as *Greens Reparation Bulletin*. It is important however to note that articles on Scots law are by no means confined to periodicals published in Scotland or even the United Kingdom.

Most of the sources described in section 8.3B cover periodicals which publish articles on the law of Scotland. In addition the *Laws of Scotland* will highlight relevant articles.

13.4   REFERENCE WORKS

13.4A   Dictionaries

13.4A1   Conventional dictionaries

Bell's Dictionary and Digest of the Law of Scotland (7th edn, 1890) is undoubtedly the classic Scots law dictionary. *Scots Law Terms and Expressions* (1982) and *Greens Glossary of Scottish Legal Terms* (3rd edn, 1992) offer more concise definitions. The *Glossary* (1992) first appeared as part of the *Laws of Scotland* and encompasses Scottish legal terminology, Latin words and phrases, and terms used in European Community law. *Trayner's Latin Maxims* (4th edn, 1894) goes into greater detail and was last reprinted in 1993.

13.4A2   Judicial dictionaries

The *Scottish Contemporary Judicial Dictionary of Words and Phrases* (1995) examines the English language as it has been interpreted in the Scottish courts. While the author concentrates on words judicially considered since 1946, useful entries derived from the *Faculty Digest*, the *Scots Digest*, and the still valuable *Scottish Judicial Dictionary* (1946) are included to extend coverage back to 1800.

13.4A3   Biographical dictionaries

Who's Who in Scotland (annual) provides information on many individuals not included in *Who's Who*.

13.4B   Directories

13.4B1   Directories for law

The principal Scottish sources of information are the *Scottish Law Directory* and the *Blue Book*. Both are annual publications. The *Scottish Law Directory* is usually referred to as the 'White Book' and provides alphabetical lists of advocates, solicitors, and law firms with contact details, and a list of law firms arranged by town and city. Information on the courts, government departments, law societies and other organisations is included. The *Blue Book* is the official directory of the Law Society of Scotland and is similar in coverage. The Law Society web site has searchable directories of solicitors and firms. It is at

> http://www.lawscot.org.uk/

13.4B2   Compendia

The *Oxford Companion to Law* (1980), having been compiled by a Scottish academic, is also of value for information on Scotland. However, works aimed at the general public, such as *Everyday Scots Law* (2000), are not recommended for use by the serious law student.

13.5   OFFICIAL PUBLICATIONS

13.5A   Description

13.5A1   Definition

Official publications relating to or having an effect upon Scotland may emanate from either the government of the United Kingdom based in London or the government of Scotland based in Edinburgh. The Stationery Office is the principal publisher in both instances. The use of government web sites to make official publications more readily available is a welcome development of recent times and virtually everything published by the Scottish Parliament and the Scottish Executive is available in this way. Indeed a well-organised official web site often represents the most convenient source of official information. Section 8.6 describes Westminster official publications so this section is confined to the publications of the devolved bodies.

13.5A1.1   Scottish Parliament publications

The *Business Bulletin* is a valuable source of information on the current, future and past business of the Parliament. It is published daily and covers announcements, the programme of business, agendas of committee meetings, oral and written questions, motions and amendments, Bills and other documents, petitions, and the progress of parliamentary business. The *Official Report* is a substantially verbatim report of proceedings in the Parliament and its committees (see 10.3B4) and potentially of considerable research value. Much will depend upon the publication of the revised text with an index compiled by the Scottish Parliament Information Centre (SPICe). The *Minutes of Proceedings* is simply a formal record of the decisions made. The *SP Papers* series mostly consists of committee reports but other important documents laid before the Parliament may also be published in this way. An important example is the report of the Scottish Parliamentary Corporate Body on the construction of a new building to house the Parliament at Holyrood. *Bills* and *Acts* have been fully described in sections 10.3 and 10.4. From its inception the Scottish Parliament has regarded information and communications technologies as central to the promotion of openness, accountability and democratic participation. All the above are therefore available on the web site at

> http://www.scottish.parliament.uk/

13.5A1.2   Scottish Executive publications

The work of the Scottish Executive and its departments covers all devolved matters and the range and nature of its publications reflect this. As it assumed the functions of the former Scottish Office most of the information previously published by that body now emanates from the Executive. Printed publications are numbered sequentially, e.g.:

> SE/2000/37

and the majority are published by The Stationery Office in Edinburgh. A substantial number are laid before the Scottish Parliament but the original citation is retained. Some documents are joint publications and are laid before both the UK and Scottish parliaments, displaying both a 'Cm' number and an 'SE' number. The Scottish Executive web site provides ready access to the majority of its publications. It is at

> http://www.scotland.gov.uk/

The Scottish Executive is wholly responsible for the Executive Agencies previously overseen by the Secretary of State for Scotland. These include the Scottish Court Service, the Scottish Prison Service, and the Registers of Scotland. Annual reports may be published by the Agency or on their behalf by The Stationery Office. Executive Non-Departmental Public Bodies (NDPBs) in Scotland, such as the Scottish Legal Aid Board, are also the responsibility of the Executive.

Reports of the Scottish Law Commission are now laid before the Scottish Parliament by the Scottish Ministers and accordingly carry an 'SE' number. Those published jointly with the Law Commission in England are also published either as Command Papers or House of Commons Papers.

Press releases and publications from the Scotland Office, the department charged with ensuring that Scottish interests are represented within the United Kingdom government, are available on its web site at

  http://www.scottishsecretary.gov.uk/

13.5A1.3   Other publications

The Scottish Law Commission also issues discussion papers which are valuable sources of information on the state of the law of Scotland. They are usually a preliminary to a report to the Scottish Ministers (noted above) which will propose reform of particular aspects of the law and often includes a draft Bill. The Commission's annual reports list recent publications and indicate which proposals have been implemented.

The publications of many other government bodies in Scotland are made freely available through the internet. A convenient way of tracing these is to consult the organisation index on the Government Information Service web site at

  http://www.open.gov.uk/

although the Scottish Executive site also provides many links.

13.5B   Finding information

Generally, as described in section 8.6B.

13.5B1   What's Happening in the Scottish Parliament

WHISP is compiled by the Scottish Parliament Information Centre (SPICe) and published each week that the Parliament is sitting. It is a treasure trove of information about the activities of the Parliament and its documentation. One particularly useful feature is the bibliography which is to form the basis of one published by The Stationery Office. It also draws attention to SPICe's research publications which like *WHISP* are available on the Scottish Parliament web site.

13.5B2   Web sites

It is worth reiterating that the Scottish Parliament site at

> http://www.scottish.parliament.uk/

and the Scottish Executive site at

> http://www.scotland.gov.uk/

are key resources. Both have search engines, but careful examination of the structure of the sites will probably lead to the required information without also retrieving a great deal of irrelevant material.

There are also many unofficial sites which act as convenient gateways to a variety of legal and official information. The web pages prepared by the Maps and Official Publications Unit of Glasgow University Library are particularly helpful in the Scottish context. The web site is at

> http://www.lib.gla.ac.uk/Depts/MOPS/

PART 3

RESEARCHING THE LAW OF THE EUROPEAN COMMUNITY AND EUROPEAN HUMAN RIGHTS LAW

Chapter 14

The European Community: introduction

On 1 January 1973 the United Kingdom joined the European Communities, and agreed to apply and be bound by the law of the Communities. The gradual movement towards the harmonisation of laws across all member States significantly quickened with the ratification of the Single European Act in 1987. In 1992 the European Union (EU) was established by the Treaty of Maastricht, and is merely a stage in the process of creating closer union among the peoples of Europe. The EU adds a new dimension to the European Communities but does not replace them. The law of the Communities can no longer be considered in isolation as a separate unit of legal study or research, but now permeates UK law as a whole. It is important for you as a law student to understand and know how to use the legal sources and materials of Communities' law, which are quite different from those of domestic UK law.

Before looking at the structure of Communities' legal materials it is necessary to understand the meaning of some terms which are frequently confused and wrongly used interchangeably.

The phrase European Communities referred to the European Coal and Steel Community (ECSC), set up in 1952, the European Atomic Energy Community (Euratom) set up in 1958 and the European Economic Community (EEC), founded under the Treaty of Rome after the city in which it was signed in 1957. The Treaty of European Union 1993 (better known as the Treaty of Maastricht) changed the name of the European Economic Community to the 'European Community' (EC). The Common Market is a phrase often used to refer to the European Community, but the term only refers to the freedoms and policies implemented within the Community and excludes external relations. The Internal Market is that part of the Common Market concerned with the free movement of goods, persons, services and capital. It was the object of the Single European Act (SEA) of 1986 and was completed at the end of 1992.

Chapters 14 to 16 of this book are about the European Community (EC). The legislation which set up the Community not only created a system of law independent of national law but also created a number of bodies, known as 'institutions':

(a) *Council of Ministers* — to take decisions on legislative proposals.
(b) *Commission* — to enforce the application of EC law and instigate new legislative proposals.
(c) *European Parliament* — to advise on legislation.
(d) *European Court of Justice* — to interpret EC law.
(e) *Court of Auditors* — to examine the accounts of all revenue and expenditure of the Communities and keep a check on the budget. It is little more than a supervisory body.

In addition to these institutions, there is an advisory body which you may come across in law studies: the *Economic and Social Committee* — a body representing economic and social interests in the Community, such as employers' organisations and trade unions, which is consulted by the Council together with Parliament, before final decisions are taken.

EC legal information sources, like those for England, Wales and Scotland, may be divided into primary (i.e., original) and secondary (i.e., commentary and description) — see figure 14.1.

The primary sources (see chapter 15) comprise:

(a) *Primary legislation* — the founding treaties and later amending treaties, concerned with the establishment of the Community, treaties of accession as the membership of the Community has been enlarged (see 15.2).
(b) *Secondary legislation* — laws setting out in detail how the objectives established by the treaties are to be met (see 15.3).
(c) *Case law* — the decisions of the European Court of Justice (ECJ) (see 15.4).

The secondary sources comprise textbooks and periodicals (see chapter 16).

Figure 14.1   The literature of European Community law.

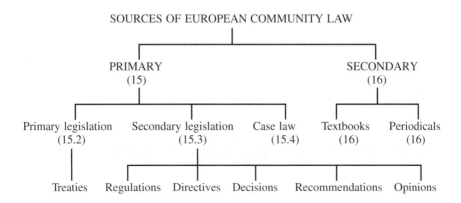

(The numbers in brackets indicate the chapter and section where discussion of the particular source will be found.)

Chapter 15

Legislation and case law of the European Community

15.1 INTRODUCTION

The authorised text of the treaties and secondary legislation of the EC is not made available in separate individual publications as the Acts and statutory instruments of the United Kingdom are, but are printed in the pages of the *Official Journal of the European Communities* (normally abbreviated to *Official Journal* or, simply, OJ). The title of OJ has not changed to reflect the altered terminology (see chapter 14). OJ is published almost daily and in several parts. The three parts in which you, as a law student, will be interested are:

(a) The L series (Legislation), which gives the text of agreed legislation.

(b) The C series (Communications and Information), which contains draft legislation, official announcements and information on EC activities.

(c) The annexe, which contains the full text of debates of the European Parliament.

Since the European Parliament has merely advisory rather than decision-making functions, the main interest, for legal research purposes, rests with the L and C series. Note that the reports of decisions of the European Court of Justice (ECJ) are *not* published in OJ, but as a separate publication, *Official Reports of Cases before the Court*.

The L series is usually divided into two sections: Acts whose publication is obligatory (which includes EC Regulations), and Acts whose publication is not obligatory (which includes EC Directives). The distinction is important for it is maintained in the Index to OJ. The contents of each issue of OJ are listed on the front cover and can occasionally extend onto the inside of the front cover, and even inside the back cover as well! Much of each issue contains legislative documents relating to agricultural policy or the customs union, which are often applicable for only a limited period of time. In the index these are listed in lighter type, whilst other measures are given in bold type with an asterisk.

Community publications are usually published in each of the languages of the member States. The covers of official EC publications are colour-coded according to the language of publication and English language publications have purple covers.

Since the publication of EC legislation and the reports of cases before ECJ is far more centralised than their counterparts in the United Kingdom, you might expect it to be relatively easy to master the necessary research skills. Regrettably this is not so, because of the sheer quantity of official publications and difficulties you will face in using the official indexes, although the advent of CDs and the internet have made this task easier. Further, the reports of ECJ cases are delayed by as much as 18 months because of the importance attached to achieving a precise and accurate translation of the judgment and opinions into all EC languages.

Therefore, as you will see, whilst the authoritative text of legal documents is given in official publications, you will have to master the use of non-official publications and databases to find your way through the vast quantity of EC publishing — the L and C series of OJ alone run to over 30,000 pages annually!

Finally, where can you find EC official publications? Most law libraries are likely to subscribe to OJ. However, the EC has made efforts to ensure publications are accessible to encourage teaching and research as well as for consultation by the general public. Over 40 academic libraries (universities and colleges) in the UK have been designated European Documentation Centres (EDC) and receive a comprehensive range of EC material. They are open to the general public. There are also two other networks: European Reference Centres (ERC), which have basic collections of EC publications and, Public Information Relays (PIR), a network of public libraries providing EC information to the general public. Finally, five EC Depository Libraries (DEP) with major collections intended for use by the general public have been designated in the UK. A list of all these organisations is given in the twice yearly EC publication: *European information on your doorstep.*

15.2   COMMUNITY TREATIES

15.2A   Description

See section 14.1.

15.2B   Finding information

15.2B1   European Union: selected instruments taken from the Treaties

The authoritative text, as we have seen, is given in various issues of OJ. However, for convenience the texts are brought together in the above set of two 'books', published in 1995. Each book comprises five volumes.

15.2B2   *Unofficial versions of the treaties in paper texts*

(a)   *Encyclopedia of European Union Law* — a loose-leaf publication in five volumes, also available as part of the CD: *European Legal Information*.

(b)   H. Smit and P. E. Herzog, *The Law of the European Economic Community. A Commentary on the EEC Treaty* — a loose-leaf publication in six volumes.

(c)   *European Union Law Reporter* — a loose-leaf publication in four volumes, also available as a CD: *EU Law Library*.

(d)   *Blackstone's EC Legislation Handbook* — edited by N. Foster. A very fat, single volume intended for use by practising lawyers.

(e)   *Blackstone's EC Legislation* (annual) — edited by N. Foster. A single volume reprint of the major materials without annotations, intended for law students.

15.2B3   *Internet and CD versions of the treaties*

15.2B3.1   *Europa Website*

The full text of the treaties is available free on Europa, the European Union's server, at

     http://europa.eu.int/eur-lex/en/treaties/index.html

15.2B3.2   *CELEX*

The *CELEX* (Communitatis Europae Lex) group of databases is the official electronic database of the European Community and runs on a computer in Luxembourg. It includes the full text of most documents. The database is divided into a number of separate files which are further subdivided into sectors. The legislative file has four sectors. Sector 1 contains the full text of the treaties. Sector 2 contains the text of enactments passed in member States when each joined the EC, including the Act of Accession of the United Kingdom. *CELEX* was originally designed for use by Commission staff and not by the public. There is a very large set of commands and the database is not easy to use. It is unlikely that your library will give you access to this version of the database.

15.2B3.3   *JUSTIS-CELEX*

JUSTIS-CELEX is a commercial version of the *CELEX* database and is much easier to use. It contains the full text of the treaties. It is available as part of a set of CDs, updated quarterly, but there is an option to subscribe to a weekly updating service available over the internet. Ask your library staff which service is available for you to use.

15.2B3.4   *Other databases*

Other databases, not so far mentioned, containing the text of the treaties include:

- *JUSTIS European Commentaries* — CD updated quarterly.
- *Eurolaw* — CD updated monthly or quarterly depending on the subscription taken and available on the internet.
- *European Law on CD-ROM* — updated quarterly.
- *OJ CD* — updated quarterly.
- *LEXIS* — in its EURCOM library and the ECLAW file.
- *EU Direct* — an internet database available from Butterworths to subscribers only.

15.2C Answering research queries

For background information on using CDs and the internet for legal research, see appendix 4.

The information given earlier should make clear how to find and use the treaties.

15.3 SECONDARY LEGISLATION

15.3A Description

Whilst the treaties provide the overall objectives of the activities of the EC, secondary legislation sets out the fine detail of how these objectives are to be achieved. There are five different types of European Community secondary legislation. Each has a different definition and purpose:

(a) *Regulations:* are addressed to all member States — to be applied in full and are directly applicable without the creation of national legislation.

(b) *Directives:* are addressed to all member States — lay down an objective to be achieved in a specific time but member States are left to legislate the details of implementation.

(c) *Decisions:* may be addressed to members States, individuals, groups of individuals or companies — the means by which EC implements treaties or regulations.

(d) *Recommendations and Opinions:* suggest a line of action or opinion and are not legally binding.

The two types of secondary legislation you are most likely to use during law studies are Regulations and Directives. They can be made by the European Commission or the Council of Ministers. A key point to remember is that whilst EC Regulations do not require national legislation to bring them into force, EC Directives can only be implemented through national legislation, which in the UK will be either an Act of Parliament or a statutory instrument. How the UK government selects which method to employ is discussed in an article by Bates (1989). It is very important when undertaking research on an EC Directive to check whether it has been implemented within the jurisdiction with which you are concerned. You will *not* find this information in the Directive itself but will have to check either, the national sources or, an EC database which includes this information.

So as to better understand the relationships between the various publications produced as part of the legislative process in the EC, it is necessary to sketch in the process itself. The following sequence is derived from a much fuller table printed in Ramsay (1997) and follows what is known as the 'co-decision procedure':

(a)   Commission sends a proposal to the Council of Ministers — the text of the proposal and the explanatory memorandum are published as a COM document (the popular title for a range of working documents of the Commission), the text alone appears in the *Official Journal* C series.

(b)   Council consults the European Parliament and, in certain circumstances, the Economic and Social Committee. A committee of the European Parliament prepares a report on the proposal which is published in series A of the *European Parliament's Working Documents.*

(c)   The European Parliament in full session considers the report on first reading. The text of the debate is published in *Official Journal,* Annexe, while the text of the opinion they express is printed in *Official Journal* C series.

(d)   The European Social Committee gives an opinion — the text is printed in *Official Journal* C series.

(e)   The Commission considers amendments — the outcome is published in the same titles as was the proposal which began the legislative process — see (a) above.

(f)   The Council prepares a common position on the proposal — text published in *Official Journal* C series.

(g)   The European Parliament issues a second report, holds debate and vote and publishes the adopted text in *Official Journal* C series.

(h)   The Commission publishes its opinion on Parliament's amendments to the Council's common position, together with any amended proposal — published as a COM document.

(i)   The Commission adopts the amended proposal.

(j)   Council informs Parliament by letter that it is unable to adopt all of the Parliament's amendments. A Conciliation Committee is convened.

(k)   A joint text is adopted by the Conciliation Committee.

(l)   European Parliament issues a third report, holds debate and vote — published in *Official Journal* C series.

(m)   The joint text is approved by Council and Parliament — published in *Official Journal* C series.

(n)   The text is signed by both Council and Parliament. It becomes law and is printed in *Official Journal* L series.

During your law studies you will be mainly concerned with secondary legislation which has become law (i.e., printed in *Official Journal* L series), though occasionally you may need information on proposals (printed as COM documents with explanatory memorandum, or text only in *Official Journal* C series).

COM documents only become public after a considerable period of consultation with interested parties, and it is only the final version which is published. This fact is reflected in the way in which the documents are cited:

COM (year) running number, final

as in the following example:

> Proposal for a Council Directive on safety glazing and glazing materials on motor vehicles and their trailers, COM (89) 653, final.

The text of this particular proposal was, as usual, published some time later in the *Official Journal* C series. References to the *Official Journal* take the following form:

> OJ series issue number, date of issue, page number

as in the following example:

> Proposal for a Council Directive on safety glazing and glazing materials on motor vehicles and their trailers (OJ No. C95, 12.4.1990, p. 1).

The L, C and S series of OJ are given a running number commencing at one in January each year, but the annexe series, covering European Parliament debates, is numbered quite differently.

A very small number of the most important proposals are given wider public notice by being published as supplements to the *Bulletin of the European Union* (see 15.3B1.6). When referring to a particular piece of EC legislation printed in OJ the citation should include the following elements, though (with one important exception) there appears to be no standard order in which they should appear:

(a) the institutional origin of the Act (Commission or Council);
(b) the form of the Act (Regulation, Directive, Decision etc.);
(c) a unique legislation number;
(d) the year of the enactment;
(e) the institutional treaty under which it is made (EEC, EC, ECSC, Euratom);
(f) the date the legislation was passed.

The important exception to note is that Regulations are normally cited with the name of the institutional treaty followed by the legislation number and then the year of enactment, whilst Directives and Decisions are cited by the year, legislation number and then the institutional treaty. It is very important to remember this system of citation when tracing references to legislation in indexes, otherwise it is easy to waste time finding the wrong document. Here are two examples of how the citations should be given; the first is an example of a Regulation, the second a Directive:

> Council Regulation (EEC) No. 737/90 of March 1990 on the conditions governing imports of agricultural products originating in third countries following the accident of the Chernobyl nuclear power station.

Council Directive 87/102/EEC for the approximation of the laws, regulations and administrative provisions of the member States concerning consumer credit.

15.3B Finding information

There are two ways of exploiting this vast output of EC secondary legislation: by using full text databases, indexes, lists and directories compiled officially by the EC; or by using the same products with easier to use software, made available by commercial publishers. The commercial publishers base their products on the official database of the EC — *CELEX* — but provide easier to use search software and include features, such as commentary, which add to the value of their product.

15.3B1 *Official sources*

15.3B1.1 CELEX

A computer in Luxembourg holds Sectors 3 and 4 of the official legal database of the EC. These sectors contain the full text of secondary legislation as published in the L series of OJ. Sector 5 contains references to draft legislation in the form of COM documents. Sector 7 contains details of national implementation of EC legislation. Legislation on the database is updated weekly and the text is added usually about three to four weeks after its publication in OJ. As was noted in section 15.2B3.2 above, *CELEX* is not easy to use, and the alternative commercial services noted in sections 15.3B2.1 and 15.3B2.2 are more widely available.

15.3B1.2 *Europa*

The text of the *Official Journal* for 45 days after publication is available free on the Europa web site of the EC, after which it is removed to the EUDOR Website which charges for each request. The Europa web site is at

http://europa.eu.int/eur-lex/en/oj/index.html

In another part of the Europa web site there is an internet version of the *Directory of Community Legislation in Force* (the paper version is described at section 15.3B1.7). If you know under which of the 20 headings in the analytical structure (i.e. Community-speak for broad subject area) the legislation you require falls, and (this is important) the legislation has been amended or interpreted within the last 45 days, it is possible to obtain the full text free, regardless of the date the original legislation was published. The site is at

http://europa.eu.int/eur-lex/en/lif/index.html

15.3B1.3 *University of Mannheim European Documentation Centre (EDC) web site*

If you know the type of secondary legislation, its year and number, you can obtain the full text free via the University of Mannheim EDC web site. Use the lower of two search forms at the site and, on clicking search, you will be sent to the EUDOR site, free, and the computer will search the complete file of secondary legislation from 1959 onwards. It must be emphasised that you have to know the details of the precise piece of legislation you require to make use of this service. There is no subject or title search facility. The Mannheim site is at

http://www.uni-mannheim.de/users/ddz/edz/biblio/opace.html

15.3B1.4   Index to the *Official Journal of the European Communities*

The index to the *Official Journal* is published monthly with an annual cumulation. It has a number of drawbacks: it only cumulates every 12 months, it excludes references to the 'C' series of OJ, and it uses un-idiomatic English for the alphabetical (subject) index. There are easier ways to search for secondary legislation using the electronic databases noted in sections 15.3B2.1 and 15.3B2.2.

15.3B1.5   *General Report on the Activities of the European Union*

This is published annually, within a few months of the end of the calendar year to which it refers. The body of the report, which in recent years has run to over 600 pages, gives a synopsis of legal and other developments during the year with footnote references to secondary legislation appearing in the *Official Journal*, both as draft and enacted law. Annexes at the back of the volume give details of the progress during the year of a selection of directives. Researching the *General Reports* over a number of annual issues will provide you with a broad view of Community legislative activity on a topic, and valuable references to the *Official Journal* or other EC sources in which the original documents were published. The *General Report* and the *Bulletin* (see below) are available on a CD.

15.3B1.6   *Bulletin of the European Union*

Published 10 times a year, this performs a similar function to the *General Report* except that the narrative synopsis of developments is replaced by brief notes on the progress and development of legislation, with full references to where the original materials were published. An annual index is published as part of an issue available early in the calendar year following. The value of the *Bulletin* is weakened by it appearing at least four months in arrears of the events it describes. It is also published on CD and on the internet at

http://europa.eu.int/abc/doc/off/bull/en/welcome.htm

15.3B1.7   *Directory of Community Legislation in Force*

The *Directory* is published twice a year and contains information on legislation in force as at 1 June and 1 December. It is currently published in two volumes.

Volume 1 contains the main body of the *Directory*, arranging references to legislation under 20 very broad subject headings and numerous more detailed subject headings. This arrangement means you will usually have to think of words of much wider meaning which include the topic in which you are interested and then narrow down once you have discovered the right major heading. For example, 'pollution' is not one of the 20 main subject headings but is a part of 'environment, consumers and health protection', which is! Volume 2 comprises chronological and alphabetical (i.e., 'sort of' subject) indexes, and the latter helps a little when using Volume 1 for a subject search.

15.3B2 Commercial sources

There is a large number of unofficial databases and publications. They may be divided into three groups (with a few overlaps), i.e. those which:

(a) provide the full text of all or a selection of EC legislation (see 15.3B2.1 to 15.3B2.4);
(b) track implementation or amendment or repeal of legislation (see 15.3B2.5 and 15.3B2.6);
(c) provide summaries of legislation or are concerned with current awareness, that is, drawing attention to new developments (see 15.3B2.7 to 15.3B2.15).

15.3B2.1   JUSTIS-CELEX

JUSTIS-CELEX is a commercial version of the *CELEX* database and is much easier to use. It contains the full text of the secondary legislation, the national implementation database and the DTI Spearhead database. The DTI database is especially useful for it contains summaries of some secondary legislation, compiled by UK government staff. The summaries detail the effect and progress towards implementation of EC legislation within the UK. *JUSTIS-CELEX* is available as part of a set of CDs, updated quarterly, but there is an option to subscribe to a weekly updating service available over the internet. Ask your library staff which service is available for you to use.

15.3B2.2   Other databases

Other databases containing the text of the secondary legislation include:

- *OJ CD* — contains the full text of the *Official Journal*. 'L' and 'C' series, from 1952 onwards. The CD is updated quarterly.
- *JUSTIS Official Journal C Series* — the full text of material from the *Official Journal* C series, including COM documents (proposed legislation), from January 1990 onwards. The CD is updated quarterly but for an additional subscription it is possible to obtain a monthly update via the internet.
- *Eurolaw* — includes the same material as *JUSTIS-CELEX*, including the DTI Spearhead database (indicated as DTI Briefings within this database).

The CD is updated either monthly or quarterly depending on the type of subscription taken.

- *EU Law Library* — the CD version of the loose-leaf encyclopaedia *European Law Reporter*, containing the text of secondary legislation with commentary by the editors of the encyclopaedia.
- *European Law on CD-ROM* — contains the *CELEX* database plus DTI Spearhead and another database: Spicers Centre for Europe, of abstracts of journal articles. The CD is updated quarterly.
- *LEXIS* — the full text of a selection of secondary legislation from the OJ L and C series, from 1980 onwards, is contained in its EURCOM library and the ECLAW file. The NATPRV file contains information on national implementation of EC provisions from January 1989 onwards.
- *EU Direct* — an internet database available from Butterworths to subscribers only. It contains the full text of secondary legislation.
- *EC Infodisk* — a CD containing a selection of legislation focusing on EU integration.

15.3B2.3   Encyclopedia of European Union Laws

This loose-leaf publication was formerly titled *Encyclopedia of European Community Law*. You will still find old binders on library shelves with this title, even though the contents are up-to-date. The whole of Volume C, which is currently published as 11 loose-leaf binders (and expanding continually), comprises reprints of EC secondary legislation, with commentary and annotation (in a smaller type) provided by the editors. It does not include draft legislation or legislation relating to customs and agriculture. Each Volume is divided into a large number of parts, and the text of each part is divided into numbered paragraphs. There is a subject index to the whole of Volume C towards the back of the last binder, and a second, supplementary index right at the back, which covers the most recent additions to the encyclopaedia. The references given in the indexes refer to the volume letter, part and paragraph number (in arabic numerals) where information is to be found. Take care not to confuse this information with the roman numerals on the spines of the binders, which have no relevance to finding material in the publication. You can find your way around the binders by looking at the guide cards, which project from the edge of the pages, and mark the beginning of each part of the text. Each broad subject, such as company law, which comprises a whole part of the encyclopaedia, commences with a checklist of the secondary legislation, in EC reference number order, included in that part. If you know the reference number of the Regulation or Directive, these checklists, or the consolidated checklist to the whole of Volume C near the back of the final Volume, or the tables of Community secondary legislation at the front of binder CI, will enable you to find the part and paragraph number where the legislation is reprinted.

The more helpful subject indexing, coupled with the provision of annotations, make this encyclopaedia a better starting-point for searching for secondary legislation than OJ and its indexes. However, updating such a large work takes time and it is still necessary to check other, official sources for amendments. This encyclopaedia is also available as a CD: *European Legal Information.*

15.3B2.4 European Union Law Reporter

Formerly known as *Common Market Law Reporter*, but despite its new name, this five-volume loose-leaf work concentrates on the secondary legislation of the European Community. It reprints secondary legislation, including some existing draft Regulations and Directives, in full, with editorial commentary. Draft Regulations and Directives are reproduced in the 'pending legislation' section, and cross-referenced to the main text of the *Reporter*. Volume 4 contains a topical index (or subject index) to the main work, preceded by a separate 'latest additions to topical index' which contains new or revised entries to the publication. From time to time these entries are incorporated in the main index to bring it completely up-to-date. Volume 4 also has 'finding lists' detailing different types of secondary legislation according to their official reference numbers. Volume 5, EU Update, contains information on current legal developments, especially new legislation and decisions of the European Court of Justice. Material remains in the Update until the main work can be updated.

Since *European Union Law Reporter* also includes the texts of European Court of Justice rulings and quasi-judicial Commission Decisions, it is consequently a more comprehensive source for EC law than the encyclopaedia noted in section 15.3B2.3. The encyclopaedia is available on CD under the title: EU Law Library.

15.3B2.5 Butterworths EC Legislation Implementator

Published twice a year, this is an invaluable guide to the implementation in the UK of Community Directives. Unfortunately, it provides an incomplete check as it covers implementation by statutory instrument and only a selection of Acts. It also focuses only on the implementation of Directives and does not cover the dates of coming into force of EC Regulations. Nevertheless, it is extremely useful. It arranges information chronologically by Directive number, and gives the target date for implementation, and references to UK legislation issued in fulfilment.

15.3B2.6 European Communities Legislation: Current Status

This publication is in several parts:

(a) two hard-back volumes;
(b) a single, soft-cover volume (this reissued annually);
(c) a soft-cover Cumulative Supplement;
(d) an alphabetical subject index both published three times a year; and
(e) a fortnightly newsletter.

These five parts, list in order of official Community reference number, all secondary legislation of the EC published in OJ since 1952, except for those instruments concerned with the daily business of the EC. Each entry comprises the title of the EC legislation or a short summary, and details of whether the whole or any part of the legislation has been amended, repealed, deleted, added to or replaced and, if so, the Community reference number for the 'amending' legislation. The subject index appears to use similar index terms to those in the EC 'harmonised vocabulary' which means references may be hidden under terms you do not expect. Recently, a sixth part has been added to the set since the main volumes had become so large. Entries for legislation no longer in force have been removed to a new, separate soft-cover volume.

15.3B2.7 Law of the European Communities Service

This publication first appeared in 1990. In four loose-leaf volumes it currently contains commentary with footnotes, on EC secondary legislation, arranged into 21 specific subject groups. Use of the full text databases (see 15.3B2.1 and 15.3B2.2) or the paper encyclopaedias (see 15.3B2.3 and 15.3B2.4) is to be preferred.

15.3B2.8 Halsbury's Laws of England, 4th edn, volumes 51 and 52

These bound volumes comprise an editorial commentary on EC law with copious footnotes giving references to where the original documents may be found. The volumes were published in 1986 and state the law correct to 30 November 1985. They have been kept up-to-date through entries in the Cumulative Supplement and service volumes to the whole Halsbury's service.

15.3B2.9 Lawtel

The internet service, Lawtel, includes an EU Interactive database containing summaries of EC legislation, both proposed and adopted, from 1987 onwards. The service is available to subscribers only and is not part of the basic subscription to Lawtel, so some universities or colleges may not take this additional service. Ask your law librarian for details.

15.3B2.10 JUSTIS European Commentaries

This CD, updated quarterly, does not contain the text of secondary legislation but summaries of a selection with access to the DTI Spearhead database.

15.3B2.11 European Current Law

This publication began in January 1992. It was formerly known as European Law Digest (1973–91). In appearance it is like Current Law Monthly Digest (see 6B2.4). The content is quite different, for it contains summaries not only of EC law, but also the domestic law of West, Central and East European countries. As far as EC law is concerned, it is sections 1 and 2 which are of most relevance. The first section is The Focus, which examines one area of recent legal development through a review article; the second section, European Union (Community Law), digests important legislation and cases, all arranged under subject headings. Each issue carries a list of the latest implementations of EC law within member States. Unfortunately, the list does not cumulate with each issue nor does it appear in *European Current Law Yearbook*, which consolidates and cumulates the rest of the contents. Unlike *Current Law Monthly Digest* there is no electronic version.

15.3B2.12   Current Law Monthly Digest

CLMD contains a table of European legislation implemented recently by statutory instrument. The list is arranged in chronological order by Regulations, Directive or Decision number. The table cumulates through the loose issues for each year but, unfortunately, does not appear in *Current Law Yearbook*.

15.3B2.13   Weekly Information Bulletin of the House of Commons

This publication is also discussed in section 4.1B1. Amongst its many listings it includes brief details of the latest COM documents containing draft legislation. Select Committees in both Houses of Parliament consider draft EC legislation and report their opinion whether the proposals raise questions of legal or political importance. Some proposals do, and of these a number are debated on the floor of the House of Commons. All the reports of the House of Lords Select Committee are debated. You will therefore find references to EC legislation in some of the other Parliamentary sources noted in section 4.1B, especially *Hansard* (see 4.1B6).

15.3B2.14   Butterworths EC Brief

This four-page newsletter covering, in summary, all proposals for legislation, all enacted legislation of the EC and all UK legislation implementing it, is published weekly.

It is a current-awareness publication, designed to keep readers up-to-date with developments, but can be used for research. No indexes are published, so it is a matter of 'skim reading' through past issues to find the information you are looking for.

15.3B2.15   European Access

Published bi-monthly, this publication is not confined to law but comprehensively lists, towards the back of each issue, new EC publications, and comment in newspapers, journals and books about the EC, including legislative developments. The journal is available on the internet at

    http://www.europeanaccess.co.uk/

15.3C   Answering research queries

For background information on using CDs and the internet for legal research, see appendix 4.

15.3C1   *Tracing the text of EC legislation on a subject*

Electronic route
Any of the databases mentioned in sections 15.3B2.1 and 15.3B2.2.

Paper route
Either *Encyclopedia of European Union Laws* (see 15.3B2.3), or:

- *European Union Law Reporter* (see 15.3B2.4);
- *Law of the European Communities Service* (see 15.3B2.7);
- *Halsbury's Laws of England* (see 15.3B2.8) — follow figure 15.1 and also see section 6B5.1 on how to use this encyclopaedia;
- *European Communities Legislation: Current Status* (see 15.3B2.6) — after identifying the reference numbers of the legislation, use OJ itself;
- *General Report on the Activities of the European Union* (see 15.3B1.5) and *Bulletin of the European Union* (see 15.3B1.6) — see figure 15.2.

Figure 15.1   Using *Halsbury's Laws* to trace EC legislation by subject.

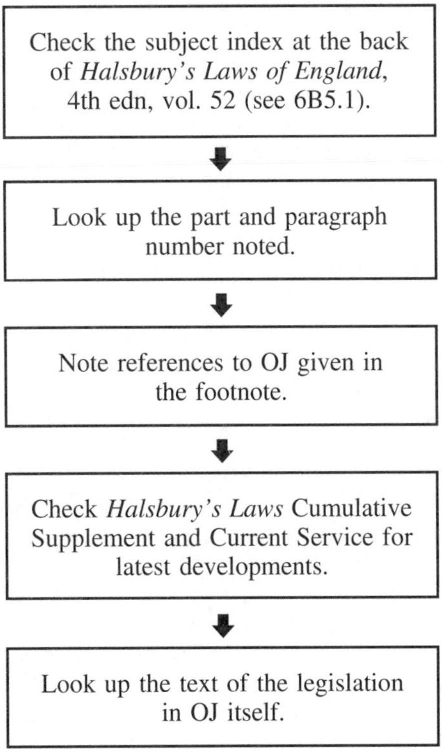

Figure 15.2   Using EC publications to trace legislation by subject.

Check the *General Report on the Activities of the European Union* (see 15.3B1.5) over a number of years and note any references to OJ. Use the contents list at the front of the *Report* to identify the broad subject area under which the legislation you require falls.

Check the *Bulletin of the European Union* for the period to date not covered by the *General Report* — use the annual index published in an early issue of the following year and the indexes to individual issues during the current year.

Look up the text of the legislation in OJ itself.

15.3C2   Tracing draft or proposed legislation

It helps to have an idea of how recent is the proposal. The system for agreeing legislation is lengthy and can take several years, unlike the annual cycle in the UK Parliament. So, unless you have a good idea when the proposal was made and can therefore go to issues of the *Official Journal* C series, it can pay to use one or more of the current awareness alerting services.

Electronic route
Use one or more of the following:

- *OJ CD* (see 15.3B2.2) — but note that the CD is updated only quarterly and is therefore no use for very recent proposals.
- *JUSTIS Official Journal C series* (see 15.3B2.2).
- *Lawtel* (see 15.3B2.9).

Paper route
Use one or more of the following, working through each backwards in time. If possible, start with one of the first three sources mentioned as they will probably carry the most current information.

- *Butterworths EC Brief* (see 15.3B2.14).
- *European Access* (see 15.3B2.15) — use the list of recent publications at the back of each issue.
- *Bulletin of the European Union* (see 15.3B1.6) — trace backwards until you overlap with the date of the latest issue of the *General Report*.
- *General Report of Activities of the European Union* (see 15.3B1.5).

- *European Union Law Reporter* (see 15.3B2.4) using the cumulative index to new developments and the pending legislation sections.
- *Weekly Information Bulletin of the House of Commons* (see 15.3B2.13), working backwards in time and checking whether the draft legislation has been considered in Select Committee of either House of Parliament. A successful result of this research will provide you with the COM document number and even the reference to OJ C series in which the draft legislation was printed. You will also have the date when the UK Parliament considered the legislation and so be able to consult other publications for reports on the debates.

If all else fails, contact your nearest European Documentation Centre listed in the EU publication: *Information on your doorstep.*

15.3C3   Has this EC Directive become law within the UK?

To become law an EC Directive must be enacted by the UK Parliament.

Electronic route
Sector 7 of the *CELEX* electronic database (see 15.3B1.1) will provide details of the national implementation of EC Directives. *JUSTIS-CELEX*, *Eurolaw*, *European Law Library* and *LEXIS* (all described in 15.3B2.2) include information about national implementation, frequently as a note at the end of the text of each Directive. *Lawtel* (see 15.3B2.9) will probably be the first database to provide information about implementation as it operates independently of the *CELEX* database.

Paper route
The publications are listed below roughly in the order with which they report new implementations — the quickest is listed first.

- *Current Law Monthly Digest* (see 15.3B2.12) — note that the table cumulates with each loose issue, so you need only check the table in the latest issue. Since the table for past years is not printed in the *Yearbook*, your research cannot go beyond the oldest monthly issue kept by the library.
- *European Current Law* (see 15.3B2.11) — but note that since the table does not cumulate each month you will need to check issues in reverse chronological order over a period of time.
- *Halsbury's Laws of England*, volumes 51 and 52 (see 15.3B2.8). Use either the tables at the front of volume 52 or the subject index at the back of volume 52 to trace commentary on the Directive. Details of implementation in the UK are given in the editorial footnotes in small type. Remember to check the Cumulative Supplement and Service volumes for the latest developments.
- *Encyclopedia of European Union Laws* (see 15.3B2.3). Use either the checklist or indexes towards the back of the final binder to volume C to find references to where the Directive is reprinted in the body of the encyclopaedia. Editorial footnotes in small type give details of implementation in the UK.

- *Butterworths EC Legislation Implementator* (see 15.3B2.5) — but it is published only twice a year.

Note that *European Union Law Reporter* (see 15.3B2.4) does *not* give details of the implementation of EC Directives in the UK.

15.3C4   Is this piece of EC legislation still in force?

Electronic route
Use one of the following:

- *JUSTIS-CELEX* (see 15.3B2.1).
- *Eurolaw* (see 15.3B2.2).
- *EU Law Library* (see 15.3B2.2).
- *LEXIS* (see 15.3B2.2).

Paper route
Directory of Community Legislation in Force (see 15.3B1.7) — authoritative but the least easy paper source to use.

European Communities Legislation: Current Status (see 15.3B2.6) — easy to use. If you know the EC reference number, look up the appropriate year and document number in the bound volume and associated soft-cover volume, then the Cumulative Supplement.

If you know only the subject-matter, check the index volume and note the reference numbers given, then turn to the hardback volume, soft-cover supplement and Cumulative Supplement, which are arranged in year and running EC reference number order.

Alternatively, use *Encyclopedia of European Union Laws* (see 15.3B2.3); or *European Union Law Reporter* (see 15.3B2.4) using either the subject indexes or checklist or finding lists to locate the legislation in the main part of the publication.

15.3C5   Has this EC legislation been considered in any cases before the European Court of Justice?

Electronic route
It is important to remember that to research this question you will need to access the case law sections of the databases for references to the legislation in question.
   Use one of the following:

- *JUSTIS-CELEX* (see 15.3B2.1).
- *Eurolaw* (see 15.3B2.2).
- *EU Law Library* (see 15.3B2.2).
- *LEXIS* (see 15.3B2.2).

Paper route
Butterworths EC Case Citator and Service (see 15.4B15) is by far the best source to use. Otherwise:

- *Encyclopedia of European Union Laws* (see 15.3B2.3).
- *European Union Law Reporter* (see 15.3B2.4).
- *Halsbury's Laws of England* (see 15.3B2.8).

15.4 CASE LAW

15.4A Description

The practice and procedure of the European Court of Justice (ECJ), based in Luxembourg and founded in 1952, is quite different from that of the national courts of the UK. As a result, the reports of cases heard and judged by the court have a quite different structure. Up to 31 December 1993 (with the exception of 1985 and 1986) individual case reports were in three parts:

(a) Report for the hearing.
(b) Opinion of the Advocate-General.
(c) Judgment of the court.

From 1 January 1994 the report for the hearing has been omitted.

The report for the hearing is a statement made to the court by a reporting judge outlining the facts of the case and giving a summary of the legal arguments. The opinion of the Advocate-General is an impartial review of the issues and prior decisions, with a discussion of the alternative choices available to the court and the Advocate-General's personal view of what in law should be done. The court usually follows the opinion of the Advocate-General in its judgment. Although the court is always composed of at least three judges, only a single judgment is given, and it is frequently short. Individual judges are not permitted separate or dissenting opinions.

In the *Official Reports of Cases before the Court*, more popularly known as *European Court Reports* (ECR), the report for the hearing is preceded by a summary of the judgment (comprising catchwords and headnote specially compiled for the publication), which has no binding force but, like its counterpart in domestic English law reports, is a useful indication of the subject-matter.

The court may deal with a case in any of the eleven languages currently officially recognised by the EC. The only authentic version of a particular case is that printed in the procedural language employed. Each of the three parts of the case could have proceeded in a different language. *European Court Reports* contains only the English version, and a footnote to the first page of each part of the report of a case indicates in which language that part was originally heard. However, most law libraries in the UK are likely only to stock *European Court Reports*, and not sets of reports for each of the 11 official languages.

The major drawback with *European Court Reports* is the time taken to publish case reports. Frequently up to 18 months can elapse between the judgment being given and the report of the case being published. This is because considerable importance is attached to achieving a precise and accurate translation of the judgments and opinions into all EC languages.

The Court has its own free web site which carries the full text of all judgments from June 1997 onwards. It is at

http://www.europa.eu.int/cj/en/index.htm

It is worth noting that the web site contains a statement about the authenticity of the reports of decisions — the paper version is definitive!

The mode of citation recommended by the editors of the *European Courts Reports* is:

Case registration number. Names of parties [year] ECR Part number (only from 1990 onwards) page number.

Here are two examples:

Case C-3/87 *The Queen* v *Ministry of Agriculture, Fisheries and Food, ex parte Agegate Ltd* [1989] ECR 4459.

Case T-119/89 *Teissonnié re* v *Commission* [1990] ECR II-7.

However, this method of citation is not suitable when ECJ cases are cited alongside English cases, which are not cited by registry numbers. Then it is better to put the case number after the names of the parties, thus:

The Queen v *Ministry of Agriculture, Fisheries and Food, ex parte Agegate Ltd* (case C-3/87) [1989] ECR 4459.

Teissonniè re v *Commission* (case T-119/89) [1990] ECR II-7.

The case registration number is given at the head of each case report in ECR. Up to 1989 it comprised a running number which started at 1 at the beginning of each calendar year, followed by the year the application was filed with the court. In 1989 the new Court of First Instance was inaugurated and cases before this court have a registration number pre-fixed by the letter T whilst cases before ECJ are now prefixed C. It is important to remember that the case registration number merely refers to when the original application was filed with the court and *not* when the case was reported, which can be several years later. If you know the case registration number it is possible to access the full text of all ECJ decisions free, using the University of Mannheim's European Documentation Centre (EDC) web site at

http://www.uni-mannheim.de/users/ddz/edz/biblio/opace.html

Complete the lower of the two search forms on the screen.

Unlike UK law reports, judgments are published in ECR in strict chronological order, so it is not difficult to trace the report of a case from its date.

The names of parties are frequently lengthy, and in common use are often abbreviated. The official index to ECR does not include these popular names, but some unofficial indexes helpfully do. Further, the official annual index to ECR is often several years late in appearing.

Reflecting the inauguration of the new court, beginning with Part 1 of 1990, ECR has been divided into two sections, each with a separate pagination. Section I contains reports of cases before the Court of Justice, Section II includes reports of cases before the new Court of First Instance.

15.4B   Finding information

Apart from ECR itself and the two internet sources noted above, the sources which will help you exploit EC case law fall into four categories:

(a)   Information about the progress of cases (see 15.4B1 to 15.4B3).

(b)   Alternative reports of cases to those published in ECR, in paper or electronic form (see 15.4B4 to 15.4B9).

(c)   Guides, indexes and summaries of decisions (see 15.4B10 to 15.4B14).

(d)   Case citator (see 15.4B15).

15.4B1   *Official Journal of the European Communitees (OJ)*

Probably the first indication that a case is being brought before ECJ is the appearance in OJ C series of a brief summary of the matter in dispute. If a case, once registered, is not pursued, the C series will again note its removal from the register. When a judgment is given by the court a brief summary — only a page or two long — will be printed in the C series.

15.4B2   *Bulletin of the European Union*

This publication appearing ten times a year, provides brief summaries of new cases and the judgments of other cases, with references to where more details will be found in OJ C series. The summaries are usually printed within section 8 'Community Law' of the *Bulletin* under the sub-heading 'Decisions of the Court of Justice and Court of First Instance', and individually grouped under subject headings. Unfortunately, the *Bulletin* is usually published at least four months after the events it documents. It is also published on CD and on the internet at

http://europa.eu.int/abc/doc/off/bull/en/welcome.htm

15.4B3   *Proceedings of the Court of Justice and the Court of First Instance of the European Communities*

Each week the Information Service of the Court of Justice issues a bulletin giving brief details of the progress of cases during the week in question. The bulletin is in four sections: the first comprises summaries of recent judgments, the second carries an extract from the conclusion of the opinion of the Advocate-General, the third section lists new cases and the fourth reproduces notices issued by the court relating to its practice and procedure. The summaries are not authoritative.

The bulletin is published within a few days of the events it describes and since ECR is so much delayed in publication, it is a valuable source of information on recent decisions. Unfortunately, use of the bulletin is not easy because indexes are published only annually, about six months after the year end.

15.4B4 Common Market Law Reports (CMLR)

CMLR, first published in 1962, is issued weekly. It does not report all EC cases, but only a selection. However, it does report EC cases more rapidly than ECR and, for this reason, you will find the series referred to frequently during your course. CMLR sets out reports of EC cases rather differently from ECR, adding after the headnote the names of those appearing in the action, with lists of cases referred to, perhaps in an attempt to make the reports look more like those from English courts. CMLR also carries reports of cases from national courts, of both member EC countries and non-members. Each weekly issue of CMLR carries an index inside the front and back covers. Each volume, there are usually three a year, carries a comprehensive range of indexes.

Since 1988 competition cases have appeared in a separate anti-trust supplement — *CMLR Antitrust Reports*. Subject collections of cases from CMLR have been published including *EEC Financial Services Cases 1964–1988, Industrial Property Law in the Common Market 1962–1988, and EEC Employment Cases*. CMLR is also available on CD.

15.4B5 All England Law Reports (European Cases)

Starting in 1995, this series of law reports prints the full text of a selection of judgments of the ECR. It is published ten times a year.

15.4B6 CELEX

Sector 6 of this official legal database of the EC contains the full text of judgments and orders of the ECJ since it was established, and opinions of Advocates-General since 1965. Case law is updated weekly and summary information is available in the database about six to ten weeks after the judgment has been delivered. The full text is not available until after the case has been published in ECR. As has been noted elsewhere, *CELEX* is not easy to use — see 15.2B3.2.

15.4B7 JUSTIS-CELEX

This CD contains the full text of the case law contained in sector 6 of the *CELEX* database but with search software which is much easier to use. The CD is updated quarterly but, for an added subscription, weekly updates can be obtained over the internet.

15.4B8   Other databases

Other databases containing the text of ECJ judgments include:

- *Eurolaw* — includes the same material as *JUSTIS-CELEX* plus, at the end of the report of each case, a list of journal articles in which the decision has been discussed. The CD is updated monthly or quarterly depending on the subscription taken.
- *European Law on CD-ROM* — contains the *CELEX* database. The CD is updated quarterly, and is also available on the internet.
- *LEXIS* — contains the full text of the reports, in English, of *European Court Reports* (from 1954 onwards), *European Commercial Cases* (from 1978 onwards), *Common Market Law Reports* (from 1959 onwards) as well as unreported ECJ cases from October 1980 onwards. All these reports are included in the EURCOM library, CASES file. The same materials may also be searched in the INTLAW library, ECCASE file. European Commission Decisions relating to competition will be found in both the EURCOM library, COMDEC file, and the INTLAW library, COMDEC file.
- *EU Direct* — an internet database available from Butterworths to subscribers only. It contains the full text of case law.

15.4B9   European Union Law Reporter

Up to 1989 a selection of ECJ cases was published in full text as part of this encyclopaedia under its former title: *Common Market Reporter*. These cases will be found in a set of 'Transfer Binders'. Since 1989, at the end of each year, a volume entitled *European Community Cases* has been produced. Cases published during the current year, will be found in volume 4 of *European Union Law Reporter*. The indexing to this wealth of material is not good: there is only an index by the names of cases to the material in the Transfer Binders.

15.4B10   Lawtel

The internet service, *Lawtel*, includes an EU interactive database containing summaries of all cases heard by the ECJ and the Court of First Instance since 1987. The service is available to subscribers only and is not part of the basic subscription to *Lawtel*, so some universities or colleges may not take this additional service. Ask your law librarian for details.

15.4B11   Digest of Case Law Relating to the European Communities

This authoritative work is prepared by the Library, Research and Documentation Division of the Court of Justice. Unfortunately, this pedigree is no guide to practical usefulness. *The Digest* eventually will be in four series of loose-leaf volumes. To date only two series have been published and only series A, covering the case law of the Court of Justice, will be of interest to law students. It contains a subject-by-subject arrangement of quotations from *European Court Reports* based on the headings employed in the treaties establishing the Communities. The main drawbacks are that (a) it currently digests only cases published between 1977 and 1985 and (b) the latest issue of the digest is published in English only every five years, according to information given at the ECJ web site. Lack of currency is a serious flaw in the research tool.

15.4B12   European Current Law

This publication began in January 1992. It was formerly known as *European Law Digest* (1973–91). In appearance it is like *Current Law Monthly Digest* (see 6B2.4). The content is quite different, for it contains summaries not only of EC law, but also the domestic law of West, Central and East European countries. As far as EC law is concerned, it is sections 1 and 2 which are of most relevance. The first section is The Focus, which examines one area of recent legal development through a review article; the second section: European Union (Community Law), digests important legislation and cases, all arranged under subject headings. At the year end *European Current Law Yearbook* consolidates the entries. Unlike CLMD, there is no electronic version.

15.4B13   The Digest

Volume 21 of this publication, fully described in section 6B2.6, contains summaries of major EC cases arranged by subject. The main drawback is that it can take many months from the date of the original report of the case for a summary to appear in either the annual Cumulative Supplement or Quarterly Survey to *The Digest*, so it is not useful for research on very recent cases.

15.4B14   Halsbury's Laws of England, 4th edn, volumes 51 and 52

These bound volumes comprise an editorial commentary on EC law with copious footnotes giving references to where the original documents may be found. The volumes were published in 1986 and state the law correct to 30 November 1985. They have been kept up-to-date through entries in the Cumulative Supplement and Service volumes to the whole *Halsbury's* service.

15.4B15   Butterworths EC Case Citator and Service

This excellent finding tool includes lists of ECJ cases arranged by official case number, name, treaty provision, regulation, directive, decision, popular case name and key phrase (rather like a subject index). Using the lists it is possible to trace whether there have been cases interpreting a particular piece of legislation. The whole service is updated by a replacement volume issued every six months. In the interim, a fortnightly case listing service is published on pink paper.

15.4C   Answering research queries

For background information on using CDs and the internet for legal research, see appendix 4.

15.4C1   Tracing a report of an EC case by name or by case reference number

Electronic route
Use one of the following:

- *JUSTIS-CELEX* (see 15.4B7); or
- any of the databases mentioned in section 15.4B8.

Paper route
To check by case name consult, in order of ease of use:

- *Butterworths EC Case Citator and Service* (see 15.4B15).
- *European Current Law* (see 15.4B12).
- *Current Law Case Citator* (see 6B3.1).
- *European Union Law Reporter* (see 15.4B9).
- *All England Law Reports (European Cases)* (see 15.4B5) — use the annual indexes.
- *Common Market Law Reports* (see 15.4B4) — use the annual indexes.
- *European Court Reports* (see 15.4A) — but the indexing is poor.

To check by case reference number consult, in order of ease of use:

- *Butterworths EC Case Citator and Service* (see 15.4B15).
- *European Union Law Reporter* (see 15.4B9) — use the index to cases at the back of volume 4 and then methodically consult the table of cases by case number in each of the dozen or so transfer volumes.
- *All England Law Reports (European Cases)* (see 15.4B5) — use the annual indexes.
- *Common Market Law Reports* (see 15.4B4) — use the annual indexes.
- *European Court Reports* (see 15.4A) — but the indexing is poor.

15.4C2   Tracing EC cases by subject

Electronic route
Use one of the following:

- *JUSTIS-CELEX* (see 15.4B7); or
- any of the databases mentioned in section 15.4B8.

Paper route
Use one of the following:

- *Butterworths EC Case Citator and Service* (see 15.4B15).
- *European Union Law Reporter* (see 15.4B9).

- *Halsbury's Laws of England*, 4th edn, volumes 51 and 52 (see 15.4B14).
- *The Digest* (see 15.4B13).

15.4C3   Has this ECJ case been referred to subsequently?

Electronic route
Use one of the following:

- *JUSTIS-CELEX* (see 15.4B7); or
- any of the databases mentioned in section 15.4B8.

Paper route
Use *Butterworths EC Case Citator and Service* (15.4B15).

15.4C4   Have there been any cases which have considered this EC Regulation or Directive?

Electronic route
Remember that to research this question you need to use the cases part of the database. Use one of the following:

- *JUSTIS-CELEX* (see 15.4B7); or
- any of the databases mentioned in section 15.4B8.

Paper route
Use one of the following:

- *Butterworths EC Case Citator and Service* (see 15.4B15).
- *Halsbury's Laws of England*, 4th edn, volumes 51 and 52 (see 15.4B14).
- *European Union Law Reporter* — the *European Community Cases* part (see 15.4B9).

15.4C5   Tracing recent judgments

Electronic route
Use one of the following:

- *JUSTIS-CELEX* (see 15.4B7);
- any of the databases mentioned in section 15.4B8; or
- *Lawtel*, EU interactive (see 15.4B10).

Paper route
The list is roughly in the order in which information about new decisions becomes available, with the quickest services placed first.

- Newspaper law reports — *The Times* and other newspaper law reports are often the first to report a judgment (see 8.3B14). Check the latest paper or internet issues first, then the CDs.

- *Proceedings of the Court of Justice of the European Communities* (15.4B3) — check the contents pages of each issue.
- Periodical notes of cases — the *Gazette, New Law Journal* and *Solicitors' Journal* carry brief details of recent decisions which may be quickly followed by longer, explanatory articles; check *Legal Journals Index* — preferably the internet version, to trace references to them (see 8.3B1).
- *Butterworths EC Case Citator and Service* (see 15.4B15).
- *Bulletin of the European Union* (15.4B2) — check recent monthly issues, which will provide references to summaries of decisions in the *Official Journal* C series.
- *Official Journal* C series itself (see 15.4B1).

Then, if you have not found what you require, continue your search following the steps outlined in 15.4C1.

Chapter 16

Commentary on European Community law

16A DESCRIPTION

Both the European Community itself and also many commercial publishers produce books, periodicals, booklets, pamphlets and reports on EC law. The closer integration of EC member countries means that many UK law textbooks and periodicals carry valuable background information and comment on legislation and cases.

As was noted in chapter 8, the most efficient way to search for secondary sources such as textbooks and periodical articles is to use either indexing services, which arrange under subject headings brief details of original publications, when and where they were originally published; or abstracting services, which provide not only this so-called bibliographic information but also a short summary of the contents of each item listed.

16B FINDING INFORMATION

16B1 Sources

16B1.1 SCAD Bulletin

SCAD (*Service Central Automatisé de Documentation*, or in English: Community System for Access to Documentation) is the Central Documentation Service of the European Commission. The *Bulletin*, published under this name since 1983, is a weekly publication listing a wide range of EC documents and also articles from non-EC periodicals. Over 1,200 different periodical titles are indexed, though only articles of substantial length are included. *SCAD Bulletin* includes references to about 15,000 new documents each year. The subject coverage is not restricted to law but covers the whole range of functions of the EC. Entries are arranged under about 30 broad subject headings. Whilst each issue includes a subject index and index to keywords (i.e., important words taken from the title of a document), the indexes are only published in French. Unfortunately there are no cumulative indexes, so to search the *Bulletin* for references to publications means searching the index of each issue. The *Bulletin* is therefore of most use for keeping up-to-date with recent developments by scanning each issue as it is published, rather than as a source for tracing references back over a long period of time.

The indexing problems are overcome if you use electronic versions of the database. The EC's Europa web site has free access to the database, called SCADplus. It is at

http://europa.eu.int/scad/

There are three CD versions: SCAD + CD, JUSTIS European References (updated quarterly) and EC Infodisk (which carries only a selection of SCAD relating to EU integration).

16B1.2   European Access

See section 15.3B2.15.

16B1.3   Legal Journals Index

This database, fully described in section section 8.3B1 has indexed articles about EC law appearing in a wide range of law journals published in the UK. In recent years it has also included references to articles appearing in over 85 English language law journals published in European Union countries.

16B1.4   European Legal Journals Index

This is a paper publication which contains the specifically EC-related material from journals indexed in the electronic version of LJI.

16B1.5   Current Law Monthly Digest

See section 8.3B4.

16B1.6   Newspapers

See sections 8.3B14 to 8.3B16

16C   ANSWERING RESEARCH QUERIES

If you are looking for some recent articles from periodicals on either a broad or narrow area of EC law, *Legal Journals Index* (see 8.3B1) or *European Legal*

Journals Index (see 16B4) are probably the easiest and quickest sources to use. The paper publication *Current Law Monthly Digest* (see 8.3B4) is also valuable but because of the less specific subject arrangement may prove tedious to use for detailed topics, and for research over more than a year or two. *European Access* (see 15.3B2.14) does not cover the range of law periodicals of either LJI, ELJI or *Current Law Monthly Digest*.

The quality newspapers sometimes carry comment and analysis of EC legal matters (see 8.3B14 to 8.3B16).

SCAD, and particularly the internet and CD versions (see 16B1), is probably the best service to use if you are researching a topic over many years and wish to draw material from the widest range of books, periodicals and other publications.

Chapter 17

European human rights law

17.1 INTRODUCTION

The Council of Europe was founded in 1949 with the general aim of enhancing the cultural, social and political life of Europe. The first aim of the Treaty which established the Council is 'to protect human rights in a pluralistic democracy'. The main institutions of the Council are the Committee of Ministers, formed from the foreign ministers of Member States, and the Parliamentary Assembly. The Secretariat is based in Strasbourg. Over 30 States are members, including many nations which are not members of the European Union, and, in addition, there are others having 'guest' status.

The first and most widely known of over 150 conventions signed by all or a small group of member States is the Convention for the Protection of Human Rights and Fundamental Freedoms, popularly known as the European Convention on Human Rights. It was signed by the then small number of member States in 1950, and came into force in 1953. The United Kingdom was one of the first States to sign the Convention in 1950, and the first to ratify it in 1951. Since 1966 the UK has accepted the right of an individual to petition the Strasbourg authorities in respect of alleged breeches of the Convention. Yet the rights and freedoms guaranteed by the UK as obligations in international law were not part of or actionable within the domestic legal system. The UK did not incorporate the Convention into domestic law until the Human Rights Act 1998 was passed by Parliament. The Act came into force fully on 2 October 2000.

As originally constructed, the Convention provides for the creation of two institutions, the European Commission of Human Rights, founded in 1954, and the European Court of Human Rights (ECHR), founded in 1959, which sits in Strasbourg. The Commission received petitions from individuals who felt that they had a grievance which could be remedied by the European Convention. The Commission acted as a filter, screening applications to decide whether they were admissible. Later in the process, the Commission drew up a report based on an examination of the facts and stated an opinion, not a decision, on whether the facts disclosed a breach by the State concerned of its obligations under the Convention. The Commission either referred the report to the Council of Ministers (a political body) or directly to the ECHR. The Court then considered the evidence and came to a decision. The proceedings of the Court were predominantly written.

From 1 November 1998, when Protocol 11 of the Convention came into force, the Commission and Court were abolished and a new, single, permanent Court of Human Rights was created. The Court now comprises a heirarchy of committees and chambers with a Plenary Court at the apex. Questions of admissibility previously dealt with by the Commission are now considered by 'Committees of three' judges before being allocated to chambers and courts at a higher level. The Committee of Ministers of the Council of Europe supervises the execution of judgments where a violation has been found.

Since the sources for European human rights research are relatively few, the organisation of this chapter differs from those which have preceded it. The documents produced by or about European human rights are discussed below under two general headings: the primary sources (see 17.2) and the secondary sources (see 17.3). The primary comprise three categories, the Convention itself (see 17.2.1), the documents produced by the European Commission of Human Rights (see 17.2.2) and, finally, those produced by the ECHR (see 17.2.3). The secondary sources comprise commentary on European human rights law and sources which help you keep up-to-date with legal developments on this topic.

17.2   PRIMARY SOURCES

17.2.1   The European Convention on Human Rights

With all the sources noted below, it is important that you check whether the source is up-to-date and contains not only the text of the Convention but also the Protocols which amend it.

17.2.1.1   Official sources

There are at least two sources:

(a)   individual copies of the Convention published by the Council of Europe, such as that in the booklet: *Human Rights today: European legal texts* (Strasbourg: Council of Europe Publications, 1999);
(b)   the Council of Europe web site, which carries the full text of the Convention and all the protocols. The site is at

http://conventions.coe.int

To research the background negotiations and preparatory documents which led up to the promulgation of the Convention in 1950, the best source is an eight-volume set published between 1975 and 1985 under the title: *Collected Edition of the Travaux Preparatoires.*

17.2.1.2   *Unofficial sources*

There are a number of textbooks on European human rights which carry the text of the Convention as an appendix at the back of the publication. Here is a selection of titles:

*   Harris, D.J., et al. *Law of the European Convention on Human Rights*, 2nd edn (London: Butterworths, 1999)
*   Dickson, Brice, *Human Rights and the European Convention* (London: Sweet & Maxwell, 1997)
*   Lester, Lord and Pannick, D., *Human Rights Law and Practice* (London: Butterworths, 1999)
*   Reid, K., *A Practitioner's Guide to the European Convention on Human Rights* (Sweet & Maxwell, 1998)
*   Grosz, S., Beatson, J. and Duffy, P., *Human Rights: The 1998 Act and the European Convention* (London: Sweet & Maxwell, 2000)

JUSTIS Human Rights internet service contains the full text of the Convention and all relevant protocols. It is available to subscribers only.

17.2.2   European Commission on Human Rights

17.2.2.1   *Collection of Decisions of the European Commission of Human Rights*

This publication in 46 volumes carries a selection of the decisions made by the Commission between 1955 and 1973. The text is in English and French.

The method of citation recommended by the Commission within its documents does not assist tracing cases within its many volumes. The usual way of citing Commission decisions, adopted by many British authors, is to refer to a decision printed in this set as follows:

Case name, year of decision, volume number, abbreviation, page number

For example:

X v UK (1967) 25 C.D. 76.

17.2.2.2   *Decisions and Reports*

This series follows on from the above and began in 1974. It is also a selection by the Secretariat of the petitions brought before the Commission. The selection is based on their significance and relevance. Generally they include the Commission's report on the merits of the petition, reports of friendly settlements achieved before the petition reached the Court and reports striking out a petition. They are published in English and French. From volume 76 onwards, two versions of each volume have been published: volume A contains the text in the original language and volume B, produced much later, contains a translation into the other official language. Indexes to the set have been produced after each block of 20 volumes has been published.

Note that the Commission ceased to function on 31 October 1998.

Decisions and reports are usually cited as follows:

Case name, year of decision, volume number, abbreviation, page number

For example:

S v UK (1986) 47 D.R. 274.

17.2.3   European Court of Human Rights

Publications may be divided into three categories:

(a)   list of cases pending (see 17.2.3.1);
(b)   those which provide the full text of the decisions of the Court (see 17.2.3.2);
(c)   summaries or digests of decisions (see 17.2.3.3).

17.2.3.1   List of cases pending

A list of cases pending is available on the Court's web site at

http://www.echr.coe.int/eng/pending.htm

17.2.3.2   Full text reports

The HUDOC database containing all the judgments of the Court is available free on the Court's web site, at

http://www.echr.coe.int/eng/Judgments.htm

Judgments and Decisions
This official paper version of the reports continued to the end of 1995. They were published in two series: series A containing the judgments and decisions; and series B containing the pleadings, oral arguments and other documents. The usual way to cite a case from *Judgments and Decisions* is as follows:

Case name, year of decision, series letter, volume number.

For example:

Golder v UK (1975) Series A, no. 18.

Reports of Judgments and Decisions
This is the name for the official Court reports adopted from 1996. They contain only the decision of the Court and any separate opinions. There is usually a delay of 9 to 12 months before the report of a case is published. The usual way to cite these reports is:

Case name, abbreviation, year of decision and volume reference, page number

For example:

Robins v UK, R.J.D. 1997-V 18, 01

European Human Rights Reports
These commercially published and unofficial reports appear 12 times a year and contain the full judgments of all court decisions. From 1993 a supplement published every six months contains summaries and extracts of selected decisions and reports of the Commission.

LEXIS
This database includes the full text of judgments in the INTLAW library and ECCAS file. It also carries the full text of *European Human Rights Reports* from 1979 onwards in the EURCOM library and the CASES file.

JUSTIS Human Rights
This internet service contains the full text of all ECHR decisions using the official texts. It is updated weekly but is available to subscribers only.

17.2.3.3 Summaries and digests

Human Rights Case Digest
Published 11 times a year, it carries summaries, running to five or six pages in length, of judgments of the Court, resolutions of the Committee of Ministers, summaries of cases referred to the Court by the Commission and admissability decisions.

Digest of Strasbourg Case-Law relating to the European Convention on Human Rights
This five volume set covers the period 1954–82 and arranges digests of case decisions of both the Commission and the Court, in order of the articles of the Convention. Loose-leaf supplements to the first two volumes appeared in 1988, but updating seems to have ceased in the early 1990s. Although issued by the Council of Europe this publication is not regarded as an official source of published case law.

Case Law of the European Court of Human Rights, compiled by Vincent Berger
Published in two volumes and covering the period 1960–90, it gives two or three page summaries of all the decisions of the Court in chronological order, with an index by article of the Convention.

A Systematic Guide to the Case-Law of the European Court of Human Rights,
compiled by Peter Kempees
This publication consists of excerpts from the judgments of the Court, arranged
according to the articles of the Convention. The first volume, covering the
period 1960–94, was published in 1996 and the first supplement, covering 1995
and 1996, appeared in 1997. Supplements are due to appear annually about six
months after the end of the year in question.

17.3 SECONDARY SOURCES

17.3.1 Commentary on human rights law

As was discussed in chapter 8 on English law, commentary is found in a number
of sources, of which the following are most relevant to the study of European
human rights law: textbooks and journals. Most of the sources described in 8.1B
will help you find books on the topic. As to journal articles, the indexes most
relevant are: *Legal Journals Index* (see 8.3B1), *Index to Legal Periodicals* (see
8.3B5) and the newspaper CDs and indexes (see 8.3B14 to 8.3B16). *JUSTIS
Human Rights Companion* database is an internet service containing commentary on the convention, protocols and case law. It is based on the text in the
two-volume book: *Companion to the European Convention on Human Rights*
by Prof. M.M. Wallace. The web site is updated only when a new edition of the
book is published. The site is available to subscribers only.

17.3.2 Keeping up-to-date

There are five sources:

(a) *Current Law Monthly Digest* (see 6B2.4).
(b) *European Current Law* (see 15.3B2.11) — new developments are
described briefly under the heading: Human rights.
(c) *European Law Review* — this journal publishes a separate Annual
Human Rights Survey covering the extent to which States have ratified the
Convention, including reviews of opinions of the Commission and decisions of
the Court and articles discussing human rights law.
(d) *Yearbook of the European Convention on Human Rights* — first
published in 1955, it is prepared by staff of the Council of Europe and published
in English and French within the same volume. It provides a selection of key
extracts from the judgments of the Court arranged according to article of the
Convention. It also describes the Council of Europe's activities on human rights
matters in general and the impact of the Convention within the Parliaments and
courts of some of the Council's member States.
(e) *European Human Rights Law Review* — published six times a year, it
includes a section of Case and Comment on the decisions of the Commission
and the Court.

PART 4

KEEPING UP-TO-DATE

Chapter 18

Getting the best out of electronic and paper sources

The bulk of this book — chapters 3 to 17 — is about selecting and using legal publications which are appropriate to answering a particular information or research need. In contrast, this brief chapter is about the skill of keeping abreast with legal development and change. A vast quantity of new legal material is published each week and it is essential for you both as a student and, later, in your career to master the technique of keeping up-to-date. There are several ways this can be accomplished and it is wise to adopt one of them early in your studies so that you have developed a valuable research habit before you enter legal practice.

18.1 DAILY NEWS SERVICES

Butterworths LawDirect is an online legal newspaper with current stories, news and features and even video clips. Access is free at

   http://www.butterworths.com/

   In another part of the same web site is *Law Online*, a subscriber access only alerting service, containing summaries of the latest legislation, cases and official publications.

   Lawtel carries a subscriber only *Daily Update* service with summaries of latest legislation, cases and journal articles. The web site is at

   http://www.lawtel.co.uk/

18.2   WEEKLY PERIODICALS

A number of major weekly law periodicals designed for practising lawyers carry news sections and articles reviewing recent legal developments; some are also available on the internet.

Gazette is the weekly journal of the Law Society of England and Wales. It contains a news section at the front of each issue with a legal update section of brief summaries on new developments in UK and EC law. Sandwiched between the news and updates are brief 'feature' articles. The text is also available at

> http://www.lawgazette.co.uk/

The Lawyer is a tabloid newspaper featuring news and reviews of people and organisations in legal practice. Longer review articles in the centre pages sometimes carry information of interest to students. An online version with an archive of some sections from past issues is available at

> http://www.thelawyer.co.uk/

New Law Journal also carries a news section at the front, but at the centre of each issue is a section entitled 'NLJ Practitioner' which has fairly lengthy reports of one or two cases followed by NLJ Law Digest of recent developments in legislation and official publications. *New Law Journal On-line* carries the contents of the latest issue only with the full text of selected items, and an alphabetical index to all articles published since the beginning of 1997. It is at

> http://www.butterworths.com.nlj/index.htm

Solicitors' Journal also carries brief news reports followed by feature articles, and at the centre of each issue is 'Lawbrief'. It contains summaries of cases and is printed on coloured paper with pre-punched holes for the supplement to be removed and inserted in a separate binder. SJ is not available online at present.

In Scotland, the *Journal of the Law Society of Scotland* and the *Scots Law Times* also provide means of keeping up-to-date.

You may wish to consider taking out a personal subscription to one of these titles as a way of ensuring immediate access to news of latest developments.

18.3   MONTHLY REVIEWS

Current Law Monthly Digest has been noted at several points in earlier chapters. It contains brief summaries of recent Acts, statutory instruments and case law (UK and EC), together with details of the authors and titles of new books and periodical articles, as well as major government publications. All this material is arranged under broad subject headings making it very easy to scan the sections of personal interest. Although *Current Law Monthly Digest* lacks the news and review content of the weekly law periodicals described above, it is an excellent alerting service to a wide range of new publications. The contents of

Current Law Monthly Digest are scattered over several parts of the *Current Legal Information* (CLI) electronic database, but by using the 'What's new' feature, it is possible to extract the latest developments.

Law Notes (published monthly) is specifically designed for trainee solicitors rather than undergraduates. Brief notes of recent cases and statutory publications are included as well as one or two articles on legal practice topics.

One of the features of *Halsbury's Laws of England* is the Monthly Review, a booklet issued to subscribers to this encyclopaedic publication. The Monthly Review is filed in the Current Service binder. Each issue includes a few pages on recent developments whilst the bulk of the booklet comprises summaries of Acts, statutory instruments and cases, with references to articles which have appeared in a limited range of law periodicals. Information in the review is arranged under broad subject headings which match those used in the rest of the encyclopaedia.

PART 5

AIDS TO IMPROVE THE
QUALITY OF YOUR RESEARCH

Chapter 19

Recording and presenting research findings

19.1 RECORDING RESEARCH PROGRESS

When you undertake a piece of extended legal research over several months for, say, your final-year project or dissertation, you may consult quite a large number of the sources noted in chapters 3 to 17. Hopefully, you will come across references to a large number of original publications which you will need to either find in your library or ask the library staff to obtain for you via the inter-library loan service. You will appreciate that keeping a record of your research progress, a check on the sources you have already consulted, those you have yet to read, items you have asked the library to obtain for you — in short, being in control and organised about the progress of your research — will assume far greater importance than when, in the past, you were merely spending a few hours or days researching for an essay, assignment or assessment. If you are not methodical in the conduct of your research you may find you:

(a)   overlook a search of some vital sources of information;

(b)   cover the same or similar publications more than once, and so waste valuable time and effort by duplicating your references;

(c)   omit some vital element in a reference to a publication (such as the title or date of the periodical in which you found a valuable article) and have to retrace your steps to ensure you give a complete and accurate reference to it in your bibliography;

(d)   discover, when finally writing up your project or dissertation, that you should have checked indexes and catalogues under a subject term or concept which you have only now realised is vitally connected with the topic of your research.

How do you avoid these common pitfalls?

(a)   In the early stages, when planning your research, define the relationship of your topic to other areas of law and other areas of knowledge. By drawing boundaries around your topic it will help to prevent you being side-tracked and spending time researching topics marginal to your interest and keep your research to the point.

(b)   Carefully consider the types of legal information you require to undertake your project — use the section headings in chapters 3 to 17 to help you decide which types of source are going to be relevant. For example, if you are researching the reform of a part of social security law, you will wish to consult a quite different range of sources as compared with research into equal opportunities in the legal profession.

(c)   Carefully consider the jurisdiction(s) your research is going to cover: England, Wales, Scotland, United Kingdom, European Communities, United States, or a comparison of practice and procedure between any number of jurisdictions.

(d)   Match your requirements in (b) and (c) above and read the relevant subsections of chapters 3 to 17, noting the appropriate sources for each relevant type of publication mentioned in each subsection B, on finding information.

(e)   Develop a system of 'bibliographic check cards' which will indicate the sources you *should* check and the sources you *have* checked already (see Pemberton, 1974, p. 48).

Either use personal computer software, such as Carddbox or Cardfile, or buy a pack of 5in 3in or 6in 4in cards (or metric equivalent) and a flip-top box made to keep them in. Most stationers stock these. Write across the top of each card the title of a publication you have noted, from reading each subsection B, as being relevant to your search for information. In the body of the card note the years over which you consider it necessary to search issues of that publication. Figure 19.1 shows the layout of a bibliographic check card for *Index to Legal Periodicals*. As your search of the *Index* progresses you can cross off the issues you have consulted, and so always have an accurate record of the progress of your research.

Figure 19.1   Example of a bibliographic check card.

Title of bibliographic source ➡	INDEX TO LEGAL PERIODICALS				
	1970	1980	1990		
	~~1~~	1	1		
Years	~~2~~	2	2	Air law	Index terms
to be ➡	~~3~~	3		Airspace	⬅ to search
searched	~~4~~	4		Space law	under
	~~5~~	5		Space technology	
	6	6			
	7	7			
	8	8			
	9	9			

Keep your bibliographic check cards in alphabetical order by the title of the publication, and occasionally review your total research progress by glancing over the whole set of cards.

This system of cards will:

(i)   make you think about your research campaign and plan your progress;

(ii)   help to ensure you check all your sources thoroughly, especially when you reach the shelves and find the next volume of a publication you wish to check is being used by someone else — on your check cards that volume will remain un-ticked and remind you to return to it later;

(f)   Devise one or more cartwheels for your topic, as described in chapter 2, and run your list of subject terms against those used in each of the publications you have selected from the appropriate B subsections on exploitation. When you have discovered the subject headings used by the compilers of a particular publication under which you find relevant references, note the subject headings either in a space on the face of the relevant bibliographic check card (as in figure 19.1), or on the back, so that if you need to return to the publication at a later time you will immediately be able to consult the most appropriate subject headings. Rarely will you find two publications using exactly the same index terms under which to place information about a topic. Making a note of the terms used by a particular publication will speed your research.

(g)   When you find a relevant reference in an index or catalogue, create a 'bibliography card' for it, which will provide you with details of information you have discovered (see Pemberton, 1974, p. 48). Use either Cardbox or Cardfile software or similar cards to the bibliography check cards but keep your collections of bibliography cards and bibliographic check cards separate.

Set out information on your bibliography cards to a standard pattern, and stick to that pattern — it will make the task of compiling the list of references, to be given at the end of your written work, much easier! Make up a specimen card for a book and a specimen card for a periodical reference and refer to them as you create new bibliography cards.

If the reference is to a book, complete the card as in the upper part of the illustration in figure 19.2; if it is to a periodical article, include the information given in the lower part.

Even if you have used electronic databases and have collected pages of print out with references to books and articles, it is still worthwhile creating bibliography cards to a standard layout. As will be explained shortly, cards are a far more flexible way of holding information than sheets of paper.

You will notice that, near the bottom of each card, the source from which the reference was obtained is noted. This is useful information, because if you have made an error in copying the reference you can quickly look up the source index or catalogue again. Further, should you need to ask your library to obtain the item on inter-library loan, the request form you will need to complete will ask for your 'source of reference', so that if any errors in the transmission of your request between libraries occur, or the book or periodical article cannot be traced, library staff can verify that the reference is correct from the source information you have provided. You can also note near the bottom of the bibliography card whether you have had to ask the library to obtain the item on inter-library loan, the date on which you made the request, and whether your request has been satisfied. If you keep these bibliography cards in alphabetical order by the name of the author, you will be able to check, when you come across further references in a different index or catalogue, whether you have already discovered the material. You will therefore ensure you do not note the same reference down twice and duplicate the list of publications you need to consult.

Figure 19.2   Examples of bibliography cards.

BOOKS

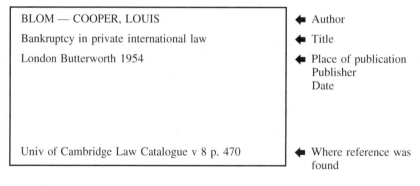

PERIODICALS

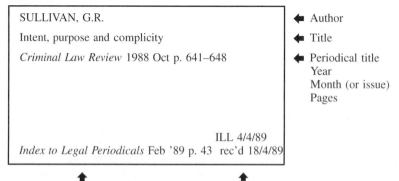

You will discover that using bibliography cards, one card for each book or article, is a very flexible way of holding information. When you come to actually write your project or dissertation, you can plan the order in which you quote or cite references merely by rearranging the order of your bibliography cards. Further, the group of cards containing references you cite in a particular chapter can then be rearranged again into the order you require for the bibliography or list of references you will need to give either at the end of that chapter or, merged with cards used in other chapters, to form a grand, single bibliography at the end of the entire project or dissertation. Always use a flexible method of holding research information, such as cards — *never* note references to books or articles as you glean them from indexes or catalogues on to separate lines of a sheet of paper, cramming 30 or 40 references down the page. You will not be able to sort or reorder the references into alphabetical sequence, subject groups or the order of quotation. You will not be readily able to check whether you have already discovered the reference earlier in your research. In short, you will not have methodically organised the products of your research effort.

If you choose to use a personal computer with a program such as Cardbox or Cardfile, remember that since most of the 'exploitation' sources you will be using will be reference-only items which you cannot borrow from the library or use at home, you will either need to use a PC in the library or fall back on the 'old-fashioned' 5in 3in cards described, and laboriously transcribe data from the cards compiled in the library to your computer file at home.

19.2   FOOTNOTING AND COMPILING BIBLIOGRAPHIES

Open almost any major law textbook and you will notice, at the bottom of some pages, numbered paragraphs in smaller type. These are footnotes; they have four main uses:

(a)   to cite the authority for statements made in the text;
(b)   to make cross-references to related information or publications;
(c)   to make incidental comments on the text;
(d)   to make acknowledgements.

Some lecturers encourage students to footnote their own essays, assignments or assessments, so it is worth remembering the precise purposes of footnotes. Overlong footnotes make the main thrust of the argument in the text less easy to follow and can be particularly off-putting if any one footnote extends over more than a page. If it really is necessary to provide that much incidental information, place it as an appendix at the end of the text.

However, lecturers are likely to be more concerned with your bibliography — the list of sources you have cited — than the construction of footnotes. The bibliography should be given at the end of your written work, and it serves two purposes: those marked (a) and (d), above.

You should get into the habit, if you have not already, of honestly acknowledging where your opinions and views came from. Lecturers are not expecting brilliant flashes of original thought from student essays, assignments, assessments, projects or dissertations — they may only come following long familiarity with a topic, and sometimes never at all! If you fail to give due acknowledgement to the authors of the textbooks or periodical articles you have used, and try to pass off their work as your own, lecturers will easily spot the change in style and use of language. Plagiarism will not be tolerated.

One of the most thorough and comprehensive guides to the citation of legal publications in the United Kingdom is French, D., *How to Cite Legal Authorities* (London: Blackstone Press, 1996), giving principles for the layout of references to every type of law source in paper format, with copious examples.

So that those who read your written work can find the books and articles you cite, can read and check the accuracy and appropriateness of your interpretation, you should use a system or standard form of citation by which the quotation or paraphrase in the body of your essay is linked to the full reference to the book or articles you provide in the bibliography at the end of your essay.

There are, in fact, at least three systems of citation in common use. Two, the numeric system and the name and date (or Harvard) system are widely used in all subjects from astronomy to zoology. The third, the Harvard Law Review Association's Uniform System of Citation, has been devised specially for use in legal publications, but its use is confined to the USA. Details of each are given in appendix 5.

Sometimes, especially when you are preparing for a longer piece of work such as a research project or dissertation in your final year, lecturers will specify which of the three systems you should use. For shorter pieces of work, such as essays, assignments and assessments, such guidance may not be given, so you will have to select one of the three systems and follow its requirements when preparing your work. Choose *one* of the three alternative systems for citing references and use it *consistently* through a single piece of work — do not mix use of the three systems.

APPENDICES

Appendix 1

Check your knowledge of how to use a law library

1. The stock of a law library is usually divided into books and periodicals. Is it in your law library?

2. How is the stock arranged on the shelves:

   (a) by subject according to a classification scheme,
   (b) by jurisdiction,
   (c) by title,
   (d) by author,
   (e) by a combination of these?

3. Are there any separate sequences for particular types of stock, such as:

   (a) large books (folios, quartos or oversize),
   (b) thin books (pamphlets),
   (c) photocopies,
   (d) dictionaries,
   (e) general encyclopaedias,
   (f) directories,
   (g) bibliographies?

If so, where are they located?

4. Over which periods of time can you borrow books, and where is the 'loan period' for a particular book marked on it?

5. Are some books available for loan for very brief periods of time and, if so, where can you obtain them:

    (a)   from the open shelves,
    (b)   by asking at an issue desk or counter for staff to obtain them from a 'closed' collection?

6. What type(s) of catalogue system does the library have:

    (a)   computerised,
    (b)   microform,
    (c)   card,
    (d)   a combination of these?

7. Which different ways can you search for books:

    (a)   by author,
    (b)   by title,
    (c)   by subject,
    (d)   by keyword,
    (e)   by other routes? (If so, what are they?)

8. Try the following searches to learn more about the information given in the catalogue:

    (a)   An author search for ATIYAH, P.S. Are several different titles noted? Select one and discover from the entry the subject classification number (class mark) and details of where it is located in the library.
    (b)   A title search for *Constitutional and Administrative Law*. Are several different editions noted? Select the most recent and discover from the entry the subject classification number (class mark) and details of where it is located in the library.
    (c)   A subject search for books on 'contract'. If you are using a microform or card catalogue, what is the classification number or class mark? Use this mark to search the classified catalogue for authors and titles. If you are using a computerised catalogue, select one of the entries in the list of authors and/or titles and identify its classification number (class mark).

9. If you are using a computerised catalogue, does it tell you whether a particular copy of a book is on loan and, if it is, when it is due to be returned?

10. If you want a book that is on loan, how do you ask the library to recall it from the reader who presently has it?

11. Which different ways can you search for periodicals:

    (a)   by title,
    (b)   by subject?

12.   Try the following searches to learn more about the information given in the periodicals catalogue:

(a)   Does the library keep the following periodical titles:

(i)   *Criminal Law Review,*
(ii)   *All England Law Reports,*
(iii)   *Modern Law Review,*
(iv)   *New Law Journal?*

(b)   If it does, which issues of each does it stock?
(c)   What information is given about the location of these periodicals in the library?
(d)   Can you find the titles the library stocks, on the shelves?

Appendix 2

The inter-library loan service

APP 2.1   WHAT IS IT?

When you discover there are books or periodical articles that you require but which are not stocked by your library, you can make a written request on forms available in the library for the materials to be borrowed from another library for you. All academic (i.e. university and college) libraries and all public libraries are members of the national inter-library loan service. A large number of privately funded libraries (such as those in firms of lawyers) are also part of the network. Most items requested are obtained from the British Library Document Supply Centre (BLDSC) at Boston Spa, West Yorkshire, but some may be obtained for you from other academic libraries. Some items may be obtained from libraries abroad.

APP 2.2   HOW DO I USE THE SERVICE?

Your library may have inter-library loan application forms on public display for you to fill in with details of the publications you require. Often there will be two different types of form available for you to use: one type should be used for books, theses and the like, the other for periodicals, conference papers, and law reports.

When you request items you have discovered from a search of bibliographies, indexes and abstracts make sure you give full and accurate details of the item you require. Lack of information could cause delays in supplying the item. There will be a place on the form for you to quote your source of reference: the author or title of the book or bibliography, with page references, in which you discovered the item. This is important as it enables libraries to recheck your source if problems arise — it can be helpful if you attach a photocopy of the reference to your request.

Some further points to remember when making an application:

(a) *Books:* give full details including the name of the publisher, date of publication and edition (very important in law where books pass through editions quickly), and the international standard book number (ISBN) — a 10 digit number which uniquely identifies one title or edition of a title from a specific publisher.

(b) *Periodicals:* give full details of each article you require, the full title of the periodical in which the article appeared, year, volume, part and page references, as well as the author and title of the article itself.

(c) *Law reports:* give full details of the names of parties to the action and the *full* title (not the abbreviated citation) to the series of reports, with year, volume and page references.

(d) *Theses:* give details of the degree/awarding institution, type of degree (PhD, MPhil, LLM etc.) as well as the year, author and title. For British PhD theses you will also need to complete and hand in with your request a thesis copyright declaration.

APP 2.3   HOW LONG DOES IT TAKE TO OBTAIN AN ITEM ON INTER-LIBRARY LOAN?

It is not possible to estimate how long it may take to obtain each item — it depends on how readily a library holding the item you require can be located and, if the item is part of the borrowable stock of the library, whether it is on their shelves and not on loan to one of their library users at the time you request it.

APP 2.4   HOW LONG MAY YOU KEEP AN ITEM OBTAINED ON INTER-LIBRARY LOAN?

If the item has been obtained from BLDSC, Boston Spa, you will have the book for three weeks with an automatic extension for a further three weeks so long as it is not required elsewhere. It is not usually possible to renew BLDSC loans.

If the item has been obtained from another academic library the loan period will be determined by the library lending the publication and this can vary. It is possible, however, to renew these loans.

Some items are supplied as photocopies of original documents and these you may keep.

Please remember to take particular care of all inter-library loans and to return promptly items obtained for you.

Appendix 3

Comparative table of generally-accepted terminology for the division of Bills, Acts and statutory instruments

(Based in part on information given in University of London, Institute of Advanced Legal Studies, *Manual of Legal Citations*, part 1, the British Isles (London: The University, 1959) and Erskine May, *Parliamentary Practice*, 22nd edn (London: Butterworths, 1997).)

Column A = division
Column B = abbreviation
Column C = symbol, i.e., an example of how the division is distinguished in the publication.

Bill			Act			Statutory Instrument		
A	B	C	A	B	C	A	B	C
Part	Pt	VIII	Part	Pt	VIII	Part	Pt	VIII
Chapter	ch.	VI	Chapter	ch.	VI	Chapter	ch.	VI
Clause	cl. (plural = cll)	3	section	s. (plural = ss.)	3	*article	art (plural = arts) or	3
						*regulation	reg. (plural = regs) or	3
						*rule	r. (plural = rr.)	3
Subsection	subs.	(2)	subsection	subs.	(2)	paragraph	para.	(2)
paragraph	para.	(d)	paragraph	para.	(d)	subparagraph	sub-para.	(d)
subparagraph	sub-para.	(ii)	subparagraph	sub-para.	(ii)	sub-subparagraph	sub-sub-para.	(ii)
Schedule	Sch.	3	Schedule	Sch.	3	Schedule	Sch.	3
Part (of schedule)	Pt	2	Part (of schedule)	Pt	2	Part (of schedule)	Pt	II
paragraph (of schedule)	para.	1	paragraph (of schedule)	para.	1	paragraph (of schedule)	para.	1
subparagraph (of schedule)	sub-para.	(2)	subparagraph (of schedule)	sub-para.	(2)	subparagraph (of schedule)	sub-para.	(2)

*terminology of division determined by whether the publication is titled an Order (article) or Regultions (regulation) or Rules (rule).

Appendix 4

Using CDs and the internet for legal research

APP 4.1   INTRODUCTION

Knowing how to use electronic databases to undertake effective legal research is now as important to a law student as knowing how to use paper sources. Virtually every law school library in the United Kingdom has access to some type of electronic database containing information about the law, and most law firms and barristers' chambers use electronic sources also.

For many years there was just one law database: *LEXIS*. Although it is the oldest and, as far as the range of jurisdictions and types of legal material included, the most comprehensive presently available, it is facing severe competition from large numbers of CD and internet databases.

Most of these electronic services have been commercially provided, that is, they are available only to subscribers. As a member of a subscribing educational institution you will have access to a selection of these services although you won't have to pay yourself. Some web sites are available free of charge; predominantly, they are government run sites providing legislation, selections of cases and official publications.

Even if you are not intending to train as a lawyer you will find electronic databases used in many occupations, so it is important that during your studies you learn the principles of searching an electronic database.

APP 4.2   WHAT YOU NEED TO KNOW BEFORE YOU GO ONLINE

You must have a clear idea of:

(a)   the topic or subject you are researching and relevant keywords (see App 4.2.1);
(b)   the type of database you wish to search: bibliograhic, full text or current awareness (see App 4.2.2);

(c)   the type of legal material for which you are searching: legislation, cases, official publications, newspaper reports (see App 4.2.3);

(d)   the time period you need to cover: the last week, month, year, decade, 50 years (see App 4.2.4).

App 4.2.1   Devising a search

Especially when you are undertaking research for a long piece of work such as an essay, assessment, dissertation or thesis, resist the temptation to go to the computer straight away. Spend some time thinking about the research topic and identifying keywords. The techniques described in chapter 2 will help you. One important point to remember is to avoid using commonly occuring legal words when searching a database: law, tax, case, will retrieve too much irrelevant material.

Electronic databases use special software to search the material they contain. Whilst each brand of search software operates differently, and the screen into which you type your request differs from one database to another, there are some common principles worth understanding.

Single word search

This is the simplest type of search, where you type in, for example, blackmail. This type of search is useful only where the topic can be summed up in a single word and the response from the database is a reasonable but not overwhelming number of relevant hits.

Phrase search

A similar type of simple search is where you type in a recognised legal phrase, such as 'landlord and tenant' usually placing the phrase in inverted commas so that the search software looks only for the specified words appearing together and in that order, rather than as words widely separated and in any order.

Compound or Boolean or advanced searches

This type of search is best used where you have a topic made up of a number of keywords, for example, legal aspects of oil pollution at sea.

Most electronic search software will not provide the best results if you type in the search phrase as given above. The computer will want to know the relationship between each word, otherwise it will assume a relationship between each word which may not be the one you are intending. For example, using the above example, you are looking for documents which are about oil and pollution. If you do not specify this relationship, some databases will use a default setting and assume you mean oil or pollution. The results will not be as relevant as you wished. Also, the concepts mentioned in your query might be capable of being expressed using similar words (synonyms) and to retrieve those documents from the database you will need to include all the synonyms in your search. In the example, to undertake an effective search you would have to include the following:

sea or ocean or marine

The logical operators or Boolean connectors which are recognised by electronic search software are:

'AND' 'OR' 'NOT'

'AND' joins concepts to make a search more specific, e.g.:

oil AND pollution AND north AND sea

'OR' widens the search especially where there are synonyms, e.g.:

marine OR sea OR ocean

'NOT' excludes words, e.g.:

pollution NOT air

Complex searches can be created using brackets, e.g.:

oil AND pollution AND (sea OR ocean OR marine)

Points to watch:

(a) Keep you search request short. Three or fewer keywords is best. If you use long 'search strings' and the search fails to find anything, it may take a number of repeated searches each removing a search term, to identify the keyword or keywords which caused the search to fail.

(b) Enter you search terms with the keyword of broadest meaning first, followed by those of narrower meaning. For example,

Contract AND breach AND damages

If the search fails it is much easier to edit a hierarchy than a jumble.

(c) Some search services, especially those on the internet, will automatically apply Boolean logic to the terms you type in. Find out whether the service uses AND or OR as this will affect what it searches for and the results it finds.

(d) Some search services require you to type AND or OR in capitals; other do not. Yet others require you to use check boxes to indicate what you require. Others use + or − as alternative commands. Some databases use + to mean something quite different: that the word in front of which it is placed must appear.

Using wildcards

If, for example, you were searching for documents on the professional negligence of lawyers, it is important to recognise that within the database, the following phrases might have been used to describe the topic:

- that someone was negligent
- that an act was done negligently
- that it was a case of negligence

To cover all the possible endings of the word negligence, many databases will accept the use of a wildcard, very often an asterisk *. The *LEXIS* database is different and uses an exclamation mark ! instead of an asterisk. If the search word is truncated to the common stem to which the different endings are applied, and the asterisk is then added, the computer will search for all endings of the word automatically. For example negligen*. This is a very powerful and valuable search technique, but must be used with care. If the stem you use could refer to several concepts the relevance of your results will be low: employ* will cover employee, employer, employment, employed and may be too general for the specific query you have in mind.

App 4.2.2   Which types of database are available?

There are three ways of categorising law databases: by their purpose, the type of information they contain and, finally, the medium in which the information is held and delivered to the user.

Purpose

(a)   Indexing or bibliographic services provide very brief details of publications and are used most frequently when starting research about a legal topic or subject. They do not usually contain the text of publications themselves, only a description (i.e., author, title, subject matter). In this respect they are rather like library catalogues, guiding you to relevant material held elsewhere.

(b)   Full text databases contain the complete text of, for example, Acts or cases or official publications.

(c)   Current awareness services provide summaries of legal information. Their main purpose is to keep users up-to-date with the latest legal developments, but as their archives develop they are valuable for research outside the very recent past. Sometimes these databases provide the possibility of ordering on-line the full text of a document at added cost (in universities and colleges this ordering service is usually not available to users because of the open-ended commitment to expenditure of library funds).

The type of information contained

(a)   Older established databases collect information on all legal topics from a wide range of different types of source. Examples include *LEXIS*, containing the full text of statutes, statutory instruments and reported and unreported cases, and *Lawtel*, containing summaries of a similar range of material.

(b)   Some databases restrict themselves to reproducing in full text form one particular type of legal information, such as cases. Examples include *All England Electronic Law Reports* or *JUSTIS Weekly Law Reports*.

(c)   An increasing number of databases gather together information on a discrete legal topic regardless of the source in which it originally appeared. Examples include *Butterworths Family and Child Law CD*, containing statutes, statutory instruments, law reports, unreported cases, and extracts from the major books on practice and procedure in the subject area.

(d)   Whilst most databases are mainly concerned to reproduce electronically information also available in paper form, a few contain information not available by any other means. Examples include *Badger*, containing brief details of government publications, press releases and press comment relevant to law, and the *Journal of Information Law and Technology*, an electronic journal specialising on law in the context of IT.

Delivery medium

(a)   *Remote on-line databases.* Before the advent of CD-ROMs and the internet, the only way to search for information electronically was by subscribing to obtain access to information held on a computer outside your university or college, sometimes outside the UK. Currently, *LEXIS* is the only law database which still operates in this way, though internet access to the database is a distinct possibility in the near future. *LEXIS* is also the only law database to operate a scheme of charges based not on a standard annual charge but on the length of time and the part of the database accessed at each search session. The *LEXIS* charging scheme is rather like a taxi meter — the longer the search, the more it costs. For this reason alone, access to *LEXIS* is not usually made available to students direct, unless they have been through a comprehensive training programme. Searches may be conducted on their behalf by library or teaching staff. Finally, *LEXIS* is not as easy to search effectively and efficiently as more modern database systems — several hours training is required even to achieve basic competency.

(b)   *CD-ROM databases.* These are widely available in law school libraries. Often the university or college will network CDs so that the same database is available from as many PCs across the campus as possible. Sometimes it is possible to access the CD network from a PC you may have at home, but circumstances vary and it is best to ask library staff if this is feasible. For technical, financial and contractual reasons it is sometimes not possible for your university or college to network a CD, so it may be loaded on a single PC in the law library or law school (this arrangement is often referred to as stand-alone access). Unlike *LEXIS*, normally there is no restriction on the use of CDs. CDs are:

(i)   often very easy to use,
(ii)   capable of offering more sophisticated search features,
(iii)   usually much faster at searching than internet-based services.

But, their biggest disadvantage is that they are up-dated monthly, at the quickest, and frequently only quarterly. In contrast, internet-based services are usually updated daily.

(c)   *Internet-based services*. These may be searched from any PC connected to the internet and loaded with a web browser, software which offers the ability to access the internet, and manipulate the information found there. Two of the most widely available browsers are Netscape Navigator and Microsoft's Internet Explorer. Although there are some free web sites of relevance to law, usually containing the text of legislation or cases, many are subscriber access only since the information they contain has had value added to it by the commercial organisation providing the service. The added value may be in the form of summaries, indexes or sophisticated search software. Access is restricted by the use of a password. Library or teaching staff will inform you of the services you are entitled to access and the relevant passwords. Internet databases:

(i)   Sometimes can be accessed from your PC at home as well as those in your university or college; ask your law librarian for advice.
(ii)   Sometimes can be slow to use because of the intense traffic at popular sites often offer less sophisticated means of searching than other forms of electronic database.

The greatest advantage of internet databases is that they are the most frequently updated of all types of database and so are invaluable if you are searching for the latest information or developments.

App 4.2.3   Which type of legal material am I searching for?

This is covered in chapters 3 to 12 of this book.

App 4.2.4   Which time period am I searching for?

(a)   Last week or month — use internet sources.
(b)   Older than 4 to 6 weeks — use either internet or CD, but carefully note how often a particular database is updated — this information is given about the majority of databases in chapters 3 to 12 of this book. However, not all electronic databases give 'frequency or update' information in the 'About this database' or 'Help' sections of the service. If in doubt, ask our law library staff if they have this information.

APP 4.3   GOING ONLINE

Since each university or college will set up its CDs differently, some on networks each using different software, others as stand-alone CDs inserted in the CD drive of an individual PC, the techniques which follow concentrate on using the internet to search for law.

The purpose of this section is not to give a highly technical introduction to using the internet but to highlight some research techniques which will enable you, as a lawyer, to be more able to find the information you require.

App 4.3.1 Some technical terms explained

To use the internet you need to use a piece of software called a browser. The two most widely available are Netscape Navigator and Microsoft Internet Explorer. The browser enables you to:

(a)   access the internet;
(b)   open and go to a specific point on the internet;
(c)   copy or save or print from web pages (pages installed on the internet);
(d)   cut and paste to other applications, such as a word processing package (e.g. Word).

The specific points on the internet are URLs or Uniform Resource Locators. They are the equivalent of a full postal address — the standard method of naming or specifying any kind of information on the internet. A web site is a group of documents or pages on the same computer — each site usually has a home page.

The home page is the 'top level' page of the site and is similar to the contents page of a book, detailing what other information can be obtained within the particular site from this point.

The documents on the web site are written in a computer readable coding system which the browser can read. The system is called Hypertext Mark Up Language (HTML).

Some web sites comprise screens of information which are split into several independent windows or frames. Only the frame in which you are working with the cursor is active at that time and linked to the menu tool bar and the button bar. Frames are a useful design device which allows you to stay in one frame but use the links in another frame to visit other sites. However, if you are printing or downloading from a frames site, only the active page will print or download.

App 4.3.2 Understanding an URL

Structure

It is important to understand what the URL means because if you undertake a subject search using a search engine (see App 4.3.3) you may be sent into the middle of a web site. The URL will provide you with information which will help you:

(a)   navigate your way around or out of the site;
(b)   indicate the origin of the information on the site and, most importantly for legal information, indicate the authority of the information (is it official, privately produced or commercial?).

URLs:

(a)   specify the name and address of the resource on the internet;
(b)   are hierarchical, reading from left to right;

(c)   can tell you the route (pathway) to the resource, the computer, directory and file;

(d)   can provide information on the organisation (or individual) providing the resource;

(e)   often contain the geographical location of the server.

An example of an URL with its component parts identified is given in figure App 4.1.

The basic structure of an URL is:

protocol://server-name.domain-name/directory/filename

- Protocol describes the access method, the most popular is 'http://www'.
- Server-name is the name of the server you need to access.
- Domain-name tells you the country in which the server is based and the nature of the organisation which owns the server. Note that the USA does not have a country code. Country codes include:
  — au   Australia
  — ca   Canada
  — de   Germany
  — fr   France
  — uk   United Kingdom

Figure App 4.1   The structure of a Uniform Resource Locator (URL).

http://www.open.gov.uk/lcd/atojfr.htm

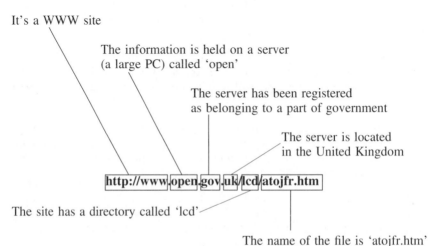

It's a WWW site

The information is held on a server (a large PC) called 'open'

The server has been registered as belonging to a part of government

The server is located in the United Kingdom

http://www.open.gov.uk/lcd/atojfr.htm

The site has a directory called 'lcd'

The name of the file is 'atojfr.htm'

- Organisation identifiers include:
  - — ac, edu   academic or educational servers
  - — co, com   commercial servers
  - — gov   government
  - — org   non-governmental, non-profit making organisations

Directories and filenames

A tilde sign ~ indicates that this is the personal directory of an individual. The information and opinions are personal and not official. It does not necessarily mean the information is of poor quality but merely it is not official. It has been known for students to ignore the meaning of the tilde sign and assume that the site is an authoritative exposition and commentary on the law when, in fact, the site belonged to a pressure group adopting a very particular interpretation of the law.

Learning about and navigating a large site by deleting part of the URL

If you delete the URL from the right-hand side back to the slash marks / you will move up the hierarchy of pages and see how the page is embedded within the site. If you wish to practise this go to the internet mentioned in figure App 4.1 by typing in the URL and then delete part of the URL so that all that remains is

   http://www.open.gov.uk/lcd

You should now be at the home page for the Lord Chancellor's Department.

Favorites and Bookmarks

If you find an web site of value, to make it easy for you to return to it on a future occasion, click on Favorites (if using Internet Explorer) or Bookmarks (Netscape Navigator) and add the URL to a list of bookmarked sites. In future, when you wish to return to the site, click on Favorites or Bookmarks and then click on the name of the site in the list and you will be taken to the bookmarked page, without the need to type in its address. You will probably find it useful to organise your Favorites or Bookmarks into 'folders', arranged by subject.

App 4.3.3   Finding legal information on the internet

There are four search tools available:

  (a)   web search engines;
  (b)   meta-search services;
  (c)   classified subject directories, sometimes called portals or gateways;
  (d)   link pages.

Web search engines

A web search engine gathers information about web sites into its own database. When you submit a search request to the search engine it searches its database index of web sites for those which are likely to contain the information you seek.

Because different search engines cover different proportions of the internet and index it in different ways, they can provide quite different results from the same search. Many have a distinctly American bias, though some European search engines are now available.

Here are the most well-known:

- AltaVista — http://www.av.com/
- Excite — http://www.Excite.co.uk/
- Infoseek — http://www.infoseek.co.uk/
- Lycos — http://www.lycos.co.uk/
- Yahoo — http://uk.yahoo.com/
- Northern Light — http://northernlight.com/
- Google — http://www.google.com/
- Webtop (formerly Euroferret) — http://www.webtop.com/search/topferret

Two web search engines that relate specifically to law are:

- Findlaw — http://www.findlaw.com/
- Internet Legal Resources Guide UK — http://www.ilrg.com/nations/uk/ (includes specialised law entry-point to Alta Vista search engine as well as links to UK law sites)

Unfortunately, web search engines have been found to be of little use for legal research for the following reasons:

(a) In a test reported by Lawrence and Giles (1999), of 11 major search engines, the best performer, Northern Light, covered approximately 16% of the World Wide Web. The web then comprised about 800 million pages.

(b) In the same test undertaken in 1997, the best performer covered approximately 33% of the web. In 1997 the web comprised about 320 million pages. The web is growing far faster than search engines can index it.

(c) Search engines have technical problems in collecting information from sites which have pages in the form of 'frames'.

(d) Some search engines index only the home page of a site and do not visit the lower level pages.

(e) Search engines cannot gain access to sites which are password protected or are entered through a 'search form'. Many subscriber only sites containing valuable legal information fall into this category.

(f) Some search engines take months to capture a new site, index it and add it to the database.

(g)   Some search engines are programmed to collect the most popular sites only — hence, many search engines are good at collecting news, current affairs and leisure sites but poor at technical or academic sites.

The conclusion to be drawn is that web search engines are the least useful way of finding large quantities of relevant legal information. They are valuable only if all other avenues have failed.

Meta-search services

Meta-search services or meta-searchers offer simultaneous searching of a number of search engines from a single point. They work in the same way as search engines but they merely search the indexes of a group of search engines and report the results as a composite list. The disadvantages are that only simple forms of search can be used, there is often some sort of cut-off which limits the number of hits retrieved and the speed of the meta-search engine is controlled by the speed of the slowest search engine accessed. They are not recommended for law research.

Classified subject lists

These are hierarchical arrangements of resources developed by humans rather than by machine. The earliest were known as subject trees — now they are often called subject gateways. Subject lists are valuable for law research because they are:

(a)   specialised by subject;
(b)   selective — they will identify key sites on a subject;
(c)   based on the usefulness of sites — in the best subject lists each site will have been appraised for its value by a human being (rather than a machine);
(d)   well organised and there is a low risk of redundant or duplicated entries, as compared with the results provided by a search engine.

The subject arrangement can be ad hoc (as with Yahoo) or to a standard library classification scheme. Some entries contain only the URL of the site, others provide annotations and descriptions. Some include an evaluation of the site.
    The most popular are:

• WWW Virtual Library: Law — http://www.law.indiana.edu/v-lib/index.html
• Yahoo — http://uk.dir.yahoo.com/Regional/Countries/United_Kingdom/Government/Law
• BUBL: Law— http://link.bubl.ac.uk/law/
• NISS (National Information Services and Systems) — http://www.niss.ac.uk/subject/alpha.html
• SOSIG (Social Science Information Gateway): Law — http://www.sosig.ac.uk/law

Link pages

These are similar to classified subject lists except that they have been developed by subject specialists in education and commerce to assist learners and impress customers. They are highly subject specific so are one of the best places to start an internet search in law. The arrangement of link varies from site to site, and some have a search facility built into the page to assist users locating a relevant site.

To use link pages, merely go to the link page, select the site most appropriate to your search need and click on the coloured HTML link. You will be taken to that information source. If you wish to return to the link page click Back as many time as necessary. Remember, that if you click Home you will return to the home page of your university or college or your own personal home page, not the link page.

Whilst there is duplication amongst the three most popular sites listed below, they have individual strengths.

- Delia Venables (http://www.venables.co.uk/) — Best for links to sites of interest to practising lawyers.
- LAWLINKS: Legal Information on the Internet (http://www.ukc.ac.uk/library/lawlinks/) — Best for links to sites of interest to academic lawyers.
- eagle-i (http://ials.sas.ac.uk/eagle-i.htm) — Best for links to sites carrying overseas law.

Many universities and colleges have developed their own subject specific link pages. Ask library staff about these valuable short-cuts to successful legal research using the internet.

Appendix 5

Systems for citing documents in written work

Recommendations for citing and referencing published material are set out in a British Standard BS 5605: 1990 which incorporates systems recognised in a more complex standard BS 1629: 1989.

Two systems of citation are generally recognised: the numeric and the name and date or Harvard system. In addition, lawyers writing in law reviews in the USA employ a hybrid system devised by the Harvard Law Review Association.

APP 5.1   NUMERIC SYSTEM

In this system cited documents are numbered in the order in which they are first referred to in the text. At every point in the text at which reference to a particular document is made, its number is inserted in brackets or parentheses or as a superscript (little number).

Examples:

'In a recent study (26) it is shown . . .' or
'In a recent study [26] it is shown . . .' or
'In a recent study 26 it is shown . . .'

When different parts of a document are cited at different points in the text add the page numbers with the reference number in the text.

Example:

'In a recent study (26, p. 629) it is shown . . .'

References describing the documents cited are given in a list at the end of the text arranged in numerical order. The sequence of elements in the reference is normally as follows:

(a)   *For a book*: name of author; title of book; name of editor, compiler or translator (if any); name of series in which the book appears (if any); number or name of edition, if other than the first; place of publication; name of publisher; date of publication.
Example:

26. Devlin, P., *The Judge* (Oxford: Oxford University Press, 1979).

(b)   *For an article in a periodical*: name of author; title of article; date of volume; volume number; abbreviated titles of periodical; page number.
Example:

27. Tang, Chin-Shih, 'The law of citation and citation of law' (1986) 10 Dalhousie LJ 124.

At the end of the text, the references are listed in numerical order. A major drawback of the numeric system is if, in the final stages of preparing a document you wish to add an extra reference or remove an existing one, all references following the change will need renumbering. Modern word processing systems can, however, reduce the work involved.

APP 5.2   NAME AND DATE (HARVARD) SYSTEM

In the Harvard system, at every point in the text at which reference to a particular document is made, its author's surname and the year of its publication are given.
Examples:

'Laster (1988) describes . . .'
'In a recent study (Brenner 1990), it is described as . . .'
'Scharf (1989a) discussed this briefly . . .'

If the author's name occurs naturally in the sentence give the year of publication in brackets; if not, then give both name and year. When the same author has published more than one cited document in the same year, distinguish between the documents by adding a lower-case letter (a, b, c etc.) after the year inside the brackets.
Bibliographic references describing the documents cited are arranged in alphabetical order of author's names and then by year and letter.
Examples:

Brenner, Susan W. (1990) 'Of publication and precedent: an inquiry into the ethnomethodology of case reporting in the American legal system' 39 De Paul L Rev 461.

Scharf, Harry M. (1989a) 'The court reporter' 10 J Legal Hist 191.

Detailed recommendations for compiling references by the numeric and Harvard systems are contained in section 4 of BS 5605.

Another method of referencing is described by Turabian (1996), who recommends that the first time a work is mentioned in a footnote, the entry should be in complete form unless a full bibliography is added at the end of the essay or paper. Once a work has been cited in full, subsequent references to it should be in abbreviated form.

APP 5.3   HARVARD LAW REVIEW ASSOCIATION

This system of citation is quite complex and employs slightly different rules for the system depending on the type of document in which the citations are made. The details and examples given below are based on the requirements for law review footnotes. For further details consult: Harvard Law Review Association, *A Uniform System of Citation*, 16th edn (Cambridge Mass: Harvard Law Review Association, 1996), sometimes referred to as The Blue Book.

In the text, references are set out as for the numeric system (e.g., 'in an authoritative study (26) . . .') whilst the sequence of elements in the footnotes or bibliography is as follows:

(a)   *For a book*: name of author — with initials placed before surname (in capital letters); title of book (in capital letters); page number(s); and then in parentheses: edition number and date.

Example:

26. W. HOLDSWORTH, A HISTORY OF ENGLISH LAW 278 (6th edn 1938).

(b)   *For a periodical article*: name of author — without initials unless there is a citation elsewhere in the work to another author of the same surname; title of article; volume number; title of periodical; page number(s); and then in parentheses, date.

Example:

27. Hutcheson, *A Case for Three Judges*, 48 HARV L REV 795 (1934).

APP 5.4   CITING ELECTRONIC SOURCES AND DATABASES

These rules are a summary of those given in Section 17.3 of the Harvard Law Review Association publication, noted above.

If a database contains documents published and available separately it is not necessary to indicate they are also available in database form unless the documents in original form are difficult to obtain.

Because of the transient nature of many internet sources, citation to the internet should be discouraged unless the materials are unavailable in printed form or are difficult to obtain in their original form. When citing to materials on the internet, provide the name of the author (if any), the title or top level heading of the material being cited, and the Uniform Resource Locator (URL). The URL should be given in angled brackets. For electronic journals and publications, the actual date of publication should be given. Otherwise, provide the most recent modification date of the source preceded by the term 'last modified' or the date of access preceded by the term 'visited' if the modification date is unavailable.

Examples:

> Mark Israel, *The alt.usage.english FAQ File* (last modified 17 Nov. 1995) < ftp://rtfm.mit.edu/pub/alt.usage/english/alt.usage.english_FAQ >

> Scott Adams, *The Dilbert Zone* (visited 20 Jan. 1996) <http://www. unitedmedia.com/comics/dilbert>

The rules do not cover CD databases specifically. However, various authors suggest the following citation order:

(a)   database (underlined or in italics)
(b)   [CD-ROM]
(c)   inclusive dates (in round brackets)
(d)   place, producer
(e)   available

For example:

> *Index to Legal Periodicals* [CD-ROM] (1981–99). New York: H W Wilson. Available: SilverPlatter.

Appendix 6

List of useful web sites

All of the web addresses listed below are correct at the time of writing, however they are subject to change at any time. If you find that an URL does not work, either try searching for the site through any of the web search engines listed on p. 310 or one of the links pages listed on pp. 311–12.

RESEARCHING THE LAW OF ENGLAND, WALES AND SCOTLAND

Primary legislation

UK Parliament
   http://www.parliament.the-stationery-office.co.uk/

House of Commons
   http://www.parliament.the-stationery-office.co.uk/pa/cm/cmhome.htm

House of Lords
   http://www.parliament.the-stationery-office.co.uk/pa/ld/ldhome.htm

Public Bills before Parliament
   http://www.parliament.the-stationery-office.co.uk/pa/pabills.htm

Publications on the Internet
   http://www.parliament.the-stationery-office.co.uk/pa/cm/cmpubns.htm

Weekly Information Bulletin of the House of Commons
   http://www.parliament.the-stationery-office.co.uk/pa/cm/cmwib.htm

Sessional Information Digest of the House of Commons
   http://www.parliament.the-stationery-office.co.uk/pa/cm/cmsid.htm

Lawtel
   http://www.lawtel.co.uk

Daily List of Government Publications
   http://www.the-stationery-office.co.uk/daily_list/

Standing Committee Debates on Bills
   http://www.parliament.the-stationery-office.co.uk/pa/cm/stand.htm

Acts of the UK Parliament
   http://www.hmso.gov.uk/acts.htm

Current Legal Information (CLI)
   http://193.118.187.160/cli.htm

   Online User Guide for Students
   http://www.smlawpub.co.uk/digital/cli/index.cfm#student

LEXIS
   http://www.butterworths.com/

UK State
   http://www.ukstate.com/portal.asp

Government Information Service
   http://www.open.gov.uk/

Secondary legislation

The National Assembly for Wales
   http://www.wales.gov.uk/index_e.html

HMSO Wales Legislation
   http://www.wales-legislation.hmso.gov.uk/

Current Legal Information (CLI)
   http://193.118.187.160/cli.htm

   Online User Guide for Students
   http://www.smlawpub.co.uk/digital/cli/index.cfm#student

Lawtel
   http://www.lawtel.co.uk/

Welsh Legal Digest Online
   http://www.welsh-legaldigest.co.uk/

Government Information Service
   http://www.open.gov.uk/

Case law

House of Lords: Judicial Work and Judgments
   http://www.parliament.the-stationery-office.co.uk/pa/ld/ldjudinf.htm

The Court Service
   http://www.courtservice.gov.uk/

The Court Service Judgments
   http://www.courtservice.gov.uk/judgments/judg_home.htm

The British and Irish Legal Information Institute
http//www.bailii.org/

Smith Bernal: Casebase (Court of Appeal and Crown Office (Queen's Bench
Division) decisions)
http://www.casetrack.com/casebase

Daily Law Notes
http://www.lawreports.co.uk/indexdln.htm

Lawtel
http://www.lawtel.co.uk

Halsbury's Laws Monthly Review
http://www.butterworths.com

Current Legal Information (CLI)
http://193.118.187.160/cli.htm

Online User Guide for Students
http://www.smlawpub.co.uk/digital/cli/index.cfm#student

The Privy Council Decisions
http://www.bailii.org/uk/cases/UKPC

Extra-legal sources

Office of Fair Trading
http://www.oft.gov.uk/

Data Protection Commissioner
http://www.dataprotection.gov.uk/

Government Information Service
http://www.open.gov.uk/

The Lord Chancellor's Office
http://www.open.gov.uk/lcd/lcdhome.htm

Commentary on the law

UK Sensitive Map (University of Wolverhampton)
http://scitsc.wlv.ac.uk/ukinfo/uk.map.html

Current Legal Information (CLI)
http://193.118.187.160/cli.htm

Online User Guide for Students
http://www.smlawpub.co.uk/digital/cli/index.cfm#student

Law Gazette
http://www.lawgazette.co.uk

New Law Journal
http://www.butterworths.com/nlj/index.htm

Web Journal of Current Legal Issues
http://webjcli.ncl.ac.uk/

Journal of Information, Law and Technology (JILT)
   http://elj.warwick.ac.uk/jilt/

Mountbatten Journal of Legal Studies
   http://www.solent.ac.uk/law/silrd.html

Index of Law Journals, by Washburn University School of Law
   http://www.washlaw.edu/lawjournal.html

Legal Journals Index
   http://www.smlawpub.co.uk/product/abbrevs/abbrevs.cfm

Lawtel
   http://www.lawtel.co.uk

The Civil Service Year Book
   http://www.civil-service.co.uk/

The Law Commission — Library
   http://www.lawcom.gov.uk/library/library.htm

Government Information Service
   http://www.open.gov.uk/

The Stationery Office
   http://www.official-documents.co.uk/menu/bydept.htm

British Official Publications Current Awareness Service (BOPCAS)
   http://www.soton.ac.uk/~bopcas/

Scotland

JUSTIS UK Statutes
   http://www.justis.com/navigate/main.html

Scottish Parliament (including What's Happening in the Scottish Parliament)
   http://www.scottish.parliament.uk/

UK State
   http://www.ukstate.com/

Scottish Parliament Law Review
   http://www.splr.co.uk/

HMSO Scotland Legislation
   http://www.scotland-legislation.hmso.gov.uk/

The Scottish Courts Website
   http://www.scotcourts.gov.uk/

Houses of Parliament (Scottish appeals to the House of Lords)
   http://www.parliament.uk/

Current Legal Information (CLI)
   http://193.118.187.160/cli.htm

   Online User Guide for Students
   http://www.smlawpub.co.uk/digital/cli/index.cfm#student

Law Society of Scotland
http://www.lawscot.org.uk/

Scottish Executive
http://www.scotland.gov.uk/

Scottish Office — Secretary of State for Scotland
http://www.scottishsecretary.gov.uk/

Maps and Official Publications Unit, University of Glasgow
http://www.lib.gla.ac.uk/Depts/MOPS/

RESEARCHING THE LAW OF THE EUROPEAN COMMUNITY AND EUROPEAN HUMAN RIGHTS LAW

Legislation, case law and commentary on the law of the EC

Europa — The European Union's Server
http://europa.eu.int/index-en.htm (for English version)

European Union Law
http://europa.eu.int/ or http://europa.eu.int/eur-lex/en/

Treaties on Europa
http://europa.eu.int/eur-lex/en/treaties/index.html

Official Journal of the European Communities
http://europa.eu.int/eur-lex/en/oj/index.html

Directory of Community legislation in force
http://europa.eu.int/eur-lex/en/lif/index.html

University of Mannheim European Documentation Centre (EDC)
http://www.uni-mannheim.de/users/ddz/edz/biblio/opace.html

Bulletin of the European Union
http://europa.eu.int/abc/doc/off/bull/en/welcome.htm

European Access Journal
http://www.europeanaccess.co.uk/

Court of Justice and Court of First Instance
http://europa.eu.int/cj/en/index.htm

SCAD: Central Documentation Service of the EC
http://europa.eu.int/scad/

European human rights law

Council of Europe
http://conventions.coe.int/

European Court of Human Rights
http://www.echr.coe.int/eng/

KEEPING UP-TO-DATE

Butterworths LawDirect and Law Online
  http://www.butterworths.com/

Lawtel Daily Update
  http://www.lawtel.co.uk/

Law Gazette
  http://www.lawgazette.co.uk/

The Lawyer
  http://www.thelawyer.co.uk/

New Law Journal
  http://www.butterworths.com/nlj/index.htm

Weekly Information Bulletin of the House of Commons
  http://www.parliament.the-stationery-office.co.uk/pa/cm/cmwib.htm

Sessional Information Digest of the House of Commons
  http://www.parliament.the-stationery-office.co.uk/pa/cm/cmsid.htm

Daily List of Government Publications
  http://www.the-stationery-office.co.uk/daily_list/

Web Journal of Current Legal Issues
  http://webjcli.ncl.ac.uk/

OTHER ONLINE SOURCES OF LAW INFORMATION

Internet Legal Resources Guide UK
  http://www.ilrg.com/nations/uk/

WWW Virtual Library — Law
  http://www.law.indiana.edu/v-lib/index.html

SOSIG (Social Science Information Gateway): Law
  http://www.sosig.ac.uk/law

eagle-i
  http://ials.sas.ac.uk/eagle-i.htm

Findlaw
  http://www.findlaw.com/

Delia Venables
  http://www.venables.co.uk/

LAWLINKS
  http://www.ukc.ac.uk/library/lawlinks/

NISS (National Information Services and Systems)
  http://www.niss.ac.uk/subject/alpha.html

BUBL: Law
  http://link.bubl.ac.uk/law/

References

Anon. (1983) 'Commencement — the latest' 4 *Statute Law Review* 42.

Bates, Jane (1989) 'The conversion of EEC legislation into UK legislation' 10 *Statute Law Review* 110.

Bates, T.StJ.N. (1986) 'Parliament, policy and delegated power' 7 *Statute Law Review* 114.

Bennett, Andrew F. (1990) 'Uses and abuses of delegated power' 11 *Statute Law Review* 23.

Brown, Paul (1989) 'Law reporting: the inside story' 20 *The Law Librarian* 15.

Clinch, Peter (1989) *Systems of Reporting Judicial Decision Making.* Unpublished PhD thesis. University of Sheffield.

Clinch, Peter (1990) 'On making law reports easier to use' 21 *The Law Librarian* 62.

Craies, W.F. (1971) *Craies on Statute Law*, 7th edn (London: Sweet & Maxwell).

Cross, Charles and Bailey, Stephen (1991) *Cross on Local Government Law*, 8th edn (London: Sweet & Maxwell). Loose-leaf.

Drewry, Gavin (1989) 'Public Bills in the Westminster 1987–88 Parliamentary session' 10 *Statute Law Review* 200.

Drewry, Gavin (1992) 'Public Bills in the 1988–89 and 1989–90 Parliamentary sessions'. 13 *Statute Law Review* 179.

Durnford, Charles and East, Edward (1786) *Reports of Cases Argued and Determined in the Court of King's Bench* (London: Whieldon).

Ferguson, R.N. (1988) 'The legal status of non-statutory codes of practice' [1988] *Journal of Business Law* 12.

Harrison, Nicholas (1984) 'Unreported cases: myth and reality' 81 *Law Society Gazette* 257.

Holland, James A. and Webb, Julian S. (1999) *Learning Legal Rules* , 4th edn (London: Blackstone Press).

Lawrence, Steve and Giles, C. Lee. (1999) 'Accessibility of information on the Web.' 400 *Nature* 8 July 1999 107.

Lee, Simon and Fox, Marie (1999) *Learning Legal Skills,* 3rd edn (London: Blackstone Press).

Lord Chancellor's Department (1940) *Report of the Law Reporting Committee* (London: HMSO).

Moran, C.G. (1948) *Heralds of the Law* (London: Stevens).

Morris, R.J.B. (1990) 'Finding and using local statutory instruments' 11 *Statute Law Review* 28.

Noel-Tod, Alex (1989) 'What's in a name? The statute book and popular titles' 20 *The Law Librarian* 29.

Ollé, James (1973) *An Introduction to British Government Publications*, 2nd edn (London: Association of Assistant Librarians).

Parry, D.L. and Rowell, R eds. (1999) *Butterworths Trading and Consumer Law* (London: Butterworths). Loose-leaf.

Pearson, R.P. (1986) 'Open justice' 130 *Solicitors' Journal* 969.

Pemberton, J.E. (1974) *Undertaking Enquiries*, part 2, Literature search and compiling a bibliography (Open University. Social Sciences. A Third-Level Course. Public Administration. Course D331. Block III, Part 2) (Milton Keynes: Open University Press).

Pollock, Sir Frederick (1896) *A First Book of Jurisprudence* (London: Macmillan).

Rait, R.S. (1924) *The Parliaments of Scotland* (Glasgow: Maclehose, Jackson).

Ramsey, Anne (1997) *European Union Information*, 2nd edn (Halifax: Association of Assistant Librarians).

Statsky, William P. (1982) *Legal Research, Writing and Analysis*, 2nd edn (St Paul, Minn: West Publishing Co.).

Transcripts of judicial proceedings: how to obtain them, (1996) 2nd edn (Hebden Bridge: Legal information Resources).

Turabian, Kate L. (1996) *A Manual for Writers of Term Papers, Theses and Dissertations*, 6th edn (Chicago: University of Chicago Press).

Walker, D.M. (1988–) *A Legal History of Scotland* (Edinburgh: W. Green/T. & T. Clark).

White, R.M. and Willock, I.D. (1999) *The Scottish Legal System*, 2nd edn (Edinburgh: Butterworths).

Winfield, Percy (1925) *The Chief Sources of English Legal History* (Cambridge Mass: Harvard University Press).

Index